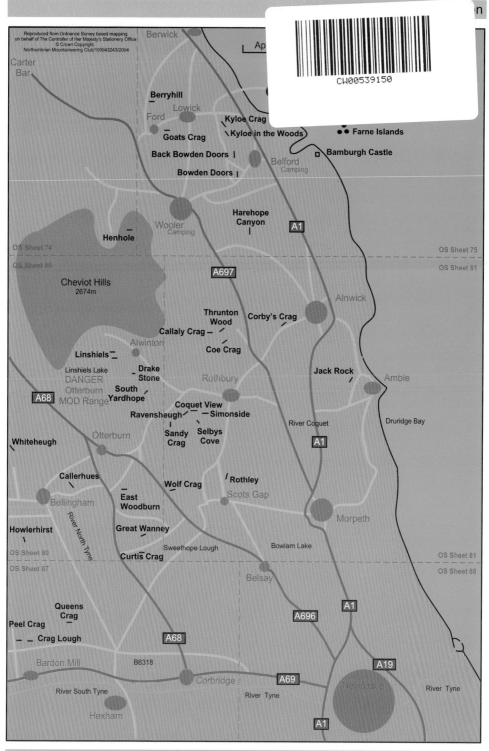

Berwick

Carter Bar

Berryhill

Lowick

Ford

Kyloe Crag

Goats Crag

Kyloe in the Woods

Farne Islands

Back Bowden Doors

Bamburgh Castle

Bowden Doors

Belford
Camping

Wooler
Camping

Harehope Canyon

A1

Henhole

OS Sheet 74

OS Sheet 75

OS Sheet 80

OS Sheet 81

Cheviot Hills
2674m

A697

Thrunton Wood

Corby's Crag

Alnwick

Callaly Crag

Alwinton

Coe Crag

Linshiels

Jack Rock

Amble

Linshiels Lake
DANGER
Otterburn
MOD Range

Drake Stone

Rothbury

A68

South Yardhope

Coquet View

Simonside

River Coquet

Druridge Bay

Ravensheugh

Sandy Crag

Selbys Cove

A1

Whiteheugh

Otterburn

Callerhues

Wolf Crag

Rothley

Scots Gap

Bellingham

East Woodburn

Howlerhirst

Great Wanney

Morpeth

Sweethope Lough

Bowlam Lake

OS Sheet 80

OS Sheet 81

Curtis Crag

OS Sheet 87

Belsay

OS Sheet 88

Queens Crag

A1

Peel Crag

A696

Crag Lough

A68

A19

Bardon Mill

B6318

Corbridge

A69

Newcastle

River South Tyne

River Tyne

River Tyne

Hexham

A1

River North Tyne

Northumberland Climbing Guide

Edited by John Earl
Layout by Steve Crowe

"There is no nobler county than that of Northumberland, as it rolls processionally northward to the Border in great waves of coloured and historic moorland, cresting upon the skyline into sudden and surprising crags, which crown for us the magnificent walking and admirable rock climbs."

Geoffrey Winthrop Young, in the foreword to the first edition 1950.

Karin Magog
53. On the Rocks (E7 6c)
Brilliant, bold and technical
P40
Photo: Paul Linfoot

Previous Editions.

Copies of some of the previous editions can be found on the NMC web site at www.thenmc.org.uk.

1950	First Edition	
1964	Second Edition	Norman E Haighton
1971	Third Edition	Norman E Haighton
1976	New Climbs Supplement	John Earl and Robert Hutchinson
1979	Fourth Edition	Norman E Haighton
1984	New Climbs Supplement	John Earl
1989	Fifth Edition	John Earl
2000	Bouldering Guide	John Earl
2004	Present Sixth Edition	John Earl

Produced by the Northumbrian Guidebook Team
for the Northumbrian Mountaineering Club
NMC © Northumbrian Mountaineering Club 2004
Page layout and graphics by Steve Crowe
Printed by The Ernest Press

ISBN 0-9504686-3-0

NMC Participation Statement.

The NMC recognises that climbing and mountaineering are activities with a danger of personal injury or death.
Participants in these activities should be aware of and accept these risks and be responsible for their own actions and involvement.

The NMC wish to thank the following for supporting the production of this guidebook.

Scarpa.co.uk
info@mountainboot.co.uk 0191 296 0212

Berghaus.com
info@berghaus.com 0191 516 5700

theBMC.co.uk
office@thebmc.co.uk 0870 010 4878

Wildtrak.com
sales@wildtrak.com 0191 261 8582

Contents

INTRODUCTION

The first meeting to discuss the production of a replacement guide for the 1989 Definitive Guide to Climbing in Northumberland was held in February 2000. A guide book team was established, crags allocated and work began. The Foot and Mouth epidemic of 2001 totally stopped crag visits as virtually all of them were out of bounds and the whole process of guide book work ground to a halt. In 2002 the process was kick started and in true climbing tradition when the party moves at the pace of the slowest member, so it is with guide book production.

As you will see from the Acknowledgements we had a massive Guide Book Team which is excellent for getting a broad spread of opinion and in theory should make the job quicker and easier. I am living proof that this is not the case.

In this guide we have followed the normal UK grading system as used in the previous guide. We have attempted to review the grades of existing routes and most of those that have been revised have been revised up. However there are a number of old routes which have not had known second ascents and therefore it is difficult to be totally consistent.

The majority of the new hard climbs have not been repeated at the time of going to print and the grades used are those given by the first ascentionist. However as stated in the last guide 'it must be remembered grades are subjective, are not an exact science and can at best only be a reasonable indication of the difficulty of a route'. This is equally true today. A graded list not to be taken too seriously has been included at the end of each major crag and these are even more subjective than the grade.

Since the last guide the grades of routes in the County, have risen significantly. There are a number of reasons for this; a more professional approach to new routing, an attempt to equate grades with those in other areas and in a few instances an increase in the level at which people are operating. The challenges remaining at the time of the last guide are being met and as a consequence a number of very hard, bold and independent routes have been produced. There are still many remaining and it is hoped that they will be left for the generation that is capable of climbing them in good style and following the true line.

John Earl

ACCESS FUND
A contribution is being made to the Access Fund based upon guidebook sales.

access &
conservation
trust

ACKNOWLEDGEMENTS

The guide although completely revised is based upon the previous five editions and the two supplements. Its publication however would not have been possible without the funding from the NMC, financial support of the BMC and the generous sponsorship from Scarpa and Berghaus.

Particular thanks are due to the crag authors, Rick Barnes, Andy Birtwistle, Alec Burns, Tim Catterall, Martin Cooper, Steve Crowe, John Dalrymple, Chris Davis, Andrew Earl, John Earl, Hugh Harris, Malcolm Lowerson, Karin Magog, Ian Murray, Steve Nagy, Graeme Read, Steve Roberts, Cliff Robson, Bob Smith, Graham Telfer, Karl Telfer, Michael Thomas, John Wallace and Martin Waugh who have put in so much hard work over the past four years. Our task in producing the guide was made easier by John Dalrymple who provided all authors with electronic drafts, me with computer advice throughout the process and finally did the templates for each crag.

We are also indebted to Steve Crowe for the final layout of the guide and also to him and Malcolm Lowerson for their excellent digital crag photographs, to Karin Magog for her informative maps, Andy Birtwistle and John Dalrymple for their Geology notes, Derek Cutts for the Early History and to Bill Renshaw the BMC area access officer for general access advice and for keeping us all up to date with the developments of CRoW. Thanks are also due to those who provided photographs and to Andy Birtwistle, Mark Savage, Darren Stevenson, Steve Crowe and Rick Barnes who as well as taking many of them helped me make the final selection. In addition to the Guide Book Team we are obliged to Dave Cuthbertson, Nick Dixon and Ron Kenyon for their support.I should also like to thank Stewart Wilson who allowed us to reproduce material previously published in 'North of England Rock Climbs' in 1992.

A special thanks is given to Mike Arnold who painstakingly read through each manuscript at least twice and when I was starting to tire continued to identify errors in grammar, layout and consistency.

Finally, I am indebted to Carol, who along with Steffie has accompanied me around many of the crags major and minor, showing exceptional patience and understanding.

I have promised that this will be my last guide and to paraphrase Steve Redgrave if anyone in the future sees me going anywhere near a guide book they have my permission to shoot me.

John Earl

YET MORE ACKNOWLEDGEMENTS

Further thanks are due to my IT support team of Stuart Magog for software support and especially the crash course on Photoshop, and Ian Crowe for hardware support including the installation of the larger hard drives required to produce this guide.

May I also add a special thanks to all the photographers for supplying me with a huge catalogue of images to select from, only a small fraction of which were able to be used, but they all did make the task of page layout a much more interesting challenge.

Special thanks must go out to Karin Magog who sacrificed many days climbing on the Yorkshire Limestone, to pose for photographs on many county routes especially for this guide, and for endless hours at home alone whilst I wrestled the text and graphics into shape.

Steve Crowe

TECHNICAL NOTES
MAPS
The location of each crag is indicated by its grid reference.
The county is covered by six Ordnance Survey 1:50,000 maps, sheets
74 (Kelso)
75 (Berwick upon Tweed),
80 (The Cheviot Hills),
81 (Alnwick and Rothbury),
87 (Hexham and Haltwhistle) and
88 (Tyneside).
Most crags lie on sheets 80 and 81.

CLASSIFICATION
ADJECTIVAL GRADES
These give an assessment of the overall difficulty of the climb taking into account technical difficulty, strenuousness, whether or not sustained, quality of protection and the nature of the landing. The grades are Moderate, Difficult, Very Difficult, Mild Severe, Severe, Hard Severe, Mild Very Severe, Very Severe, Hard Very Severe, and Extreme and appear in the text in their abbreviated forms.
The Extreme grade is sub-divided into E1 to E9 and although this is the highest grade used in this guide it is an open ended system.

TECHNICAL GRADES
These are an assessment of the technical difficulty and strenuousness of each pitch. The grades are 4b, 4c, 5a, 5b, 5c, 6a, 6b, 6c, 7a, 7b and again, this is an open ended system.
Routes below 4b receive only an adjectival grade, whilst most routes 4b and above receive both an adjectival grade and technical grade. There are however a small number of routes/problems which, although of a high level of technical difficulty because of their short nature or because the hard move is off the ground followed by relatively easy climbing have been given a technical grade only. The grades assume chalk, sticky boots (but not resin which is totally unacceptable in Northumberland) and a comprehensive rack of modem protection.

ROUTE QUALITY
A system of stars is used to indicate the quality of the route, these have been awarded on a crag by crag basis but only the very best routes have been given three stars.

FURTHER INFORMATION
The NMC's web site www.thenmc.org.uk includes more detailed information on some of the Minor Crags.

NEW ROUTE INFORMATION
This is also be available on the NMC's web site www.thenmc.org.uk

NEW ROUTES
Descriptions of new routes should be sent to John Earl, 7 Hornsea Close, Brunswick Green, Wideopen, Newcastle upon Tyne NE13 7HG and should include length, grade and date.

FACILITIES
CAMPING

Although there are numerous camp sites in the County the following are known to have been visited by climbers.

Belford: South Meadows Caravan and Camping Site 01668 213326
Crag Lough: Winshields Farm, Once Brewed. 01434 344243
Wooler: Highburn House A small and friendly site at the north end of town. 01668 281344

Other Caravan and Public Campsites

Bridge End, Wooler	GR 995278	01668 81447
River Breamish, Powburn	GR 054185	01665 78320
Byrness Park(Plus Bunkhouse)	GR 780015	01830 20259
Kielder Castle	GR 632934	01434 250209
Clennel Hall, Alwinton	GR 928072	01669 50341
Bellingham	GR 840832	01434 220258
Stonehaugh	GR 796762	01660 30251
Leaplish (Kielder Lake)	GR 660877	01434 250278
Hawkhirst	GR 658893	01434 250317

ACCOMMODATION

The National Park Visitor Centre at Ingram, (GR NU020163) Tel, 01665, 578890
A small informal camping field with arranged access to toilets and drinking water.
Barrowburn Camping Barn – (GR NT868107)
Booking at National Park Headquarters, Hexham 01434 605555.
Camping permitted.

Self Catering Cottages in Northumberland and the Border regions of England and Scotland
http://www.northumbria-byways.com/coastal_region1.htm

Check with your local Tourist Information Centres before your visit to ensure that this information is still up to date.

THE COUNTY CODE
ETHICS
Up to the time of the last guide both first ascents and repeat ascents were in the main done in what would be described as very good style, virtually no new routes having been top roped or extensively practiced prior to leading, with abseiling, cleaning and minimal inspecting the norm. However, in the period since the publication of the last guide, along with trends in other outcrop areas 'headpointing' (the practice of extensively top roping prior to leading or soloing) has been deployed on most of the hard new routes. Unfortunately this style has also been adopted by some on many of the 'old' routes which had originally been climbed in better style. Pegs must not be placed for either protection or aid, as the sandstone is particularly fragile and easily damaged. No bolts have been placed in modern times and it is essential to preserve the nature of Northumberland climbing that this situation continues. Prior to the last guide a number of routes had been produced as a result of extensive wire brushing and/or chipping, these were not included in that guide and have not been included in this guide. Perhaps that stance has been effective because we do not appear to have had any further problems with chipping. However, excessive top roping and careless abseiling is continuing to cause damage to our fragile crags. Indeed some areas particularly at Bowden Doors are just wearing away due to their popularity. We really all must start using this finite facility in a more considerate way.

ROUTES AND BOULDERING
Some might say (John Gill for instance) that much of the sandstone climbing in Northumberland is bouldering, albeit of the high ball variety. However in this guide we have tried to include only routes, the bouldering being comprehensively covered in the Northumberland Bouldering Guide also published by the NMC. I accept this is a fine line and almost certainly everyone will not agree with where we have drawn the line. The simple criterion is bouldering should be fairly safe, when protected by a mat, should you fall off. If this is not so, or a rope and runners are necessary then it should be considered as a route.

BRUSHING
Sandstone can be very soft and even those crags that appear to be iron hard may only have a thin outer layer of hard rock retaining a sea of sand. Once this skin is damaged the rock is ruined for all time.
If a route has lichen on it, brushing with a soft bristle brush should be sufficient. If it is sandy even this minimal brushing can cause damage and it should only be ragged. 'Tooth brushing' pockets to death is liable to eventually destroy the outer surface and always remember the back of a toothbrush is hard plastic.

RESIN
The use of resin in the county is totally unacceptable.

John Earl

Lichen at Shaftoe
Photo: Steve Crowe

ACCESS AND CONSERVATION

Northumberland has always been a uniquely special and quiet place to climb, a real pleasure, for local climbers and visitors alike. Perhaps inevitably the pressure from climbers has continued to increase, particularly on the popular crags, as has the use of crags by organised groups. The Northumberland crags are our special heritage and we want climbing in the County to carry on being the unique experience it has always been. With your help in making sure that the crags are used responsibly we can make sure that this happens.

Access to crags in Northumberland has always been taken with the agreement or aquiescence of landowners. Over the years good relations have been built up with many landowners and their support for climbing is valued most highly. For many crags in the county access will continue to be taken by agreement. Climbers should make sure they seek permission where this is required. In particular permission must always be sought before a group uses a crag.

Climbers should always respect the needs of landowners and tenants and should follow the Country Code. Leaving litter is perhaps the easiest way to put access at risk and crags should be litter free zones. Always take all litter home, even if someone else has left it. Car parking can also be a problem and bad parking can threaten access. Remember that other people need to use the roads and that farm vehicles need access at any time. Climbers should not disturb any livestock, nor should their dogs. Dogs should only be taken to crags where this is permitted. They must be kept on a lead if there is any stock near a crag or at lambing time.

There will soon be a right of access to some crags in the County, for the first time ever, under the Countryside and Rights of Way Act 2000, CRoW. This gives a right of access to mountain and moor for recreational use, including climbing, and will come into force in Northumberland in mid 2005. Until then there is no access to any crag in the County as of right and climbers should respect existing access arrangements.

The crag descriptions indicate the crags that are covered by CRoW. Even when the right of access is in force there may be some restrictions on access to crags, where, for instance there are birds nesting on a crag. There are also restrictions on dogs on CRoW access land. CRoW access restrictions will be posted on the NMC, Climb*online* and BMC websites. Please make sure to check these sites regularly, particularly in the nesting season.

Crag flora should always be treated with the greatest respect. Plants on established routes should be left untouched at all times and route preparation on new crags and routes should be sensitive to existing vegetation. Insensitive route preparation on crags on CRoW access land or in designated areas, (SSSIs, SACs, SPAs), could be an offence and could trigger the involvement of English Nature, the National Park or the Countryside Agency. Information on this will appear on the NMC, Climb*online* and BMC websites. Keep yourself informed.

Crags are not indestructible. Our treasured sandstone crags are extremely soft and are particularly vulnerable to over use. Damage to holds, routes and the crag environment is irreversible and is an increasing concern. Over use can also result in tensions between climbers and threats to access. In particular there must never be any chipping or modification of holds on Northumberland crags and rope damage must be avoided at all times, by the use of rope guides if necessary. None of the sandstone crags in the County can sustain winter climbing, the rock is too soft and damage is irreversible. Winter climbing and the use of crampons should be restricted to only the highest crags and only then when the conditions are such that there will be no damage to the rock.

Bill Renshaw

Access updates can be found on these websites:

NMC: www.thenmc.org.uk

Climbonline: www.climb*online*.co.uk

BMC: www.thebmc.co.uk

GEOLOGY

The Northumbrian landscape and the crags we climb on today are the result of millions of years of geological activity and wildly varied climates. The scenery reflects the many events that have taken place over this enormous period of time and when interpreted tells a fascinating story.

If we could transport ourselves back 380 million years to what is now Northumbria we would witness a scene straight out of Mordor! Massive volcanoes would be spewing out lava. Explosions hundreds of times louder than the Otterburn firing ranges would rent the air and the only life would be in distant seas. When we climb at Henhole or the Bizzle it is these andesite lavas that provide our routes and holds. The volcanoes have now been eroded to their roots and magma from deep in the vent forms the granite domes that lie just underneath the peaty rounded summits at the heart of the Cheviot range.

The volcanic events subsided and millions of years of erosion by fast flowing rivers and streams gradually wore the mountains away. Sediments were flushed into the shallow seas which by now surrounded the old volcanoes. These sediments created beds of conglomerate, sandstones and mudstones known collectively as the Cementstones. These softer rocks which form the Coquet, Aln and Till Valleys and the Millfield Plain have no climbing worth.

About 340 million years ago a vast river on the scale of the Mississippi developed to the north east, depositing sand in a huge delta and so creating the Fell Sandstone. This magnificent 1000 feet thick deposit contains much evidence of this sandy delta. Wave Wall at Bowden Doors shows this well. The lower part of the wall, left of The Wave, has a cross section of one of the channels in the delta whilst the "wave" above shows the 'cross bedding' formed as the sand eddied in the strong currents. When you crimp the rock you are in the bed of a long gone river that had seasonal variations in its flow. Plants were washed in as well, evidence of which can be seen in the large tree fern fossils on the ledge at the top of Hazelrigg Wall at Back Bowden Doors.

Fell Sandstone appears in an arc of escarpments from the Kyloe Hills in the north, down past Alnwick and along the Simonside Hills where crags such as Ravensheugh, Corby's, the Bowdens and the Kyloes offer some of the very best sandstone climbing in the country. At the time the climate would have been Tropical, similar to the Amazon today, so the friction wouldn't have been up to much!

Gradually the delta gave way to swamps with tree like ferns, areas of coral sea and smaller rivers depositing sand. The first creatures were beginning to crawl from the seas to the land, fossil amphibian footprints have been found near Craster. The result of this sedimentation was beds of sandstone, shale, limestone and coal known as The Limestone Group. These rocks dominate the landscape in the south east and centre of the county. The sandstones are not as extensive as the Fell Sandstone and tend to be coarser in nature becoming very gritty in places. They do however form major climbing crags at Jack Rock and The Wanneys, with smaller bouldering venues at Shaftoe and Rothley. The few limestone outcrops are too small and insignificant to be of value to the climber

Around 300 million years ago came a period of large scale earth movements. This built mountain ranges the size of the Himalaya elsewhere, but only folded and faulted the rocks in Northumbria. The movements tilted the sedimentary layers so they dipped away from the Cheviot massif. The subsequent erosion of these rocks has resulted in escarpments which for the most part face the hills, so from the tops of the crags both north and south one gets magnificent views of the Cheviots.

Earthquakes are also to thank for our superb routes and scenery.

Towards the end of this period renewed igneous activity in the south of the region resulted in the intrusion of magma into the sedimentary rocks. Like jam in a sandwich hot magma was squeezed between the layers. The legacy of this is our most extensive and famous geological feature, the Great Whin Sill. This major outcrop is composed of quartz dolerite (not to be confused with dolomite which is a type of limestone). It runs in an arc from the south west of the county right up to the north east. The Whin Sill can be seen at the coast at the Farne Islands, Dunstanburgh and Cullernose Point. However it is at its best at Peel Crag and the largest climbing cliff in the county, Crag Lough. Its defensive capabilities were well utilised by the Romans who used it for their Wall as it is thought the Picts and Scots did not have access to sticky rubber and chalk.

In contrast the latest geological event involved ice. This was the recent sculpting of the landscape during and after the last Ice Age only about 15,000 years ago. If the rocks are the building blocks then ice was the builder. As the ice sheet moved over the harder rocks they broke away along the vertical lines of weakness leaving the faces we climb on, a process known as 'plucking'. The Pinnacles at Ravensheugh are remnants which were torn from the main crag, but were not moved away completely. The gaps left under the ice where this occurred filled with water under enormous pressure which scoured the rock leaving overhangs at the foot of some of the faces. Other features were formed by fast flowing meltwater, the most prominent being Selby's Cove on Simonside. Wetsuits at the ready for the next Ice Age!

So the next time you climb on any of the crags in this guide you can reflect on the strange sequence of events that put them there. Whether you are crimping sand grains from a delta, pinching a piece of lava from a volcano or jamming up an ice widened crack, it all has a story to tell.

Andy Birtwistle and John Dalrymple

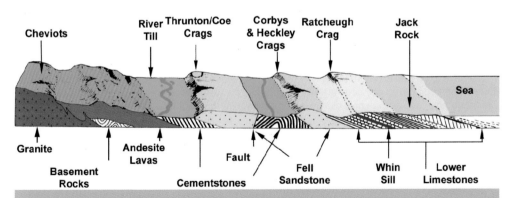

Andesite Lavas; Henhole

Fell Sandstone; Bowden Doors Group, Kyloe Crags, Simonside Hills

Coarse Grained Fluvial Sandstone - Jack Rock, Shaftoe, Rothley

Whin Sill - Crag Lough, Peel Crag

HISTORY

The crags before the climbers

Climbers are probably the biggest group of visitors to most crags. Therefore, they have an important part to play in discovering and preserving 8,000 years' worth of human activity there. Informed and sensitive attitudes are vital to support continued access. Anyway, when you're at the foot of the crag choosing your next brilliant route, it's fascinating to think that on the same spot, people have butchered the deer they have hunted, burnt their grannies, chipped the crag without complaints and blown lumps off it with gunpowder. Bored seconds, when the backside above hasn't moved for ten minutes and the neck muscles are aching can look around and spot clues for all these activities.

Northumberland crags have been a focus for human activity long before the first climbs were recorded in 1902. The first people to be drawn to them arrived as early as 8,000BC. Bearing in mind that the view from the top of Bowden Doors then would be of a vast forested plain stretching to Germany, not of the North Sea, we should remember things have changed a bit. Some unrecorded first ascensionists might have been proto-Germans.

Don't let your second read the next bit if their concentration is already a bit suspect. It's easy to spot evidence of early activity at nearly every crag. Patches of erosion caused by climbers' feet often turn up the tiny flint blades about 10mm long that middle stone age hunters used for their arrow heads and knives. They often turn up at Bowden Doors and Back Bowden and show that people were sheltering under the overhangs 7000 years ago, sorting their gear and having their bait just like now. Many hundreds of these microliths have been excavated below an outcrop in the Rothley area and there must be more sites to find. Bigger flints from the New Stone Age and the Bronze Age also turn up. The quarry area at Kyloe Crag was where a New Stone Age lumberjack lost or dumped the polished stone axes he (or she) had got all the way from Langdale in around 3000 BC, so maybe people were already picking up some of their gear on trips to the Lakes. A spectacular Bronze Age arrow head was found by a climber at Corby's Crag. If you pick up any flints, put them in an envelope with the find spot written on and pass them to the Museum of Antiquities, Newcastle University. They will help to build up a picture of a lost world.

Goats Crag and Corby's Crag were also used by prehistoric Northumbrians to bury their dead. Bronze age corpses (none of them unfortunate climbers we hope) were cremated. The burnt bones were smashed up and buried in big pots under overhangs at the crags. These have been found and excavated. A find like that is so rare and important, it would be vital to report it at once.

Then there's the mysteries. Goats Crag has its goats, carved at an unknown date but possibly very old. More important still are the prehistoric spirals at Jack Rock. There are some near Ancient Briton. Once you've got your eye in, there are several more along the crag. Bored seconds can play I spy. These have to be preserved from any sort of wear, so please stay off them. There's a good chance of more on other crags, so any seen are worth reporting. It's worth remembering that Britain's first known Old Stone Age cave art was only discovered in Derbyshire this century.

The quarrying must have started very early, but some was still going on in the 19th Century when hand drills of about 50mm diameter were used for placing gunpowder charges. What you get left is half a drill hole, split lengthways. Look near the Introductory Staircase end of Bowden Doors or in a few places at Corby's. Millstone quarrying was a bit slower and probably earlier. You chipped a circular groove; undercut it at the bottom, hammered wooden wedges in, poured in water and waited for the wood to swell and split the millstone away from the rock. There are dozens of them near the Drakestone, traces at Corby's Crag and on top of other crags such as Berryhill.

By this stage, your second may have dropped you while distracted by the rock art. The consolation is that your impact may well have dislodged some vital prehistoric clues from the foot of your route.

Derek Cutts

Rock Carvings in Northumberland
Photos: Derek Cutts.

Up to 1939

The earliest climbing reference is dated 1902 when G.W. Young, writing in the C.C. Journal, drew attention to climbs on Simonside and Wanney. Simonside is given the lesser prominence ... "The north face offers a close succession of fine chimneys and scrambles of varying difficulty from twenty to fifty feet in height. Some of these ... are not yet known to have been climbed." On Wanney, Young describes ascents of West Chimney and Ravens Nest on the Western Section and, on the main crag, Central Gully, Foxes Hole ("the foot held by a fierce family of wild goats") and "the reward of the day, a curving chimney with smooth equidistant walls and a smooth back parting two large overhanging bluffs. Every part of this can be climbed back and toe." This can only be Great Chimney. Both Doves Nest Crack and Boundary Corner were mentioned as unclimbed lines.

The S.M.C. Journal for 1907 records an ascent of Bizzle Chimney ' This is called Northeastern Chimney and Tarver and Glover, who made the ascent on 5th March 1899, also describe how to reach the cannonhole on Henhole. These two articles indicate a fair amount of development on the Northumbrian crags around the turn of the century though Young, later, (on High Hills, P 21) appears to preclude earlier climbers; "But later each day and within a walk or a drive, we might be striding over moor and dale to some cliff unclimbed since England had a history. The crags were still unknown and unexplored in those days and they were waiting in rain and solitude and grandeur for us."

There seems little doubt that M.B. Heywood discovered Crag Lough. Young and his companions, the Trevelyans of Wallington, only visited after Heywood's discovery, reported in the C.C. Journal for 1912. The Journal contains a long article and sketch of Crag Lough. The topographical information is at first easy enough to follow. Peel Crag is described as "... too much broken to offer many definite climbs." He does describe one route at the west end of Peel Crag which could be Sunset "...a clean climb up a very stiff slab, which necessitates exceptional contortions" Unfortunately the accuracy of his description disappears when he changes from the narrative to the visual. The sketch shows five routes on Crag Lough which could include Hadrian's Chimney and East Central Chimney. Though he only shows five routes on the sketch, Heywood says that the crag "... provides climbs at short intervals throughout its whole length. The majority are difficult, some exceptionally so."

Although there were other parties climbing in Northumberland during this period the scene was dominated by the parties based on Wallington. Many of these climbers, including Young, were not local but friends of the Trevelyan family. Charles Trevelyan of Cambo and G.M. Trevelyan of Wallington seemed to be the centre of activity with Young, Heywood and R. Bicknell as the earliest group. By the 1920's the next generation was continuing the climbing activities. George Trevelyan, H. Trevelyan and P. and C. Bicknell were introduced to the crags by their fathers and the parties in the twenties also included Jack Longland and F.R.G. Chew. The crags visited included Crag Lough, Henhole, Wanney and Simonside but, because of their proximity to Wallington, Shaftoe, Rothley and Wolf crags were given much attention. There appears to have been a good deal of serious climbing but hardly any of the lines can now be identified.

Some names receive frequent mention; "The Skull" and "Chew's Choice" on Wanney and "Great Auk Chimney" on Simonside but unfortunately these colourful names were forgotten by the time of the first guide. The best documented crags during this period are the Wanneys. The Gun (Armstrong Arms) at Ridsdale kept a visitors book in which many of the climbers recorded their successes and failures. This book is still held by Mrs. Nesbitt, the tenant at the time, who lives nearby. The first entry, by Messrs. Vineycomb and Fletcher, is dated 1912. They mention a number of chimneys and end up with the enigmatic sentence "Think well marked chimney just East of Wall on Great Wanney difficult." This leaves doubt as to whether Great Chimney was climbed or just assessed and later entries in the book suggest the latter. Later the same year they recorded an unsuccessful attempt, obviously unaware of Young's ascent. Boundary Corner was climbed and Idiot's Delight attempted (then known as Raven Nest climb). After the failure to climb Great Chimney by a different party in 1918 it was ascended on slack rope by Messrs. Wilson and Hughes in 1919. The first ascent without top rope was finally claimed by Wilson in 1920.

One interesting aspect of the visitors book is the prominence given to Aid Crag and Little Wanney. The majority of routes described are on these crags and not on Great Wanney. There was no co-ordinated development of the crags until the appearance of A.P. Rossiter towards the end of the 1930's. By the mid thirties most of the county's crags had been climbed on but extensive development was restricted to the Wanney's, Simonside and the smaller crags in these areas. Crag Lough does not seem to have been popular and a note by Longland in Oxford & Cambridge Mountaineering 1928/29 does not mention Crag Lough though covering Rothley, Wanney and Tosson. Bowden Doors and Kyloe crags were similarly unpopular though probably visited occasionally and the same journal in 1935 records several climbs on the Lion Rock, Belford Moor (probably Colour Heugh) by Robin Hodgkin.

Towards the end of the thirties, activity on the crags became more intense A.P. Rossiter was a frequent visitor to the Wanneys, where in one week he climbed 57 routes. He became the undisputed expert on the area and was later to provide the material for the guide. Basil Butcher and Keith Gregory began their exploration of Crag Lough and the Cheviot and a short climbing guide to the Simonside area was prepared by the King's College M.C. presided over by Ermrys Williams. Jack Longland was now working in the area and climbing with Rossiter at Wanney and elsewhere. In 1940 he made a fine lead of Rothley Crack.

1940 - 1950

The outbreak of War slowed down activity but the King's College Club was still active. As well as frequent visits to Simonside the College Club did routes on Crag Point, Yardhope and Sandy Crag. Transport was difficult and the crags were in relative solitude; the vegetation gave many the impression that little climbing had been done and the lack of written material seemed to confirm this. When the College climbers turned their attention to Crag Lough they met Basil Butcher, Keith Gregory, Charlie Gosman, Syd Walker, Joan Edwards and Muriel Thorpe; Bracket, Pinnacle Face, Hadrian's Buttress and Chimney, Trapezium and Tarzan were already favourites. Throughout the period this group, augmented by Brian Cooke, Bob Conn and others developed the crag until by the end of the decade 46 routes could be recorded. Main Wall was climbed by Butcher and Gregory, Grads Groove by Cooke and Conn.

Two other wartime climbers deserve mention, Derek Maling, who began the work on the guide to Crag Lough, and John Sally Lunn. Both were involved in falls on Crag Lough, neither serious, but these accidents led to the formation of the first Northumbrian Climbing Club which, after a short life from 1942-1943, disbanded with the exodus of most members to the Forces.

The return to the crags began in 1945-46 and the present Northumbrian Mountaineering Club was formed almost immediately. Its first hut Antic Hay, near the Twice Brewed, was the base for further

To the crags during the winter 1955-56.
Eric Rosher, Bill Troup, Frank Caroll and Geoff Oliver.
Sporting all the latest climbing equiptment!
Photo: Nev Hannaby

assaults on Crag Lough. During 1947 Tony Moulam, stationed at Catterick, led Impossible Buttress Route 1 with Alf Mullan belayed to home-made pitons. Having roped down to inspect the traverse across Impossible Wall, Cooke pioneered the Girdle traverse of Main Wall with Butcher and Mullan. During his short stay in the area Moulam also climbed The Organ Pipes, Hoozits Crack (he was Hoozit), Centurion's Crack and Helix, with Gosman, T.P. Snell and other locals.

Surprisingly Peel Crag was regarded as too loose and broken for good routes. One route (probably Sunset) called Garden Wall was well known but, the crag received little attention. Cheviot was very popular however. Early work by Butcher and Gregory led to bus meets by the NMC. to Henhole, Bizzle and Dunsdale. The latter was particularly popular. A fatal accident at this time gave the crag a bad reputation. Philip McGill, a leading climber at the time, was attempting a new route when he was hit by a rock from above and killed and his second, Harry Warmington, injured. In the Henhole, the steep rock walls were a great attraction; Zig Zag, Cannonhole Direct and Black Adam's Corner had already been climbed by Butcher and Gregory while McGill and Warmington had led Long John (then Rib and Wall), College Groove and Tombstone.

Towards the end of the decade the NMC. concentrated on producing the first guide which appeared in 1950. It contained three main sections. The Crag Lough section was prepared by Butcher, Gosman and Cooke; Simonside area was based on the original King's College work brought up to date by Jack Pickeford and the Wanneys section was the work of A.P. Rossiter. G.W. Young was still alive and took an interest in the work, contributing a foreword (in fact an article by Gregory in the F.R.C.C. Journal for 1946 mentioning his early ascents on Crag Lough brought forth a sharp rebuke from Young in the next Journal). It is surprising however that Cheviot was not included and some of the routes done by them on Crag Lough and elsewhere were similarly missed.

1950 - 1964

The fifties saw further development of Crag Lough and Peel Crag. This was largely due to the efforts of Albert Rosher, an enigmatic and indefatigable character with an eye for good lines and the ability to force them. Albert began his activities in the forties. In 1952 a group known as the Crag Lough Club was formed with Albert as the key figure and Frank Carroll, Don Laws and Geoff Oliver as early members. The group was responsible over the subsequent years for most of the harder routes on Crag Lough including Sciatica, Crescent Crack, Why Not, Impossible Buttress Route 3 and Y Climb. Peel Crag was also developed. The group, always small, continued into the sixties and its success was attested by an increase in the number of routes on Crag Lough in the 1964 guide of 32 plus a new section of 22 routes on Peel Crag. Nev Hannaby, responsible for a number of new routes, had previously completed a full guide to Crag Lough and Peel Crag which was unfortunately never published. Other active members included Eric Rayson, Terry Sullivan and John Cheesmond. Members of the group added one or two lines to Wanney and developed the quarry in Rothbury into a fierce climbing gymnasium.

During this period there came the development of a number of unexploited crags. In 1954/55 Peter Biven was stationed at Boulmer and put up a score of routes on Ratcheugh and about 10 fierce routes on Cullerose. The Northumbrian M.C. was active and produced a short guide to Kyloe Crags (Collar Heugh) showing sixteen routes put up largely by G. Lewis, E. Clarke and B. Butcher in 1957/58. Another member, Malcolm Lowerson, put up solo the main routes on Jack Rock around 1960. Crag Point was tackled as a serious climbing ground and a number of routes were added to Henhole where E.A. Wrangharn was a frequent visitor.

As with the 1950 guide, the 1964 edition was not a true statement of the position at the time. Many more crags had been explored and routes worked out than the guide gave credit for, but neither of these guides attempted to be comprehensive. The 1964 guide was a hurried and piecemeal affair which would never have appeared at all if an attempt had been made at complete coverage of the county's climbing. Work had been going for some years on preparation of the guide but inactivity had set in when Norman Haighton took over in 1963. Adding only Peel Crag and Jack Rock to the material inherited the guide was published without further ado to fill the immediate need.

Nev Hannaby
83. Main Wall Route Two (VS 5a), Crag Lough
circa 1956
P111
Photo: Nev Hannaby Collection

1965 - 1971

The Crag Lough group, though diminishing, continued and Albert Rosher, at his own expense, brought out a small guide to new routes (some 70) added to Peel Crag and Crag Lough, most of which were his own work. The Border Climbing Club was formed and concentrated its early efforts on Crag Lough but a list of routes on Bowden Doors was produced which showed the crag to have been well worked by members of the club. Climbing spread on all fronts, climbers and clubs proliferated and crags of all types were sought out. Causey Quarry, first discovered by Nev Hannaby, was developed into a popular evening centre. Coe Crag, Cullernose Point, Belling Crag, Kyloe Crags, all had their devotees and it is doubtful whether any crags remained unvisited or easier lines unclimbed. What was lacking was some co-ordination and attempt at documenting the position. Since 1968 Allan Austin had been visiting the county occasionally and, with David Roberts, tackling some hard lines on the lesser known crags. Most of the lines on Coe Crag, The Sorcerer on Colour Heugh, and new lines on Bowden Doors and Kyloe were all climbed. By 1970 it was becoming popular to visit many of these crags on summer evenings and the arrival of Hugh Banner and John Hiron on the scene led to regular assaults on the local crags. The NMC. had long been neglecting its own county for the bigger climbing areas and it was decided in July 1970 to attempt a new and comprehensive guide to the county. Several people shared the work. While the main crags were being developed the county was searched for other climbing areas and over 200 possibilities visited by Norman Haighton. As a result, the number of major crags described rose from 7 in the 1964 guide to 14, and 26 minor crags could also be mentioned.

The Crag Lough and Peel Crag area was covered by John Roberts while working at the YHA and his feat of cataloguing, climbing and describing more than 150 routes in less than a year warrants recognition. On the Simonside area Geoff Jackson had a similar task but with the added problems of distance. Apart from the addition of one or two harder lines like Sagittarius and The Quiver, the main efforts on the Simonside face were in tidying up, rationalising and rewriting. The major effort was required on Ravensheugh where a number of impressive crack lines had no recorded ascents, though some undoubtedly had been climbed. Hugh Banner, Dennis Lee, John Hiron, David Roberts and Jim Patchett assisted Geoff Jackson and ascents were made of Pendulum, Baluster Crack, The Trouser Legs, Honeymoon Crack, Cave Crack and Ravensheugh Crack. Sandy Crag was also developed by the same team, providing a handful of hard lines.

Another area of considerable effort was Kyloe. John Hiron started the work which was finished by Dennis Lee. Some good lines had been added on the traditional Kyloe Crags by Allan Austin, particularly Penitent's Walk and Coldstrearn Corner, but the main development came on Kyloe-in-the-Wood. This crag, deep in the wood, was only discovered in the sixties and by 1970 there were a number of good lines. The same group as at Simonside augmented by Malcolm Lowerson, Ken MacDonald and John Earl, made some fine ascents including The Elf, Thin Hand Special, The Harp and The Crucifix, Hugh Banner leading Thin Hand Special and The Crucifix.

Bowden Doors area was written up by Hugh Banner with the help of the material prepared by the Border C.C. Other lines were successfully attempted particularly Main Wall and First Leaning Groove led by Malcolm Rowe, and some new routes recorded on Colour Heugh. The Cheviot area was brought up to date by Malcolm Lowerson and together with Jim Patchett and Norman Haighton, new routes were added on the main crag and some outlying buttresses were developed. Jim Patchett made fine leads of Misconception, Conception Corner, The Brute, Fingery Jim and Steerpike. David Roberts prepared the Coe Crag and Cullernose Point sections. Having done much work on these crags in the past he was in a good position to record the results. Malcolm Rowe had been responsible for some fine leads on Cullernose Point including Zero G. Corby's Crag, long known but never extensively climbed, was assaulted by Ken MacDonald and John Earl and with a number of friends, many lines were worked out including Sunshine Superman and the long routes on North Buttress. The work of preparing the Causey Quarry section fell to Ed Thompson (father and son), Ed (Junior) having soloed all the routes on numerous occasions, had doubtless made first ascents of some and certainly added The Haunt.

Bob Hutchinson
38. Northumberland Wall (E2 5c), Great Wanney
Bob changed the face of Northumberland
climbing during the early 1970s
P140
Photo: David Reay

1971 - 1979

Following publication of the guide in 1971 Hugh Banner's influence continued to be felt for another year or so through such climbs as Thunder Crack on Simonside and a number of lines on Wanney including Patchett's Plunge and Great Wall on which he was joined by Mick Foggon who led the excellent first pitch.

In the autumn of 1972 Bob Hutchinson, who in subsequent years was to change the face of Northumberland climbing, appeared on the new route scene with his ascent of the Trial. This was probably the hardest route in the county at this time, an impressive achievement from this newcomer to the sport.

Around this time he and John Earl struck up a partnership which, between 1973 and 1976, was responsible for most of the significant developments in the county. These included at Jack Rock, The Butcher and free ascents of Ancient Briton and The Girdle; at Ravensheugh - Sandrider, Rampart Crack, Candle in the Wind and Gates of Eden; at Sandy Crag - Angel Fingers and Sandy Crack (perhaps one of the best hard routes in the county); at Bowden Doors -free ascent of Overhanging Crack, Stretcher Wall and The Sting; at Back Bowden Doors - The Enchanter; at Corby's Crag - Gibbon's Gambol and at Kyloe - Bad Finger and Australia Crack. Hutchinson's ascent of this last route was again a significant step forward and it was not repeated for two years. In addition they found time for the development of South Yardhope, Linshiels and Goats Crag.

The most significant developments by other climbers during this period were the free ascent of the Dangler at Stanley Quarry (possibly by Bob and Tommy Smith). Malcolm Rowe's ascent of the Witch at Back Bowden Doors and the extensive gardening at Thrunton Crag by Gordon Thompson.

In 1976 details of these new routes were published in a "New Climbs Supplement." This limited edition once more stimulated interest in the area, though in the early stages most teams were working their way through the new routes in the guide, leaving Hutchinson and Earl to add more scalps to their belts with such fine routes as Whinstone Churchill at Crag Lough; Idiot Wind and Northumberland Wall at The Wanneys; Red Rum, The Pearler and The Entertainer at Kyloe; Salvation at Sandy Crag; Last Straw at South Yardhope; On The Verge at Back Bowden Doors; Childhood's End, Plumbline and free ascent of Honeymoon Crack at Ravensheugh; Overdrive at Goats Crag and The Deep at Cullernose Point Towards the end of this period however other climbers began to make their presence felt. Dave "Cubby" Cuthbertson made a free ascent of Monty Python at Kyloe (introducing chalk for the first time on a new route in the county), Jeff Lamb ascended The Manta at Bowden Doors, Martin Doyle and Karl Telfer climbed Ranadon at Corbys Crag and Paul Stewart led Bad Company (later given an independent finish by Earl) and Elf Direct at Kyloe.

By 1978 the heat was on, the prospect of a new guide no doubt fanning the flames. Hutchinson and Earl managed a good quota of fine climbs, notably; Nerve Wrack Point and Jonathan Livingstone Seagull at Cullernose Point; Endless Flight at The Wanneys; Culloden at Great Dour; High T at Kyloe; The Gauleiter, The Goose Step, The Wave and The Boomer at Bowden Doors and Octopus and Childhoods End at Ravensheugh. The contribution from other teams was hardly less significant and included the development of Callerhues Crag into a hard gymnastic climbing ground by Bob and Tommy Smith who also put up a number of excellent routes around the county, notably The Barbarian and The Rajah at Bowden Doors. Steve Blake's new routes included the very good Poseidon Adventure, Prime Time and Original Sin. Jeff Lamb plucked two plums, Over the Edge on Simonside and Impossible Wall at Crag Lough and Bill Wayman put up two very hard routes at Peel Crag Ritual and Sacrifice.

Tragically on 31 st August 1978 when the preparation of the guide was well under way Bob Hutchinson, who had done more than anyone to render the old guide obsolete, was killed in the Lake District doing the thing that mattered most to him, prospecting for a new route.

A final fling of activity led right up to the closing date for inclusion in the guide with the addition of new routes, particularly in the Bowden Doors area where Bill Wayman and Paul Stewart made successive solo ascents of Cruel Dude and the Smith brothers climbed Lost Cause and Crater Maker.

Paul Stewart
39. Bad Company (E2 5c), Kyloe in the Woods
Paul climbing one of his most popular routes.
P192
Photo: Bob Smith

1979 - 1988

Towards the end of the period covered by the last guide a new force in Northumbrian climbing, in the spindly shape of Bob Smith, had emerged. Initially climbing with brother Tommy, Callerhues was developed and then they spread their efforts far and wide across the county.

In the early period following Bob Hutchinson's tragic death in the Lake District a number of people were vying with Bob for the significant routes, including Steve Blake, John Earl, Tommy Smith, Paul Stewart and Bill Wayman. The best of these routes were Hitchhikers and Underpass by Steve Blake, Outward Bound and Quiet County by Paul Stewart and John Earl, Lost Cause and Barracuda Roof by Tommy Smith and Rising Damp, High Tide, His Eminence, Dulalai T.A.P., Thin Ice, Sabbath, First Born and Thunder Thighs by Bob Smith.

The main competition slowly disappeared however, Tommy Smith retired (it has since become an annual event), John Earl developed tendonitis Paul Stewart, Bill Wayman and Steve Blake all left the area leaving Bob to dominate the scene. Their departures seemed to coincide with the numbers getting harder and the consequences becoming ever more serious, a situation which Bob relished. Following Tommy's retirement and Paul's departure Bob Smith and a partially mended John Earl teamed up and the next few years resulted in the following hard classics; Merlin, Macbeth, Absent Friend, Rock and Roll Star and Leonardo.

In the early eighties a powerful local youth, one Peter Kirton, spurned the appeal of routes to direct his not inconsiderable strength to the art of bouldering, producing; Vienna at Bowden and Playing Rudies at Kyloe-in-the-Woods. Bouldering with Peter honed Bob's competitive edge extending in the process many problems into routes such as the fine Bowden Doors selection of Toffs, Liberty, The Bends and Poverty. Elsewhere in the county highly technical routes the like of Bonneville, Kremlin, Crouching the Mahogany and Second Born ensued.

In the last couple of years quality climbs have continued to be turned out by the locals the majority of the best and hardest including Morgan, Right of Reply, Mordreth, Trial Separation and Upper Crust fell to Bob Smith accompanied on the last three by Earl. Throwback on the esoteric Broomlea Lough Crag, was also discovered by the same team but this time the roles were reversed. Other contributions have come from Karl and Graham Telfer with When the Wind Blows at Back Bowden, John Wallace who ascended Stairway to Heaven at Great Wanney, Kev Howett with Breakout at Jack Rock, Tim Gallagher and Tommy Smith who alternated leads on High Society and Crucifixion at Kyloe In and at Kyloe Out where Tommy emerged yet again as the Elder Brother. Probably the major event of this time however was Bob Smith's lead of the very technical and equally serious On The Rocks which tackles the centre of the Tube Wall. The invaders also got in on the act with Tony Courts toughing it out on Peak Technique (no doubt appropriately named) and Mark Liptrot adopting professional tactics to conquer Death Knell.

Finally the significant routes of 1988 were: Rough Passage where the addition of an independent finish by Bob Smith and John Earl gave a superb and serious route over The Wave. Imminent Break Crisis, a hand traverse across the quarry wall at Goat Crag courtesy of Andy Moss; and Karl Telfer's Ruth Route, a technical piece of climbing, this time up the centre of the Goat Crag's quarry wall. Regrettably however, immediately adjacent to this route a number of chipped holds have appeared. This brings the recent history of climbing in Northumberland up to date but it does seem an unfortunate note on which to finish. Let us hope however that the current bouts of chipping are isolated incidents and do not prevail. We the local activists are determined that they shall not and will do everything in our power to preserve our delicate and beautiful crags.

Bob Smith
77. First Born (E4 6b), Kyloe Crag
Bob on the first ascent
of one of his many new routes
P182
Photo: Phil Swainson

1989 – 2004

Following the completion of the last guide Smith and Earl together with most of the guide book team directed their energies elsewhere leaving the field free for a new wave of young local climbers including Hugh Harris, John Wallace, Steve Roberts and Tim Gallagher who were joined by itinerants Dave Pegg and Richard Davies.

The guide was only just published when Richard Davies was stretching his legs to produce Agape E6 at Ravensheugh, Imagery at Bowden and Devils Soulmate E6 at Howlerhirst. Hugh Harris who in the next few years was to make a significant contribution to Northumberland climbing started at Ravensheugh with an impressive string of hard new routes, First Among Equals E6, Lapse of Reason E5 and, he also partnered Tim Gallagher on his lead of Castaway E6.

In 1990 raiders from north and south made their attacks. The evergreen Dave Cuthbertson promoting County Ethics at E7 7a possibly the County's technically hardest route at the time, which wasn't repeated for 13 years due to a combination of difficulty and the loss of a hold, and Ian Cummings who had repeated a number of Bob Smith's harder routes went into battle with Rip the Lip E6 at Bowden. In the same year Hugh Harris added Living on Borrowed Time E6 and Victim of Circumstance E5 at Sandy.

In 1991 things really did take off with all of the young guns involved. Dave Pegg producing his trilogy of hard routes at Back Bowden, Big Ariel Dynamite E5 7a, King Lear E6 and The Pixies E6, Richard Davies climbing Katana E6 at the Wanney's, Tim Gallagher The Dungeon E6 at Goats Buttress and the relative novice Joe Webb did Time and Motion E7 at Sandy. But this was really Hugh Harris's year. With John Wallace and Dan Patterson on Bowden he did Inner Space E6 and Narcosis E6, at Ravenshugh he found Paradise Lost with Rhian Webb and at the Wanneys there was a Policy of Truth with Ian Cummings. All of these are major routes but the event of the year was his audacious and futuristic Crisis Zone E7 at the Wanneys.

Between 1992 and 2000 significant new routes were few but the ones climbed were another step forward. Malcolm Smith climber extraordinaire in 1994 made his contribution to Northumberland routing with Transcendence E8 and Leap of Faith E6 and in the same year Steve Roberts matched Malcolm with the very pumpy and serious I Bet He Drinks Carling Black Label also at E8. In 1995 Nick Dixon repeated On the Rocks and added a hard companion route Off the Rocks E8. In 1996 Noel Crane who lived for a few years in the north east stretched further than anyone had stretched before to give Border Reiver E7 at Ravensheugh.

This dearth of new routes at the cutting edge may have had something to do with the rise in the popularity of bouldering and the publication of the Northumberland Bouldering Guide. However in 2000 perhaps because a New Definitive Guide was being produced routing came back into fashion and Andrew Earl made his first important contribution to new routes with the technically hard and serious The Young E8 up an immaculate wall at the secluded Callaly Crag, and the difficult Masterclass E7 and bold Master Blaster Arête E7 at Rothley.

In 2001 the Foot and Mouth epidemic put new routing on hold. In 2002 Andrew Earl gave an indication of what was to follow with The Ayes Have It E8 7a at Ravens Crag but it wasn't really until 2003 that it got going again. Mark Savage smeared his way up the bold eliminate Savage Slab E7 at Back Bowden. However the year provided Andrew Earl with the opportunity to reach another Northumberland milestone. He climbed the impressive Crocodile Arête at Ravensheugh E7 but then moved grades up a notch with Northumberland's first E9's The Prow at Kyloe in the Woods and The Darkside at Back Bowden, two superb, difficult and serious routes. Over this period Steve Crowe as well as the new routes at Linshiels, did a number of second and third ascents of some of the County's harder climbs such as Where Angels Fear to Tread, Master Blaster Arête, Master Class, Off the Rocks and Charlottes Dream Direct.

In 2004 as the guide was being brought to a close Mark Savage produced a number of eliminate type routes but his best effort was a direct start to his route AKA Mr Vegas to give a fine independent climb. Finally Andrew Earl using his finely honed climbing competition skills produced a very hard Direct Start to Endless Flight, eliminating in the process Steve Crowe's alternative entry.

TommySmith
7. Guardian Angel (E5 6a), Howlerhirst Crag
Tommy had long arms and a longer neck!
P162
Photo: Bob Smith Collection

How to use this guide....

Major Crag Section Author	National Grid Reference Aspect Metres above sea level Approach time from parking place in minutes

History
As well as the general history in the introduction there is a short historical section for each major crag.

Situation and Character
A colourful description of each major crag. The colour band for each crag indicates the rock type, more details can be found in the geology section on page 13.

Approaches and Access
Driving distances are measured in miles whereas the walking distances are described in kilometres. A selection of the crags have approach maps. Other crags may refer to a map on another page. Always seek permission if the section indicates that this is the norm.

Minor Crag **Web Guide**	**National Grid Reference**

Many of the crags in this section have good routes and are well worth a visit for a short day or evening. More information can be found on some of the minor crags by visiting the NMC web site at www.thenmc.org.uk

John Earl
55. Duke of York (E1 5b)
The first Earl of Northumberland
battles with the Duke of York.
Photo: Andrew Earl

Back Bowden Doors (Colour Heugh)

NU 065336
West Facing
170m
10 minutes

Steve Roberts

History

Back Bowden Doors has a fairly early history with climbing first recorded in the 1935 Oxford and Cambridge Mountaineering Journals under its local name of Lion Rock. It mentions routes that sound suspiciously like those on the south end of the crag. Unfortunately the routes ascended up to 1965 are without documentation. In 1965 Rodney Wilson climbed the brilliant Arches, a soaring diagonal traverse on the north crag. 1968 saw Allan Austin and Dave Roberts climbing the ferocious Sorcerer which still demands respect today. Also around this time Ken Wood climbed The Sorcerer's Apprentice. In 1973 Hugh Banner, doing what he does best, jammed over Roof Route. 1974 saw the first ascent of the Central Wall on the North crag with The Witch by Malcolm Rowe and Nev Hannaby. In 1975 Bob Hutchinson and John Earl produced two bold companion routes for The Witch, The Enchanter led by Hutchinson and the Broomstick by Earl. 1976 saw four more routes climbed, Magic Flute and Glass Slipper by Hannaby and Rowe, and the bold On The Verge by Earl and Hutchinson. Later in that year Hutchinson climbed Black Magic. In 1977 Earl and Hutchinson came across The Duke of York. The following year produced a spate of fine hard routes with Earl and Hutchinson (again) climbing Broken Glass and The Wand. The same team, this time led by Hutchinson, climbed the brilliant Tube and Hard Reign. Unfortunately this was to be Bob Hutchinson's last route on the crag. Also in 1978, Steve Blake and Jeff Lamb came under The Spell.

1979 saw Tommy Smith going head over heels with the very impressive Lost Cause and Dwarfs Nightmare with brother Bob. Meanwhile Paul Stewart along with Earl stretched it out on the intimidating Outward Bound. 1981 was to see the first breach of the impressive overhanging North Wall with Merlin by Bob Smith and Earl. Later in the year Earl and Bob Smith collected Pyewackit and Shackletack with Ian Kyle. In 1982 the second route on the North Wall fell again to Bob Smith and Earl with the bold and technical Macbeth. On a summer's evening in 1985 Bob Smith and Earl extended The Tube with Uncouth Youth and Smith stretched it even further with the relentless but well protected Right of Reply. The following year Bob Smith was at the North Wall again this time with brother Tommy producing Morgan. 1987 proved to be a popular year for bold technical routes starting with Bob Smith's ascent of the much sought after On The Rocks while Tony Coutts smeared his way up Peak Technique in slippers. Karl and Graham Telfer woke up with Charlotte's Dream and the bulging When The Wind Blows. Leading up to the publication of the 1989 guide, activity was rounded off with Bob Smith and Earl climbing the very sustained Mordreth also on the North Wall.

Cutting edge development continued on the impressive North Wall in the early nineties with a Scottish raid from Dave Cuthbertson adding the desperate County Ethics. In 1991 Dave Pegg brought his new routing eye and not inconsiderable fitness to claim the very bold Pixies and the powerful but safe King Lear. Whilst working at Proctor and Gamble, Pegg added his last new route to the crag in the form of the very short and very hard Big Aerial Dynamite. 1994 brought two big routes with big numbers. I Bet He Drinks Carling Black Label, by Steve Roberts, added the longest and hardest route on the North wall to date, whilst Malcolm Smith picked off one of the County's last great lines with the fantastic Transcendence. 1995 saw the addition of yet another fine bold climb on the Tube wall with Nick Dixon going Off the Rocks.

Recent years have seen a slow down in terms of new routes or significant repeats of the harder lines, as most eyes turned to the quality of bouldering found at this venue, however in the build up to this guide a number of fine repeats and quality variations have been added. Mark Savage added the audacious Savage Slab and straightened Charlottes Dream. This development culminated with the ascent of perhaps the counties hardest route to-date, an awesome addition, The Dark Side on the North Wall by Andrew Earl, following in his fathers footsteps with a last minute addition to this outstanding piece of rock just before the guide goes to print! It is hoped that this trend of activity

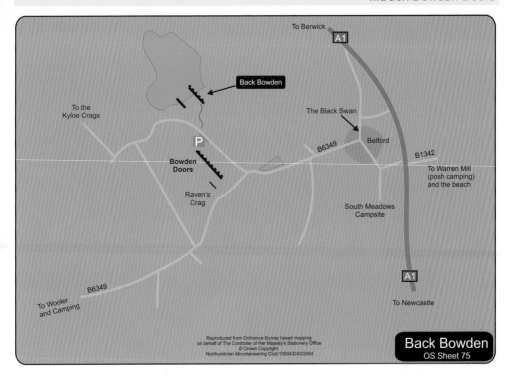

will continue and that the routes on this crag, which offer one of the finest collection of outcrop extremes in the country will continue to be enjoyed in the future. To this end, descriptions and accurate grading for on sight attempts have been carefully examined to encourage activity on the extremes.

Situation and Character

Shown as Dancing Green Hill on the map, Back Bowden Doors lies approximately 3 miles west of Belford in an unusually sheltered position looking west across a shallow valley. The rock is Fell Sandstone of the same good quality as that found at Bowden Doors. The crag tends to dry very quickly with the exception of the North Wall, which needs a number of days to fully dry after heavy rain. Routes on this wall can suffer from holds snapping, particularly after a damp spell. Excessive use of the routes should be avoided at these times in order to prevent damage. This crag offers a fantastic selection of some of the best extremes in the area, with a superb contrast of climbs, including bold technical walls, intricate smearing tests and the legendary North Wall, the crucible of steep and powerful climbs. Unusually many of the harder lines offer reasonable protection. While containing many routes in the upper extremes, plenty of routes exist in the easier grades.

Approaches and Access

From Belford take the B6349 Wooler Road. Continue for 3 miles, turn right at the Hazelrigg sign and follow this for ½ mile to the brow of the hill and a large steel gate on the right. Park here, being careful not to block the gate. Pass through the gate and continue left to another gate. Follow the track and the main crag soon comes into view. This track can be very damp and muddy and approach footwear is recommended. There is no public right of way and the relationship between the landowner and climbers has been strained. Visitors should ensure they park cars well away from the gates and off the road. Please also take care to avoid disturbances to the livestock.

Andrew Earl
10. County Ethics (E7 7a)
Cubby's route remained unrepeated for 13 years
Photo: Steve Crowe

The Quarry Face

The Climbs

The rocks are arranged in two main buttresses separated by an arc of lower rocks, which contain many small problems, too short to merit individual description. The climbs are described from left to right when facing the crag. Although a number of micro routes exist, the first climb of note is the rightward trending crack line of Diagonal.

Quarry Face

1. Diagonal 6m VD
After an awkward start the crack leads, without further difficulty, to the top.

2. The Toppler 6m HVS 5b
Start 4 metres to the right at a short scoop. Climb this to gain the two broken flakes followed by an awkward mantel. An easy finish is soon at hand.

3. Lichen Groove 7m D
The obvious, vegetated leaning corner just right, with a large wedged block at its top is climbed direct.

4. The Tippler 7m HVS 5b
Immediately right of Lichen Groove, beneath the slab, is a cramped overhung ledge which runs up from the ground. Move awkwardly right along this to straighten on a small foothold in the middle of the slab. Climb straight up on improving holds via the easy groove above.

5. The Bogie 9m MS
Start at the undercut 2 metres right of The Tippler where a strenuous pull leads to good holds and a small ledge. Continue up the cracked slab slightly right, then up to the overlap to finish up the right side of the blunt nose.

6. Quarry Face 10m MS
The slabs to the right appear to have been quarried in antiquity. Climb easily up to a crack in the centre of the quarried face. Up the crack and finish with difficulty on the right via a good flake hold. The blunt nose 2 metres left of the flake may also be climbed at much the same standard.

7. Glass Slipper 12m VS 5a
Climb the lower slab just to the right and cross the overlap to a good foothold. Climb delicately up the slab to a recessed ledge. Traverse 3 metres right and pull over the upper wall to gain the top.

8. Broken Glass 11m E2 6a
A very deceptive route. Start 2 metres left of Twisting Crack. Climb the lower slab to the overlap, which is surmounted on small holds, move slightly left and then ascend the slab trending right to the ledge. Climb the upper wall.

9. Twisting Crack 8m HS 4c
Lies in the right hand corner of the quarry face at its junction with the overhanging wall. The crack is undercut but once the niche 3 metres up is gained, excellent hand jams lead to the top.

To the right is the stunning North Wall. All the routes to the right on the overhanging wall are of a high standard and quality to match.

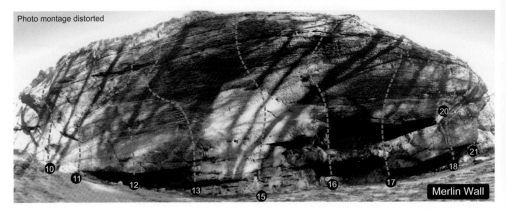

Photo montage distorted

Merlin Wall

North Wall

10. County Ethics 10m E7 7a ***
A route with a very hard crux. Start 5m right of Twisting Crack beneath the obvious hanging scoop in the head wall. Climb the overhanging wall to reach a line of pockets (Rock "n" Roller/ Slug protection), move into and up the scoop to finish.

11. Merlin 11m E5 6a ***
The original and arguably still the best way up this wall. Gains the left hand end of the obvious ledge, which is at one third height on the overhanging wall. Hand traverse the ledge to the centre then move up to the horizontal crack (Good friend protection). Climb the wall above, insitu thread, on pockets and rounded holds to an exciting grapple with the heather!

12. The Pixies 11m E6 6b *
A fingery and powerful climb, protection is available but is poor and difficult to place. Start right of Merlin below the middle of the ledge at one third height. Climb the boulder problem wall to the ledge and then move up the steep wall above, 2m left of Merlin, to a typically rounded finish leftwards.

13. Morgan 14m E5 6a *
After a bold start this route offers fine climbing with excellent protection. Climb to the right end of the large shelf/ break via two large potholes. Pull up to the upper break using two small pockets, gear in Merlin. Traverse right to a good hold and a good threaded wire, pulling over the bulge directly above to finish.

14. I Bet He Drinks Carling Black Label 20m E8 6c **
A long, bold and very sustained climb. A fall from the latter part of this route is possible but not advisable! Climb Morgan to its thread and good hold, continue rightwards following the seam on very poor holds to reach the hanging corner, pull up into this, committing yet tempting given the fall potential and finish rightwards.

15. The Dark Side 11m E9 7b ***
Bold and outrageously hard climbing up the central line of this wall. Start just right of the centre of the white shield, making ever harder and more committing moves following a curving line of non holds!, to the sanctuary of the three quarter height break, where poor protection is available before finishing direct.

16. Mordreth 11m E6 6b **
A great bold climb, sadly friable. Start 8m right of Morgan at the back of the cave. Climb the short pillar to the roof, swing out of this to gain a good hold on the wall above. Pull across right and climb the wall to the first horizontal break, move back left to another horizontal and finish over the bulge above.

17. Macbeth 11m E6 6b ***
A classic route which can be protected in proportion to your stamina. Start under the overhang left of the start of The Arches. Climb under the roof. Pull out right to the lip using a large pot hole and then use another pot hole to pull onto the wall. Traverse to the rightmost of three pot holes, friend 2½ and then climb up the wall to the break using the deep mono. Move right to finish on the obvious fluting.

Andrew Earl
15. The Dark Side (E9 7b)
Perhaps the hardest route in The County
Photo: Steve Crowe

Witch Wall

The right hand of the three pot holes can be gained from The Arches.

18. The Arches 16m HVS 5b ***
An awesome line offering excellent protection, taking the soaring left to right overlap. Make an awkward move to gain the start of the overlap and follow this to its end, finishing up the flutings.

19. Cauldron 14m E1 5c
Start up The Arches and finish via the obvious break right of Hard Reign.

20. King Lear 11m E6 6c *
A powerful but protectable boulder problem type route up the wall right of Macbeth. Start as for the Arches and climb this route for 3m. Move left through the roof (no 1 Rock in small hidden pocket) to gain holds at the base of the small hanging flake. Climb the headwall (crux) using very small holds and the flake to reach the flutings and finish as for Macbeth.

21. Hard Reign 14m E3 5c **
An excellent route crossing The Arches. Climb the arête to the right of the start of The Arches to a good thread beneath the overhang. Move left, surmount the overhang with difficulty and continue more easily to the top.

22. Holly Tree Corner 14m MS 4b *
The corner is climbed direct, the section through the holly tree being the hardest.

The crack running left from Holly Tree Corner is climbed to flutes and the grooved slab.

To the right of Holly Tree Corner is an area of pocketed slabs with the prominent Sorcerer Roof at the right hand end.

Central Wall

23. Pyewackit 12m E4 6a
Follow the Witch to the overhang then traverse delicately left to the overhanging groove just right of the chimney. Finish up this. The wall on the left of the initial runnel provides a harder start.

24. The Witch 12m E2 5b ***
Start 3 m right of Holly Tree Corner. Climb the runnel to the overhang. Move boldly onto the wall on the right and gain an undercut crack beneath the overhang. Continue right until the overhang recedes at a shallow scoop and climb this.

25. Shackletack 12m E3 6b *
Start beneath four short flakes approximately 2 metres right of The Witch. Climb up past a crescent shaped feature to the roof. Finish directly above over the bulge.

The wall to the right offers excellent bold climbing although route finding and protection can prove difficult.

26. The Wand 14m E3 5b *
Start just left of the central weakness. Go over a bulge and gain a ledge via a short diagonal crack. Climb directly up the wall on small holds to finish just right of The Witch. Magic.

27. The Broomstick 14m E3 5b *
Start up the central weakness and continue straight up the wall above, making a long reach to gain some flutes at the top of the crack.

28. The Enchanter 14m E3 5c **
Start at a shallow scoop midway between The Broomstick and Bottle Crack. Climb the shallow scoop to a horizontal ledge and continue directly up the wall above until a traverse right can be made to gain some flutings and hence the top.

29. Strange Brew 17m E3 5b
Climb the wall immediately left of Bottle Crack to the flutings at the top (runner in flutings), step down and hand traverse the break to finish immediately right of the Wand.

John Mountain
24. The Witch (E2 5b)
Photo: Steve Crowe

Neil Anderson
38. Straight Crack (HS 4b)
Photo: Steve Crowe

30. Bottle Crack 14m MVS 4c **
The crack is undercut and hard to start but once entered it leads on steeply to finish on good holds and jams.

To the right of Bottle Crack is an impressive overhanging section with three prominent weaknesses above. All of the routes in this area have alternative starts or variation finishes, only the best versions have been described.

31. The Wizard 15m E3 5b *
This excellent route takes the obvious hand traverse just to the right of Bottle Crack finishing up the left hand weakness. Follow the traverse and pull over on the flutings. Step back left and climb the broad arête above.

32. Black Magic 14m E1 5c
Start 5 metres right of The Wizard where the roof is at its largest. Using pockets and flakes make an awkward entrance to the hanging, vegetated corner and finish up this with more ease.

33. The Vole 14m E1 5c
From the ankle threatening nose on the right climb the thin diagonal roof crack to vegetated jams. Continue into the bilberries and finish up the shallow groove on the right.
Alternative Finish E1 5c *
From the nose pull out right to good holds just below the lip of the roof. Either pull over and continue direct up the flutings above or pull across left and gain the central fluting.

34. Sorcerer's Apprentice 14m E1 5c *
Gain a small nose at the back of the overhang and swing out onto the lip. Pull up using a prominent flake crack (the central weakness). Move left and follow easier rocks to the top.

35. The Sorcerer 14m E1 5c ***
An excellent route. The right hand weakness takes the form of a shallow groove near the right edge of the wall. The start entails a long reach and strenuous arm pull to surmount the overhang. Step right and climb the delightful groove finishing up the flutings.

36. The Charm 14m E1 5c
Pull through the roof as for The Sorcerer then step up and left and go up the wall keeping just right of the arête. Finish by using the obvious undercut to reach the final flutes.

37. The Spell 13m E2 5c *
Start left of Straight Crack and climb up to good holds, move up to the pothole using a flake and a smaller pothole. Gain the short flake and continue to the horizontal break. Finish up the flutings above.

38. Straight Crack 13m HS 4b **
On the south facing wall to the right of the overhangs is a prominent crack starting as a chimney and narrowing to hand jamming width. The final crack is not as fierce as it appears.
Alternative Finish E1 5b
From the top of the crack traverse diagonally right to finish up the fluting.

39. Magic Circle HVS 5a
The obvious traverse just above the roofs. Climb Straight Crack for 3 m to a traverse line going left which is followed to Holly Tree Corner.

Golden Stairs Area

The next prominent feature is a stepped corner with three risers just to the right of Straight Crack and immediatley left of the impressive hanging slab.

40. Golden Stairs 13m VD
The first riser is the most difficult. Start from a boulder at the right hand side and move up until good holds lead back left. The second and third steps are straightforward.

Direct Start S 4c
Climb the crack in the left corner with difficulty at the top.

41. Magic Flute 12m E2 5b **
Ascends the hanging slab right of the corner of Golden Stairs. Start up Golden Stairs and make an awkward move right onto a ledge at the bottom left of the slab. Climb delicately up the slab to reach an improving fluting. Poorly protected.

42. Bolder Lands 11m E5 6b
The name gives a clue to the style of this route. Climb the cracked corner beneath the left arête of the hanging slab to join Magic Flute and arrange poor protection in the base of the slab. From the lip, traverse 1metre right to the base of a solitary flute, climb up this and finish slightly right.

43. Dead on Arrival 15m E6 6a
Follow Magic Flute to the foothold on the lip of the slab. From here traverse gingerly diagonally rightwards on smears to finish as for Peak Technique.

The counter diagonal line has also been climbed from the crescent break on Peak Technique.

44. Savage Slab 14m E7 6c *
An exciting addition combining the hardest sections of this buttress to give a committing experience. Start with the boulder problem dyno right of the Magic Flute. Gaining the break traverse right to where the bulge of the slab eases and using pockets pull up direct onto the slab keeping left of the crescent shaped break, trend left to the centre of the slab and finish direct.

45. Peak Technique 12m E6 6b ***
Testing your rubber and mental tenacity! This bold route takes the right hand side of the slab. Start as for On The Verge. From the foot ledge on the lip, step left and make your way gingerly up the slab via the diagonal smearing holds using faith and friction. Dubious protection in the crescent shaped break.

46. On the Verge 12m E4 6a **
This fine, bold route takes the right hand side of the slab. Climb the thin crack in the wall left of Woodcutter's Crack and pull out onto a ledge beneath the slab. Poor camming devices in crescent shape break. Make a high rock-over to gain a position of relative comfort before a series of bold and committing moves lead up the arête until a crack is gained, which provides an easy finish. Can be started direct, with a running jump up the arête!

47. Woodcutter's Crack 12m HVD
Climb into the recess by the left hand crack. Exit by the bulging crack on the left on good finishing holds.

48. Forester's Corner 12m D
Gain the halfway ledges from the right via a diagonal crack and finish by the corner crack in the back of the recess.

Dave Rudge
46. On the Verge (E4 6a)
Photo: Mark Savage

Tube Wall

Tube Wall

All of the routes are of superb quality.

49. Tube 15m E4 5c ***
A mega classic. Start behind the fence post 2 m right of Woodcutter's Crack. Climb the flake trending left to a ledge. Boldly follow the rightward trending scoop to beneath the overhang, traverse 4 metres right via better protection, to beneath the obvious slit and swim over the bulge onto the slab above.

Left Hand Exit E3 5b
From the top of the scoop hand traverse left to the arête and climb direct to the top.

Direct Finish E5 5c
From the top of the scoop continue direct over the roof. Bold

50. Uncouth Youth 20m E4 6a *
Follow the Tube to where it goes over the roof and continue around the arête to the lowest point in the crown of flutings, pulling over on these. A long sling is advisable to protect the finishing moves.

51. Right of Reply 23m E5 6b ***
A superb climb taking all that is best of the Tube and doubling it. Follow Uncouth Youth to below the crown, continue traversing down on the diagonal break (small cams) only to make a very hard move up and across right to the second arête. Climb flutings above and, Thank God, the top.

52. Charlotte's Dream 14m E5 6b *
A wandering route. Start in the middle of the wall. Climb the central flake for 3m to a good pocket. Traverse left to the short horizontals, protection as per the Tube. From the horizontals pull up diagonally right to a good hold then lunge for the break. Continue directly over the bulge above.

Direct Variation E7 6b **
This straightened version offers some of the best climbing on the buttress. Instead of moving left to the gear placement on the Tube, continue directly up the wall, finishing direct over the bulge.

53. On the Rocks 14m E7 6c ***
Brilliant, bold and technical climbing on immaculate rock. Start as for The Duke. From the sanctuary of the overhung ledge, step left and climb the centre of the wall above via the fading flakes making some very technical and committing moves on small ripples to gain the Tube. Finish up this, or...

Direct Finish 6b *

From the good hold on the break reach straight over the bulge to a small crimp, pull over powerfully on two sidepulls.

54. Off The Rocks 14m E8 6c *

A direct and harder variation on the previous route, offering little new, yet excellent climbing. Follow On the Rocks to the committing moves away from the main break. From a comfortable standing position, where On moves leftwards, use the good finger edge to move up and right passing very poor holds to gain the Tube break directly beneath the crack in the roof. Finish over this as for the Tube.

55. Duke of York 13m E1 5b **

Takes the obvious horizontal fault which runs across this impressive piece of rock at half height. Climb the flake crack to reach the overhung ledge, move right to the fault, hand traverse around the arête and across the wall to finish at Angle Corner. Then reverse it for fun.

56. Transcendence 13m E8 6c ***

A magnificent route with desperate bouldery moves, taking the impressive right prow of the Tube Wall. Start up the faint groove just right of the Duke, make a long reach from an undercut pocket to gain the Duke shelf, move slightly right along the break (good friends). A long pull to and leaving an obvious edge followed by some very difficult moves on poor pockets, leads to easier but bolder moves and a junction with Uncouth Youth, finish up this.

57. Lost Cause 12m E4 6b ***

A wild but safe route requiring boulder problem qualifications. Start at Angle Corner and reverse the last 3 m of the Duke of York. Pull up to the prominent broken flake and use this to gain the break above with more difficulty, move up easily to the flake finish.

58. Leap Of Faith 14m E6 6c *

A wilder direct start to Lost Cause, start in the middle of the Duke of York wall. Climb up to the obvious hole (poor large cam), use this to connect with the break, before finishing as for Lost Cause. The style of ascent depends on your reach or dynamic ability!

59. Angle Corner 10m VD

The obvious right angled corner to the right. Climb easily up to the twin cracks which lead steeply to the top.

Alternative Finish E3 6b

From two thirds up the corner traverse across the wall above to finish up Lost Cause.

60. Back To Back E5 6b

Although this route features no new climbing it is worthy of mention, as it gives yet another fantastic trip along this fine piece of rock. Climb Lost Cause, just below the top traverse left to reach the finish of Right of Reply, reverse this finishing up the Tube Left Hand. Hanging stances not allowed.

61. Gangway 10m MVS 4c

Climb the gangway just right of Angle Corner to a ledge at its top. Either the slab or the crack on the right may be taken to finish.

To the right of Gangway the rocks become lower but yield several interesting problems before they gather themselves together to form the Southern Section.

Ian Murray
49. Tube (E4 5c)
Photo: Bob Smith

Hazelrigg Wall Area

Southern Section
The first climb is marked by a holly bush.

62. Hollybush Crack 6m MS
An easy but vegetated crack is followed by a rightward traverse, which leads easily to the top. The holly proves the most difficult problem.

63. Scabby Hand 7m E4 5c
Climb the obvious scoop to the right of Hollybush Crack, as bold as it looks!

64. When The Wind Blows E6 6b *
A very bold route with a short, hard, technical section. Start below the hanging broken flake. Climb the overhang to the ledge, then make an awkward move rightwards from a layaway to the aforementioned flake. Move quickly up and left to a good hold and small wire before an easier finish above.

65. Peace At Last 12m E5 6a
Yet another bold line up this buttress. Start left of Outward Bound. Climb easy large overhangs, to a large ledge. Climb the overhanging wall by a rightward trending line of snappy holds to finish just left of Outward Bound. A harder start can be made through the large roof with a pothole in it leading to the ledge.

66. Outward Bound 12m E4 6a **
This excellent and well protected route, gives a

much safer outing than the previous three lines. It takes the right side of the impressive buttress left of March Line. Go over bulges to a horizontal crack and, using this, reach a flake and good holds above. If you used a knee lock, check your tights, Missus.

67. March Line 12m VD
Climb the crack to the left end of the ledge. Either semi hand traverse awkwardly left from the back of the ledge to a standing position on the nose at the front or reach the same point by a huge arm pull (I like it). Easier cracks lead to the top.

68. Roof Route 13m E1 5b ***
Excellent climbing. Starting 3 m right of March Line climb the obvious diagonal crack to the ledge. Climb the overhanging roof crack with difficulty to excellent finishing holds. Move right and up easily to the top.
Direct Finish E2 5c
Above the roof crack climb the crack to the overhang, move left and surmount the final overhang with difficulty.

69. Wall and Crack 13m S 4b *
As for the first pitch of Roof Route to the ledge. Climb the corner crack on the right on good holds and jams.

70. Hazelrigg Wall 8m HVS 5b *
Start 5 metres right of Roof Route. Climb the diagonal weakness leftward to the ledge. A long arm is advantageous.

71. Pinup 8m E2 6a *
The overhanging wall immediately right of Hazelrigg Wall is climbed direct via some firm but worrying nipples to the ledge.

72. Risk and Hope 15m E1 6a
The hanging corner left of Original Route. Climb this to the ledge. Directly above is an overhang with some small flakes, use these to surmount the overhang and climb the wall above.

73. Original route 14m VD **
This fine climb takes an improbable line up the highest point of the buttress just right of Hazelrigg Wall. Start at the foot of a weakness and climb on good holds via a corner to a stance below the overhangs of the upper tier. Take the overhangs at their weakest point, just right of the crack of Wall and Crack.

74. Highland Fling 15m E1 5c
Start 2 metres to the right of Original Route. Climb the centre of the slabby wall to the ledge. Surmount the roof using a large hold on the lip. Continue up the wall above.

75. Final Wall 13m VD
The wall on the right gives this route's raison d'etre. Finish via the easy corner crack which leads quickly to the top.

The Final Wall

76. Bullet 6m E1 5c
Start at the far right hand end of the heather ledge. Climb the short but bold wall via the small shell holes. Harder than it looks.

77. Big Aerial Dynamite 9m E5 7a *
A classic extended boulder problem. Easier for the small and flexible. Start between Bullet and Dwarfs Nightmare. Pull around the roof on good holds to gain the undercut flake. Achieving a standing position to reach tiny holds on the wall up and left provides the crux. A quick pull leads to better holds and the top. Small, carefully placed wires offer protection.

78. Dwarfs Nightmare 10m E2 6b *
The hanging corner in the centre of the long wall is gained with great difficulty. Spotters advisable. Once the lip is gained a short pull into the corner leads easily to the top. Desperate for the short.

79. A Short Sharp Shock 10m E3 6a
The wall right of Dwarf's Nightmare. Climb the wall on sharp flakes to the shot holes and the break. Move left along the break to the nose, a good hold on the lip leading to an awkward mantel.

80. Griffon 10m HVS 5b
At the far right end of the wall where the buttress is severely undercut an awkward move may be made to reach a hold on the lip of the overhang. From this, swing right to a flake then onto a short wall which leads to the central break. Traverse 3 metres left to a prominent crack which is climbed to the top.

Alternative Finishes
From the edge of the roof finish left or right at a similar standard.

81. Rays Roof 7m MVS 4c
The isolated buttress right of Griffon gives a pleasant roof climb. Start beneath the roof, following the cracked line up to and over the roof via large holds.

82. Footless Fulmar VS 4c *
A left to right traverse starting just right of Scabby Hand and taking the obvious break above the half height ledge and finishing right of Griffon. Superb stuff.

Alec Burns
66. Outward Bound (E4 6a)
Photo: Bob Smith

Back Bowden Doors Graded List

E9
The Dark Side 7b ***

E8
Transcendence 6c ***
I Bet He Drinks 6c **
Off the Rocks 6c *

E7
County Ethics 7a ***
On the Rocks 6c ***
Savage Slab 6c *
Charlottes Dream Direct Variation 6b **

E6
Peak Technique 6b ***
King Lear 6c *
Pixies 6b *
Mordreth 6b **
Macbeth 6b ***
Leap of Faith 6c *
When the Wind Blows 6b *
Dead On arrival 6a

E5
Big Aerial Dynamite 7a *
Charlotte's Dream 6b *
Right of Reply 6b ***
Morgan 6a *
Merlin 6a ***
Bolder Lands 6b
Back to Back 6b
Peace at Last 6a
The Tube Direct Finish 5c

E4
Lost Cause 6b ***
On the Verge 6a **
Scabby Hand 5c
Uncouth Youth 6a *
Outward Bound 6a **
Tube 5c ***
Pyewackit 6a

E3
Shackletack 6b *
Short Sharp Shock 6a
Hard Reign 5c **
Strange Brew 5b
The Wizard 5b *
The Broomstick 5b *
The Wand 5b *
The Tube Left Hand Exit 5b
The Enchanter 5c **

E2
Dwarfs Nightmare 6b *
The Witch 5b ***
Pinup 6a *
Broken Glass 6a
The Spell 5c **
Magic Flute 5b **

E1
The Charm 5c
Roof Route 5b ***
Bullet 5c
Risk and Hope 6a
Highland Fling 5c
Cauldron 5c
The Vole 5c
The Sorcerer 5c ***
Sorcerer's Apprentice 5c *
Black Magic 5c
Duke of York 5b **

HVS
Magic Circle 5a
The Arches 5b ***
Hazelrigg Wall 5b *
The Toppler 5b
Griffon 5b
The Tippler 5b

VS
Glass Slipper 5a
Footless Fulmar 4c *

Mark Savage
52. Charlotte's Dream Direct (E7 6b)
The direct line of most resistance!
Photo: Steve Crowe

Berryhill Crag

Rick Barnes

NT 938403
South Facing
75m
5 minutes

History

The crag has been climbed on for a long while, Ken Macdonald ascended Marcher Lord in the early seventies, but it was only in the 1979 edition of the guidebook that the routes were named and graded. Since then development has been sporadic, many new lines attempting to fill already small gaps or providing variations to existing routes. There have, however, been some notable exceptions.

In 1982, Bob Smith accepted the challenge of the big roof to lead Death or Glory. At the same time he climbed the equally difficult, but slightly less scary, Do or Die. Eight years later Bob returned and, on one day, climbed three new lines including Much Ado About Nothing and, with Andy Birtwistle, the difficult Legal Separation.

In 1992 Karl Telfer, in the company of his brother Graham, added Faye of Flying to the main overhang while in the previous year the pair, with Joe Gilhespy, found an excellent and independent line to the right of Marcher Lord to give This Pedestrian. Tim Catterall, visiting the crag in September 1994 added a number of additional lines, A Pocket Full of Lichenight being the best.

Situation and Character

A pleasant sandstone crag facing south and reaching a height of 15 metres. Although the rock in places must be treated with care, this crag is a beginner's paradise; there are numerous routes in the easier grades on slabs, walls and cracks and some harder lines are also available. Only the longer climbs are described here.

Approaches and Access

The crag lies roughly mid way between Wooler and Berwick, close to the village of Etal. About 1 mile north of Etal on the B6354, a farm lane leads off to the east. Parking is available on the side of the lane before the main farmhouse is reached. The top of the crag lies beyond the farm and can be reached in 5 minutes.

It is essential that all visiting climbers ask permission at the farm before proceeding to the crag.

It is highly unlikely that there will be a refusal but the approach routes may differ from time to time depending on the operational requirements of the farm. Note that this applies to organised parties as much as individuals and just because you have been given permission once does not mean you can go on without asking in the future. As with every crag, take every piece of litter away when you leave. Please do not jeopardise future access to this crag by ignoring these requests.

The Climbs

The crag is described from left to right. The bay to the left of the main crag offers a wide variety of attractive problems on slabs and a short wall. These have been left to individual enterprise. The main crag begins with a steep, west facing wall high above the main approach path.

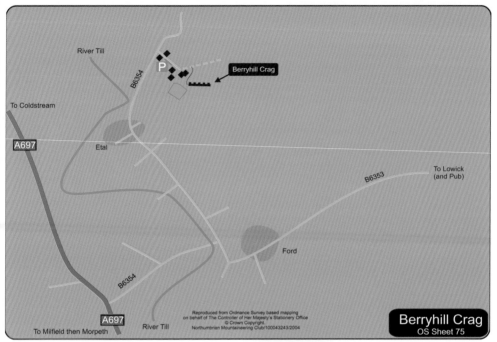

Berryhill Crag
OS Sheet 75

1. No 'O' Levels Required 8m E3 5c
The overhanging prow high up on the left.
Monkey up the black prow, taking care with
brittle flakes, to an awkward finish.

At the next level down is:-

2. Overhanging Crack 8m MVS 4c
An obvious line above and to the left of the steep
wall.

3. Much Ado About Nothing 6m E1 5b
1metre to the right of the previous route and left
of a shallow, overhanging corner is a steep wall.
Climb the wall on good holds to an easier finish.

4. Legal Separation 7m E4 6a
Delicate and difficult moves up the shallow
corner lead to a finish on the right.

Down to the next level and the start of the
obvious…………

5. Western Arête 11m VS 4c **
Climb the arête in a fine position, starting from
either side.
Direct Start 5b.

The next three climbs lie to the right of the
arête above a substructure of broken rock and
vegetation.

Bob Bennett
5. Western Arete (VS 4c)
Photo: Steve Crowe

Berryhill

6. Cheat 12m VD
Climb easily to the small overhang and pull over on good holds. Then follow the arête or the slab on its right.

7. Kinmont Willie 12m VD *
Easily up to the central crack and climb it direct.

8. Jock O' the Syde 12m VD
Scramble to the foot of the high right hand crack and start it via a slab on its right (or direct, slightly harder).

Some 15 metres further right, on a southeast facing wall, there are two short Severe problems (easy descent to the left or continue to the top, leftwards, on huge jugs), a vegetated corner crack of Difficult standard which is best avoided and a short Severe slab (descent to the right).

The next climb lies further right and takes the obvious steep crack leading to a large ledge at half height.

9. Reiver's Way 15m D *
Straight up the steep crack to the ledge. It is possible to scramble off down right but the proper finish lies up left. The upper slab has a high initial step.

To the right is a small tree in an open, vegetated, gully. This gully gives access to two routes on the upper wall.

10. Steep Fluted Wall 12m HVS 4c
From the bay behind the tree climb the overhang with good holds but on dubious rock and continue up the obvious flutes.

11. A Pocket Full of Lichenight 12m HVS 5a
A more pleasant route than it's companion but with only one good gear placement, at mid height. Climb the obvious line of pockets at the right hand side of the wall to a tricky finish.

20 metres right brings you to a large west-facing slab.

12. Slab Crack 12m D
Easily up the short corner and then climb the left trending crack. A well protected and enjoyable climb.

13. The Flutings 12m VD *
An excellent route. Climb the lower wall direct or by the right edge and then direct up the sculpted slab.

Andy Birtwistle leading **15. Marcher Lord VS 5a**
One of Northumberland's most pleasant and popular VS's

Photo: John Earl

Berryhill

The square faced pillar provides some entertaining problems and alternative starts to the previous routes. To the right, a large bay contains the following routes…

14. Hi Diddle Diddle 12m HS 4b *
The crack left of Marcher Lord. Start in the overhung corner and continue, in the same line, up the steep wall above and the flutings to finish.

15. Marcher Lord 12m VS 5a ***
The classic of the crag which takes the obvious crack line to the overhung top. Pull up the short corner and climb the crack. At the top, move right to a small cave and pull leftwards over the final overhang on superb holds. It is also possible to finish by crawling through the cave.

16. This Pedestrian 12m E3 5c *
A bold route which takes the centre of the smooth, pink, wall right of Marcher Lord. Cross the roof and continue direct to a pocketed wall of softer rock. Finish 2m right of the cave.

17. Footsloggers Trip 15m VS 4c *
Climb the groove 3 metres right of Marcher Lord to the first break then traverse left to Marcher Lord. Continue left to finish up the flutings as for Hi Diddle Diddle.

18. Potters Way 14m VS 5a
Start as for Footsloggers Trip and climb to the break beneath the final roof. Traverse left and take the right-hand exit from the cave of Marcher Lord.
Variation 14m E3 5c
This climbs the overhanging groove direct but otherwise has little independent climbing.

To the right of Potters Way lies a steep, broken wall: holds are huge but the rock is not above suspicion. Three lines can be detected, all of Difficult/Very Difficult standard. The obvious chimney on the left, the rocks to the right of the chimney and a line passing to the right of a small yew tree.

The next two routes lie slightly to the right.

19. Slanting Crack 9m MS 4a *
From a square recess, climb direct to the obvious feature and continue to the top.

20. Eastern Arête 9m MS 4a **
Start 1metre right of the previous route and climb up and right to the arête. Go round the corner then straight up. An excellent, exposed route.

At the eastern end of the crag is an obvious large two - tier boulder that provides a suitable reference point. The next five routes lie to the left of the boulder.

21. Do or Die 12m E4 6a
In the centre of the overhung bay, and 2m left of a more obvious crack, start at the thin diagonal crack. Climb up on good holds and make a hard move left to the shelf, which is followed left, to the arête. Continue to the top.

22. Faye of Flying 12m E5 6a
A hard climb that fills in the gaps between Do or Die and Death or Glory. Start as for Do or Die and continue to the obvious rock scar in the centre of the roof. Reach right, to Death or Glory, and climb to a ledge. Finish more easily up the wall on the left.

23. Death Or Glory 12m E4 5c

The big roof! Often top roped due to the extremely dubious quality of the rock. Start below the right hand side of the bay at the foot of Border Ballad. Follow the obvious line of holds across the roof, hoping that they stay attached for just a few more seconds.

24. Border Ballad 12m HVS 5b *

Climb to and across the roof crack and pull up to a standing position at the top of the chimney. The climb can be abandoned at his point but it is much better to continue up the fluted wall on the left that provides an enjoyable, exposed continuation.

25. Thrutch 8m MS 4a

The obvious chimney is climbed direct. A route for traditionalists!

The west-facing wall of the boulder, at a right angle to the main crag, provides a few short, but pleasant routes.

26. Boulder Direct 6m HVS 5a

Climb the slab on its left side, pull over the bulge with difficulty and trend left to the top.

27. Boulder Right Hand 6m VS 5a

Better protected than its neighbour, this route takes the centre of the slab, trending right to cross the overhang and so to the top.

The boulder itself offers a pleasant traverse, starting from the left and using the horizontal break to round the corner where you reach...

28. Lunger's Leap 6m E1 5b

Start below the overhanging triangle and climb to the break. Reach direct to the fluted nose and the top above. The rock is delicate here, treat it with care.

Above and behind the boulder is a steep, slabby wall that provides some short but enjoyable routes. Variations are possible but the best are described below.

29. Route One 5m M

The open chimney and crack to the left of the slab.

30. Route Two 5m HVS 5b

The steep wall can be climbed on small but satisfying edges.

31. Route Three 5m VS 5a

Further right, a thin crack and wall provide a tricky route.

32. Route Four 5m M

5 metres to the right is an easier crack.

Berryhill Graded List

E5
Faye of Flying 6a

E4
Do or Die 6a
Legal Separation 6a
Death or Glory 5c

E3
This Pedestrian 5c *
No 'O' Levels Required 5c

E1
Much Ado About Nothing 5b
Lunger's Leap 5b

HVS
Border Ballad 5b *
A Pocket Full of Lichenight 5a
Route Two 5b
Boulder Direct 5a
Steep Fluted Wall 4c

VS
Marcher Lord 5a ***
Potters Way 5a
Footsloggers Trip 4c *
Boulder Right Hand 5a
Route Three 5a
Western Arête 4c **

Bowden Doors

Andrew Earl

NU 070325
West Facing
170m
2 minutes

History

Very little is known about the early years of Bowden Doors, although a few notes were made in the Oxford and Cambridge Journals in 1935 and Peter Biven did some seven routes in 1955. Unfortunately most of the routes ascended from then to the late sixties went undocumented and any attempt to catalogue them would prove a difficult venture. In 1967 Eric Rayson climbed Canada Crack and Alan Austin with Dave Roberts picked off Woolman's Wall and Pitcher Wall. The following year saw the first known on sight lead of Lorraine by Malcolm Rowe. Austin with Ken Wood climbed Scoops 1 and 2. In 1969 Malcolm Rowe collected a couple of gems with Main Wall and First Leaning Groove. 1971 saw the first aided ascent of the Overhanging Crack involving a rest on a large chockstone near the top. In the autumn of 1972 Hutchinson, who had only been climbing some twelve months, created the crag's first extreme with his excellent route The Trial. Not only was this a test piece on Bowden but a significant step forward in the county. He soon joined forces with John Earl freeing the aforementioned Overhanging Crack and picking up Stretcher Wall.

The period from 1976 to 1978 saw the only significant first ascent by a raider. Jeff Lamb slipped across the border to pick the ripe plum; The Manta, while Hutchinson and Earl collected The Sting. Another local activist Steve Blake produced some fine routes, in particular Transformer and Don't Let Go. He also turned out what seemed at the time insignificant problems but in later years became stepping stones for the up and coming Hard Man. Climbs like The Harvest Bug, Big Splash and Y Front have become routes in their own right. By far his best achievement however, was the Poseidon Adventure, which was the first route to break through the long wave formation at the left end of the crag. This was soon challenged by Hutchinson and Earl who produced an even harder and bolder route up the white flakes on the left to give The Wave. In 1978 the same team went on to collect a string of brilliant routes such as The Gauleiter, Goose Step and Boomer.

Two new faces, Bob and Tommy Smith, started to climb new routes and in 1978 Tommy provided The Judge, and Jury either side of The Trial, and slipped his way up The Flying Fish. Meanwhile Bob climbed The Rajah, the first 'unrecognised' 6b on the crag, and the brutal Barbarian. In 1979 other local climbers also got in on the scene, namely Bill Wayman and Paul Stewart who competed over Cruel Dude, a solo duel which Wayman only just won; revenge was close at hand for Stewart with Brutally Handsome. Bob Smith started to hot things up with the strenuous Rising Damp and High Tide, together with Crater Maker and Street Runner. The following year was quiet for Bowden seeing only a few routes by Bob Smith; His Eminence, Kaiser Bill and Dog Eat Dog, an oft tried problem. 1981 and 1982 were years of short, hard problems; Pete Kirton leapt for joy on Vienna and Bob Smith climbed Toffs, Rough Passage and Liberty. Karl and Graham Telfer found Outer Limits whilst Bob Smith and Earl picked up its Direct Finish and Child's Play. 1983 and 1984 saw only two significant routes, The Bends and Poverty, both on sight solos by Bob Smith, whilst Ian Kyle clenched his cheeks and pushed his way to the front of the queue on The Belford Pie Shop. Bowden had a sleepy few years until 1988 when Mark Liptrot returned and like one of the railway children shunted his way up and down the very bold Death Knell before soloing it. The end of the 1988 summer saw Bob Smith and Earl making Rough Passage a hard and independent route.

As the last guide was going to print, Richard Davies did Imagery and shortly after publication in 1990, a fit Ian Cummings produced the stamina fest Rip the Lip. This was followed in 1991 by Narcosis and Inner Space courtesy of Hugh Harris, Joe Webb and Dan Patterson. It was not until 1999 that further significant development took place with the ascent of Hangover Wall by James Ibbertson and Heaven Can Wait by the 6 foot 5 inch Andy Cowley (which may be harder for the vertically challenged). The new millennium saw Mark Savage filling gaps with Please Stop Me in 2000, A Grave Mask in 2001 and See You in Disneyland in 2002. Who knows what the future will bring, hopefully no more chipping or heavy wire brushing, only more brilliant routes with which this crag abounds.

Situation and Character

This splendid open crag dries extremely quickly although like all sandstone, it remains weak after being wet. However, its proximity to the road and the low rainfall makes it a most valuable climbing ground. The majority of climbs are steep and often technically difficult. The rock is Fell Sandstone, with a hard outer crust which is easily damaged and top roping and abseiling is to be discouraged. Also, the leader should at all times make sure, when belaying, that the rope to the second is not rubbing across the top of the crag, resulting in irreparable grooves being created. We only have the rock once so please look after it. Too much faith should not be placed in wires and friends behind small flakes and in shallow breaks.

Approaches and Access

The crag lies just north of the B6349 Belford Wooler road. Coming from the south, turn left from the A1 at the B1342 Belford Wooler sign. Follow this into Belford then turn left at the B6349 Wooler road. Coming from the north turn right at the B1234 Detchant Middletown sign and follow this into Belford then turn right at the B6349. Continue for 3 miles keeping left when the road forks at 2½ miles. Continue for 200 metres until just over the brow of the hill. The south end of the crag is visible about 100 metres north of the road. DO NOT PARK IN FRONT OF THE GATE.

The part of the crag north of the wall is on Open Country. Climbing on this part of the crag will be as of right when the CRoW access right comes into force. The area of Open Country extends to the Back Bowden road to the east of the crag so it will also be possible to take access to the crag from this road as of right.

The part of the crag south of the wall is not on open country, nor is the traditional access route from the Belford to Wooler road to the south of the crag. Please respect the wishes of the farmer when using this part of the crag and taking access from the road

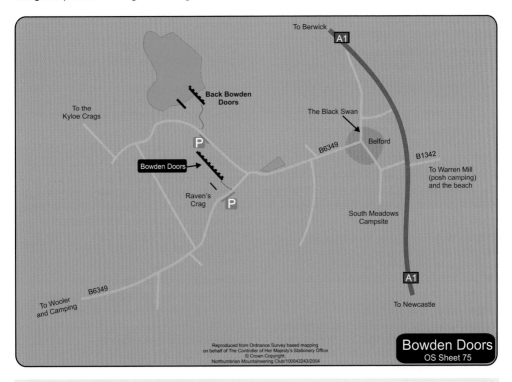

Reproduced from Ordnance Survey based mapping on behalf of The Controller of Her Majesty's Stationery Office © Crown Copyright. Northumbrian Mountaineering Club/100043243/2004

Bowden Doors
OS Sheet 75

Main Wall Area

The Climbs

The climbs are described from right to left.

1. Banister Crack 10m VD
From the first step of Introductory Staircase. Climb the crack on the right wall.

2. Introductory Staircase 12m M *
An obvious line which requires no description.

The next eight routes take the first major wall of the crag Main Wall.

3. Handrail 10m VS 4c
A very pleasant climb immediately left of Introductory Staircase. Climb the flake and the wall above, moving slightly left to the top.

4. Handrail Eliminate 10m HVS 5c
The fading flake 1 metre left of Handrail offers an eliminate problem. Finish up the wall above just left of Handrail.

5. Main Wall Eliminate 15m HVS 5b *
A classic despite its name. Climb the third flake on the wall to the break. Make a couple of delicate moves up the wall above and continue with more ease.

6. Main Wall 15m HVS 5b ***
An excellent route. Start at a small corner just right of the centre of the wall. Climb the corner, exit on the right and climb back left to finish up the stepped diagonal crack.

7. Hissing Sid 14m E1 5c
Climb the blunt arête 1m right of The Viper. After a tricky move reach the second break, move right a little and climb straight up the wall above, heading for the rightward facing flake. Continue direct to the top.

8. The Viper 16m E1 6a *
Start in the corner just right of Stretcher Wall and hand traverse horizontally right for 3 metres to where a difficult pull can be made into a thin crack. Follow this to the junction with Main Wall, break out right and climb the wall on good holds to the top.

6a alternatives have been done either side of the thin crack of The Viper.

9. Stretcher Wall 14m E1 5c *
A fine climb. Start at the left end of the first wall at a flake leading up to a small overhang. Climb the flake and make a long reach to gain the horizontal fault. Continue straight up, making another long reach. Steep but easier climbing to the top.

10. Deception Crack 12m VD
Start at the righthand end of the slab. Gain the cracks on the right and follow them via a V chimney to the top.

11. Second Staircase 12m D
Climb the crack splitting the slab. Continue up the slab to finish up the overhanging blocks.

The wall left of Second Staircase is known as Red Wall and contains several excellent climbs. At the extreme right end is the next climb.

12. Y Front 6m HVS 6a
The wall and thin ramp line left of Second Staircase

13. Jock Strap 6m E2 6b
Start as for Y Front and finish on the left.

14. Black and Tan 14m S 4b **
Climb onto an obvious flake and go up diagonally right to gain a crack which gives easier climbing to the top.
Alternative Finish HVS 5a
From the top of the flake move left and climb the wall as for Black and Tan Direct.

15. Black and Tan Direct 10m E2 6a
Climb the flake 1 metre left of Black and Tan. Move left to a small hold in the horizontal. Use this to gain a layaway and make a long reach to good holds. Continue directly up the wall above.

16. The Scoop 14m VS 4b ***
The shallow scoop 5 metres left of Black and Tan gives an excellent route, which is easier than it appears. Climb the short corner and follow the scoop to finish on good holds.

17. The Gauleiter 12m E3 6a **
A rather deceptive climb taking the centre of the rust coloured wall 2 metres left of The Scoop. Climb the wall crossing a horizontal fault at 2 metres. Continue up the wall, making some very thin moves, to the top.

18. Please Stop Me Before I Kill Myself 12m E3 6b
The wall between The Gauleiter and Grovel Groove Alternative Finish. Climb to the horizontal break and then make a hard move up the wall to easier moves, finishing direct.

19. Grovel Groove 12m MS *
The most prominent feature of Red Wall is a Y shaped recess in its centre. Climb the obvious, awkward, leftward sloping groove to finish steeply on the left.
Alternative Finish HVS 5a
From the ramp finish up the flakes on the right.

20. Kaiser Bill 12m E4 6b *
A route requiring a certain amount of commitment. Climb the two short corners left of Grovel Groove to a foothold below the thin flake.

John Earl
9. Stretcher Wall (E1 5c)
Photo: Andrew Earl

Red Wall Area

Climb this with great difficulty to gain a hold high on the left; move up to good holds and the top.

21. Goose Step 10m E3 6a **
Start at a pedestal 2 metres left of Kaiser Bill. Put your best foot forward and climb up to an obvious block, traverse right to two slots and continue up the centre of the wall.

22. A Grave Mask 10m E4 6a
Start as for Goose Step, but instead of moving right to the slots, continue directly up the wall.

23. Flake Crack 7m S 4b
Start up a short slab below the left end of the wall and climb up past the flake. Exit on the right.

24. Crater Maker 10m E4 6a
Start 2 metres to the right of The Corner. Climb the upward curving fault with difficulty to a horizontal crack. Then climb the wall above using flakes until an awkward move leads to good finishing holds.

25. Maginot Line 18m E3 6a
A traverse at one third height from Black and Tan to Flake Crack. Climb Black and Tan to a thin crack running leftward, follow this to the scoop. Move up to another obvious traverse line across Gauleiter to Grovel Groove. Traverse Kaiser Bill moving up to the slots on Goose Step, continue left to finish at a large flake.

26. The Corner 7m HVS 5a
The obvious corner at the left end of Red Wall, climbed with a little help from cracks high on the left wall.

27. Girdle Traverse of Main Wall 55m VS 4c
If the Handrail section of the first pitch is avoided the climb is Severe and provides good climbing at this grade, in a fine position. Climb Handrail to near its top, then traverse left on good holds to belay on Second Staircase. Continue traversing at the same level (avoiding the temptation of the top of the crag) to finish above The Corner.

The crag now forms a short wall facing south, which gives the next climbs.

28. Pinkie Peeler 7m VS 5a
The thin crack is climbed to the broken crack in the wall above, which is followed to the top.

29. Guard's Exit 7m VD *
There is an overhung recess up and just left of the corner. Gain the recess with difficulty via a short crack and finish on the left or right with about equal difficulty.

30. Brown Ale Wall 7m E1 5b
Climb the wall between Exhibition Crack and Guard's Exit with long reaches.

31. Exhibition Crack 7m HS 4c *
Just left of Guard's Exit is an obvious hanging crack starting 3 metres up. The start is the most difficult part.

32. Red Nose 8m VS 4c
An artificial but pleasant climb taking the nose to the left of Exhibition Crack. Start up a shallow groove and move right to finish at the top of Exhibition Crack. It is always possible to escape onto Russet Groove.

33. Russet Groove 10m VD ***
An excellent climb. Round the corner from Exhibition Crack is a well marked groove with an overhang at the top. Holds are sharp and good all the way with a bulge halfway up as the most troublesome section. Finish to the left.

34. The Overhanging Crack 10m E2 5c ***
The classic of its type in the county and a test piece at the grade. Climb the crack with increasing difficulty to just below the top on baggy jams. Make an awkward move to a large hole, then squirm your way up to the top.

35. Hangover Wall 12m E5 6c
Climb Overhanging Crack to two-thirds height, arrange your last protection then traverse out rightwards along a diagonal line of crimps, finishing with a lunge to the break.

36. Death Knell 10m E6 6c *
The wall to the left of Overhanging Crack. A very bold and sustained climb. From the right hand side of the wall, climb the shallow groove running across diagonally left to the scoop and then finish up right.

37. Heaven Can Wait 10m E6 6b
The first ascentionist was 6ft 5in tall; it may be hard for the short. Pull up from a small flake and pocket and move right to join Death Knell just below the scoop.

The next buttress starts just to the right of the arête with a jumble of boulders beneath. There are two short chimney and crack climbs in the bay to the right; one has been called Shadow Crack (Difficult) but the next route lies on the wall to the right of the chimney.

38. Family Pressure 7m E1 5c
The wall with a large pot hole. Climb the short flake just left of the large pothole and the wall above moving slightly left at the start.

39. Canada Dry 10m VS 5a
Start 5 metres right of the arête just left of the chimney. Climb the wall using a horizontal ledge to gain the large leftward trending ramp. Move along this until it is possible to move up right and reach the lip.

40. Dog Eat Dog 4m E2 6a
The bulging wall left of Canada Dry.

41. Quatra Twinkley 10m E3 6a
The arête left of Dog Eat Dog. Start just left of the arête. Easily up flake and gain good undercut. Use this to gain the top of the bulge, which is surmounted with difficulty. Wander easily up to the top.

42. Canada Crack 10m HVS 5a ***
An excellent route. Start up the obvious flake crack just left of the arête. Climb the flake and continue left along the rounded break, make an awkward move up to gain the obvious flake crack above. Climb this to the top. The upper flake crack can also be gained using the start of Klondyke Wall.

Laura Johnson
16. The Scoop (VS 4b)
Photo: Bob Smith

Leaning Grooves Area

43. Klondyke Wall 10m E2 5c **
Very good wall climbing on pockets. Start 3 metres left of Canada Crack, climb over the bulge and continue directly up the wall above until a reach right gains a good hold and the top.

44. First Century 11m E4 6a *
Very similar climbing to Klondyke only much harder. Start 2 metres left of Klondyke, climb up on rounded holds to a jug at half height and use a small undercling to reach better holds.

45. Long Crack 11m HVS 5a **
The obvious deep corner crack on the left offers a brilliant route with a very very interesting top Enough said, climb the crack.

46. Jackdaw Crack 10m HVS 5b
A good climb just left of Long Crack. Climb the crack until a move across left can be made into a wider crack. Continue up this with difficulty to a nice rounded finish.

47. Transformer 10m E2 6a *
A nice little number taking the arête on the left. From the righthand end of the overhang swing left onto the arête. Pull up and swing right and finish up Jackdaw Crack or climb the bulging arête above at 6a.

48. Long John 10m S 4c
The nose on the left is split by a prominent hanging chimney. Gain and climb the chimney. An awkward move up leads to good holds on the right.

49. The Big Splash 10m E2 5c
The two horizontal cracks on the wall left of Long John can be connected by a long and awkward reach. Finish up Long John.
Direct Finish E3 5c
From the second break go straight up the wall.

50. Street Runner 10m E4 5c *
Gain the large flake right of First Leaning Groove from the right, traverse diagonally right to the obvious horizontal break and up to the top on good holds. Try to resist the temptation to put a runner in the groove.

To the left of Street Runner are two shallow grooves leaning right (the Leaning Grooves).

51. First Leaning Groove 10m HVS 5a **
Climb the thin crack on the left until standing on the flake. Continue up the groove following it rightward to the black overhang. Pull over this to finish. A slightly easier finish may be made by moving left at the top of the groove.

52. Second Leaning Groove 8m VS 5a *
The left hand groove is climbed until a difficult move gives access to good holds on the top of flutings on the left.

53. Blocked Chimney Corner 7m HS 4c
The right angled corner left of the Leaning Grooves. Climb straight up into the chimney and over the block.

54. Broken Crack 7m E2 5c
Climb the broken crack just left of Blocked Chimney. A hard move to gain the top crack leads to a good finishing jug.

The arête to the left of Broken Crack without using the nose of Brutally Handsome has been climbed at HVS 5b.

55. Nose Chimney 7m D
A prominent chimney just left of Blocked Chimney Corner.

56. Brutally Handsome 7m E2 5c
A strange feature with an even stranger move. Start directly below the nose, climb up and slightly left to the roof. Reach across right to a good hold on the lip then cut loose and grab anything you can to gain the top.

The next section, which ends in a bay just right of the wall, has a leftward leaning scoop in its right half and well marked flake cracks in the centre.

57. Nutcracker 8m HVS 5b
The broken flake to the left of Brutally Handsome is followed until it is possible to move right to the arête, which is followed to the top or finish direct at 5c.

58. Scorpion 8m VS 4c **
A well named climb. The wide leftward leaning scoop is deceptively awkward at the top.

59. Crab Wall 8m S
The prominent flake cracks to the left of Scorpion are reached and followed to finish on good holds.

60. The Lobster 10m E3 5c
Start 1 metre to the left of Crab Wall. Climb the large flakes to a small wall, climb the wall (crux) to the faint flake which is climbed to the top.

61. Woolman's Wall 10m VS 5a
Start 1 metre left of The Lobster. Climb the thin flakes leading left across the wall to the dubious flake. Up this to finish.

62. Listen to the Rain 10m E4 5c
Start as for Woolman's Wall but continue up the wall passing two parallel cracks, with the crux at the top and the gear below half height.

63. The Harvest Bug 8m E1 6a
The wall left of Woolman's Wall. Gain some flakes just left of the start of Woolman's Wall, move left delicately to an obvious flake and up this to the top.

64. Creepy Crawly 7m E1 6a
Gain some small finger holds just left of The Harvest Bug. Move left then climb the wall direct.

Left of the short corner crack is another short crack, about Very Difficult in standard and just to the right of the dry stone wall are 3 offset cracks, leading up to the right.

65. Triple Cracks 7m HS 4c *
A little gem. Climb the cracks, transferring awkwardly from one to another.

The boundary wall, which meets the crag at this point, should be treated with care and crossed using the stile. Directly above the wall lies the next climb.

66. Wall Crack 7m MVS 4c
The crack is overhanging to start but the finish above the crack is easier.

67. Castle Wall 7m MS 4b
The left hand side of the buttress containing Wall Crack has a grooved and castellated appearance at the top. Climb up the obvious line, trending right and finishing steeply on good holds.

Martin Waugh
52. Second Leaning Groove (VS 5a)
Photo: Bob Smith

Lorraine Area

The bay to the left of Castle Wall contains two short cracks and a prominent flake chimney at its left hand side.

68. Flake Chimney 7m D
The chimney is climbed direct.

69. Flake Wall 7m D
The outside of the flake may also be climbed.

70. Sue 8m S 4c *
Starting at a horizontal crack in the centre of the wall, climb cracks leading slightly left. At the highest break move diagonally right to finish at the top of Flake Wall.

71. Sue Direct 8m HVS 5b
Instead of moving righ,t finish up the centre of the wall via some shallow pockets. Delicate.

72. Bella 8m E2 5c
Start from the boulder on the left. Climb directly up into the niche. Continue awkwardly up the wall to the flutings.

73. Castle Crack 8m VD ***
One of the best climbs of its grade at Bowden Doors. The crowned crack is climbed direct on excellent holds.

74. The Belford Pie Shop 8m E3 6a
A naughty little number. Climb the wall just left of Castle Crack to a short overlap. Continue up the wall to a shallow flute (crux), finish direct.

75. The Keep 8m E1 5b
Start as for Pitcher Wall Direct, move right then up to the short flake. Good holds to finish.

76. Pitcher Wall Direct 10m E2 6a
Start 2 metres right of Pitcher Wall and climb directly upwards to join that route. Where Pitcher Wall goes left, continue straight up.

77. Pitcher Wall 10m HVS 5a *
The fine wall to the left of Castle Crack is climbed on friable holds. Start just right of the shallow groove and follow the line up and slightly rightwards until it is possible to move left at the top.

78. Pitchfork 8m E2 5c
Start at the groove just left of Pitcher Wall, climb this to a good ledge and the wall above using the obvious undercut.

79. Crescent Wall 7m MS 4b
Gain the ramp to the left of Pitcher Wall and finish by a crescent shaped hold on the right.

80. Pride Before a Fall 8m VS 5a
The stepped buttress left of Crescent Wall, gained on the left by an awkward move and climbed at its centre.

To the left of Pride Before A Fall is a short chimney of no particular merit. Further left still the rocks increase in height and form an impressive, cracked corner facing left (Slab Crack). The next four climbs lie on the front of the buttress, just right of Slab Crack.

81. Runt 10m VS 5a
Climb cracks on the right edge of the buttress.

82. Little Red Rooster 10m E1 5c
Climb the flake 1 metre left of the Runt. Climb the bulge above to the horizontal break. Use this to gain the most leftward fluting and the top.

83. Lorraine 11m VS 5a ***
A brilliant route. Climb the prominent layback on the left to gain the upper horizontal crack and move left until a standing position can be gained, whence the top may be reached.

84. Don't Let Go 10m E2 5c *
The arête left of Lorraine is climbed via a finger flake on the right to the overhang, then swing left to the arête. Climb this to better holds above.

Direct Start 10m E2 6c
Climb the arête direct on its left side to gain the hanging arête after the swing left.

85. Slab Crack 10m E1 5b *
The crack is difficult to start and the bulge at half height is even more troublesome.

86. Imagery 12m E4 6b
Climb Slab Crack to the overhang (runners). Use holds on the lip to move left and make hard moves onto the slab to finish.

87. The Rajah 11 m E6 6b ***
A tremendous route, although not strenuous it is both bold and technical. Start 4 metres left of Slab Crack. Climb the wall making an awkward move to gain a stance below the overhang. Move right to gain the large jug just over the roof. Now kick start your pacemaker and pull over the roof, continue up the wall above with more ease.

88. The Cheetah 11 m E2 5c
Climb the scoop right of Tiger's Wall to the small overhang, pull over and climb the wall and crack above.

89. Tiger's Wall 11m VS 5a ***
A fantastic route 2 metres left of The Rajah, taking the prominent narrow flake crack in the upper part of the face. Start directly below this. Climb the slab and go over the overhang on good holds. Finish up the flake crack.

The flakes to the left of the upper section of Tiger's Wall provide an interesting alternative to that route.

90. Leo 10m E2 5b *
A good route. Climb the left arête of Tiger's Wall for 3 metres, then traverse diagonally right to the 3 small flakes and up the wall to finish.

The next feature left of Tiger's Wall is a shallow recess containing two cracks.

91. Red Crack 10m HS 4c
The right hand crack is taken direct and proves more strenuous than its neighbour.

92. Black Crack 10m VD
Climb the left crack to the overhang when a move right leads to the easy rocks at the top of Red Crack.

93. Banana Groove 10m HVS 5a
Climb Black Crack for 2 metres then traverse left onto a ledge. Climb the slabby groove above, trending left to finish up the scoop above.

94. Abanana 10m E1 5c *
A bold unprotected climb. Start at the lowest point of the buttress 3 metres left of Black Crack. Using the incut, climb straight up to the horizontal ledge 2 metres off the ground. Move delicately up the bulge to a small ledge in the middle of the slab. Finish direct.

95. Banana Wall 10m MVS 4c **
The slab left of Black Crack has a ledge at 2 metres. This may be gained in several places but Banana Wall proceeds by an obvious diagonal flake sloping up to the left. From the flake finish more easily on sharp holds.

96. The Runnel 10m HVS 5a *
A fine route which climbs the thin fluting to the left of Banana Wall. Climb directly to the fluting, which is gained awkwardly and followed to the top.

97. Yellow Peril 10m E2 5c
Just left of The Runnel, the most leftward flake is climbed and then the short wall above.

98. Wall End Direct 8m HS 4c
2 metres left of The Runnel the wall may be climbed by a prominent flake, finishing on the left as for Wall End.

99. Wall End 7m VD
The extreme left end of the wall gives a short but pleasant climb.

Broken rocks now follow for 15 metres until the crag reappears with a long horizontal overhung shelf as the main feature.

Crunchie Area

100. Retreat 8m E1 5b
A good route at the right end of the buttress. Climb onto the shelf at 2 metres and climb the shallow corner to an awkward pull out. Finish on the left or right.

101. Brothers in Arms E5 6b
Climb the wall on the left to a faint flake, use this to gain the top.

102. No Surrender 10m E4 6a
Climbs the bulging wall just left of Brothers In Arms. Move up via the slender hollow thread to the flakes. Reach left for a good hold then straight up to finish.

103. Boomer 10m E4 5c *
A sustained route on surprisingly good rock. Start in the centre of the wall at a large black flake. Use this to gain a flake over the overhang and follow the flakes right to a bowl in the wall at three-quarter height. Continue right to finish.

104. Cruel Dude 10m E4 5c
Yet another committing route. Start 3 metres left of Boomer. Climb the pocketed wall, reach over the bulge to the flakes using the obvious undercut and follow the line of flakes up the wall.

A corner below the left hand end of the shelf provides the start for the next two climbs.

105. Hanging Crack 10m E1 5b *
A lovely route. Climb the corner and gain the hanging crack on the right by an awkward movement, wriggle up the crack above.

106. Blind Wall 10m MS
From the top of the corner on Hanging Crack climb up left on surprisingly good holds.

107. Temptation 10m E3 6c *
Climb the wall on the right of Crunchie making a very awkward move on two pockets to gain the break. Climb the wall above with more ease.

108. Crunchie 10m E2 5c
The black wall between Blind Wall and the arête is climbed at its centre to a hollow flute.

109. Billy Liar 8m E2 6a
The arête to the left of Crunchie.

110. Arrow Crack 7m VD
An obvious flake crack 5 metres left of Blind Wall.

Left of Arrow Crack is a boulder in a shallow recess. Behind the boulder lie several short cracks and chimneys of no particular importance. The left rib of the recess provides the next route.

111. Robber's Rib 7m VS 5b
Climb the rib by means of a crack and then an awkward move left.

112. Bull's Lug 8m E2 6a
The undercut wall to the left of Robbers Rib is climbed direct.

113. Giant's Ear 10m VS 5a
Starts 7 metres left of the recess at an interesting, wide crack lying behind a rounded flake, halfway up the buttress. Gain the flake crack from the left and follow it with difficulty (try a headlock) to easy rocks.

114. See you In Disneyland 10m E3 6c
The hanging arête immediately left of Giant's Ear. Start as for that route and from the flake make a couple of moves up the arête to gain the ledge.

Chris Sowden
34. The Overhanging Crack (E2 5c)
The stunning classic.
Photo: Andrew Earl

Chipping and intense brushing has spoiled the bulging wall on the left, and the route recorded has consequently not been included.

115. Barbarian 10m E5 6b ***
A ferocious looking line with climbing to match. Saunter up the initial flake following it left until it runs out. A couple of strenuous moves on the smaller flakes only lead to an awkward reach for the final flutings and a fighting finish.

116. Green Crack 10m E1 5a
A route of substance, your skin! Climb the prominent crack. Strenuous.

117. Rip the Lip 24m E6 6a **
A technically reasonable but very strenuous, predominantly Friend protected pitch along the break under the wave. Start up Green Crack as far as the break line. Go left on rounded holds to a rest on The Bends. Reasonable climbing leads to Rough Passage. It now gets hard again with no more gear until The Wave where the route finishes.

118. The Bends 12m E5 6c *
A delicate and technical route. Climb the wall just left of Green Crack to an undercut flake, make a hard move diagonally left to a scoop and then a long reach to the break. Surface as for Poseidon Adventure.

119. Narcosis 11m E6 6c
Climb The Bends to the break under the wave, decompress, and then pull rightward round the bulge to finish on slightly better holds. Bold.

120. Poseidon Adventure 12m E4 6a ***
An extremely fine route. Start 5 metres left of The Bends. Climb the rightward trending weakness and the short wall above to the break. Traverse right to a short flake, use this to gain the arch, pull over in the centre.

121. Rough Passage 15m E6 6b ***
A bold and well named route. Start 2 metres left of Poseidon Adventure. Climb up the left edge of the triangular shaped shield to its apex and then up the wall above passing two old bolt sleeves. Traverse left for 3 metres until below a bowl high on the wave. Gain this with difficulty and pull over to a flat finish.

122. The Wave 14m E5 6a **
A magnificent route taking the centre of the wave formation. Start at the obvious white flakes 5 metres left of Rough Passage. Climb the flakes to the ledge and make a difficult move to gain the break. Traverse right for 2 metres until below the largest gash in the wave. Roll over this (crux) and continue right pulling over on good finishing holds.

123. High Tide 15m E5 6a **
A superb route. Climb the Wave to the break, traverse left for 7 metres to a shallow scoop just below the traverse line. Climb over the bulge using a good hold (strenuous).

124. Inner Space 11m E5 6b **
An excellent companion route to The Wave. Climb the wall 3m left of The Wave via the small flake to gain the break. Move 1m right and pull strenuously through the roof to a good hold. Continue to a precarious rounded finish.

125. Rising Damp 15m E4 6b **
A very sustained route. Climb the flakes 2 metres left of The Wave to the lower break. Traverse left making an awkward move to link up the breaks. Continue left with more difficulty to gain the large recess. Traverse left to a good side hold, pull up left on better holds.

The horrendous rock scars, is the line of an historical boulder problem.

Craig Smith
115. Barbarian (E5 6b)
Craig takes on the barbarian!
Photo: John Earl

The Trial Area

126. The Manta 10m E3 6a ***
A very deceptive and awkward route. Start 10 metres left of Rising Damp beneath the obvious leftward trending flake. Move up to the flake and then left with extreme difficulty until better holds are gained. Continue up the wall to the top.

127. Honeycomb Wall E4 7a
Climbs the wall between The Manta and The Sting to the break and finish as for The Sting.

128. The Sting 10m E3 6a **
A satisfying and bold route. Starts 3 metres left of the previous route where a series of three small flakes run directly up the wall. Climb the flakes then continue over the bulge on rounded holds (the sting) to the top.

128a. Flying Stag 8m E4 6c
Start just right of Flying Fish. Using small undercuts gain a small layaway up right to a rounded break and right to a ramp and up to top.

129. Flying Fish 8m E1 6a
Start 4 metres left of The Sting at the undercut flake. Use this to pull right to two small flakes above, one of which is highly friable, lunge left to a rounded hold and finish up the wall above.

130. The Skate 8m E1 5c
Climb the same flake as Flying Fish only this time move left and make a good move back right to gain a loose jam. Finish up the wall.

131. The Shiner 9m HVS 5b
Start 2 metres to the left. Climb the flake to an awkward bulge, continue up the wall.

132. Bloody Nose 9m HS 5a *
The round arete on the left with three thin flakes to its right. Climb these moving left then up the wall above via another flake.

133. Bloody Crack 9m VS 5a *
The steep crack in the leftward facing corner yields to jamming and laybacking and anything else you can get in.

134. The Jury 10m E3 5c
Start 1 metre left of Bloody Crack. Climb the curving flake and short wall to a good hold in a hole. Step right and finish over the bulge.

135. The Trial 10m E3 5c ***
A classic at the grade. Start up the black stain in the middle of the wall making some varied and interesting moves to gain the first horizontal break. Step left and climb directly up with long reaches to finish up the flake.

136. The Judge 10m E3 6a *
A good climb. Starts 2 metres left of The Trial. Climb the wall on small holds to the top horizontal ledge, traverse left and finish with difficulty over bulges.

The wall now reduces in height and has three rightward leaning, shallow scoops:

137. Scoop One 8m E1 5b *
Start on the left at a boulder. Climb the bleached flakes with more difficulty than first appears.

138. His Eminence 8m E4 6a **
Takes the bulging wall 2 metres left of Scoop 1. Improved footholds make the first hard moves to gain the shot hole somewhat easier than before. Use this to climb the wall above and finish with a further hard move.

139. Poverty 9m E5 6c *
The wall 2 metres left of His Eminence. Gain the fist sized pothole and flake just above and right and then climb the wall moving diagonally left to a small hanging flake at the top.

Malcolm Smith
128a. Flying Stag (E4 6c)
Malcolm is making the first ascent
of this bold solo
Photo: Darren Stevenson

140. Toffs 7m E3 6b

A painful route taking the arched shaped roof 4 metres to the left. Make a long reach or jump to gain a good hold below the roof. Move over the roof to an awkward undercling and use this to gain the horizontal break. Climb the bulge above using a small curved flake on the right.

Alternative Start 6b

Come in from the left on small fingerholds.

141. Scoop Two 7m E1 5c *

Start at the obvious yellow flake with a block at its base. Climb the flakes to the break and straight up the wavy wall above or first move right at the break.

142. Liberty 20m E3 6a

Climb Scoop 2 to the obvious break, follow this rightward to Scoop 1, up this to the break which is followed across The Trial to finish at Bloody Nose.

The crescent shaped flakes left of Scoop 2 provide several problems.

143. Scoop Three 8m E1 5b

This takes the left to right diagonal flake with an eyehole at its top. Climb the flake and the bulging wall above.

The wall to the right of The Scoop has been climbed directly up the centre of the arch and then via the short thin flake at 6c.

144. Finale Wall 7m E1 5c

The overhanging wall with two conspicuous pockets at its top, 2 metres left of the previous route.

145. Another Heap of it 7m HVS 5c

The wall 2 metres left of Finale Wall is climbed on awkwardly spaced holds.

146. Evening Wall 7m MS 4b

Climb the right hand end of the slab following the obvious scoop.

Numerous problems have been done on the slabs left of Evening Wall.

90 metres left of the main crag past some pinnacles and a smooth wall is a good compact buttress. Child's Play climbs the right arete of this buttress. The arse like feature in the huge boulder opposite Childs Play gives a 5b problem.

147. Entrebaillement 6m E1 6a

Undercut wall below the finish of Parisienne Walkway. Using a slit in the wall, make a long reach to a jug and then finish up the wall to meet Parisienne Walkway.

148. Parisienne Walkway 6m E1 6b

Takes the slab right of the wide crack, 7 metres right of Child's Play. Climb the slab from left to right.

149. Child's Play 6m E1 6a

The blunt arete (flat landing). Sadly made easier by erosion the chicken heads are no more and the smears have become steps.

150. Outer Limits 10m E2 5c *

Climb the flakes at the left side of the buttress making a long reach to pockets and another long reach right to a rounded ledge. Move up onto the ledge using a small well brushed pocket above and then step right to easier ground and the top.

Direct Finish E2 5c

From the ledge climb the wall directly above on widely spaced holds.

Brian Teasdale cruising
149. Child's Play (E1 6a)
At the end of another brilliant Bowden day.
Photo: Steve Crowe

Mark Adamson
33. Russet Groove (VD)
The most popular VD in the County
Photo: Andy Birtwistle

Bowden Doors Graded List

E6
Rough Passage 6b ***
Death Knell 6c *
Narcosis 6b
Rip the Lip 6a **
The Rajah 6b ***
Heaven Can Wait 6b

E5
Barbarian 6b ***
High Tide 6a **
The Wave 6a **
Brothers in Arms 6b
Poverty 6c *
The Bends 6c *
Inner Space 6b **
Hangover Wall 6c

E4
Honeycomb Wall 7a
Rising Damp 6b **
His Eminence 6a **
Kaiser Bill 6b *
Poseidon Adventure 6a ***
Boomer 5c *
Cruel Dude 5c
Street Runner 5c *
No Surrender 6a
Imagery 6b
A Grave Mask 6a
Listen to the Rain 5c
First Century 6a *
Crater Maker 6a

E3
The Gauleiter 6a **
The Sting 6a **
Goose Step 6a **
The Jury 5c
The Judge 6a *
Toffs 6b
Liberty 6a
The Belford Pie Shop 6a
Maginot Line 6a
Temptation 6c *
See You In Disneyland 6c
Please Stop Me Before I Kill Myself 6b
Quatra Twinkley 6a
The Lobster 5c
The Manta 6a ***
The Trial 5c ***

E2
Don't Let Go Direct Start 6c
Jock Strap 6b
Yellow Peril 5c
Brutally Handsome 5c
Billy Liar 6a
Pitch Fork 5c
Leo 5b *
Black and Tan Direct 6a
Outer Limits Direct Finish 5c
Broken Crack 5c
Don't Let Go 5c *
Transformer 6a *
The Big Splash 5c
Bella 5c
The Overhanging Crack 5c ***
Klondyke Wall 5c **
Outer Limits 5c *
Dog Eat Dog 6a
The Cheetah 5c
Bulls Lug 6a
Pitcher Wall Direct 6a
Crunchie 5c
The Cheetah 5c

E1
Parisienne Walkway 6b
Entrebaillement 6a
Child's Play 6a
Abanana 5c *
Little Red Rooster 5c
The Viper 6a *
Hissing Sid 5c
Family Pressure 5c
Retreat 5b
Stretcher Wall 5c *
The Keep 5b
Hanging Crack 5b *
Family Pressure 5c
Flying Fish 6a
The Harvest Bug 6a
Creepy Crawley 6a
The Skate 5c
Finale Wall 5c
Brown Ale Wall 5b
Scoop Two 5c *
Scoop One 5b *
Scoop Three 5b
Slab Crack 5b *
Green Crack 5a

HVS
Y Front 6a
Sue Direct 5b
Main Wall Eliminate 5b *
Jackdaw Crack 5b
Main Wall 5b ***
First Leaning Groove 5a **
Banana Groove 5a
Canada Crack 5a ***
The Corner 5a
Long Crack 5a **
Grovel Groove Alt.Finish 5a
Pitcher Wall 5a *
Another Heap of It 5c
Nutcracker 5b
Handrail Eliminate 5c
The Shiner 5b
The Runnel 5a *

VS
Robbers Rib 5b
Lorraine 5a ***
Runt 5a
Giants Ear 5a
Tigers Wall 5a ***
Canada Dry 5a
Pride Before a Fall 5a
Woolmans Wall 5a
Scorpion 4c **
Red Nose 4c
Bloody Crack 5a *
Girdle of Main Wall 4c
The Scoop 4b ***
Handrail 4c
Second Leaning Groove 5a *
Pinky Peeler 5a

Callaly Crag

John Earl

History

Developed by Andrew Earl, John Earl and Ian Murray during the summer of 2000. The Young, which climbs the centre of Tombstone Buttress, is a technical and sustained route as good as any in the County and at E8 7a is on a par with the hardest routes in the County.

Situation and Character

These independent pinnacles and buttresses lie in Thrunton Wood close to Callaly Village on the steep north facing slopes. Although north facing they are reasonably clean and take very little drainage.

Approaches and Access

Turn left off the A697 at the Whittingham crossroads. Follow the unclassified road to Whittingham and turn left towards Callaly. Park at some large beech trees on the east side of the wood some 2 miles from Whittingham. Follow tracks up through the wood to McCartney's Cave via Castle Hill. The location of all of the buttresses is referenced to McCartney's Cave.

There is a right of access to the crag under CRoW.

The Climbs

The routes are described from right to left.

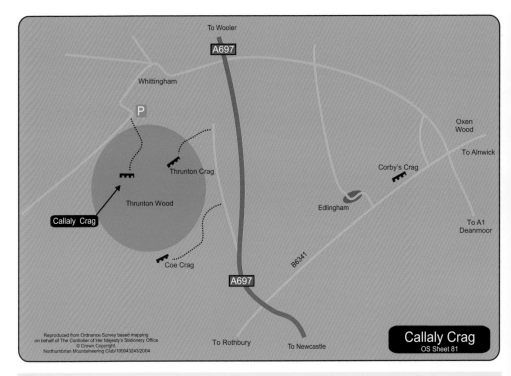

Slab Buttress

This buttress which has a prominent flake up its centre and is topped by a slab is reached by traversing the hillside leftwards for 50 metres from McArtney's Cave.

1. Summers End 10m E1 5c

A good route. Climb the corner to the overhang, gain the flake awkwardly and quit it for the slab even more awkwardly. Follow the slab direct to the tree.

Tombstone Buttress

This superb buttress is approximately 100 metres left of McArtneys Cave. It has a jam crack to the right of a smooth overhanging pancake-covered wall, which is The Young.

2. Parental Guidance 7m E4 6b

The right arête, which provides good, if slightly contrived climbing. Climb the arête on the left making use of the hole in the centre of the wall. Avoid the temptation to bridge across the gully right of the arête.

3. The Auld 8m HVS 5b **

The fine well protected crack.

4. The Young   9m E8 7a ***

A superb, very bold unprotected route. Start beneath the shield in the centre of the wall, left of the crack. Make difficult moves up the shield to gain a good hand hold, move left to two, two finger pockets which are used to gain a pancake above. Move back right to stand on the good hand hold and yet another pancake. A hard move enables a small crimp, a jug and then the top to be reached, if you are good enough.

Callaly Crag Graded List

E8
The Young 7a ***

E4
Parental Guidance 6b
Family Affair 6b ***

E3
Sleepless Nights 6a *

E2
Deet Crack 6a **
Eaten Alive 5c

E1
Summers End 5c

HVS
The Auld 5b **

VS
Mossie Net 4c

5. Family Affair 10m E4 6b ***

A fine route up the left arête. Gain the ledge with some difficulty. Climb the arête which is hard to start. Use holds on the right wall until the slab can be gained using the fluting near the top.

Ant Buttress

Situated 50 metres left and a little higher up the hillside.

6. Eaten Alive 7m E2 5c

The wall right of the arête is climbed using a pocket and the arête.

7. Sleepless Nights 8m E3 6a *

The wall left of the arête. Climb the arête to the break and then up the wall on ironstone crimps.

8. Deet Crack 8m E2 6a **

The thin crack up the centre of the wall provides good well protected climbing.

9. Mossie Net 8m VS 4c

The groove at the left side of the buttress.

Andrew Earl on his own route
4. The Young (E8 7a)
Photo: John Earl

Callerhues Crag

Steve Crowe and Karin Magog

NY 852863
South West Facing
323m
30 minutes

History

Callerhues has a very short history. Although climbers had visited the crag over the years, there are no documented records of the routes. In 1976 John Earl and Bob Hutchinson visited the crag and climbed the classic Callerhues Crack and the dark Callerhues Chimney. They also soloed a few other lines. At this time the crag was in poor condition and nothing else was considered worthwhile. The crag was rediscovered in 1978 by Tommy and Bob Smith accompanied by Pete Alderson, who took it upon themselves to clean the crag up. Within three months it had yielded some fifty new routes. Other people to climb new routes were Steve Blake with Boulevard and Earl with Arkle.

Although the crag was climbed on regularly there were no further developments until 1979 when Bob Smith climbed Dulalai T.A.P., Sheer Temptation and the technical Crouching The Mahogany. In 1984 Alan Moist with Dave Carr popped up Toshiba Receiver. A visit to the crag in the summer of 1985 found the overhanging crack left of Callerhues Chimney cleaned but unclimbed. An on sight solo by Bob Smith gave Second Born in celebration of his daughter. 1988 saw only a couple of short routes, with Bob Smith as the author of Chouca and The Storyteller.

Four routes were added in 1990, the best being New Kids on the Rock and Shadow Players by John Boyle and Gavin Ellis. Nothing significant has been recorded since then.

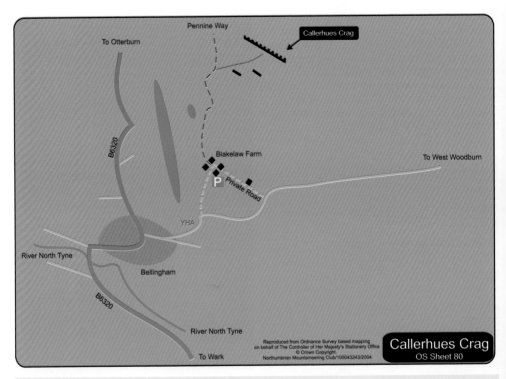

Callerhues Crag
OS Sheet 80

Bob Smith
14. Footpath (E1 5b)
Bob and brother Tommy put up
most of the routes at Callerhues
Photo: Andy Birtwistle

Situation and Character
A beautifully situated crag, overlooking Bellingham at the south end of Corsenside Common. The rock is Fell Sandstone and gives a variety of climbing techniques including the use of flakes, cracks, walls and small finger pockets. The majority of the routes are of a bouldering nature as the crag rarely reaches a height of over 10 metres. Care however should be taken as most of the tops are rounded; fortunately the landings are generally good, if you don't mind jumping.

Approaches and Access
Follow the B6320 into Bellingham turn right (east) following the West Woodburn road for 1 mile up the hill to a sharp right hand bend.Continue further up the road to a left turn marked private road. Follow this over a cattle grid to Blakelaw Farm (limited parking). From here follow the Pennine Way north to the small copse of trees on top of the hill. The crag can be seen in the east (on the right) and reached after a pleasant thirty-minute walk across the moor. Permission to climb on the crag should at all times be sought from the farm. Large groups and dogs disturb sheep so are not welcome. There is a right of access to the crag under CRoW.

The Climbs
Useful landmarks to this long and broken crag are the obvious pinnacle at the left hand end, the large detached wall, the main central buttress and a square bay. The climbs are described from left to right.The first route is on the second buttress 13 metres right of the pinnacle.

Steve Crowe
20. Tom's Peeping (VS 5a)
Photo: Karin Magog

1. Flake Wall 8m VS 4c *
A fine climb at the left end of the wall. Climb this direct on small holds to the prominent flake. From the top of the flake use four pockets on the left to pull over onto a rounded finish.

2. The Felter's Teapot 8m VS 4c
The wall to the right can be climbed direct on small nubbins to a cluster of potholes at the top.

3. Chockstone Crack 8m MVS 4b
The obvious crack with the obvious chockstone to the right. Obviously an obvious route.

4. Bait Cabin Wall 8m VD
5 metres to the right and just left of four very large boulders is a slab, which is climbed direct, the crux is at the top.

The next routes are 20 metres to the right on the wall containing the flutings to the left of the detached wall area. At the extreme left hand side is a square cut corner with a roof.

5. Pinched 7m HVS 5b
Step into the corner and try to get out via the roof.

6. Thunderclap 7m VS 5a
Up short slab to bulge, surmount bulge to good pocket, continue up slab to top. (No use of cracks either side of the slab/bulge).

7. Pincher Wall 7m VS 4c
Climb the slender flutings on the left, identified by the hump on the left shoulder.

8. Twin Cracks 7m MVS 4c
The obvious cracks 2 metres to the right. Short, dirty and awkward.

9. Arkle 7m VS 5a
Climb the wall 1 metre right of the large boulder wedged between the buttresses.

10. Side Walk 7m MVS 5a
From the boulder climb the arête on the left of the arch direct.

Detached Wall Area

11. Handrail 5m VS 5b
The left-hand arête of the detached wall, one hard move leads to easy ground.

12. Boulevard 7m E3 6b **
Climb the thin flake 1 metre right of the arête to the horizontal seam, make a hard move to gain a narrow slot on the right. Use this to gain the top.

13. Curbside 7m E1 5c
2m right are two diagonal seams, use these to gain the hanging flake then pull up and left to the top.

14. Footpath 7m E1 5b *
A fine climb up the centre of the detached wall via the single seam, making some strange mantelshelf moves to gain the top.

15. Paving 5m MVS 5a
The far right hand side of the wall.

16. Ta Mac 20 m E1 5c
An interesting traverse of the detached wall following the upper fault. Goes either way.

17. Blocked Chimney 8m D
Just right and behind the detached wall enter under the block and climb the left wall. A 30-inch chest is an advantage.

18. The Mall 8m HVS 5a
Climb either side over the block filling the chimney to a large pothole on the right; use this to pull right then follow the arête on small holds.

19. Quarrel Arête 7m E1 5b *
Start 5 metres right of The Mall directly beneath the undercut arête. A long reach over the roof is made to good holds, which lead to small finishing holds on the broad arête.

20. Tom's Peeping 7m VS 5a **
Just around the corner to the right are two flutes, which are climbed easily to an awkward finish up the crack.

21. Monocle 7m VS 5a
Straight up and over the bulge between the two cracks. Finish delicately up the slab.

22. Coppers Nark 7m HVS 5a *
The right hand crack also has a very good finish. 'Start from the ground you cheat'.

A few small poor climbs are possible before the next large wall is reached.

Andrew Earl
23. Crouching the Mahogany (E4 6b)
Photo: Steve Crowe

23. Crouching the Mahogany
8m E4 6b (Twice!) ***
'A short bastard but it's at ya straight away.' The wall and thin flake left of Weeping Fingers. Climb the wall to gain the thin flake and climb this to gain the pot hole (crux 1). Use the pothole to gain a good hold on the left (crux 2). Now do as the name suggests.

24. Weeping Fingers 8m E1 5c ***
An excellent route taking the flakes on the left hand side of the wall.

25. The Storyteller 8m E3 6b *
Climb the wall on the right direct. Side runners in Weeping Fingers reduces the grade to E1.

26. Task Master 5m VS 4c **
3 metres to the right is another weakness of flakes, which also gives fine climbing. Finish slightly to the right via the slab and a pothole or on the left following the crack at E1 5c.

27. The Whip 7m HVS 5a
1 metre to the right is a short flake. Climb this finishing on the right.

Main Central Buttress

28. Gully Wall 6m HVS 5b
The wall in the gully left of Dolcis Arête.

29. Dolcis Arête 7m E3 6a **
Starts at the left end of the main buttress. Climb the arête direct. The crux is at the top.

30. Rain Drops 8m E1 5b *
Just to the right of the arête is a groove line. Follow it, finishing slightly to the left.

31. Shadow Players 9m E3 5b
The wall right of Rain Drops, with a hard crux at the top.

32. Pot-Hole Wall 10m E4 5c
Gain the ledge under the pothole by climbing up the right side of the wall. Use the pothole to finish above on small holds. A direct start and a direct finish are both possible at the same grade.

33. Shoe Horn 12m HVS 5a
2 metres to the right is a small cave at 3 metres. Gain the cave and climb the groove above finishing slightly right.

34. Tossin a Wobbler 12m E2 5b
Climb Callerhues Crack for a metre until a move can be made onto the wall to the left. Pull over the overhang and continue directly up the wall above.

35. Callerhues Crack 12m HVS 5a ***
A classic up the large diagonal crack splitting the nose of the buttress. Follow the crack with adequate protection.

36. Twin Hats 12m E2 5c
Start 2 metres right of Callerhues Crack at a short flake in the arête. Climb this to the ledge. Pull right and climb the crack above.

37. Ned Kelly 12m E3 5c ***
Start 1 metre right of Twin Hats at the undercut corner. Climb the overhanging stepped corner until a pull across right gains the curving crack. Follow this and titter, totter or teeter up the slab above.

Alternative Start
Climb the overhang on the right to join Ned Kelly.

38. Second Born 12m E5 6b ***
The incredibly overhanging crack left of Callerhues Chimney, technically demanding but protectable. Start at the large boulder in the bog. Move left to the crack and climb this on vicious layaways and jams.

39. Callerhues Chimney 12m VS 4c *
The large obvious chimney - a fine route.

40. Rice Krispies 12m E3 5c *
To the right of the chimney is a thin crack up the left end of the large steep wall. Climb the crack and leave it for the wall on the right. Move back across left above the crack and finish direct.

41. Toshiba Receiver 10m E3 5c **
The obvious line up the potted wall right of Rice Krispies. The rock is better than it looks.

20 metres to the right is a buttress providing short routes. The next climb is on the prominent overhanging arête.

42. Pilot's Licence 10m E1 5b
Climb the overhanging arête with the flutes at the top.

43. Air Time 8m E1 5b
Climb the arête right of Pilots Licence on its right hand side to a long reach for hidden pockets over the top.

The next area is the square bay. To its left is a large wall with a hanging flake.

44. Cold Start 8m VS 6a
A very awkward move sometimes leads to the hanging flake. Romp up this to the top.

45. Green Fluff 10m E2 6a **
This hard climb goes up the arête to the right. Layback the blunt nose to some small holds, use these to make a hard move to a small pocket on the left wall which leads to easier ground.

46. Dulalai T.A.P. 10m E4 6b
From the rock shelf on the right gain the pocket in the wall. Pull up and right to the parallel cracks, climb these to an easy finish.

47. Sheer Temptation 10m E4 6b **
Climb the arête direct until standing on the obvious ledge. Continue up the arête until it is possible to move onto its right side, then finish direct.

48. The Mongrel 10m E3 5c *
Start in the left corner of the bay. Climb the wall 2 metres right of the arête to the large pockets. Move left to the arête, which is climbed direct (as for Sheer Temptation).

49. Flake Corner 7m S
Climb the corner crack on the right.

50. Polo 6m D
Climb the dark recess on the right in or out of the hole.

51. Micro 10m E2 5c
The rightward leaning flake is climbed until a bold move leads to the sentry box on the right.

The following three parallel cracks can be each climbed at Very Severe standard:-

52. Tom 7m VS 4c *
Unfortunately Tom is usually in poor condition.

53. Dick 7m VS 4c *
The second tick.

54. Harry 7m VS 4c *
To tick all three is some achievement.

55. Hanging Crack 7m E1 5b *
Just around the arête to the right, climb the wall on small holds to the hanging crack. Grab the pommel on top to finish.

56. Chouca 7m E3 6a *
From the base of Bracken Crack use the small shoulder on the left to gain the pocketed wall. Climb this and have fun. Not as steep as the name suggests.

57. Bracken Crack 7m HVS 5a
The crack on the right. Hard at the top.

The next buttress, which is 15 metres to the right, has an arête and curving scoop right of an obvious chimney.

Bob Smith bouldering out the start of
47. Sheer Temptation (E4 6b)
25 years after making the first ascent in 1979
Photo: Steve Crowe

58. Cut and Dried 10m E1 5b *
Climb the arête on the left, moving into the scoop and finishing awkwardly up the arête on the left on small but nice pockets.

59. White Rock 10m VS 5a
Gain the shoulder of rock on the right. Follow this until a traverse right gains the flake. Up this to the top.

60. The Lurcher 8m E2 5b *
Climb the overhanging corner scoop on pockets, finishing on the right.

61. Country Downfall 7m D
Climb the stepped slab on the right.

The crack on the left and channels on the right have also been climbed at Severe.

62. The Hyena 10m E1 5b *
3 metres to the right is a split block on the ground, start from this. Climb the undercut crack to the large hole with difficulty. Traverse right on small holds then straight up.

63. New Kids on the Rock 10m E3 6a
Climb through the double overlap left of The Thoroughbred then straight up to finish as for The Hyena.

64. The Thoroughbred 10m E3 6a ***
Takes the right arête of the crag direct. Jump or make a long reach for good finger holds, pull onto the arête and climb the crack to the roof. Surmount this with difficulty.

65. Horse Play 6m E3 5c
The wall around the corner to the right of The Thoroughbred is climbed to a long reach (jump), which leads to a mantelshelf to finish.

Steve Blake climbing the popular and well protected
37. Ned Kelly (E3 5c)
Photo: Steve Crowe

Callerhues Crag Graded List

E5
Second Born 6b ***

E4
Crouching the Mahogany 6b ***
Sheer Temptation 6b **
Dulalai T.A.P. 6b
Pot-Hole Wall 5c

E3
The Thoroughbred 6a ***
New Kids on the Rock 6a
Dolcis Arête 6a **
Boulevard 6b **
The Storyteller 6b *
The Mongrel 5c *
Ned Kelly 5c ***
Rice Krispies 5c *
Toshiba Receiver 5c **
Horse Play 5c
Chouca 6a *
Shadow Players 5b

E2
Green Fluff 6a **
Micro 5c
Twin Hats 5c
Tossin a Wobbler 5b
The Lurcher 5b *

E1
Weeping Fingers 5c ***
Pilot's Licence 5b
Air Time 5b
Hanging Crack 5b
Cut and Dried 5b *
The Hyena 5b *
Curbside 5c
Footpath 5b *
Quarrel Arête 5b *
Rain Drops 5b *
Ta Mac 5c

HVS
Pinched 5b
Gully Wall 5b
The Mall 5a
Coppers Nark 5a
Shoe Horn 5a
Callerhues Crack 5a ***
Bracken Crack 5a
The Whip 5a

VS
Cold Start 6a
Handrail 5b
Arkle 5a
Monocle 5a
Thunderclap 5a
Tom's Peeping 4c **
Task Master 4c **
White Rock 5a
Callerhues Chimney 4c *
Tom 4c *
Dick 4c *
Harry 4c *
Pincher Wall 4c
Stringer 4c
The Felters Teapot 4c
Flake Wall 4c *

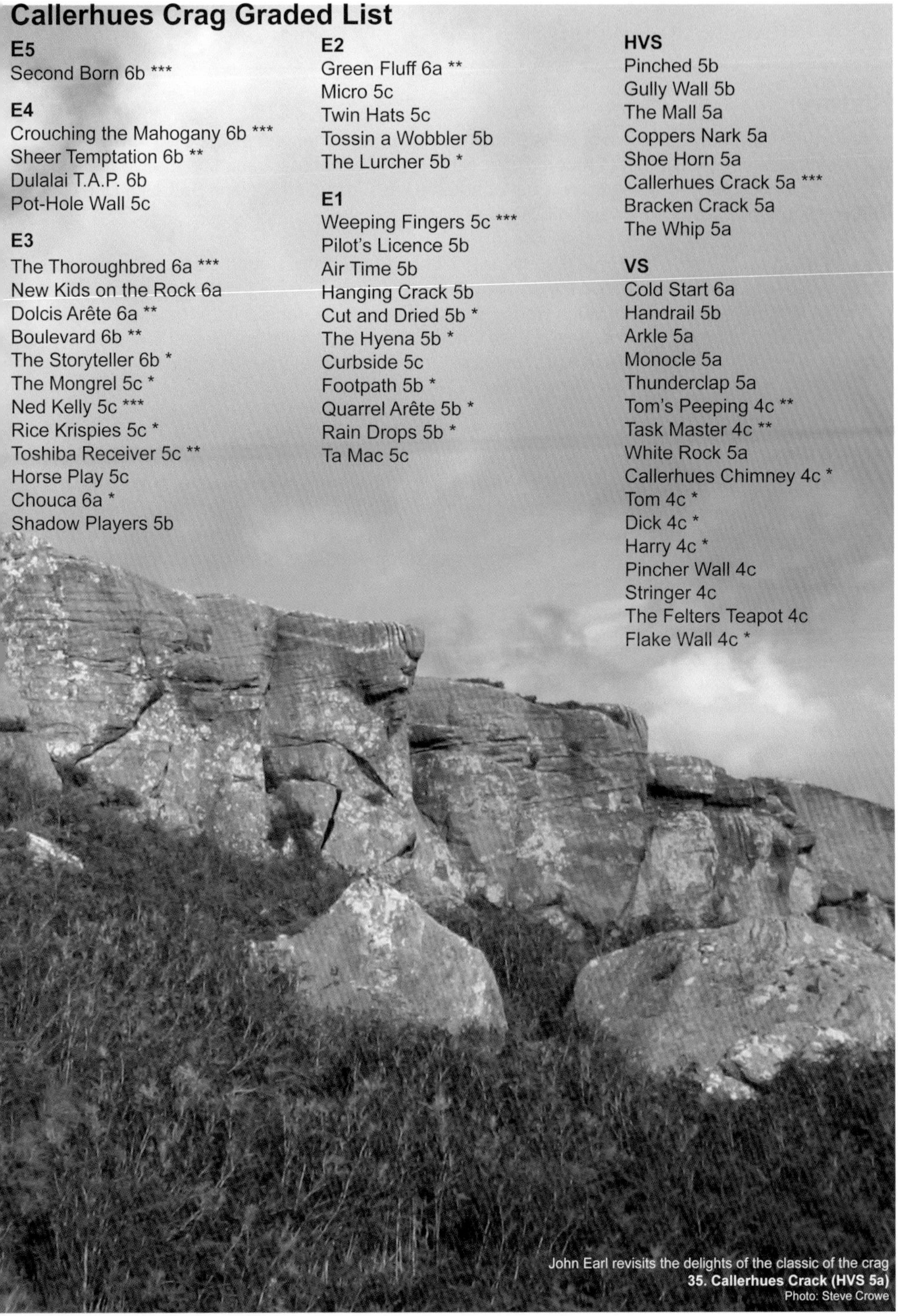

John Earl revisits the delights of the classic of the crag
35. Callerhues Crack (HVS 5a)
Photo: Steve Crowe

Coe Crag

Andy Birtwistle and John Dalrymple

NU 074073
North Facing
304m
30 minutes

History

Prior to 1968 it is likely that most of the easier lines had been ascended as the crag had been visited occasionally for years, but records of specific routes cannot be traced. In that year Dave Roberts and Allan Austin climbed a number of notable lines including Ravens Buttress, Coe Crag Corner, Hippopotamus and Honeycomb Wall.

Roberts returned in 1971 with Ernie Goodyear to climb the excellent Rough Castles Crack and in the same year Hugh Banner added the problematic Neb Crack. The crag lost popularity for many years but in 1984 a few visits by Hugh Harris, John Wallace and Graham Telfer resulted in Cave Wall, Rampart Wall and the large overhang of Orion Roof, albeit with a pre-placed friend. Andy Birtwistle added The Turret in 1988 whilst checking the crag for the previous edition.

Situation and Character

Situated on the northern scarp of Coe Crag Hill with a splendid prospect over the Aln Valley to the Cheviot Hills, Coe Crag provides an excellent venue for those seeking a peaceful atmosphere and its altitude gives a fine mountain character to the routes. The crag faces north and is at its best on warm summer days but climbing is possible throughout the year. After periods of wet weather however, it is lichenous and slow to dry. It comprises a compact area of well-weathered sandstone buttresses reaching 20 metres in height.

The rock is generally rough and sound but care should be taken when using thinner flakes that are brittle. There are three main buttresses which contain all the major courses but many smaller outcrops litter the scarp containing numerous short climbs and potential boulder problems. Only the major lines are described and it is left to the visitor to explore the many small but interesting climbs. In recent years the crag has not been popular, undeservedly so as it has much to offer and although most of the routes are middle grade the harder lines are very worthwhile.

Approaches and Access

The best approach is from Rough Castles, just off the A697 Morpeth-Wooler road. See map on page 72. Turn left off the main road half a mile north of the crossroads with the B6341 at a bend, signposted to Thrunton Wood. Park about 200 metres from the junction where a forestry road leaves on the left. Cross a stile, then walk along the forest road until the trees on the right end, just before the pylons. Trend right off the track and follow a slight depression under the pylons to pick up a good path that takes a break in the forest up the hill then contours round rightwards emerging at the moors edge. Continue up the well-marked path that follows the shoulder of Coe Crag Hill. Follow this to the top of the crag. The distance is 3 kilometres and it takes about thirty minutes. See approach map on page 72.

There is a right of access to the crag under CRoW.

The Climbs

The climbs are described from left to right beginning at Raven's Buttress. Small boulder problems are available on outcrops to the left.

Julie Price
11. Honeycomb Wall (HVS 4c)
Photo: Mark Savage

Raven's Buttress

1. Kestrel 9m HVS 5a
Start at the obvious hole on the left of the buttress. Climb to a square ledge then step right onto a small slab. Move back left and climb the steep wall to a tricky mantelshelf finish.

2. Raven's Buttress 14m HS **
Begin at the toe of the buttress and climb it on good holds through an overhang to the ledge. Move right and surmount the second overhang using a wedged block.

3. Raven Mad 10m E2 5b
Climbs the overhanging wall 5 metres right of Raven's Buttress. Climb through the lower overhang via a loose looking block and continue up the steep upper wall. Good climbing marred by dubious rock, a serious route.

A wide cave that splits the face at one-third height identifies the next buttress.

Cave Buttress

4. Battlement 12m HVS 5b
A rather artificial route which deliberately avoids easier ground. Start at the far left end and climb the wall and faint crack to gain the base of the deep crack. Pull up and move leftwards round the bulge to finish more easily up the wall above.

5. Rough Castles Crack 12m VS 5a ***
A good well protected route that takes the shallow groove followed by the deep crack. Climb up the groove to the ledge, step left and jam the deep crack above.

6. Rampart Wall 12m E2 5b **
Excellent climbing up the large bulging wall right of Rough Castles Crack. Steep and satisfying. Climb the first thin crack a metre right of the last route to reach the ledge. Step left onto the shelf and scale the wall above, utilising a hidden pocket on the right to gain the flake above. Climb straight up to finish.

7. Cave Wall 15m E1 5b *
Another good climb. Take the obvious twin cracks a metre right of Rampart Wall to the cave. Step onto the shelf and make a long blind reach for a good hold in the back of the horizontal break. Pull over and climb the wall above using the crack and finish between the two noses.

8. Black Walter Chimney 15m S **
A classic of its grade. The shallow scoop in the buttress leads to the cave. Pull up on enormous flakes then struggle up until it is possible to proceed in a more dignified manner to the top.

9. Devious Way 15m MS
Climb the crack at the left end of the overhang in the lower tier to the cave. Move right and climb the chimney through awkward bulges.

10. The Turret 15m HVS 5b
Start from the top of the detached block. Pull onto the wall and climb the crack and rib to the cave. Take the overhanging crack that splits the 'turrets' and finish by moving right up the bulging wall above.

11. Honeycomb Wall 17m HVS 4c **
A good, bold climb. The top section has little protection. Take the 'S' crack on the right side of the buttress to the right end of the cave ledge, then follow the pock-marked wall above on somewhat sloping holds to the top.

Alternative Start VS 5a
Take the crack through the overhang to the left of the 'S' crack.

12. Bumble Bee Connection 12m S
Start at the centre of the wall and move up into a recess in the middle of the wall. Climb steeply out of the recess and move right to finish.

13. Worrisome Wasp 15m HVS 5a *
A direct variation on Bumble Bee Connection. Climb the centre of the wall to gain the recess at half height. From this carry on direct up the steep wall to the top.

An easy descent gully intervenes before the next unnamed buttress.

14. Twin Cracks 14m MVS 4c
Steep and satisfying. Climb the steep hanging cracks in the centre of the buttress. Finish easily up the recess behind.

15. Hippopotamus 17m MVS 4c *
A good route. Start immediately right of Twin Cracks. An overhanging wall is climbed followed by a capped groove. Move out left and finish up a flake in the rib above.

16. Nagging Wives' Groove 15m HVS 5b *
Interesting and exposed. The groove just left of Fiddler's Climb is ascended with difficulty to a small crack splitting the overhang. Go up this to the bottom of the ramp that trends right. Step up left onto the wall and climb this to the top.

17. Fiddler's Climb 15m S
The awkward crack in the corner is climbed. Move left onto the main crag and follow a ramp delicately back right to the top of the tower.

Neb Buttress

18. Soldier of Fortune 18m E3 6a
There is a hanging groove midway between the descent gully and Neb Crack. Climb the wall direct to the groove and then up this to the slab finishing up the arete above.

19. Neb Crack 17m HVS 5a **
The wide crack in the roof of the neb can be surmounted by achieving a horizontal position just below the roof using a narrow ledge for a backrest. Stand with difficulty and jam the crack above. The chimney crack above the ledge can prove awkward.

20. Orion Roof 12m E3 6a
This route climbs the large overhang direct between Neb Crack and Coe Crag Corner. Start 3 metres left of Coe Crag Comer and climb the crack to the pocket at the back of the overhang. Use holds just right of this to make a long reach up and right to gain the traverse line. Swing left until the `good' holds run out at the lip. Then make a hard pull over to attain a standing position on the slab. Continue to the terrace.

21. Coe Crag Corner 17m HS *
A good climb that takes the left-facing corner at the right end of Neb Buttress. Gain the rib on the right or climb the corner, moving left to the foot of a short crack. Climb this over a bulge and a sloping shelf to a large ledge. The steep, wrinkled wall above is climbed trending left.

22. Coe Conut 12m VS 5a
Takes the wall to the right of Coe Crag Corner, moving slightly left to the foot of a deep narrow crack that is surmounted with difficulty.

The crack/chimney lines further right are Severe and VDiff respectively, but are not recommended.

Lower down than the main crag and some 200 metres from its right hand end is a small isolated buttress with three prominent cracks. This is the most westerly of the small buttresses and although the routes are short and not without interest their names aptly suggest their nature.

23. Sty Crack 9m S
This is the wide central crack that leads to an awkward heather finish.

24. Pig Crack 7m HVS 5b
At the right end of the buttress is a crack with an overhang at half height. This is climbed, the crux being to establish oneself above the overhang.

25. Porky 7m VS 5a
Round the arête from Pig Crack is a wall that provides an amusing problem when climbed direct.

Coe Crag Graded List

E3
Soldier of Fortune 6a
Orion Roof 6a

E2
Rampart Wall 5b **
Raven Mad 5b

E1
Cave Wall 5b *

HVS
The Turret 5b
Nagging Wives' Groove 5b *
Kestrel 5a
Battlement 5b
Neb Crack 5a **
Pig Crack 5b
Worrysome Wasp 5a *
Honeycomb Wall 4c **

VS
Coe Conut 5a
Honeycomb Wall - Alternative Start 5a
Porky 5a
Rough Castles Crack 5a ***

Coquet View

Hugh Harris and John Wallace

NZ 994014
North Facing
350m
45 minutes

History

The early history of this overlooked crag will probably remain a mystery though it is probable that some of the easier routes may have been climbed previously. A tip-off from a well known NMC member in 1990 initiated the development reported here and the routes recorded were climbed over a couple of years by the "Wildtrak Crew". The names are those given by the most recent ascentionists. There has been no development since then.

Situation and Character

This well hidden crag is situated only a short distance east from Ravensheugh but cannot be seen from any of the approach paths, which only adds to its secluded nature. It is of similar rock to its larger neighbour but also offers some quite unique and impressive features of its own. It suffers from the same problems of early season dirt and greenness but there are some good little routes that make it worth a visit, especially on a fine summer evening later in the season when the crag catches any available sun.

Approaches and Access

The rocks can be reached in about forty five minutes from the Forestry Commission car park on the road between Great Tosson and Lordenshaw (037997). The Forestry Commission road is followed through the forest to beneath the west end of Simonside where a minor track leads west across the plateau to a fence and sometimes a stile. This is the same approach as for Ravensheugh. At the stile turn right and follow the path, next to the fence, down hill for about 200m until the right end of the crag is reached. There appears to be no problem with access. For approach map see page 237. There is a right of access to the crag under CRoW.

The Climbs

The crag is divided into six major buttresses split by gullies, some of which give descent routes. The routes are described from left to right. This is not where you logically arrive at the crag.

Needle Buttress

The furthest left buttress, so named because of the obvious 'Eye' through the projecting hanging arête. The first route starts 1m right of the left hand end of the wall with a pocket at head height.

1. The Nick 6m E2 5c

Climb the wall direct, passing the pocket; with a difficult move to reach the top holds.

2. Helen of Trowel 6m VS 5a

Start 3 metres right of The Nick below the twin hanging cracks. Climb the awkward wall and gain the right crack, which leads to an easy finish.

3. Ky's Route 9m HVS 5a **

An excellent route that climbs the open corner and crack crossing the left end of the 'Eye' at half height. Start 2 metres right of Helen of Trowel and climb direct to the 'Eye'. The crux is leaving it to enter the crack above. Finish on good holds.

4. Broken Thread 9m HVS 5b *

Start below the centre of the right end of the 'Eye'. Climb up to the 'Eye' then use the thin crack to gain the wall above. Climb this boldly on good holds.

5. To the Point 6m HVS 5b

The blunt arête at the right side of the 'Eye' 1.5 metres right of Broken Thread is climbed direct with a long reach to start.

There is now a gully. The next buttress is:

Watch Buttress

The next route takes a thin crack, with a diamond shaped pod, in the centre of the left wall of the buttress.

6. Flight of Fancy 7m VS 5a *
Climb the crack with awkward moves to leave the pod.

After a gully the next buttress takes the form of an impressive steep arête.

The Prow

7. The Put Off! 6m E1 5c
Climb the wall left of Avoiding the Issue to large ledges at half height. Finish as for The Issue.

8. Avoiding the Issue 7m E1 5c
Climb the wall and groove 1metre left of the arête to large ledges at half height. Finish as for The Issue.

9. The Issue 13m E3 6a **
A good feature. Climb the arête direct on its right hand side to the half height ledges. Finish up the rounded arête above.

The next buttress is the largest of the crag and has some strange convoluted rock features and a large smooth block standing at its top.

Convolution Buttress

10. The Garden Path 10m VS 5a
The once cleaned line on the left side of the buttress that has reverted to nature.

11. Arseburner 11m 5.10d (E3 5c) *
Start at the right toe of the buttress. Pull up, move left and climb up to the arse shaped, impending but well protected off-width crack with a distinctly American feel. Climb this by any means possible - arm bars seem to help! A classic struggle.

Alternative Finish HVS 5a
The much easier cleaned groove to the right and definitely not in the spirit of the route.

To the right of Convolution Buttress is a deep crevasse leading round behind the next buttress which is set back slightly.

12. Hanging Slab Buttress
So named because of the obvious unclimbed feature. There are no routes on this buttress.

Chimney Buttress

The final buttress has an open chimney splitting its centre.

13. Finale 7m E2 5c *
Start 3m right of the central chimney below twin flutes. Climb these to a large pocket. Move slightly left and up to a tricky exit onto sloping holds.

Coquet View Graded List

E3
The Issue 6a **
Arseburner 5c *

E2
Finale 5c *
The Nick 5c

E1
Avoiding the Issue 5c
The Put Off! 5c

HVS
Broken Thread 5b *
To the Point 5b
Arseburner Alternative Finish 5a
Ky's Route 5a **

VS
The Garden Path 5a
Helen of Trowel 5a
Flight of Fancy 5a *

Corby's Crag

Cliff Robson and Michael Thomas

NU 127101
North West Facing
184m
1 minute

History

Surprisingly for somewhere so accessible the first recorded activity was not until July 1970. Ken Macdonald, John Earl and friends visited the crag and a large number of lines were climbed out in the following months. Climbs included Plonka, Man Friday, Audacity and the hardest route at the time, Sunshine Superman. The following few years saw development come to fruition. In 1973 Bob Hutchinson added Corbeau and in 1974 he swung his way up the powerful Gibbon's Gambol.

In 1977 Martin Doyle and Karl Telfer claimed Ranadon and Jeff Lamb snapped up Tenacity on one of his raids east. Bob and Tommy Smith brought the crag into the 1980s with the difficult Ash Wednesday climbed in late 1979. Only two lines have been put up since then. Sam's Route on the North Buttress was squeezed in at the end of the cave in 1989 by Stu Ferguson. The other, an obvious but never recorded line,

Situation and Character

Corby's Crag is a pleasant sandstone outcrop with a very scenic north west facing aspect in a relatively sheltered position on the flank of Alnwick Moor. It overlooks the Vale of Whittingham with excellent views northwards to the Cheviots and provides a pleasant venue for visits from spring through to autumn. In winter it tends to suffer from damp and lichen, being slow to dry after prolonged rain and taking drainage from the road above.

The rock is a softer sandstone than most in the county but contains harder bands and although sound to climb on, it has suffered badly from top roping in recent years with deep grooves being gouged out on some routes. This, together with heavy use of the crag by training groups has led to some serious erosion and pollution problems. Although an excellent middle grade crag, it is not very suitable for beginners as the climbing is often delicate and technical. Constant abseiling on North Buttress has damaged both classic routes and the crag top.

Approaches and Access

The crag is about 3¾ miles east of the A697 (Morpeth-Wooler) and B6341 (Alnwick- Rothbury) crossroads along the B6341. Quite a number of small outcrops are to be found in this area and Corby's lies about 50 metres down off the road to the left. There is a small car park at the north end of the crag near the top of the long hill overlooking Edlingham. Approaching from the east it is about 5 miles from Alnwick. The South Buttress is best reached by taking a path past a large oak which grows at the top of the crag. Time, one minute or faster if the car brakes fail. See approach map on page 72. There is a right of access to the crag under CRoW.

The Climbs

From right to left the crag comprises a Far South Buttress, South Buttress, Upper Middle Section, Lower Middle Section and the impressive North Buttress. Apart from the latter area, routes are short but the steep bulging nature of the rock and hidden pocket holds create an interesting and varied challenge and compensate for the lack of height.
The climbs are described from right to left.

Far South Buttress

1. Mr. Jones 12m D
Start at the right hand end of the crag about 2 metres down from the fence. Climb to a ledge. Then break right up a ramp to finish.

2. Little X 6m VS 5a
Left of Mr. Jones is an "X" shaped feature. It provides an interesting problem with harder variations possible if taken direct or from the right. Start left of the "X" and climb straight up for about 2 metres, traverse right to the cross and then climb up to a sloping ledge. A good tick.

3. Two Tree Chimney 12m D
Climb the tree filled chimney by its left side to the bay. Follow the chimney above by backing up inside. A flake just left of the upper chimney provides a second pitch at Very Severe.

4. Bloody Sunday 12m VS 5a
Just left of Two Tree Chimney is a small cave. Climb the wall to the right of this on flakes until a traverse right can be made to a crack and groove which is climbed to a large ledge. Move easily left about 2 metres. Then finish awkwardly up the wall above. An interesting climb.

5. Reject 11m E1 5b
Takes the bulging slab direct. Start a few metres left of Bloody Sunday. Climb the first bulge to a break. Then make a delicate and poorly protected move up the short wall to the ledge. Finish up the final wall right of Bloody Sunday.

6. L.P. 11m VS 4c
Good climbing up the open corner formed by a slab and wall 4 metres left of Bloody Sunday. Climb the slab and then go up the wall to the right of a small overlap to reach a groove leading up diagonally left for a few metres, before going straight for the top.

7. Nut's Wall 10m VS 4c
Climb up to the foot of the smaller of the two flakes left of L.P. and continue up until an awkward step right can be made to a large foothold on the wall. Continue more easily via the arête or the groove.

8. Misrepresentation 10m MVS 4c **
A good climb which starts up the left edge of the buttress. Move up to the foot of the large flake and climb it to a rounded finish.

9. Bluebird 10m E3 6a *
The overhanging arête to the left of Misrepresentation provides a bold and unprotected route. Once established under the overhanging wall make a very long reach for sloping holds above and then pull right to the final flute.

South Buttress

At the left end of Far South Buttress is an obvious easy way down. South Buttress extends from here to a large overhang. Immediately left of the easy way down, a small buttress and bay provide some short but worthwhile courses of Very Difficult to Severe standard but the best route takes the buttress direct.

10. Chicken Run VS 4c
Climb the buttress by a flake to the nose, then continue straight up on small but positive holds or chicken out and traverse off right.

11. Prediction 10m VS 5a
A slab about 3 metres left of a reddish overhang in the bay may be climbed by laybacking to reach an awkward stance facing the overhanging wall. From here a rather unpredictable manoeuvre is required to gain another slab about 2 metres higher.

12. Temptation 10m HVS 5a *
Climb the enticing wall left of Prediction towards an overhang about halfway up. A long reach to a hollow sounding flake gains the wall, which is followed to the top.

13. Overunder 10m HS 4b
Follow the series of overhangs left of Temptation leading left and diagonally upwards, but go up over the final one to a sloping ledge. From here the wall is climbed right of a tree.

Variation 10m VS 5a
From the first overhang pull over and right via a broken flake onto the wall. A few delicate moves are required to reach the top.

14. First Opportunity 10m MS
The obvious wide crack with a dead tree stump at the top is climbed with unexpected awkwardness.

15. Scotsman's Way 10m VS 4c
A climb which starts up a flake just left of First Opportunity. Jockey up to the overhang then move right across the slab to the rib, which is followed to the top.

Corby's Crag

16. Wheatcroft's Delight 12m
Hard Severely Vegetated
This route, of interest to botanists, starts up the flake described above. Climb upwards until a traverse left may be made to a small holly beneath the overhanging nose. Climb the overhang on the left, thence to the top, mainly by the use of vegetation.

17. Missed Opportunity 10m HVS 5b
Start one and a half metres left of the start of Scotsman's Way. Follow small flutings to the undercling. Make a tricky move rightwards over the small overlap to a thin flake and finish straight up.

18. Watering Can 10m VS 4c
The wall above the cave is often dripping but when dry provides a short route. Pull through the overhang at the right end of the cave and climb the wall to finish by a sapling.

A short route of Severe standard follows a right diagonal crack above the cave to a tree left of Wheatcroft's Delight.

19. The Plonka 12m S ***
A classic involving some delicate climbing. Follow a ramp leading left diagonally upwards from the cave to meet a right diagonal crack. Follow this to a tree and either finish direct or make a short traverse left and finish by a large block.

20. Crossover 16m S
Start at a red, crescent shaped feature on the buttress about 3 metres left of The Plonka. Continue awkwardly up over a bulge to join with the crack of Wonderland and traverse left across the wall below a tree to finish up the arête above Garden Gully.

21. Wonderland 11 m S
The obvious, rightward slanting, wide crack.

22. Gibbon's Gambol 12m E2 5c *
Gain a large flake under the overhang left of Wonderland. Monkey along this to the end and make some difficult moves over the overhang to finish up the slab above.

Direct Start 5c
Climb the wall 3 metres to the left and move out under the overhanging flake to join the normal route at the top of the flake.

23. Ken's Caper 12m HVS 4c
Begin by climbing the left corner of the overhang by the end of South Buttress on juggy rock until it is possible to move right to a ramp. From this position climb delicately straight up the wall.

24. Tiger Feet 10m E1 5a **
The overhanging arête avoided by the previous route provides a bold and enjoyable climb. Ascend the ramp then move left with difficulty to reach the bottom of a flute. Follow this to the top.

25. Tiger's Tale 10m HVS 5b
The obvious slab right of Garden Gully is gained with difficulty via pockets on the arête. Often damp and not much gear.

Upper Middle Section
This section, which is about 30 metres long, lies at a higher level above the fence marking the end of South Buttress. It starts with a recess above which is a short grassy gully known as Garden Gully.

26. Crab Walk 11m D
6 metres left of Garden Gully the wall is climbed to reach a ramp on the top of a large detached flake. Follow this right to the apex and then climb the slab to reach a block on the top. The flake can also be taken in its centre at 5b.

27. Point Blank 12m E3 6a
A serious route up the wall between Crab Walk and Sunshine Superman. Climb the wall on small incuts to gain the base of a flute and make a long reach from this to the top.

28. Silent Freeway 12m E2 5c
Climb to below the crux of Point Blank and then move left to the bottom of the top niche of Sunshine Superman. Hand traverse a few metres left along the obvious break to the small rounded flake and the top.

29. Sunshine Superman 10m HVS 5a***
Excellent climbing taking the obvious, clean, overhanging crack which runs diagonally right from a small niche to a larger one surmounted by an overhanging block. The upper niche can be quitted on the right or the overhang taken direct on good holds. A great test piece.

30. Corbeau 10m E1 5a *
A good route taking the bulging wall between Sunshine Superman and Hole in One. Start at a flake left of Sunshine Superman and climb up to the overhang. Step left and then make for the top on deep but slightly suspect incuts and little gear. Usually soloed by the locals.

The wall between Corbeau and Hole in One can be climbed at 5c.

31. Hole in One 10m MVS 4c *
4 metres left of Sunshine Superman a flake by a small hole in the rock, about 3 metres above the ground, leads diagonally right towards some blackish rock. Follow this, then move left to finish up the crack on the left.

32. Super Spooky 10m E2 5c
The wall just left of Hole in One is climbed on small holds.

33. Birdie 10m HVS 5a
The wall immediately right of Bogeyman is climbed to the pod. Finish direct.

34. Bogeyman 6m VS 5a *
Climb up the short, strenuous, overhanging crack which goes straight through the bulges 6 metres left of Hole in One.

Lower Middle Section
Follow the path from the left end of the South Buttress down to a lichenous buttress marked by a tree at its right end and by a gully between a series of large boulders at its higher, left end. Various short problems have been climbed as well as the two described routes.

35. Rough Cut 15m S
Traverse above the cave from right to left, finishing up Dog Rough.

36. Dog Rough 12m S
The climb starts right of a cave near the left end of the buttress, below a rounded block on the top. Climb easily up to a wide ledge. Then follow the right hand crack diagonally up and left until it is possible to make straight for the block above which is climbed direct.

John Earl
29. Sunshine Superman (HVS 5a)
Photo: Bob Smith

North Buttress

North Buttress

North Buttress is about 50 metres long. It is bounded on the right by two large boulders and extends to the north end of the crag. Main Wall is that part of North Buttress extending from the north end to a dark recess left of an arête beneath a large oak tree.

37. Boulder, Crack and Slab 11m VD

Left of the two large boulders forming the limit of this section a crack is formed. Climb this to a heather ledge and ash sapling from which a traverse left may be made across the slab by the easiest line.

38. Cake Walk 12m D

Start beneath a line of overhangs left of the large blocks of Boulder, Crack and Slab. Move up to gain handholds beneath the overhangs. Traverse left to cross over a short chimney and continue to the top.

39. Amorous Antics 10m E3 6b

A naughty route which climbs the shallow groove above Cake Walk. Climb the wall to a diagonal undercut.   Then pull onto the slab using a shallow pot hole and climb the shallow groove to finish.

40. Misunderstanding 10m MS

Starting about 4 metres left of Cake Walk, climb the wall by the line of least resistance.

41. Black Wall 12m VS 4c *

Begin at a black patch of rock left of Misunderstanding. Layback up to the bulge and climb upwards until stopped by the overhang which is climbed direct. Finish up the short wall.

42. False Impression 12m VS 5a

Start midway between Black Wall and Easy Rider. Climb up, trending right to the small overhang. Pull over on good holds and finish up the wall.

43. Easy Rider 12m S

4 metres left of Black Wall. The arête by the right end of Main Wall is climbed to a large oak tree. Work to the right beneath it, finishing up the arête on the right.

44. The Chest Expander 15m HVS 5b

A low line traverse of Main Wall. Start in the dirty corner left of Easy Rider. Ttraverse left under the first roofs of Audacity and Tenacity and continue traversing until it is possible to go up to the finish of Man Friday.

45. Combo 15m HS 4b

Bridge up the sides of the dark recess left of Easy Rider until a short left traverse can be made. Move up and continue the traverse to a shallow groove. Climb up past this then traverse right above it, finishing up the pinnacle.

46. Plumbline 11m VS 4c
Climb directly upwards to a nose about 4 metres left of Combo and continue up to and between two small overhangs, to finish up a slab.

47. Cauliflower Lug 15m E3 6a
Starts with a swinging pounce for the obvious large ear right of Audacity. Move up and right to a set of flutings, climbing these on the right and the wall above to the old tree. Not many opportunities for using the gear you lug up!

48. Tenacity 15m E4 6a
Climb Audacity for 3 metres then move right to climb the obvious twin flutes to a hold above. Traverse right and climb up to the tree and from this climb the thin crack above by means of a bold layback.

49. Audacity 15m HVS 5a ***
An impressive direct route up the centre of Main Wall. The classic of the crag. Start by using a large flake and the wall on its left to reach the overhang. Move left and climb the flutes above on good holds then move right and continue upwards, passing right of an overhanging bulge, to a corner. Finally, trend leftwards up a slab to finish.

50. Man Friday 18m VS 4c
Starts in the same place as Audacity but traverse left using handholds on a ledge for a few metres to an overhanging flake. Climb this and then traverse left again to a bulging nose about 3 metres left, which is climbed direct to a heathery finish.

51. Ranadon 15m E2 5b ***
Climb the blank looking wall left of Audacity to the obvious break and go straight up the wall left of the obvious flutes. At the second horizontal break trend left (crux) to finish up a scoop. An excellent route.

52. Ash Wednesday 13m E4 6a
A difficult direct route up the North Buttress. Begin at the shallow cave left of Ranadon and climb straight up from its right side to the break. Follow Ranadon up the wall. Then climb the overhang directly above, moving slightly right up the overhang to do so.

53. Friday's Child 13m E3 5c*
From the left side of the cave, climb the overhanging wall above by means of the obvious flake to a break. Follow the deep flakes to a small roof and using an undercut on the right of a thin crack, pull into the scoop and then move out rightwards to an awkward finish.

54. Sam's Route 12m E2 6a
Start 2m left of Friday's Child. Climb directly up the overhanging wall and continue straight up the wall above. Lacking good gear and unfortunately often damp.

The following two routes go up the extreme left end of Main Wall taking the two obvious lines of weakness.

55. Crew 10m MVS 4c
A good climb with a rather worrying finish. Climb the enormous pockets 4 metres right of the arête. Then go up the wall above on flakes. Jibber up a heathery groove on the right to finish.

56. Sow 10m HS 4b
Climb the left arête of Main Wall on hidden flakes and pockets trending left to finish.

57. Shadow Crack 8m VS 4c
The strenuous overhanging crack at the extreme north end of the crag, finishing left of the tree.

58. Girdle Traverse 42m VS 4c
Begin as for Cake Walk but move left from the chimney towards Easy Rider. Continue left below the oak tree, then downwards until the dark recess above the start of Combo can be bridged. Follow the traverse of Combo to a ledge just beneath the tree. Traverse left with some delicate moves until good footholds are reached. Progress on these until a diagonal move leads on to the small cave. Continue left then up a bulge as for Man Friday.

Corby's Crag Graded List

E4
Ash Wednesday 6a
Tenacity 6a

E3
Amorous Antics 6b
Point Blank 6a
Bluebird 6a *
Cauliflower Lug 6a
Friday's Child 5c *

E2
Sam's Route 6a
Gibbons Gambol 5c *
Super Spooky 5c
Silent Freeway 5c
Ranadon 5b ***

E1
Reject 5b
Tiger Feet 5a **
Corbeau 5a *

HVS
Sunshine Superman 5a ***
Temptation 5a *
Tiger's Tale 5b
Audacity 5a ***
Missed Opportunity 5b
The Chest Expander 5b
Birdie 5a
Ken's Caper 4c

VS
Prediction 5a
Bloody Sunday 5a
Overunder Variation 5a
Bogeyman 5a *
Little X 5a
False Impression 5a
Scotsman's Way 4c
Man Friday 4c
Black Wall 4c *
L.P. 4c
Nut's Wall 4c
Chicken Run 4c
Watering Can 4c
Plumbline 4c
Girdle Traverse 4c
Shadow Crack 4c

Andy Birtwistle
24. Tiger Feet (E1 5a)
Photo: Mark Adamson

Mike Arnold attacking the classic
99. Whinstone Churchill (E2 5b)
during the NMC anniversary meet in 1995
Photo: Steve Crowe

Crag Lough
by Malcolm Lowerson

NGR NY 932822
North Facing
Alt. 250m
15 minutes

History

Crag Lough was probably first discovered in 1907 by Marcus Beresford Heywood who recorded a number of routes in the Climbers Club Journal published in 1912. The article referred to five routes that are shown in a rather featureless diagram but from the descriptions it seems possible to identify what are now Hadrian's Chimney, Great Chimney and Main Wall. In the 1920's there were further visits by the next generation of climbers and though no doubt much was climbed nothing was recorded at that time.

In the 1940's activity increased with a keen band of climbers including Basil Butcher, Keith Gregory and other members of what was to become the Northumbrian Mountaineering Club climbing many routes; by that time Pinnacle Face, Main Wall, Hadrian's Wall and Grad's Groove were receiving regular ascents. Impossible Buttress and Route I were led by Tony Moulam, the latter giving possibly the hardest move on the crag at that time.

In the 1950's the Crag Lough Club was formed and many harder routes were ascended including Crescent Crack, Y Climb, Why Not and Impossible Buttress Route Three.

Further exploration continued into the 1960's but towards the end of that decade interest in the crag began to wane as increasing mobility among climbers brought the more distant sandstone outcrops into reach, resulting in many obscure and some worthwhile climbs returning to a vegetated state.

The last routes of significance were added in the 1970's. Bob Hutchinson and John Earl made a rare diversion from the sandstone to free climb Smooth Bastion and rename it Whinstone Churchill, Jeff Lamb freed the previously aided Impossible Wall to produce the hardest route on the crag and Bob and Tommy Smith added the bold Stephenson's Rocket.

Since the publication of the 1989 Guide Book only three new routes have been recorded and many of the existing routes have become heavily vegetated due to too few ascents. Despite this, the more popular lines are in good condition and Crag Lough has some of the longest and best quality Severe and Very Severe climbs in Northumberland.

Crag Lough seen from Milecastle 39
Photo: Steve Crowe

Situation and Character

The crag, which is dolerite and forms part of the Whin Sill, is impressively situated above the lough, which provides its name and is the largest and most extensive crag in the county. However, the northerly aspect and the smooth nature of the rock makes climbing here in the winter months a character building experience; the rock is virtually frictionless when wet, even when completely clean and this is certainly no all-weather crag. The rock is formed into large columns and many of the better routes follow definite natural lines. Some of the best routes are in the lower/middle grades which bear comparison with the best outcrop routes anywhere.

Approaches and Access

The crag lies about 1 mile north of the B6318 Newcastle Carlisle road (the Military Road). Cars can be parked at the Steel Rigg car park, which is reached by turning due north from the Military Road at the Once Brewed Youth Hostel. From the car park a clear pathway (right of way) leads beneath Peel Crag and Crag Lough is reached in about twenty minutes. The land is owned by the National Trust and camping is forbidden but there is a small farm campsite at Winshields Farm about 200 metres west of the Twice Brewed Inn. An alternative access route lies along the farm track leading to Hot Bank Farm until the Roman Wall is reached and followed west to the top of the crag. This approach is shorter but parking on the Military Road is limited, dangerous and probably illegal. Crag Lough has not been mapped as CRoW access land. It is, though, on National Trust land and so will be shown as open country on the new Explorer map. Access rights and arrangements remain as described above.

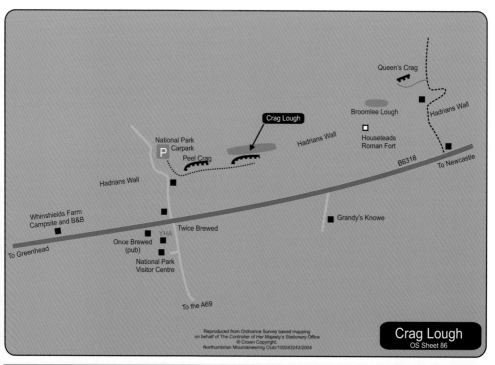

Pinnacle Face | Impossible Buttress | West Buttress

The Climbs

The climbs are described from right to left.

West Buttress

1. West Chimney 8m M
Climb the obvious chimney on substantial holds.

2. West Corner 11 m S
An interesting little route. Climb a short corner and pull round left onto the face. Move up and back right to finish up the crack.

3. Wall and Crack 11m D
Start just left of the toe of the buttress. Climb the conspicuous chimney for 5 metres then traverse left across the wall to reach cracks which lead to the top.

4. Fifth Avenue 11m D
The route meanders up the left side of the buttress.

Monolith Wall
8 metres left of Fifth Avenue, a smooth, steep wall with a peculiar hatchet shaped protruding rock provides the next two routes.

5. Face Route 15m S
Start below and to the left of the protruding rock. Climb the crack to the rock then follow a line of footholds slanting up left. The ascent of the final short wall is the crux.

6. Original Route 15m S
Start 4 metres left of the previous route. Climb the broken wall, below and well to the left of the protruding rock, to a sloping ledge. Move down this slightly then step up onto the wall above. Traverse right and finish up the edge.

Impossible Buttress
This prominent buttress begins just left of Monolith Wall.

7. Route Three 18m VS 5a *
The narrow corner crack high up at the back of the right wall of the buttress. Climb the crack on awkward jams to a ledge. Move left with difficulty to the overhanging corner then pull up right to finish on good holds.

8. Intermediate Treatment 17m E2 5c
Start 1metre left Route Three. Using small ledges climb leftwards to the arête. Move back right and use a scoop as a foothold to reach the base of the ramp. Follow this and the crack to the top. It is easier (HVS 5a and more logical) to reach the crack by climbing just to the left of the arête.

9. Route One 18m HVS 5a **
The final moves are testing. Climb the broken groove on the front of the buttress moving right to a small ledge at half height. Move up to the small overhang, then make a delicate step up left onto a sloping spout from where the top can be reached. Two variations are possible from the ledge.

The Right Variation HVS 5a
Traverse right to the edge, which is then climbed.

The Left Variation HVS 5a
Go down slightly until a step can be made onto the left wall, which is climbed to the top.

10. Route Two 20m VD
Start as for Route One. Climb up for 3 metres until it is possible to traverse left via a large flake into the chimney. Climb the chimney then the arête on the left.

11. Impossible Slab 20m E3 5c
Start 3 metres left of the previous route. Climb the wall direct to the top of the large flake and continue to the horizontal break. The crack above is followed to the top.

12. Impossible Buttress Obverse 17m HVS 5a
Start high up and left of the chimney of Route Two. Climb the short wall to a stance on the arête overlooking the chimney. Descend the chimney for 2 metres until a horizontal crack can be seen crossing the blank wall. Using this for the hands and a similar one for the toes, cross onto Route One, which is then followed.

Pinnacle Face
This buttress is identified by the pinnacle at its foot. It is next to the Appian Way (the wide gully).

13. Pinnacle Crack 7m D
Climb the obvious broken edged crack high up on the west wall of the buttress.

14. Bracket 15m VD **
To the right of the pinnacle on the north west corner of the buttress is a shiny, narrow slab with a deep crack on its left. Follow the crack line and finish on the left or right.

15. Pinnacle Face 14m VS 4c ***
A delightful climb. Ascend the block beneath the sentry box. From here move up and right out onto the face and follow the steep cracked wall to the top. It is possible to climb the pinnacle and step across or back and foot between pinnacle and face.

16. Pinnacle Face Obverse 8m S
Climb the steep crack up the left side of Pinnacle Face.

The Appian Way is the earth and rock slope to the left of Pinnacle Face. It provides an easy means of descent. On the left side of the Appian Way lies the compact Hadrian's Buttress.

Karin Magog leading
15. Pinnacle Face (VS 4c)
Photo: Steve Crowe

25 | The Appian Way | 14 | 21 | 18 | 20 | Hadrian's Buttress | Pinnacle Face

Hadrian's Buttress

17. Hadrian's Recess 15m S *
The recess faces the Appian Way just above the toe of the buttress. Climb the narrow crack in the left side of the recess to a small ledge. Continue up the wider crack above.

18. Hadrian's Buttress 17m S ***
A classic, possibly the best of its grade on the crag. Start at the foot of the buttress immediately left of Hadrian's Recess. Climb a crack moving left to a ledge. Follow a crack until forced to the right. Finish with two mantelshelves.

19. Hadrian's Rib 17m VS 4c *
Start at the toe of the buttress to the right of the conspicuous chimney and climb directly up the rib on widely spaced holds. An artificial but entertaining route.

20. Hadrian's Chimney 17m S
Climb the prominent hanging chimney.

21. Hadrian's East 20m VD
Start 3 metres left of the chimney; follow the broken face and upper chimney.

22. Crescent Climb 18m VD
Begin to the left of Hadrian's East at the foot of a short deep, open corner. Climb the corner to a big ledge. Move right onto a slab, which is followed onto the upper reaches of Hadrian's East.

23. Hadrian's Highway 17m S
Follow Crescent Climb to the big ledge. Move up the wall behind to a small ledge from where a difficult semi layback move is required to bring easier ground within reach.

24. Hadrian's Necklace 35m MVS 4b
An interesting excursion round the buttress. Follow Crescent Climb until just below the big ledge. Pull round into Hadrian's East and go down that climb to just below a projecting block. Using hand holds just below an overhang, traverse the steep wall into Hadrian's Chimney. Descend this until below the chimney, then move right under the overhang and make an airy move round onto Hadrian's Buttress, which is followed to the top.

25. Ash Tree Wall 15m S **
The steep wall to the left of Crescent Climb with an ash tree growing at its top. Follow the obvious line of cracks finishing at the tree.

Mark Armitage leading
18. Hardian's Buttress (Severe)
"Possibly the best severe on the crag"
Photo: Steve Crowe

Jezebel Buttress

Tarzan Buttress

26. Amendment VD
A small buttress high up at the back of a grassy recess 20 metres left of Ash Tree Wall. Mantelshelf into the big niche. Move up and step around to the right into the chimney and continue up this.

Tarzan Buttress

The next buttress, Tarzan Buttress, lies approximately 50 metres to the east of Hadrian's Buttress, the area of rock between the two buttresses being overgrown. The buttress reaches down to the path and has a short deep chimney set into a corner, at its foot.

27. Evasion Groove 26m HVS 5a *
Start in the corner at the foot of the deep chimney. Follow Tarzan to the cleft and take the right wall to a ledge. The awkward corner above leads onto a ramp below a wedge shaped block. Bridge up and pass the block with difficulty onto easier ground.

28. Tarzan 26m VD ***
Start in the corner at the foot of the deep chimney. Work up the wall to the right until it is possible to step across the top of the chimney and onto a ledge below a deep cleft. Climb up

this until the top of the wall can be reached. A strenuous pull leads to a ledge. Climb the gap between the pinnacle above and the wall, then finish up the wall trending right.

Direct Start MVS
The cleft can be reached direct from the ground.

29. Easy Picking 10m HVS 5b
Start immediately left of the obvious crack on the narrow north facing rib. Climb right to the arête and follow it up the hanging crack to a ledge. Move left to Tarzans Mate then back right to the arête, which is followed to a large ledge and a junction with Tarzan.

30. Tarzan's Mate 26m VD **
Start immediately to the left of the obvious crack on a narrow north facing rib. Climb this to a platform and continue up cracks to join Tarzan at the pinnacle.

Direct Start S
Climb the obvious corner crack direct.

31. Cheetah Traverse S
A short traverse using either of the two starts of Tarzan's Mate. From the platform traverse right under the overhang and move round to the deep cleft of Tarzan. Continue as for Tarzan.

32. Jane 26m MVS 4c
Start immediately left of the rib of Tarzan's Mate. Climb broken rocks to the overhang and pull up right onto the rib. Step back left into the thin serpentine crack and climb up to join Tarzan at the pinnacle. Follow Tarzan until that route veers right and climb the steep crack straight above.

Belfry Buttress
Midway between Tarzan and Jezebel Buttresses and situated high up, is a steep, pointed buttress, Belfry Buttress.

33. Belfry Buttress 23m S
Work up the lower rocks, then follow the right side of the buttress until a move left can be made onto the arête using a good handhold. Continue up the face trending left.

Jezebel Buttress
The next prominent buttress is Jezebel Buttress. It appears to consist of several ill fitting blocks.

34. Sinister Corner 23m S *
A pleasant series of interesting problems. Jam the narrow crack between the face and a tall pillar, to a block at the top. Step right onto the wall and move diagonally right to a ledge. Take the corner at the right end to another ledge. Move back left round into a corner and climb this to the top.

35. Jezebel Direct 23m MVS 4b
At the front of the buttress lies a narrow corner crack between a short slab and the face. Follow the crack to the top, then step right and ascend a cracked wall to a ledge with a flake. Step off the flake and follow a groove to the top.

36. Jezebel 23m D ***
Start on the left side of the buttress below a deep crack containing jammed blocks. Climb the crack. Step right onto the cracked wall and climb it to a large platform. From the left side of the platform climb the cracked wall, then the chimney to the top.

37. Hara Kiri 17m HS 4b
Follows the left edge of the upper buttress. Climb the wall until the large upper cracks can be used.

To the left of Jezebel Buttress and higher up lies a steep wall, which contains two short but excellent routes.

38. Wooden Tops 15m E1 5b **
The old peg crack. Climb the crack for 2 metres and traverse right to the arête. This is climbed until a hard move back left leads to the central finishing cracks.

39. Spot the Dog 15m HVS 5b *
Climb a flake on the left of the buttress. Move slightly left to a thin crack, which is followed awkwardly until a move right leads to a hand crack to finish.

Raven's Tower
The next buttress forms the left edge of an amphitheatre

40. Raven's Arête 15m E1 5b
The arête to the right of Raven's Tower is climbed direct. It is delicate and poorly protected with some doubtful holds.

41. Raven's Tower 15m MVS 4b ***
Climb up to the gap between the perched block and the tower. Move up and right into the crack on the right face. Climb the crack to the top. It is possible to reach the gap by a crack in the front of the lower buttress.

42. Crescent Cracks 15m VS 5a **
Start as for Raven's Tower. Go straight up and pull over the small overhang to reach the two parallel, crescent shaped cracks and using these climb to the top.

Angus MacDonald (founder member of the NMC) on
1. West Chimney (M)
Photo: Andrew Birtwistle

Broken Ash Buttress   Dexter Buttress   Raven's Tower

Dexter Buttress

The next buttress, Dexter Buttress, reaches down to the path and can be recognised by the steep, north facing corner, which reaches from the bottom to the top of the buttress. This forms the line of Why Not Direct.

43. Sweet Violets Bitter Almonds 22m D

The deep gully 5 metres right of the main corner of Dexterity is climbed to a small wooden fence on the path above the crag.

44. The Central Girdle 90m MVS 4c *

A worthwhile route. Climb the corner some 3 metres right of Dexterity and move right, round the corner to a sharply defined 1 metre overhang. Climb this using a crack on the left. Traverse across left to Why Not then move round the exposed corner to a ledge on Block Chimney. Move left into the corner and climb up 5 metres to a ledge then cross the steep wall. Continue the traverse at the same height into Deep Gully. Traverse across Centurion's Crack to the big crack of Praetor, which is climbed to a large ledge. Descend the crack on the other side to sloping ledge. Cross the ledge and ascend the corner for a metre. Continue left into Punch Line and descend this until it is possible to move across to the top of Back Alley. Dirty in parts.

45. Dexterity 22m S **

Start in the main corner and climb up moving right to a large ledge. Move right along the ledge and climb the right edge of the wall, moving back left over blocks to a platform. Climb the short wall at the back of the platform.

46. Why Not 23m VS 5a **

Start in the main corner and climb up to the long ledge as for Dexterity. Take the groove at the left end of the ledge and climb up on poor holds to the top of the large flake. Climb the corner crack above to the top.

47. Why Not Direct 23m HVS 5b **

Start in the corner and climb up 3 metres to a ledge. Move left into the bulging corner and layback up the thin crack to the top of the flake. Finish up the corner crack as for Why Not.

48. Chariot Race 17m E3 5c **

A more direct line to the upper groove of Block Chimney Super Direct. Start immediately right of Block Chimney. Climb a short groove, pull onto the right arête then step left onto the face and move up, using side holds, to the horizontal break. Continue up the groove above.

49. Block Chimney 17m D **

The obvious chimney with a large jammed block

round to the left of Why Not. Climb up to and under the block. Traverse right onto the front of the buttress and climb the staircase to the top.

50. Ben Hur 17m E1 5c
Start as for Block Chimney. Climb up past the jammed block and follow the thin crack up the steep wall above. Continue up the arête to the top.

51. Block Chimney Super Direct 18m HVS 5a*
Follow Block Chimney for 8 metres to a horizontal crack in the right wall. Using the crack move right to the foot of a groove. Make an awkward pull up into the groove, which is followed to the top.

The following two routes are reputed to exist on the loose and vegetated area between Block Chimney and Deep Gully.

52. Naissance 10m VD
An indeterminate line on the right side of the buttress.

53. Catherine 20m VS 4c
4 metres right of Deep Gully. A narrow, slanting crack ,widening to a ledge, followed by a wall.

54. Deep Gully M
This deep conspicuous gully has a 5 metres rock pitch of Moderate standard. It is very useful as a way down after climbing on the central section of the crag though care is needed near the top where the rock is loose.

Deep Gully to Central Buttress
Many of these climbs are covered with heavy vegetation and are not recommended. They are recorded for historical interest only.

55. Centurion's Crack 11m S
Start in the left hand corner of Deep Gully. Climb the crack to an overhanging block, pass this and finish up easier rock. Vegetated.

56. Praetor 15m VD
Start 3 metres left of Centurion's Crack at the foot of an overhanging crack. Climb the crack to the top of the pillar and the wall behind to the top. Vegetated.

57. Doomsday Crack 17m HS 4b
Takes the steep crack in the upper part of the pillar. Climb the wall direct to the crack and follow the crack to the top of the pillar. The wall behind is then ascended. Vegetated.

58. Gargoyle 20m HVS 5b
A few metres or so left of Doomsday Crack is a corner with prominent overhangs above it. Climb the crack in the right wall of the corner to the overhangs. Move left under the overhangs, making a hard move up into a shallow groove and step right above the overhangs to continue. It is easier (and better protected) to climb the crack on the right through the overhangs.

59. Punch Line 20m HS 4b
Start in the corner just right of the conspicuous chimney. Climb up to a ledge and then up the corner direct with increasing difficulty.

60. Back Alley 20m D **
Start as for Punch Line. Climb the crack for 2 metres then traverse left to the foot of the obvious chimney. Climb the chimney to a platform and tree. Easy climbing to the top.

61. Trapezium 22m D
Start as for Back Alley but continue traversing left behind the big detached block. Strenuous climbing up the fissure leads onto the top of the block. Traverse left onto the face and climb the deep crack up to the tree on Back Alley.

Variation Start One VS 4c
Climb the direct line leading to the right side of the detached block.

Variation Start Two S
Traverse round the front of the block from Waterloo.

62. Waterloo 40m HS 4b
A tall pillar lies against the buttress below the detached block of Trapezium. Climb the crack between the left side of the pillar and the face, to its top. Enter the deep crack of Trapezium (from the opposite direction) and struggle up to the top. Traverse delicately into Back Alley. Continue the traverse below the overhangs of Gargoyle to a ledge. Step up onto a sloping ledge and balance across to a crack behind a large pillar. Follow this and the wall above to the top.

63. Spuggies Gully 25m VD **
A good line, which follows the large chimney on the front of the buttress ending on the platform at the top of Trapezium.

64. Abseil Wall 17m VS 5a
The steep wall left of Spuggies Gully, keeping to the centre and finishing up the V groove.

Central Buttress

65. Broken Ash Buttress 27m VD

A long route, better than it looks. It follows the broken face to the left of Abseil Wall. Climb 5 metres to a shallow chimney which is then followed, over steeper rock, to a large ledge. Move up right, from the right end of the ledge, into a corner on the west side of the upper rocks. Ascend this to finish.

Between Broken Ash Buttress and Central Buttress lies a small but prominent buttress.

66. Sombrero 17m S

Start on the right side of the buttress. Jam the crack, which is just the wrong size, to its top. Step round right into a groove containing a large rowan. Follow the groove trending right.

67. Chimney and Mantelshelf 17m D

Climb the chimney on the left side of the buttress to a ledge. A mantelshelf leads into a short chimney, which is followed by a wall.

68. Castor 7m D

5 metres left of the previous climb a pinnacle leans against the crag. The crack between pinnacle and crag forms this route.

The longest climbs on the crag are to be found on Central Buttress.

Central Buttress

69. Y Climb 15m HVS 5a **

The Y shaped crack on the west wall of the buttress. From the grass slope on the right use a sharp though doubtful flake to traverse in. Make an awkward pull up into the crack where good jams can be used to reach the upper, easier crack.

70. Crystal 21m HVS 5a ***

An exposed and sustained route. To the right of the toe of the buttress lies an obvious overhanging corner, which is climbed to a ledge. Move a little way up Grad's Groove until a traverse right into the crack is possible. Follow the crack to a ledge. The flake crack above is followed to an awkward move at the top. Once a standing position has been attained, traverse right along a narrow ledge to the top of Y climb or climb directly to the top using small rounded holds.

Variation HVS 5b

From the ledge climb the crack direct.

71. Grad's Groove 21m MVS 4b **

The overhanging groove in the front of the buttress just left of Crystal. The main difficulties are only 3 metres up. Climb the groove on small sloping holds to a ledge. The chimney above is then followed. If the section below the ledge is avoided the grade is Very Difficult.

72. Brutus 21m HVS 5b
Start just left of Grad's Groove. Climb a series of cracks to a smooth wall split by two thin cracks and follow the right crack to the overhang. Step right and climb the prominent nose by a strenuous crack.

73. Neglect 25m HVS 5a **
A good line with the crux at the top. Start just left of Brutus. Climb a wall on small holds to a very shallow chimney. Continue by bridging to a high ledge. The strenuous pull over the final overhang left of the corner, is awkward for the short.

74. Right Organ Pipe 27m HS
The first chimney left of Neglect. Nowhere technically difficult but long and steep, often damp and vegetated. Follow the chimney to the very top where a narrow foot ledge allows escape to the right.

75. Central Organ Pipe 27m HS
The next chimney to the left. Somewhat cleaner than the neighbour on its right but similar in standard.

76. Left Organ Pipe 25m HVS 5a **
Climb the chimney until it overhangs, then continue up the crack on hand jams until a difficult move left can be made to gain a flake. Pull up on the flake to a ledge. Follow obvious cracks and grooves.

77. Midnight Watch 27m HVS 5a
Takes the arête between Left Organ Pipe and Bisector. Start up the crack of Bisector and step right onto the arête above the small overhang. Move up to the horizontal break, climb over the overhang to a ledge and finish up the arête.

78. Bisector 27m S
Left of the Organ Pipes lies a very steep, smooth wall, bounded on its right edge by a crack and a groove. Climb the crack into the groove and continue past large blocks, trending left, to the top. Dubious rock in places.

79. Impossible Wall 27m E4 6b ***
Originally artificial, this is now a difficult but protectable climb. Start in the centre of the impending wall and climb for 3 metres to a sloping foothold. Using poor layaways make a hard move up to a small handhold. Achieve a

standing position below a thin crack and ascend this to a small ledge. Up a groove and pull left to another groove. Continue for 5 metres, then move right across the face and up to the top.

80. Great Chimney 27m HS ***
A classic route up the conspicuous chimney left of Impossible Wall. Climb the chimney to the large jammed block. Using good holds on the block, swing out and mantelshelf onto the top. Climb the short wall to the top of the crag.

81. God Lives Under Water 34m E2 5b
Climb the right arête of Main Wall on its right hand side to a ledge on that route. Step right and climb the blocky wall to finish.

82. Main Wall 34m HS ***
A splendid route. Start on the left of the foot of the buttress. Climb up towards the right side of the wall to a small ledge. Make a difficult move using twin cracks then move right to a small, clean cut stance on the right edge. Continue on up the groove on the right side of the buttress, finishing up a short chimney to a large platform. Climb the short wall above.

83. Main Wall Route Two 34m VS 5a *
Start just left of Main Wall below a short corner with a small overhang at its top. Climb up the corner and move out over the overhang to a sloping stance. Continue delicately up the wall above to a large ledge on the left. Step left into Botany Crack and climb up for 3 metres. Traverse out left onto the face and make two mantelshelf moves. Pull up onto a ledge.

Direct Finish VS 5a *
From the large ledge on the left move up and right and continue to the top directly by cracks.

84. The Girdle Traverse 58m VS 5a
Starts as for Main Wall Route Two. Climb the corner to a spike runner. Traverse delicately right on two minute, horizontal cracks. Pull up onto the right edge of the buttress (as for Main Wall). Traverse right into Great Chimney and climb it until a line of footholds is seen crossing Impossible Wall. Traverse delicately across Impossible Wall to Bisector. Climb Bisector up to and over the large jammed block. Step right and descend the crack to the earthy ledges of the 'garden path'. Traverse right to the perched block and continue moving right under the overhang into Grad's Groove. Climb the final chimney of Grad's Groove.

85. Main Wall Link 34m S/VS 5a
Start as for Main Wall (Severe) or Main Wall Route Two (Very Severe) and climb up to the final chimney of Main Wall. Traverse right below the overhang into Great Chimney and finish over the jammed block.

86. Botany Crack 20m S
The deep crack to the left of Main Wall is followed throughout. The final open corner is made more awkward by an old protruding peg.

87. Stephenson's Rocket 23m E4 5c **
A very good climb between Botany Crack and Overhanging Chimney. Climb the central rib to the first groove and move up this to the roof, pull over and move left to below the obvious hanging groove. Enter the groove and move up to the twin holds on the shoulders (rest), exit right to a good hold and thin crack.

88. Overhanging Chimney 20m VS 5a
The chimney just left of Botany Crack. The upper half is a struggle.

89. Treetop Buttress 20m MS
The buttress to the left of Overhanging Chimney. Start from a pointed rock and make an awkward move up a flake. Another difficult move up the edge leads to easier ground, which is climbed bearing left.

90. Sciatica 20m VS 4c
The deep leaning crack on the left of the buttress. Climb the crack, then the corner above to the top.

91. High Level Girdle Traverse 83m VS 5a
Climb the initial crack of Sciatica and move right to Treetop Buttress. Step into Overhanging Chimney and descend 2 metres. Swing round the rib to the right and climb up to the belay on Botany Crack. Continue traversing right onto Main Wall and climb up to the final chimney. Move right into Great Chimney and descend the chimney to a line of footholds crossing Impossible Wall. Cross the wall to Bisector. Using hand jams move right round the monolith and across to Central Organ Pipe. Traverse right into Right Organ Pipe, step up to the right and move across to the upper ledge of Neglect. Continue round to Grad's Groove. Move right round the edge onto the narrow ledge (as for Crystal) and traverse it into Y Climb to finish.

92. Treetop Grooves 20m S
Climb the vegetated groove to the left of Sciatica.

93. Sensitol 22m E1 5b
Start at the buttress left of Sciatica. Climb the crack in the front of the buttress to a scoop. Climb the back of the scoop to a bulge. Pass this on the left and make a hard move up and right above it, to gain holds leading to a ledge. Easily to the top.

Notched Buttress
This buttress lies to the left of a grassy area and has a prominent semi detached finger of rock at the top of it. It is fairly continuous and terminates in a narrow smooth wall bounded on its right by a grass gully and on its left by a large tree.

94. Titus 17m VD
A fine, steep climb, on the right side of the buttress. Start in the corner and climb the broken groove to a clean cut stance. Climb up another 2 metres, then traverse left onto a steep wall containing jagged cracks. Follow these to the top.

95. Helix 17m S **
A clean, sustained climb. Start just left of the toe of the buttress. Climb a crack to a short rock gangway, which leads to the foot of a crack. Climb this to a ledge. Traverse right over a slab to the corner and up the semi detached finger. Finish up the zigzag crack.

96. Helix Direct 25m HVS 5a
Start at the lowest point of the buttress. Climb a crack for 3 metres to gain the arête which is followed to a bulge (poor protection). Take the bulge on the left to gain a corner. Follow this and the crack above to the top (as for Helix).

97. Julia 17m VD
Takes the left side of the broken rocks, left of Helix. Halfway up, cross right to a ledge on Helix then continue straight up.

98. East Central Chimney 20m VD
The obvious chimney 15 metres left of Helix. Follow the cracks, which widen into a chimney. Continuous pleasant climbing throughout.

Rick Barnes
70. Crystal (HVS 5a)
Sustained climbing with great exposure.
Photo: Malcolm Lowerson

Karin Magog taking on
99. Whinstone Churchill Direct (E3 5c)
A splendid objective, well worth seeking out.
Photo: Steve Crowe

Smooth Bastion

The steep, compact buttress further left was originally an artificial route, which now goes free.

99. Whinstone Churchill 17m E2 5b **

The corner on the right of the buttress is climbed and the overhang crossed moving right to a ledge. Move back left and use a flake to make a long reach into the upper groove. Climb this on good holds to the top.

Direct Start E3 5c **

Start at the toe of the buttress and gain the upper groove direct by means of the notched crack.

100. The Stone Warrior 17m E1 5b

A parallel route to Whinstone Churchill starting just left of the Direct Start. Climb the cracked groove to a block. Pull up into the cracks above and climb these to a sloping ledge. Move up and then right to gain the crack and climb this to an awkward finish.

The Ivy Tower Area

The narrow ivy covered face of Ivy Tower will be found 50 metres east of Smooth Bastion. Immediately to the right of it is a large cracked buttress containing three routes.

101. Hoozit's Crack 13m S **

Start on the right side of the buttress below the long overhanging crack. Climb the open chimney for 5 metres before traversing into the crack and climbing it. The crack is harder if climbed direct.

102. Oversight 13m MVS 4c

A pleasant line. The crack on the front of the buttress is climbed until a ledge on the left can be gained. A move right onto the steep face gives delicate climbing to the top.

103. Poker Chimney 13m VD

The chimney on the left of the buttress turns into a crack in its upper reaches.

104. Ivy Tower 15m VD

Heavily overgrown. Start to the left of the foot of the tower. Climb up to the ivy then traverse right into the gully. Climb the vegetated wall above.

Though the crag continues eastwards the buttresses are heavily overgrown and broken.

Crag Lough Graded List

E4
Impossible Wall 6b ***
Stephenson's Rocket 5c **

E3
Whinstone Churchill Direct Start 5c **
Chariot Race 5c **
Impossible Slab 5c

E2
Whinstone Churchill 5b **
Intermediate Treatment 5c
God Lives Under Water 5b

E1
Ben Hur 5c
The Stone Warrior 5b
Wooden Tops 5b **
Sensitol 5b
Raven's Arête 5b

HVS
Spot the Dog 5b *
Easy Picking 5b
Brutus 5b
Evasion Groove 5a *
Midnight Watch 5a
Gargoyle 5b
Why Not Direct 5b **
Block Chimney Super Direct 5a *
Left Organ Pipe 5a **
Neglect 5a **
Y Climb 5a **
Crystal 5a ***
Route One 5a **
Helix Direct 5a
Impossible Buttress Obverse 5a
Route One 5a **

VS
Route Three 5a *
Impossible Buttress Route Three 5a
Main Wall Route Two Direct Finish 5a *
Main Wall Route Two 5a *
Crescent Cracks 5a **
Why Not 5a **
Pinnacle Face 4c ***
Hadrian's Rib 4c *
Catherine 4c
Abseil Wall 5a
The Girdle Traverse 5a
Main Wall Link 5a
Sciatica 4c
Overhanging Chimney 5a
High Level Girdle 5a

Curtis Crag
Malcolm Lowerson

History
It is assumed that due to their prominence from the road that the crags must have received some attention from climbers in the past, although to what extent, little is known or recorded. The evidence of a rusting piton in the large recess at the left end of the North Buttress is proof of some aid climbing in the 60's. Gordon Thompson recalls doing some routes, also in the 60's and Bob Smith has soloed the overhang but cannot remember when. Malcolm Lowerson developed the crags during the summer of 1994 and with the help of Jeff Breen and Trevor Iceton recorded over 30 lines. Steve Crowe stole in to add Natural Line.

Situation and Character
The crags face west overlooking open moorland. The rock is a hard compact sandstone of variable quality. There is a good range of grades from Difficult to E3. The climbs are mainly on two distinct buttresses separated by 60 metres of broken rock. The North Buttress is up to 10 metres high with a large overhung recess at its left end. The South Buttress has the best rock and is up to 8 metres in height and most of the routes can be soloed.

Approaches and Access
From Knowesgate on the A696 or the Bellingham crossroads on the A68, drive to Sweethope Loughs and park beside the cattle grid. Walk in a westerly direction for 100 metres along the road and follow the stone wall onto the moor to reach the North Buttress after a 5 minute walk. For an approach map see page 122. There is a right of access to the crag under CRoW.

The Climbs
These are described from left to right.

North Buttress

1. Shooting Gallery 9m HVS 5a
Climb up the left edge of the overhung recess and make an awkward move left to follow a vertical crack line to ledges and the top.

2. Shot in the Dark 11m E3 5c *
Spectacular and strenuous climbing with good protection (if you can hang on long enough to put it in). From the back of the overhung recess, climb up to the right to the first roof at 4 metres. Pull over it on the left, up to below the next roof and make a difficult move up to the final roof, level with a ledge and old bird's nest. Move out to the right to gain flakes beneath the lip, just left of the arête and reach for a good jug above the lip. Cut loose and pull into the shallow scoop above to gain the top.

3. High Velocity 10m HVS 5b *
A good climb up the right side of the arête and wall above. Start below the undercut arête split by a thin crack. Climb straight up via the crack to reach a pedestal at 5 metres. Move up left on the wall above past a letterbox slot and up into a shallow scoop to reach the top.

4. The Enforcer 10m VS 5a
Start just right of the previous route below the left end of the 2 metres high roof. Pull over the roof and climb up onto the pedestal from the right hand side. Climb the wall up to the zigzag crack and follow it to the top.

5. Friendly Fire 10m VS 5a
Start below the right end of the 2 metres high roof. Pull over the roof and climb up to the ledge at 4 metres, below the broken overlapping wall. Climb up to and follow a faint vertical crack line past a downward pointing block to reach the top.

6. Loose Cannon 11m S
Start 2 metres right of the previous route at a broken crack. Climb up easily onto the large ledge. From the left hand end climb up the runnel and flutings above to below the overhang, climbing left to finish.

7. Magnum 10m VD
Climb up onto the right end of the large ledge. Move up left past a flake to climb the right hand side of the block up to the overhang and pass it on its right hand side.

North Buttress

8. Lock 8m E2 5c
Start right of the right end of the large ledge and 1 metre left of the short rib below the arête. Climb up to the left to gain a narrow ledge at 3 metres, below a short vertical crack with twin runnels above. Climb the steep wall and runnels to a ledge and pull over the short bulging wall above to reach the top.

9. Stock 8m E2 5c *
Start 1 metre left of the short rib below the arête as for Lock. Climb up to a small ledge at 3 metres and follow the faint meandering crack line up the steep wall to a ledge. Then climb more easily up the short wall above to the top.

10. Barrel 8m E2 5c
Climb up the short rib to below the left side of the arête. Climb the arête on its left side up to the ledge and then more easily up to the top.

11. Naked Gun 7m VS 4c
Start at the short rib below the arête. Climb up the right side of the arête to the ledge. Reach the top passing the small roof on its left side.

12. Bushwhacker 6m S
Climb up the right side of the shallow scoop, past flutings to below a small roof. Pass the roof on its right side to reach the top.

13. Dum Dum 5m VD
Start from the split block. Climb the wall to finish up the short crack at the top.

The small buttress to the right of North Buttress gives three climbs.

14. Small Bore 5m HVS 5b
Pull up onto the hanging arête and climb the short wall above.

15. Sharpshooter 6m S
Climb the good looking stepped crack.

16. Pop Gun 6m D
Climb the right edge of the buttress,

A number of lines on the smaller broken buttresses to the right have been climbed but are not described here due to their poor quality. The exception is a small prow shaped buttress some 40 metres to the east of North Buttress, which provides 3 bouldering lines.

17. Cap 4m 5a
Climb the steep left wall to the slot at the top.

18. Butt 4m 5a
Climb the arête on its right to an awkward mantelshelf at the top.

19. Sight 4m 5a
Climb the centre of the right wall.

20 metres to the right is the South Buttress.

South Buttress

South Buttress
There are 4 routes on the wall left of the ragged corner crack.

20. Sitting Duck 8m HS 4b
Start 5 metres left of the corner crack. Climb the left edge of the wall, past a ledge at 3 metres up to a large ledge at 5 metres. Move up left below the roof and pull up onto the top using good jugs above the flutings.

21. Decoy 8m VS 5a
Start 1 metre right of the left edge of the wall. Climb the wall to below the right end of the roof and pull over with difficulty.

22. Game Cock 8m VS 5a
Start 3 metres left of the corner crack. Climb up the wall past a small overlap at 4 metres to reach a broken wall and finish up a short crack at the top.

23. Turkey Shoot. 7m VD
Start 1 metre left of the corner crack. Climb onto the ledge at 2metres and up the wall above past a small roof to reach the top.

24. The Gobbler 7m D
Climb the ragged corner crack.

25. Glorious 12th 8m HS 4c
Start 2 metres right of the corner crack. Climb up the wall over the broken overlap onto a ledge at 5 metres and up to the top.

26. Big Shot 8m VS 5a
Start 3 metres right of the corner crack. Climb up the wall past the block on the right to finish up the left side of the overhang.

27. Victim of Circumstance 8m HVS 5a *
Start 4 metres right of the corner crack. Climb the wall to the top of a block at 4 metres. Pull past a small roof and move right below the larger roof onto the blunt arête and pull up onto the top.

28. Endangered Species 8m E1 5c
Climb up left of a shallow groove to below the blunt arête. Make a difficult move up onto the wall right of the arête and up this to the top on small holds.

29. Natural Selection 8m E1 5b *
Climb the shallow groove to below the roof at 3 metres. Pull up right onto the centre of the steep wall above and climb to the top.

30. Line of Sight 11m VS 4c
Start in the corner below the overhang at 3 metres. Climb the corner to below the overhang. Traverse left beneath it, past the block, then up the wall to finish on the left of the overhang.

31. Natural Line 7m E1 5b
Climb the corner to below the overhang. Pull over the overhang at its right edge, move left onto the steep wall and climb straight up to the top.

32. Fair Game 7m HS 4c
Climb the overhanging corner to finish with difficulty up the crack at the top.

33. Prime Suspect 7m VS 5a
Start 2 metres right of the overhung corner. Pull onto the undercut wall via a flake and hidden pocket. Climb straight up to the right end of the overhang at the top.

34. Second Thoughts 7m HVS 5b
Start 3 metres right of the overhung corner. Pull onto the undercut wall via a small side hold and climb the wall with difficulty to the horizontal break, then more easily to the top.

35. Suspicious Mind 7m VS 5a
Start 4 metres right of the overhung corner. Climb up to beneath the small overlap at 3 metres; pull straight over it and up to the top.

36. Above Suspicion 7m VS 4c
Climb straight up to the right end of the small overlap at 3 metres. Pull round its right side to a ledge, then more easily to the top.

37. Hook 7m VS 5b *
Start 2 metres right of Above Suspicion. Climb the wall via a shallow horizontal pocket at 2 metres. Initially difficult with holds improving towards the top.

38. Line 6m VS 4c
Climb up past the left end of a ledge at 2 metres to finish up the wall left of a short vertical crack.

39. Sinker 6m VS 4c
Climb up onto the left end of the ledge at 2 metres and continue straight up the wall, to finish up the vertical crack at the top.

40. Float 6m VS 4c
Climb onto the centre of the ledge at 2 metres and up past a horizontal slot, to finish to the right of the short vertical crack.

41. Cast 6m HS 4b
Climb onto the right end of the ledge at 2 metres and continue straight up the wall, near its right edge to the top.

Curtis Crag Graded List

E3
Shot In The Dark 5c **

E2
Stock 5c *
Barrel 5c
Lock 5c

E1
Endangered Species 5c
Natural Selection 5b *
Natural Line 5b

HVS
Small Bore 5b
High Velocity 5b *
Second Thoughts 5b
Victim of Circumstance 5a *
Shooting Gallery 5a

VS
Hook 5b *
The Enforcer 5a
Friendly Fire 5a
Decoy 5a
Game Cock 5a
Big Shot 5a
Prime Suspect 5a
Suspicious Mind 5a
Naked Gun 4c
Line 4c
Sinker 4c
Float 4c
Above Suspicion 4c
Line of Sight 4c

Drake Stone
Cliff Robson and Michael Thomas

NT 921044
North Facing
275m.
10 minutes

History

It is almost certain that the Drake Stone has been climbed for many centuries. Until recent times the huge boulder was thought to have miraculous healing powers, sick children being passed over the summit to aid their recovery. Obviously a place worth visiting for the modern tendonitis stricken climber. Details of early ascents have become lost in the mists of time, the first recorded activity being in November 1977 when Bob Hutchinson and John Earl added the Very Severes and Hard Very Severes with Hutchinson soon returning to climb Sir Francis. Andy Moss led Rhumba in 1983 and Bob Smith soloed Powder Monkey a short while afterwards. Lubbers' Hole, first climbed by Andrew Philipson in 1958 has been recorded here for the first time. Cliff Robson and Calum Mayland squeezed in Sol Pelicanos in 1995, the last recorded route on the crag.

Situation and Character

The Drake Stone, the name of which is derived from the Anglo Saxon word for dragon, is Northumberland's largest isolated boulder. This good quality sandstone crag lies in an exposed but scenic position on Harbottle Hill. It is quick drying and gives a number of good and varied routes. The extreme routes on the south face are largely unprotected. There are numerous bouldering possibilities nearby but the exposed position of the crag makes it a warm summer evening venue rather than a year round crag.

Approaches and Access

A short way beyond Harbottle on the Alwinton road is a Forestry Commission car park. A path leads from the south east corner through the Harbottle Crags Nature Reserve to the Drake Stone in about ten minutes. For approach map see Linshields One. There is a right of access to the crag under CRoW.

The Climbs

The routes are described in a clockwise direction beginning with the north face.

1. Pieces of Eight 7m HVS 5b

The blunt rib at the right end of the north face is climbed until a move left leads to the top. Interesting but unprotected.

2. Plymouth Hoe 7m S **

The fine crack to the left.

3. Garden Hoe 7m HS

Climb the slab about 2 metres left of Plymouth Hoe.

4. Tourist Route 8m M

The obvious chipped steps provide the easiest way up and down.

5. Cape Horn 11m VS 4c

The slabs on the east side are climbed trending left to finish up the arête. Unprotected.

6. Powder Monkey 9m E4 5c

Start at the right hand side of the south face 2 metres right of Rhumba. Move up rightwards then back left, climb the wall on widely spaced holds to a thin hanging flake and a delicate finish. Interesting and bold.

7. Rhumba 9m E4 5c

Start at the base of a rightwards trending undercut feature 3 metres right of Sir Francis. Step up, and trend slightly left to the first horizontal break, then straight up to good holds in a less prominent break 2 metres higher. Move up and right with difficulty to the top. Scary.

8. Lubbers' Hole 15m S *

Climb the thin crack in the middle of the south face (Sir Francis) until the first horizontal break is reached and a traverse left to the groove of The Golden Hind can be made. Climb this to the next break. Traverse left round the overhanging arête then climb more easily to the top.

9. Sir Francis 9m E3 5c *

A superb and bold climb up the obvious thin crack in the centre of the south face. Jibber more or less up the wall above trending slightly right towards a small flake at the top.

Drake Stone

10. The Golden Hind 12m VS 5a**
Start at the left end of the south face and climb into a groove at 3 metres. Climb this to a slab which provides an interesting finish.

11. Hispaniola HVS 5a
Climb the left arête of the south face to a horizontal crack, continue directly up the wall.

12. The Pelican 9m E1 5b *
The obvious line on the west face left of the arête, is difficult and strenuous to start. The rest is easier. A pumpy but satisfying route.

13. Sol Pelicanos 12m E2 5b
Start at the arête of Good Hope. Traverse right along the obvious lower break for 3metres. Then make strenuous moves to climb straight up to gain an obvious curving flake and crack. Finish direct.

14. Good Hope 8m HVS 5b
The left arête of the west face. Awkward and unprotected.

15. Rhumb E1 5c
A traverse of the obvious horizontal break

Drake Stone Graded List

E4
Powder Monkey 5c
Rhumba 5c

E3
Sir Francis 5c *

E2
Sol Pelicanos 5b

E1
Rhumb 5c
The Pelican 5b *

HVS
Pieces of Eight 5b
Good Hope 5b
Hispaniola 5a

VS
Cape Horn 4c
The Golden Hind 5a **

East Woodburn (Staniel Heugh)

John Dalrymple

NY 917873
South Facing
250m
5 minutes

History

Gordon Thompson and John Grey climbed extensively here in the 1960's and 1970's and did most of the obvious lines, including Woodburn Wall, Ridsdale Wall and Capstone Direct. Unaware of this, Paul Linfoot and Andy Winter rediscovered the crag, climbed and renamed many of these routes and added Autobahn and Death Wish. Karl Telfer, Graham Telfer and Joe Gilespy added The Arbitrator and the remaining lines were finished off with Oliver Went A Huntin' and Autoerotic from Mark Savage and Flying Scot and Foxey, squeezed in by Malcolm Lowerson and Graeme Read.

Situation and Character

This is a compact south facing crag with good clean rock and some quality routes. It is on the hillside about 1 km north east of East Woodburn. The crag dries quickly and is climbable at any time of year.

Approaches and Access

Take the minor road north out of East Woodburn and turn right along a gated no through road, signposted to Blakelaw. This road passes under the crag. A couple of cars can be parked just past the crag at a wooden post, but take care not to block access onto the moor.
There is a right of access to the crag under CRoW.

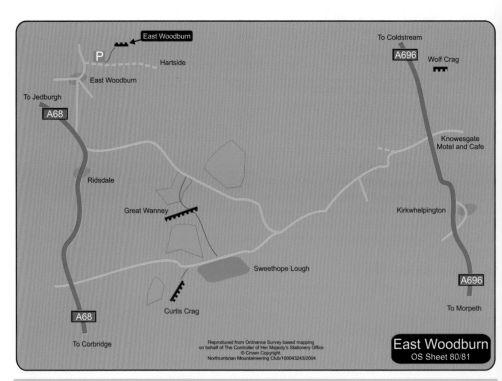

Paul Linfoot climbing
3. Woodburn Wall (E1 5b)
Rediscovering the delights
of this quality climb
Photo: Steve Crowe

The Climbs

The routes are described from left to right. Several short routes of 4c-5b have been climbed on the walls to the left of the West Buttress.

West Buttress

1. Old Ash Crack 9m D
The cracked chimney groove to the left of Woodburn Wall.

2. A Fox For President 18m HVS 5a
Start in Old Ash Crack, climb this to a break at 5 metres and follow it rightwards to the arête. Traverse just beneath the overhang, across Ridsdale Wall, and on to the right arête, finishing up the wall by a tree.

3. Woodburn Wall 10m E1 5b **
Climb the centre of the west wall, trending right to finish up a small flake high on the wall.
Direct Finish E2 5c *
Instead of trending right, climb direct to a thin finish.

4. Oliver Went A Huntin' 12m E2 5c **
Climb the front face of the slabby arête to the overhang and good gear placement. Traverse along the lip and climb the arête in an exposed position. A poor 1.5 Friend protects the crux.

5. Ridsdale Wall 11m E1 5b **
The centre of the south face of the west buttress. Climb the centre of the wall and the overhang.

6. The Arbitrator 11m E1 5b *
Climbs the wall and overhang 1.5 metres right of and parallel to Ridsdale Wall.

7. Foxey 11m VS 4c
Climb up the right of the wall passing the overhang on the right and continue to finish left of the rowan tree.

Central Buttress

8. Papa Lazaroo 9m E3 5c
From the first ledge in the gully climb straight up the wall to the left of Autobahn, on small slightly suspect holds.

9. Autoerotic 11m E2 5c
From the good hold halfway up Autobahn climb diagonally up and left to finish at a short crack.

10. Autobahn 10m E2 5c *
The left arête of the Central Buttress, left of the crack, is climbed direct throughout. There is a belay stake a few metres back from the crag at this point.

11. Green Slab 10m VD *
Climb the west facing wall of Central Buttress, just right of the crack, to a sloping ledge on the right. Finish up the crack on the left.

12. The Arête 10m HS 4b *
Takes the arête between Green Slab and Green Wall. Start on the left and follow the arête to the sloping ledge on Green Slab. Finish up the crack above.

13. Green Wall 10m HVS 5b *
Right of the arête, climb the centre of the wall to the right hand end of the sloping ledge and finish up a short corner scoop on the right.

14. Patties Route 10m VS 5a
Climb the right hand side of the wall to a small runnel then step right and climb the short crack.

Capstone Buttress

15. Flying Scot 9m HVS 5a
Climb the wall between Capstone Wall and the crack and rowan tree.

16. Capstone Wall 10m E1 5b *
The left wall of the buttress is climbed at its centre with a long reach to start.

17. Death Wish 12m E1 5b
The left arête of the buttress is climbed to the slab. Surmount the overhang directly above using the fluting.

18. The Pandemonium Carnival 14m E1 5b
Climb the centre of the face to the left of Capstone Direct and continue straight up through the overhang making a long reach from the obvious pocket.

19. Capstone Direct 12m E1 5c *
Easily up the front of the buttress and over the roof by means of the thin crack.

20. Capstone Traverse 18m MS
Climb Capstone Direct for a few feet into an awkward sentry box then traverse left across the wall under the roof, to finish up the centre of Capstone Wall. The original finished up the crack further left.

21. Overhanging Heave 8m S 4c
The short overhanging wall at the right hand end of the buttress is split by a large horizontal crack. Straight up the wall to good finishing holds.

East Buttress

22. Stilton 8m VD
The arête. Start at the lowest point of the buttress and climb the arête to the short wall.

23. Cheese Wedge 7m S
Takes a direct line up the centre of the buttress. Follow a faint crack line to a ledge and then a short wall to finish.

East Woodburn Graded List

E3	E1	HVS
Papa Lazaroo 5c	Capstone Direct 5c *	Green Wall 5b *
	Ridsdale Wall 5b **	Flying Scot 5a
E2	The Pandemonium Carnival 5b	A Fox For President 5a
Woodburn Wall Direct Finish 5c *	The Arbitrator 5b *	
Autobahn 5c *	Death Wish 5b	**VS**
Oliver Went A Huntin' 5c **	Woodburn Wall 5b **	Patties Route 5a
Autoerotic 5c	Capstone Wall 5b *	Foxey 4c

Goats Crag

Andy Birtwistle

NT 976371
South Facing
115m
10 minutes

History

There is evidence that human use of the crag dates back 3,000 years, as the site was used as an ancient burial ground. Excavations by archaeologists in 1967-8 yielded two burial pots with cremation remains in the area beneath the Guano Buttress. Extremely rare carvings of animals, possibly goats, are to be found on the smooth wall beneath Guano Groove. These are similar to examples found in Scotland and Scandinavia and are thought to be from around 100BC-400AD. This would make Goats the only crag in the county with a prehistoric picture of its name on it and also suggest that raiders got to the routes first! Please take extreme care to preserve these rare carvings by not climbing on this small section of rock.

During the last century the crag was probably explored on and off, many times. However, no records have come to light of ascents previous to a visit by Bob Hutchinson, John Earl, Dennis Lee and Ian Cranston in November 1972, which resulted in thirty-two routes up to HVS standard. Earl and Hutchinson made another visit in January 1973 to climb The Dagger with Earl adding a direct start four years later. During October 1977 Hutchinson returned yet again producing Overdrive, probably the crag classic. A selection of climbs was included in the 1979 guidebook but unfortunately records of remaining climbs were lost. Following publication of the 1979 guide, Bob Smith, Paul Stewart and Earl added more routes. These included Undercarriage, Convoy and Juggernaut. Steve Blake climbed the strenuous Underpass and Smith, found Lost Arête and Hard Shoulder in the quarry.

In 1987 Andy Moss climbing with Colin Murley added Imminent Break Crisis and while working on the 1989 guide re-climbed and named many of the obvious unnamed lines. A few lines remained to be climbed, in particular the steep wall left of Hard Shoulder, which had been well cleaned and attempted by several teams. It finally succumbed to the persistent efforts of Karl Telfer late in November 1988. Around this time some deliberate chipping or improving of holds took place to the left of this route. Prospective routes of this type are not welcome. They have not been included nor will they be considered for any future publications.

The 1990's saw the crag's bouldering potential develop but no more significant lines have ensued.

Situation and Character

Goats Crag is an exposed and quick drying sandstone outcrop with two small quarries near by. The outcrop lies on Goatscrag Hill, east of Ford Village. The situation is splendid, with views of the Cheviots and the Milfield Plain to the south and west. The rock is coarse-grained, occasionally brittle sandstone with more compact sections near the base. The natural edge consists of a series of buttresses, often overhanging and generally well supplied with holds, and pockets. Due to its south facing nature it is often a suntrap on good winter days and it makes a rewarding venue especially when combined with other local outcrops.

Approaches and Access

The crag is best reached from the A697 by turning right just before Milfield or from the A1 by following the B6353 Lowick road. Access from the A697 is to take the unclassified road through Kimmerston to Roughtinglinn (a well known archaeological site of cup and ring marks and a scenic waterfall). From Lowick continue for half a mile after the junction with the B6111 then turn right to reach Roughtinglinn. A limited amount of parking exists opposite a farm track by a small plantation. Follow this track on foot to the farm which lies directly beneath the crag. At present a good relationship exists with the farmer; to help maintain this it is ESSENTIAL that visitors ask permission before climbing. No large groups please. During spring and early summer access may be withheld or restricted to the quarries because of nesting birds. There is a right of access to the crag under CRoW.

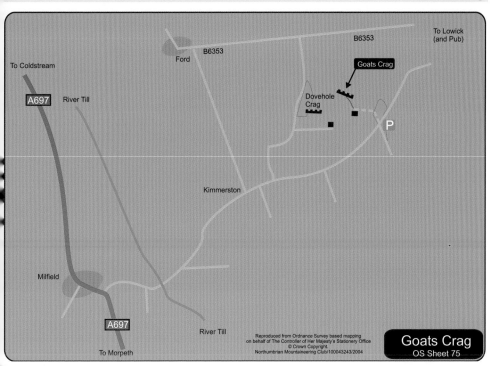

The Climbs

The routes are described from right to left. Walking up the hillside from the farmhouse the first buttress is:

Right-hand Buttress

The first route climbs a crack 5 metres from the right hand side of the buttress.

1. The Jester 5m VS 5b

Gain and follow the crack strenuously to an easy finishing corner.

2. The Juggler 6m MVS 5a

Climb the overhanging prow 3 metres further left on jugs to easier angled rock.

3. Kangaroo Court 6m E2 5c *

The roof 3 metres left. Reach around the lip using a small deep hole, then make a committing move to reach the break above and easier ground.

4. Flyover 7m E2 5b *

Another route tackling the big roof. Start directly behind the right side of a large boulder and climb to an overhung ledge. Using a pinch reach good holds on the lip and pull into a short groove to finish.

5. Snap, Crack & Plop 7m S

The crack splitting the overhangs just left. Start behind the large boulder and finish rightwards.

6. Nice Krispies 8m D

3 metres left the slab behind the boulder is climbed to steeper rock. Continue up this moving right to avoid the final overhang.

7. Bodger's Wall 7m MS

Left of the boulder is a bramble filled groove with easy slabs and a small juggy overhang to its left. Pull through the overhang to reach a thin crack at 5 metres. Continue direct to another small overhang and the top.

8. Double Trouble 8m MVS *

Start 1 metre left of Bodger's Wall. Follow the obvious line of jugs trending left and pull directly over the capping double overhangs on huge holds.

9. Ramp Art 17m VD

Start as for Double Trouble but trend left onto the obvious ramp which is followed to the top. Moderate after the start.

Guano Buttress

10. Castles in the Air 8m VS 4c
Start 4 metres left of Double Trouble. Grapple with the initial overhang using good holds to reach an easy left trending ramp line (Ramp Art). Climb straight up the wall above, right of a diagonal crack, and attack the top overhang directly on mega jugs.

11. The 48 Hour Tiler 8m HS 4c
From the boulder 2 metres left climb the overhang, then follow a diagonal crack to a large pocket in the wall above. Finish just left of the capping roof.

Variations are possible anywhere on this section and short routes can be done to the left of this route.

Guano Buttress
Continuing leftwards the crag lies back to form a corner. The left wall of the corner provides two routes.

12. Billy Goats Gruff 6m S
The flake 5 metres left of the corner leads to a horizontal break continue up the wall above.

13. Troll's Recipe Book 6m VD
The juggy arête 2 metres left and just right of a grassy groove is hardest at the start.

At this point the buttress is split by a grassy groove. To the left is a pocketed lichen covered wall and the next routes are located here.

14. Goat Pie 7m HS
Start 2 metres to the left. Climb over a bulge, trying not to make a meal of it, to reach the slab. Finish right-wards.

15. Wool Ball 8m HS *
2 metres further left is a small square niche just above the ground. Climb past the niche and up the pocketed slab.

16. Woolly Derg 8m VS 5a
Another 2 metres left is a short arête. A tricky move gains a small ledge. Stand on this and continue directly up the slab.

17. Bull Wall 9m VS 5a **
This good route climbs a short groove capped by a bulge and a crack. Climb the groove and make an awkward move left to the blunt arête, follow this to a crack and the top.

Direct Start 5a
Climb the wall 3 metres left to join the original route at 5 metres.

18. Bull Ring 9m E1 5a
A good route on slightly suspect rock. Start at the right hand of the triangular slab. Climb straight up trending left at a bulge to superb finishing holds. Finishing rightwards from the bulge is easier and less worrying.

19. Triangular Slab 9m S *
Climb the right side of the triangular slab.

20. Guano Groove 9m VS 4c *
Climb the corner on the left of the slab.

An exhausting route Tail Pipe Gas E1 5b has been squeezed up the wall to the left, starting about half way up Guano Groove.

21. Underpass 9m E4 6a ***
Make hard moves up the overhanging arête left of Guano Groove to gain the difficult groove and bulging arête above.

22. Overdrive 12m E3 6a ***
A superb route. Start beneath the bottomless corner just left of Underpass. Strenuously climb the corner, then change gear and undercut right, until a hard move leads to better holds above the overhang.

A number of climbs have tackled the overhang and wall to the left. The best and most independent is:-

23. Undercarriage 10m E3 6a
Start as for Overdrive but thug out leftwards across the roof. Climb the flutings right of The Dagger to the top.

24. The Dagger 11m HVS 5b *
From a boulder at the left end of the overhang reach good holds on the lip and hand traverse rightwards, until an awkward move leads to a hollow flake. Step right to a ramp and the top.

Direct Start 6a
Climb the overhang directly below the hollow flake aided by clever footwork. For the not so clever a soft landing awaits!

25. Twin Cam 9m E2 5b *
Follow The Dagger traverse then climb the overhanging arête on the left.

26. Convoy 8m E2 5c *
The fluting left of Twin Cam.

27. The White Pheasant 8m HVS 5a
The fluting left of Convoy. Finish rightwards.

28. Cave Wall 8m VD
The fluting and shallow cave left again.

29. Wave Call 7m HS
The thin flake 1 metre left and the wall above.

Just left small buttresses jut out of the hillside forming two arêtes.

30. Pick Pocket 5m VS 4c
Begin immediately left of the right hand arête. Climb the wall to an area of pockets. Step right onto the arête to finish.

The short wall 2 metres left and the cracks on the right have also been climbed.

31. Carb Arête 5m MVS 4b
The second arête 4 metres to the left is started on the left and finished on the right.

The fingery wall 2 metres left is 5b.

Martin Waugh motoring up
22. Overdrive (E3 6a)
Photo:Andy Birtwistle

CrackedButtress

Cracked Buttress

A further 20 metres to the left is an obvious buttress split by several cracks. At the right hand end is a short wide crack above a block, which has been climbed. The first route climbs the hanging crack just left.

32. Chip Shop Crack 5m HVS 5a
From the boulders at the back of the cave climb the overhang on friable rock. Avoid the temptation to stand on the large block to the right. A long reach gains a line of quartz holds and the easier crack above.

33. Mushy Peas 5m S 4b
The easy peasy wide crack to the left is reached by a tricky leftwards move from the boulders.

34. Catching the Belford Bus 6m VS 4c
Climb the corner and hanging crack bounding the right side of the slab. Not to be missed!

35. Belford Chip Shop 6m VS 4c *
Layback the thin diagonal crack to gain the slab, climb this rightwards on quartz holds. Finish to the left on the protruding band of harder rock.

36. Twin Cracks 6m MVS 4c
An overhanging start gives access to either of the cracks above. The left hand crack is slightly harder.

37. Juggernaut 8m E4 6a **
A bold route up the left arête of the buttress, via the thin crack in the right wall. Beware of the alarming finish.

38. Nauter jugg 6m VS 5a
The single flute in the wall left of Juggernaut can be reached directly from the small pocket below.

39. The Powerhouse of Athleticism 6m VD
The shallow corner, flake and wall just left.

The short wall 2 metres left and the even shorter corner 2 metres left again have both been climbed.

The crag now fades into boulders.

Bob Smith leading
42. The Hard Shoulder (E4 6a)
Don't be fooled by the rope into thinking there will
be any protection where you really need it!
Photo: Andy Birtwistle

The Quarries

The first quarry is a further 100 metres around the hillside. Its most obvious feature is a steep smooth wall bounded on the right by a square cut arête. To the right is a slabby area of rock providing a few easy routes, the best of which takes the central slab beginning on the left trending ramp.

40. Two Slips Slab 11m VS 4b

Start at the left trending ramp. Climb the slab and mantle onto a small ledge. Continue up the slab and faint crack above to the top.

41. Imminent Break Crisis 22m E5 6a *

A traverse of the steep wall. Climb the corner then hand traverse the break to the arête. Continue along the break with increasing difficulty to a very thin crack at the left end of the wall. Lunge for the top. By approaching the break via the fingery wall 2 metres left of the thin crack it is possible to reverse the route at the same grade.

Variation Finish E3 5c

Reach the top using a flaky hold 5 metres left of the arête.

42. The Hard Shoulder 8m E4 6a **

The arête is started on the left side with a bold swing onto the right side at half height. Well named!

43. Ruth Route 9m E5 6c **

Start about 3 metres left of the arête. Bridge out left from the block at the base of the wall, snatch ruthlessly up then rightwards to the break. Step left and climb up the final wall.

A second smaller quarry lies beyond the gate:

44. Mule Train 7m HVS 5b

Climb the wall right of the arête. Start in the middle of the wall below a small ledge. Gain this then climb the wall moving left on small crimps.

45. Lost Arête 7m HVS 5b *

Find and then climb the obvious sharp arête. A little gem well worth finding.

Goats Crag Graded List

E5	E2	The White Pheasant 5a
Ruth Route 6c ***	Kangaroo Court 5c *	**VS**
Imminent Break Crisis 6a *	Twin Cam 5b *	Woolly Derg 5a
	Convoy 5c *	The Jester 5b
E4	Flyover 5b *	Bull Wall 5a **
Hard Shoulder 6a **		Nauter jugg 5a
Juggernaut 6a **	**E1**	Castles In The Air 4c
Underpass 6a ***	Tail Pipe Gas 5b	Belford Chip Shop 4c *
	Bull Ring 5a	Guano Groove 4c *
E3		Pick Pocket 4c
Overdrive 6a ***	**HVS**	Catching The Belford Bus 4c
Undercarriage 6a	The Dagger 5b *	Two Slips Slab 4b
	Mule Train 5b	
	Chip Shop Crack 5a	
	Lost Arête 5b *	

Steve Roberts made the second ascent of
23. Crisis Zone (E7 6c)
Photo: John Houlihan/Vertebrate Graphics

Great Wanney

Bob Smith

NT 933835
North West Facing
310m
30 minutes

History

The early history of climbing on Great Wanney is in many ways the history of climbing in Northumberland as a whole and as such this early period is quite well documented in the front of the guide. The first routes were recorded by G.W. Young in 1902 and over the next thirty years or so a significant number of routes were recorded by him and his companions. The popularity of the crag continued and towards the end of the thirties A.P. Rossiter had become the local expert, climbing most, if not all, of the routes on the crag, at that time.

Things stagnated somewhat after this and no recorded, significant developments took place until 1971 when Great Wall was climbed by Mick Foggin and Hugh Banner. In 1976 Bob Hutchinson and John Earl added Idiot Wind and the magnificent Northumberland Wall. Following the first ascent of the latter, an enormous hold was chipped which Hutchinson promptly filled in with concrete using sand from the base of the crag to obtain the correct colour match. 1978 was an eventful year with the same team producing the awesome Endless Flight, which was repeated within a matter of weeks by Karl Telfer and Martin Doyle thinking they were doing a first ascent. Nosey Parker and Broken Wing were two more significant routes by Hutchinson and Earl, the former had a dubious flake which although it housed all the runners wasn't secure enough to be used as a hold, all that now remains is the scar. That year also saw the arrival of Bob and Tommy Smith with two very bold routes, Last Retreat and Blue Arête.

In 1980 Bob Smith added Thin Ice with Martin Doyle and Thunder Thighs with brother Tommy. It was some three years later however, before Bob accompanied by Earl added the latter routes dynamic and serious independent start. Also in this year Earl and Stewart added Osiris, discovering in the process that Pharaoh's Face up which it finishes was E3 and not Very Severe. On 24th July, 1981 whilst most of the country was watching the Royal Wedding; Smith and Earl were freeing the old aid route Swing High to produce the superb and sustained Absent Friend. Things remained peaceful until 1986 when John Wallace climbed Stairway to Heaven, which received its second and third ascents in the same day

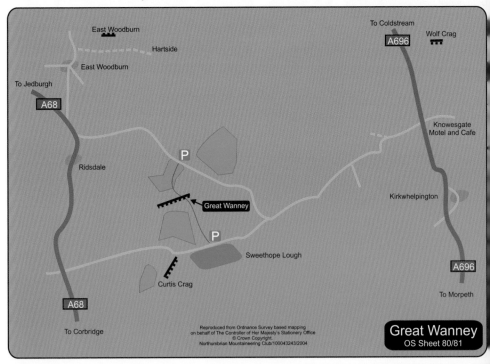

134

by Hugh Harris and Bob Smith respectively. In 1987 Harris broke through the Chapter House roof to give Willing to Sin. Hugh Harris returned in 1990 accompanied by Ian Cummings and climbed the very technical Policy of Truth, raising the crag standard to E6.

In the following year the Wanneys was brought crashing into the nineties. Richard Davies and Andy Wilkinson climbed Katana with well spaced but good protection (falling off is not recommended), whilst Hugh Harris and John Wallace left their spring time calling card with the magnificent Crisis Zone E7, again raising the standard at the crag and collecting one of the counties most striking lines. Later that year Steve Crowe and Karin Magog presented Eastern Promise, the high level traverse of East Buttress. Stu Ferguson and Paul Morgan finished 1991 off with Marquee Metal. Ten years passed until Steve Crowe and Karin Magog, late in September 2001, spotted Skyline - a series of boulder problems up the Pharaohs Face. As the guide was being finalised Andrew Earl added a very hard start to pilot Endless Flight into the twenty first century.

Situation and Character

This impressive crag adopts a commanding position atop a triangular area of moorland and forest. The rock is a hard compact sandstone of excellent quality, although its northerly aspect does make it exposed to the elements. It has some of the best quality 'easy' grade routes in the county (its V Diffs and Severes having tested many Very Severe leaders over the years) and the harder routes although often intimidating, provide quality and often well protected climbing in superb situations. The Great Wanney fault which lies behind the crag line a few hundred meters to the east of the main crag, provides a quantity of subterranean climbing, but many of the entries have been blocked.

Approaches and Access

The best approaches are reached from the A696 Newcastle-Otterburn road which is left at Knowesgate. To reach the crags from the south, park at Sweethope Loughs and follow the line of the right of way over the moors to the top of the crag, this can often be boggy after a spell of rain. Perhaps the easiest approach is to walk in from the north along a Forestry Commission track which, which is a designated permissive path. From Knowesgate follow the Sweethope Loughs road but take the right fork and park at an obvious wide gateway in a dip just beyond the cattle grid on the road bounding the area on the north and east. The distance to the crag from either direction is about 1½ kilometres and takes approximately thirty minutes. There is a right of access to the crag under CRoW.

The Climbs

Eastern Section
These are described from left to right.

200 metres left of the East Buttress of the Main Crag is a series of steep vegetated walls split by cracks. A number of routes have been climbed in this area but only the best of the worst have been described. A metal stake provides the only belay.

1. Left Crack 8m MVS 4c
Start at the niche 10 metres from the left end of the wall. Climb the crack direct to the stake.

2. Dennis 8m E2 6a *
Climb the wall left of the Right Crack passing the obvious diagonal fault.

3. Right Crack 8m VS 5a
5 metres right of Left Crack is an obvious hand jam crack with an overhang at its base. Follow the crack throughout.

100 metres left of East Buttress is a prominent isolated buttress with a crevasse at its base. The next three climbs take the front face of the buttress.

4. Pitfall 9m E2 5b *
Start directly below the right hand niche, trend slightly left to good holds at the base of the left hand niche. Pull rightwards and finish up the right hand niche.

5. Aces High 9m E2 5b
The wall right of Pitfall. Start beneath a hole half way up the wall. Climb up to the hole and directly past it using the horizontal faults. Reach right for flutes at the top to finish.

6. Marquee Metal 9m E3 5c
The arête right of Aces High with a bold finish.

Main Crag

The main crag starts with the East Buttress which is capped by a large roof and has the conspicuous boundary wall/fence leading up 10 metres to its right.

7. Eastern Promise 9m E2 5c

Start in the corner at the left side of East Buttress and climb up to the obvious break. Hand traverse rightward to finish up Jungle Warfare.

8. Eastern Ecstasy 15m E4 6a

A high level traverse of the East Buttress. Start as for Eastern Promise, traverse right along the obvious break to finish up Idiot Wind.

9. Jungle Warfare 9m E3 6b

At the extreme left hand side of East Buttress is a flake crack in the upper wall. Start beneath the undercut arête directly beneath the flake crack. A difficult move to get a foot onto the ledge beneath the roof is followed by a harder move to reach a finger jug and the break. Continue up the flake crack to an earthy hold and heather finish.

10. Eastern Traverse 11m HS 4b *

Starts in an overhanging corner high on the left side of the buttress. Make a bold move from a ledge up right to reach the arête. Traverse right under the overhang to reach Great Chimney.

Finish up Great Chimney or continue traversing and finish up the top slab of Great Chimney Obverse.

11. East Buttress Direct 15m E3 5c **

A thin unprotected lower section is followed by a strenuous but well protected roof. Start at the left side of the wall beneath Eastern Traverse and follow a faint groove up and leftwards onto the arête, which is followed to the level of Eastern Traverse. The fine roof crack directly above is climbed to a groove which provides a heathery finish.

12. Thunder Thighs 15m E5 6b *

Intimidating and committing climbing up the centre of the wall between East Buttress Direct and Idiot Wind. The crux being a long reach or jump to gain a jug halfway up the wall. The large overhang above and left of the finish to Idiot Wind is climbed via the large flake.

13. Idiot Wind 15m E4 5c **

Bold climbing up the right arête of East Buttress overlooking Great Chimney. Go directly up the arête to Eastern Traverse (unprotected). Swing out left across the lip of the overhang to good holds on a bracket. Surmount this and continue to the top.

14. Great Chimney 12m VD **
A classic chimney climb. The obvious square cut chimney immediately left of the boundary wall/fence.

15. Obverse Direct 14m HS 4c *
Climb the overhanging crack immediately right of Great Chimney to a recess. Continue upwards on the slab on the right and finish over a jammed block.

Direct Finish 5a
The crack in the left side of the recess provides a harder finish.

16. Absent Friend 14m E5 6b ***
A superb and sustained route. Start where the boundary wall/fence abuts the crag. Climb the four diagonal peg scars to the horizontal break, up the crack and bore holes to the next break and then move left up the crack to the shoulder. Pull back right and up the wall above on the right hand side.

17. Crisis Zone 15m E7 6c ***
A stunning sustained route that starts as for Absent Friend. Follow Absent Friend as far as the three shot holes. Climb these and from the top one reach the sloping ledge (very old bolt runner, trust it at your peril). Strenuous climbing up the wall above, via a further shot hole and holds on the left edge leads to an eventual pull round onto flutings.

18. Endless Flight 15m E5 6a ***
A sensational and serious route up the magnificent left arête of Boundary Corner. Climb Boundary Corner for 5 metres. Hand traverse left along the upper of two horizontal breaks to a ledge on the left of the arête (insitu threads). Using a layaway hold on the wall awkwardly gain a standing position on the ledge. Move up and swing around the arête in a sensational position (poor wire on left) up to good holds on a break, where one more long reach leads to jugs and easy climbing.

Direct E8 7a *
A fitting start to this magnificent route. From the stile climb the sloping steps until the arête can be clamped. Keep clamping to the break. Move directly up the arête to gain the threads. Continue directly up the arête to finish.

19. Policy of Truth 15 m E6 6c *
A fiercely technical route, which climbs the wall and hanging crack right of Endless Flight.

Ascend Boundary Corner for 5 metres and move left along the upper horizontal break for 1.5m to a hollow flake. Arrange protection below this and then climb the wall directly above to gain the thin hanging crack and good hold to the left. Make a long reach for improving holds that lead to the top.

20. Boundary Corner 15m VD ***
A justly popular route up the deep corner right of the boundary wall/fence. Climb up to the nose using cracks. The nose is surmounted with the aid of a high foothold and exit made through the cave.

21. Hawk Slab 15m HVS 5a *
Start at the short arête immediately right of Boundary Corner. Up the short arête to a small ledge where a slab leads to another ledge. The arête above is climbed until it is possible to step right onto the slab and finish up this near Dove's Nest Crack.

22. Dove's Nest Crack 11m HVS 5a
Start to the right of the last climb and at the top of a grassy bay. Climb the green looking chimney into a small cave. Pull round the overhang with difficulty and finish straight up.

23. Patchett's Plunge 12m E3 5b **
Pleasant but poorly protected climbing up the hanging rib between Dove's Nest Crack and Idiot's Delight finishing up the arête direct.

24. Idiot's Delight 12m HS 4c ***
A superb climb. Starts just right of the hanging rib. Climb two triangular slabs to a cave. Make an airy traverse left to the arête and then go straight up.

25. Loony's Lament 12m HVS 5b
A contrived but interesting climb which fills in the gap between Great Wall and Idiot's Delight. Start just left of Great Wall and trend left up an awkward, slabby scoop. Climb this to the base of a thin crack which is followed to the cave of Idiot's Delight. Finish up the steep crack above.

26. Great Wall 15m HVS 5b ***
The impressive wall to the right of Idiot's Delight provides a magnificent climb. The short chimney leads to a ledge. Up the corner crack until it peters out, then traverse right until a long reach allows a crescent shaped crack to be reached. Up this until it is possible to pull out onto a ledge on the right. Finish up the short overhanging crack on the right.

Great Wall Direct Finish E5 6a *
From the top of the crescent shaped crack go up the wall via the slightly leftward trending weakness. A long reach from a sloping ledge to the break being the crux.

27. Katana 15m E6 6b
An eliminate and hard line crossing Great Wall at its large ledge. From the ledge 3metres up Foxes Hole climb the blunt arête 2m right of Great Wall to the large ledge. Climb direct up blunt arête above, to the left of Great Wall normal finish.

28. Foxes Hole 12m D
The obvious deep chimney right of Great Wall leads to a terrace. Continue up the obvious chimney on the right.

29. Spare Rib 6m E4 6a
The rib to the right of Foxes Hole.

30. Karabiner Crack 6m VS 5a
A good exit from the terrace of Foxes Hole is provided by the crack at the left hand side of the terrace and right of the finish to Great Wall.

31. Bilberry Wall 8m VS 5a
Start at the faint groove and thin crack immediately left of Nose Chimney. Climb the groove until a move left across the wall can be made to finish near the arête.
Direct Start E3 6a
Gain the upper wall direct.

32. Nose Chimney 14m VD
A hanging chimney on the nose bounding Central Gully to the east. Start to the left of the chimney and traverse into it. A direct start can also be made at Severe standard.

33. The Wine O 8m HVS 5b
Start as for Nose Chimney but instead of traversing right, climb the thin crack above.

34. The Last Retreat 14m E4 6a *
To the right of Nose Chimney. Gain the arête by traversing in from either left or right. Climb the overhang and short wall to a good stance. Continue idly up the wall just right of the arête.

35. Nosey Parker 14m E5 6a *
Takes the left wall of the Central Gully to finish boldly up the crescent shaped weakness in the upper wall. Start at the left edge of the wall and climb to the traverse line. Move up onto the base of the crescent (rock scar) and continue directly up the wall to the top.

Charlotte Telfer
26. Great Wall (HVS 5b)
Photo: Darren Stevenson

36. Central Gully East 11m D
From the top of a small pinnacle climb a steep wall to a ledge on the right. Finish up the slab and corner crack.

37. Central Gully West 14m S
Climb the cracked right corner of Central Gully to a ledge. Finish via the slab and crack.

38. Northumberland Wall 15m E2 5c ***
Superb strenuous and well protected climbing makes this one of the best and most popular routes of its grade in the county. The big groove and crack line on the right wall of the gully is followed throughout to an awkward traverse right at the top. Alternatively, it may be finished direct which is somewhat harder.

39. Osiris 15m E3 5c
The second crack right of Northumberland Wall leads to the arête, which is climbed to the flutings of Pharaoh's Face and so to the top.

40. Skyline 18m E5 6b
Climb the wall below the hanging arete to the first ledge and continue directly up the arête to finish up the flutings above.

41. Pharaoh's Face 18m E3 5c
The extreme left hand edge of Main Wall which used to be the hardest Very Severe in the county. Climb up easily into a slot and continue up with difficulty to a vegetated ledge. Up just right of the edge until it becomes necessary to make a sensational pull up the overhanging nose on the left to the final flutings.

42. Main Wall 12m MS **
The fine, steep and well worn slab on the west face of the snout bounding the west side of Central Gully. Start on the right of the slab, move up and left to broad ledges. Traverse back right and up to a flake to finish.
Variation Start MS
The flake can be reached direct by a series of mantelshelves.

43. Lichen Chimney 9m M
Climb the corner to the right of Main Wall. Finish up an open groove at the top.

44. Broken Blocks Staircase 9m M
A vague climb up the broken rocks right of Lichen Chimney.

45. Dirty Flue 9m M
A shallow corner just left of the overhanging recess. From a ledge at half height, finish up slabs to the right.

46. Blue Arête 8m E4 6a
A bold and serious route up the arête to the right of Dirty Flue. Climb Dirty Flue, then traverse right onto the arête and climb this direct to the top.

47. The Brute 8m HVS 5a *
Strenuous but well protected. The obvious overhanging recess immediately right of the broken rocks. The difficulties begin at half height. Surmount two bulges by bridging and/or laybacking.

David Murray
42. Main Wall (MS)
Photo: Andy Birtwistle

48. Enery's Ammer 11m E2 5b *
The exposed scoop to the right of The Brute. Climb easily up to good holds beneath the scoop. Pull into the scoop and continue with difficulty to the top.

49. Sweethope Crack 11m HS 4b *
The crack and groove just left of the deep chimney (Squeezy Bill). Climb a short wall and pull up right onto ledges below a steep V groove which contains a narrow crack. An awkward move up the crack brings good holds into reach at the top.

50. Squeezy Bill 11m D
Climb blocks to the foot of a deep cut, narrow chimney. Force a route up the chimney.

51. Rake's Crack 12m E1 5b **
The groove and crack line just right of Squeezy Bill and left of the sharp arête is climbed direct throughout. A fine, well protected climb with the crux at the top.

52. Rake's Arête 15m VD
The fine arête just right of Rake's Crack. Climb the arête for 8 metres then traverse right onto Jacob's Ladder and finish up this.

Direct Finish E3 5c
The upper arête is climbed absolutely direct.

53. The Jibber 12m E1 5c
Climb the wall to the right of Rake's Arête direct to a prominent flake. Climb this and go direct to the top.

54. Jacob's Ladder 12m VD **
The broad, open corner to the right of Rake's Arête. Climb the corner, using the crack, to a ledge half way up below an open chimney. Move up to the top chimney and bridge to the top.

55. Stairway to Heaven 13m E5 6a
Bold climbing up the hanging arête right of Jacob's Ladder. Climb the wall to the base of the arête and make a precarious move up this. Finish up the wall above just to the right.

56. Rake's Progress 12m VD

Start 4 metres right of the open corner of Jacob's Ladder. The right edge of the wall is climbed to a ledge on the corner at 5 metres. Using the short crack on the right, gain the ledge above. Continue up to and climb the obvious back and foot chimney. The foot of the chimney may also be reached by a traverse from the ledge on Jacob's Ladder.

57. Epitaph 11m MVS 4b

Follow Rake's Progress until a traverse right can be made and the crack above attained and followed to the top.

Alec Burns below on
52. Rake's Crack (E1 5b)
Photo: Andy Birtwistle

Andrew Render above climbing
54. Jacob's Ladder (VD)
Photo: Steve Crowe

58. Girdle Traverse 150m HVS 5b

Start as for Eastern Traverse and follow this into Great Chimney. Descend Great Chimney and traverse round into Boundary Corner at one third height. Move out right and up Hawk Slab to belay at the top of Dove's Nest Crack. Move round onto Idiot's Delight and descend it. Traverse across Great Wall to the Foxes Hole. Move round across Nose Chimney to Central Gully. Climb down and traverse Northumberland Wall then round Main Wall to Lichen Chimney. Follow broken rocks across to a small arête and descend Dirty Flue almost to ground level, where the arête is passed by an awkward swing and the foot of the Brute is reached. Cross the overhung cave and work down to a horizontal traverse into Sweethope Crack. Step across to the terrace at the top of Squeezy Bill. Descend right into a V groove and hand traverse across to the arête. Continue round into Rake's Progress then move right to finish up the end chimney. (The section of this climb from Main Wall can be done as a separate climb at Severe)

Western Section

An isolated buttress 20 metres west of the main outcrop provides the following four climbs.

59. Spider Crack 12m MVS 4c
Start left of Raven's Nest. Climb the short corner to a ledge. Up the corner above to gain a short overhanging crack which leads to the top.

60. Broken Wing 12m E3 5c
Climb directly up the wall left of Raven's Nest to a good ledge beneath the final wall. Climb this with difficulty.

61. Raven's Nest 12m VD **
The splendid corner splitting the left hand side of the crag. Climb the corner on the left wall. Near the top transfer to the right wall and finish through the cave.

Variation Finishes VS 5a
Exit out right or left below the cave.

62. Thin Ice 12m E4 6a ***
Bold and technical climbing up the hanging ramp right of Raven's Nest. Climb the easy crack 2 metres right of Raven's Nest to the horizontal crack at 8 metres. Follow the hanging ramp which is both strenuous and technical, until a move left can be made to a good hold near the top.

The following five routes are on the overhanging buttress to the right of the Raven's Nest area.

63. Heather Slab 8m D
The left side of the buttress is slabby in its upper half. Climb steeply up to the slab and traverse right below overhangs to an easy finish.

64. Old Holborn 12m E1 5b
The corner left of Golden Virginia to the terrace, then the open corner above. Exit as for Golden Gate.

65. Golden Virginia 17m E1 5b
The thin crack left of California Crack to the terrace. A long reach from the boulder leads to the overhang, pull over at the obvious break.

66. California Crack 18m HVS 5a *
A good climb up the overhanging buttress which starts directly below the prominent roof crack. Climb a short nose on incut holds to the terrace below the overhanging upper wall. Start the wall either direct (long reach) or enter from the right and climb up the corner to the roof. Good jams lead round the overhang to the finish.

67. Arête and Groove 13m VD
The arête right of California Crack to a very large belay, followed by the short groove behind.

68. Task Force 13m E3 5c
Climb the centre of the lower wall, right of California Crack to the ledge. Gain the top of the huge block beneath the overhang, climb up to a niche and follow the fault to the top.

69. Golden Gate 15m MVS 4c
A traverse of the overhanging buttress between the upper and lower overhangs. Start on the wall round to the right of the ledge on California Crack. Traverse left to a block on the corner and continue left below the crack to a stomach traverse slot. Follow this, then up and left onto ribs to the finish.

70. West Chimney 12m D
The unmistakable deep chimney 10 metres right of Task Force.

71. The 16 ½ Pint Pig 13m E1 5b
The overhang right of West Chimney is climbed from the left to the ledge. Finish up the two obvious arêtes above.

72. War Monger 9m E1 5b
The wall round to the right. Climb the thin rightward curving flakes to the shattered block, this and the thin crack lead to the platform. Climb the flakes up the centre of the back wall.

73. Lee's Leap 9m MVS 4c
The wall right of War Monger is climbed near its centre to a ledge on the left at half height, up the wall above to a dirty finish. The corner at the right end of the back wall leads to the top.

Chapter House
30 metres further west is a buttress with a large overhang and a ledge just above ground level, the Monk's Bench.

74. If Looks Could Kill 6m E1 5c
Climb the crack splitting the nose at the left end of the buttress and go directly up the slab above via small flutes to the heather.

75. At the Witches Trial 6m HVS 5a
Start left of the Monk's Bench at ground level. Pull onto the wall at its centre and climb it direct. Move left at the top, above a small scoop, to heather finish.

76. 'A' Crack 5m VD
The thin crack at the left end of the overhang.

77. Willing to Sin 9m E4 6a *
A strenuous route with the crux at the top. Start 3 metres left of 'B' crack and climb the wall to the break. Pull over both roofs and finish via a small pocket.

78. 'B' Crack 7m HVS 5a *
Climb the overhanging crack on the right of the roof.

79. Blowin Free 7m E1 5b
Start 2 metres right of 'B' Crack, just left of W.L. carved on the rock. Climb straight up and over the overhang at the obvious break on small but good holds. Step left and straight up the slabs above.

80. Corned Beef 7m E1 5b
The wall left of 'B' Corner via the vague scoop.

81. 'B' Corner 7m D
The deep corner at the right end of the buttress.

82. 'B' Arête 7m VD
The flaked arête right of 'B' Corner, finishing over the perched boulder.

Two Tier Buttress
40 metres further west is an impressive two tier buttress giving four climbs.

83. Games Without Frontears 12m HVS 5b
The roof to the left of Two Tear Crack Climb the groove in the lower tier. Up the wall to beneath the roof, move right and break through at the weakness.

84. Two Tear Crack 9m E1 5c *
A good climb up the centre of the two tier buttress.

85. War Without Tears 9m E1 5c
The huge double roof system 5 metres right of Two Tear Crack.

86. Veil of Tears 30m HVS 5b
A right to left traverse of Two Tier Buttress, from gully to gully between the overhangs.

27 metres right of Two Tear Crack is a short buttress at a slightly lower level.

87. Silently Snitched from Stu 6m E1 5b
Climb the corner crack at the left hand side, very green. Step right and climb the slab to the top.

50 metres further west lies a smaller but very overhung buttress with a cleft nose.

88. Rather Bolder 7m E2 6a
Climbs the overhung and blunt arête to the left of the cleft. Pull up on good holds below the crack right of the overhang, then monkey out on decent holds to the arête. Move up to flat holds on the blunt nose and make a committed slap for the arête, one more haul then finish easily.

89. Hey Up Me Duck 6m VS 4c
Start as for the previous route, make a slightly tricky move to gain the overhanging crackand follow it pleasantly on layaways to an easy finish.

Great Wanney Graded List

E8
Endless Flight Direct 7a ***

E7
Crisis Zone 6c ***

E6
Policy of Truth 6c *
Katana 6b

E5
Absent Friend 6b **
Thunder Thighs 6b *
Nosey Parker 6a *
Endless Flight 6a ***
Stairway to Heaven 6a
Skyline 6b
Great Wall Direct Finish 6a *

E4
Willing to Sin 6a *
The Last Retreat 6a *
Blue Arête 6a
Thin Ice 6a ***
Spare Rib 6a
Eastern Ecstasy 6a
Idiot Wind 5c **

E3
Jungle Warfare 6b
Marquee Metal 5c
Rake's Arête Direct Finish 5c
Broken Wing 5c
East Buttress Direct 5c **
Osiris 5c
Pharaoh's Face 5c
Bilberry Wall Direct Start 6a
Task Force 5c
Patchett's Plunge 5b **

E2
Northumberland Wall 5c ***
Eastern Promise 5c
Dennis 6a *
Enery's Ammer 5b
Aces High 5b
Pitfall 5b *
Rather Bolder 6a

E1
If Looks Could Kill 5c
War Monger 5b
War Without Tears 5c
Two Tear Crack 5c *
Blowin Free 5b
Corned Beef 5b
Golden Virginia 5b
Old Holburn 5b
Rake's Crack 5b **
The Jibber 5c
Nosey Parker 6a
The 16½ Pint Pig 5b
Silently Snitched from Stu 5b

HVS
Loony's Lament 5b
Great Wall 5b ***
Hawk Slab 5a
The Wine 0 5b
'B' Crack 5a *
Dove's Nest Crack 5a
California Crack 5a *
Girdle Traverse 5b
Veil of Tears 5b
Games Without Frontears 5a
At the Witches Trial 5a
The Brute 5a *

VS
Bilberry Wall 5a
Right Crack 5a
Karabiner Crack 5a
Raven's Nest Variation Finishes 5a
Hey Up Me Duck 4c

Bob Smith dancing on
62. Thin Ice (E4 6a)
Photo: Mark Savage

Harehope Canyon

Tim Catterall

History

Although the crag has undoubtedly been 'discovered' numerous times, the first known route was climbed by Andy Birtwistle in 1986 when he soloed the obvious central crack of Peregrine Buttress. Nothing more was added until Malcolm Lowerson, Nick Steen and Nigel Jamieson returned in October 1993 when they climbed the crack to the left and a left to right traverse of Pirate's Buttress from a hanging stance above the stream. Paul Linfoot also visited the crag, climbing but not recording a number of routes.

The main activity however, took place during the dry summer of 2003. At the beginning of August, Tim Catterall and Phil Brereton visited the crag and climbed three routes. Tim returned a number of times, in quick succession, with various partners including Steve Nagy, Malcolm Lowerson and Phil Brereton to climb all the routes described.

On Pirate's Buttress the unorthodox use of a 2 metre long scaffold plank was used to gain access to Keel Hauled. All the other routes were climbed without the plank, although it was used to gain the grassy recess at the left hand end of the buttress.

Situation and Character

The crag straddles Harehope Burn high up on Bewick Moor. It has buttresses facing east, west and north-northwest and is up to 13 metres high. The east buttress has the burn following along its base; some of the climbs here have interesting starts. The rock is very hard, excellent quality sandstone. To date routes have been recorded on the north-northwest, east and west facing buttresses. The crags have a pleasant sunny outlook and are situated in a sheltered river canyon on the moor. The routes are quite deceptive, often looking easier than they actually are. A stake has been placed 8 metres back on Peregrine Buttress because of the lack of an adequate belay, this can be used on all the routes on that and Wagtail Buttress. The only belays available on the Pirate's Buttress side are the dying trees although a stake may be in place (it is still in Tim's garage at the time of going to print).

Approaches and Access

Follow the A1 past Alnwick to North Charlton, turn left onto an unclassified road and follow this for about 4 miles until you pass Quarry House and a large mast. Park a quarter of a mile past this by a bridleway sign on your left, which lies just below a wood on the left side of the road. Follow the bridleway across the moor in a south-westerly direction for 1½km to a fence and a small burn crossing. Just after going through the gate, turn left and follow a faint path along the burn to the crag 400 metres to the south. The crag can be seen from an earlier point on the approach but lies hidden at this point. The crag is 40 minutes from the car. Alternatively follow the description for Corbies Fortress and carry on up the burn for a further ten minutes to the crag. There is a right of access to the crag under CRoW.

The Climbs

The routes have been described from the upstream end, starting with the upstream buttress which is Peregrine Buttress.

Peregrine Buttress

1. Bewick Arête 10m E1 5b

Climb the arête on the left-hand side of the buttress. Move from the arête onto the front face and gain the ledge. Quite delicate moves off the ledge sometimes lead to the top.

2. Andrew's Grovelly Groove 12m HS 4b

Climb the short wall and curving crack to the rowan tree, climb the chimney behind the tree to the top.

3. Philipson's Folly 12m VS 5a **

Start in the centre of the face below the bottomless crack. Climb the wall to the crack, which is followed to the cave. Strenuous moves lead to a small niche and the final crack is climbed to the top.

4. Scorpion 12m E3 6a **

Start 2 metres right of the central crack. Climb the wall to a horizontal pocket; fingery climbing leads to an overhanging ledge. An awkward reach gains the next break and the eye socket above. Very strenuous moves using the eye socket and the sloping ramp lead to the top.

The wall to the right can also be climbed via a small letterbox to the large pocket using a long reach at 6a. It is possible to finish up either Scorpion or Terminated Tern.

5. Terminated Tern 13m E1 5b *

Climbs the right-hand arête. Climb into the recess from the left-hand side and gain the crack to the right of the arête. Layback the crack until it is possible to move left onto the arête. The arête is climbed on its left-hand side to the top.

6. Cunning Stunt 9m E2 6a

Just right of the fist sized crack is a short arête with a letterbox to its left. Start below the arête and use the rounded overhung break to gain the letterbox. Use this and the arête to gain the ledge above. Pull left over the bulge above.

7. Thread Flintstone 9m HVS 5a

Start at the bottom of the gully, left of the prow. Climb the large detached flake on the left wall from the left hand end, use a hidden flake to gain the ledge and a thread. Move right and continue up the crack in the wall above to a jammed block, heather mantel to finish.

Wagtail Buttress

The prominent prow and broken wall to the right.

8. Slap Happy 9m E3 6b *

Climbs the front of the overhanging prow. Start directly below the pointed nose just left of a small undercut slab. A strenuous dynamic move gains the nose and the overhung ledge above. The overhanging prow is climbed up its front face direct, via some very powerful committing climbing to the top.

9. Fat Slapper 9m E1 5c

Starts just right of the previous route, use a small flat hold on the undercut slab to gain the ledge, being able to put your foot by your shoulder is an advantage. Climb the wall above just right of the arête, passing a faint groove. A poor last runner can be placed in a small letterbox. Continue to the top on friable holds.

10. The Mistress 9m VS 5b

Start at two undercuts 1 metre left of the large pocket on the west face. Lunge up to a small flat flake. Pull up onto the ledge, move slightly right and follow flakes and flutings to the top.

11. Jabberwocky 10m E1 5b

Climbs the short undercut wall of the west face, directly below the wide crack in the wall above. Climb the wall until a hard mantel leads to the ledge, climb the crack above with surprising difficulty.

Pirate's Slab and Buttress

The east facing buttress consists of a dirty slab with large through cave to the left; and an impressive buttress, with a burn flowing across the very bottom of it. Most of the bottom of this part of the buttress is blank. At the left hand end there is a grassy recess and some smaller broken buttresses left again. In times of spate or for Keel Hauled and Walking the Plank it will be necessary to use the gangplank. This can be found in a cave to the south and should be returned there after use.

Pirate's Slab
The next two routes climb the slab with the bulging steep wall at its base.

12. Pieces Of Eight 10m S 4a
Start in the middle of the face about six metres right of the large through cave at the obvious weakness. An awkward move using this and the small blunt boss to its right gains the slab. Move up the slab to a series of grassy ledges directly below the obvious broken crack. Climb the ledges and the crack to the top.

13. Scurvy 12m S 4b
Start as for Pieces of Eight. After the awkward move onto the slab, traverse left passing a small open cave to the steeper slab. Ascend this just left of the cave to the top.

14. Captain's Chasm 15m E3 6a *
Hand traverses the right wall of the through cave looking in, to the arête. Use two small crimps to gain the left-hand end of the hand traverse, this is followed to the arête. Move up the arête to a rock over and an awkward finish.

15. Nocturnal Adventures 10m HVS 5b (Caving Grade 4)
Climb the overhanging boulder choke at the back of the cave towards the light, until it is possible to re-enter the real world above.

Pirate's Buttress

16. Skull And Cross Bones 16m E3 6a
Start below the arête in the mouth of the cave. Bridge up between the two opposing walls until a hold can be reached below the small roof. Use this to gain the large ear above the roof, pull over and climb the slanting crack above to a constricted ledge. Traverse left onto the larger ledge and climb the broken crack to the right of the tree, use the tree to gain the top.

17. Mutiny, Mr Christian 27m E2 5c **
A right to left girdle. Start by a large boulder in the through cave at the right hand end of the buttress. Hand traverse leftwards towards a blunt flake and the arête; move round the corner onto the front face and the obvious thread. Keep heading left to a sloping ledge and some small cracks. A committing move left leads to a horizontal fist jamming crack, follow this to the bottomless crack in the centre of the face. Move up and left to a series of small ledges, keep traversing to the left arête and finish up Walking the Plank.

Tim Catterall on the first ascent of
18. Keel Hauled (E4 6a)
Photo: Tina Nagy

18. Keel Hauled 13m E4 6a **
Climbs the centre of the wall. Levitate across the burn or layback your way up the plank until a tiny pinch enables you to stand upright. A committing move gains a sharp crimp below a flute or the burn if you're unlucky. Use this to gain the flared break above where gear can be placed in a crack to the right. Move left over the bulge to a small break; the top is gained via a heather mantel.

19. Watery Grave 17m E5 6b **
From the grassy recess traverse right past the two bottomless cracks to a horizontal slot. Move up using a sharp hold to another sharp hold and a poor flute above, follow this to the flared break. Climb the bulging wall above to gear, continue via small breaks to a heather mantel to finish.

20. Abductors Antics 15m E2 5c
Traverse in as for Walking The Plank. Climb the crack until it is possible to traverse right across the large flared break to the vertical crack in the centre of the buttress. Climb this trending slightly right to finish up the flute.

21. Walking The Plank 15m E2 5c *
Climbs the right-hand bottomless crack on the left-hand side of the buttress. A plank may be used to gain the sloping ledge on the far side of the burn (as on the first ascent) or wait for a drought and walk across. A delicate traverse right gains the large stone filled pothole. Climb the right-hand crack to the break and continue up the blunt arête above to the top. It is also possible to traverse in from the large recess to the left at the same grade.

22. The Black Pig 13m E3 6b
From the grassy recess traverse right to the first crack. Climb the crack until it stops. Make a hard move left to a flake and use this to gain the ledge. Climb the wall above just left of the blunt arête to the top.

23. Boarding Party 13m HVS 5a
To the left of the smooth wall is a grassy bay where the burn narrows. Jump across this and climb the bulging right-hand crack to the ledge. Climb the rounded slabs above to the right of the arête. A worthwhile route for the adventurous climber.

24. Shiver Me Timbers 13m HS 4a
Start in the same place as the previous route. Use the crack at the back of the bay to gain the ledge. Climb the overhanging corner above using the cracks to a small recess on the right. Carry on up the crack in the right wall above, just left of the arête.

Black Beards Buttress
This buttress lies at the southern end of the crag and is set slightly up the slope on the east side of the burn. A very clean buttress with a blackened arête in its middle.

25. Goatee Beard 8m S
Climb the slab on the left-hand side. Start directly below the obvious flutes at a broken crack. Use the crack to gain the flutes, climb these and head right up a ramp at the top.

26. The Black Spot 8m HS 4b *
Climb the blackened arête on its left-hand side.

27. Stubble 8m E1 5b
Climb the steep wall right of the arête via a long reach.

Harehope Canyon Graded List

E5
Watery Grave 6b **

E4
Keel Hauled 6a **

E3
Captain's Chasm 6a *
Scorpion 6a **
The Black Pig 6b
Skull And Cross Bones 6a
Slap Happy 6b *

E2
Abductors Antics 5c
Mutiny, Mr Christian 5c **
Cunning Stunt 6a
Walking The Plank 5c *

E1
Bewick Arête 5b
Fat Slapper 5c
Jabberwocky 5b
Stubble 5b
Terminated Tern 5b *

HVS
Boarding Party 5a
Nocturnal Adventures 5b
Thread Flintstone 5a

VS
Philipson's Folly 5a **
The Mistress 5b

Henhole
Martin Cooper and Graeme Read

NT 888203
South Facing
610m
60 minutes

History

The Cheviot massif shares with Great Wanney the claim to be the birthplace of climbing in Northumberland. The crags were at their most popular from the end of the Second World War, through the fifties and into the early sixties. During the second World War the remoteness of their location made the Henhole crags a specially treasured haven of escape for Tyneside climbers. In this first wave of development a number of routes were recorded, including Black Adams Corner, Zig Zag and the classic Cannon Hole Direct. Phillip McGill and Harry Warmington added, amongst others, Tombstone and College Grooves before McGill, sadly, was killed and Warmington injured in a rockfall on nearby Dunsdale Crag. Towards the end of the sixties Malcolm Lowerson and (fingery) Jim Patchett went to work on the crag to produce a series of excellent routes including Misconception, Fingery Jim and The Brute, the latter two routes being both hard and bold. Development then ceased for a number of years before Nev Hannaby added Forgotten Wall, while in 1983 Steve Crowe climbed Funeral Pyre. Calum Henderson and Lee Clegg climbed the 'Cannon Hole Superdirect', Zeus the Mighty Bull in 1987. Finally, Graeme Read and Richard Pow produced two new routes in 2002 with Hooly's Horror and the bold Conclusion Superdirect.

Situation and Character

The Henhole Crags are situated on both sides of the College Burn high on the west side of Cheviot which is the highest mountain area in Northumberland, rising to 815 metres and consisting of a vast stretch of wild moorland uncrossed by road. The Henhole is composed of igneous rock which in general is sound. It is a most impressive situation, the crags looming high above the burn.

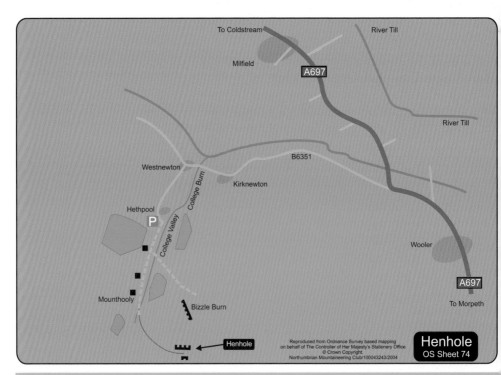

The approach is long and the situation exposed to the elements. However, the crag dries quickly after rain and if the weather is good the rewards are great, providing good climbing in the lower grades with a definite mountaineering flavour. The igneous rock of these crags provide a strongly contrasting climbing medium to most of the rest of the county and, while the rock is generally sound, care must be taken on some lines.

Approaches and Access

From Wooler continue on the A697 towards Coldstream, branching left about 2 miles from Wooler at Akeld. Continue for a further 3 miles to West Newton where a left turn is made to Hethpool. The road from Hethpool to Mounthooly Farm (5 miles) is a public right of way on foot, but to take a car requires written permission from John Sale & Partners, College Valley Estate Office, 18-20 Glendale Road, Wooler (closed weekends) which should be sought in advance. Telephone 01668 281611.

From Mounthooly a good track leads south into the Henhole (3 kilometres); allow an hour. A mountainbike ride from Hethpool to just short of the crags gives access at any time without the need for a permit.

An alternative approach from the north is to drive to Cocklawfoot, then walk east following the Cheviot Burn for 1200 metres, ascend Auchope Rigg and cross the col between Auchope Cairn and The Schill. The Henhole lies below and to the right. Walking time again one hour.

A walk direct to the Henhole Crags over the summit of Cheviot from Langleeford in the Harthope valley will give a long but potentially rewarding approach for enthusiasts, best saved for a spell of dry weather.

There is a right of access to the crag under CRoW.

The final approach to Henhole
Photo: Steve Crowe

Henhole Wall

The Climbs

The routes are described from left to right.

Rowan Buttress

The first crag to be met on the north side of the College Burn, which is to the left of, and separated from the main crag, by a wide gully of grass and scree.

1. Mortuary Slab 9m HS 4c

Starts at the left end of the wall up the steep, red flecked slab. Climb the centre of the slab. Move onto the arête after 6 metres and follow it to the top on clean rock.

2. Baptismal Fire 12m VD

Starts on the left wall 3 metres left of the corner. Climb to a perched block at 5 metres and pass it on the right. Trend left to finish up the steep grooved and vegetated chimney.

3. Honeymoon Corner 12m S

Climb the vegetated corner using the occasional rock hold.

4. Funeral Pyre 12m VS 4c

Climbs the arête right of Honeymoon Corner (small wire protection).

The following climbs lie on the Narrow Buttress left of Henhole Wall.

5. Jacob's Ladder 12m VD

Climb the groove with a series of steps in it on the left side of the face. Steeper than it looks.

6. The Egg 14m VS 4c *

A good route. Starts at the foot of the buttress, which is climbed mainly on the right to the top.

The main crag lies right of the narrow buttress and separated from it by a steep, dirty, grooved gully. The crag comprises of a large face split up its centre by a shallow gully (Central Gully). The rocks on the right have an overhung base but are more broken near the top where the angle eases.

Henhole Wall

7. Misconception 21m HVS 5b **

An excellent climb, strenuous and well protected Start at the left end of the crag, below the left end of the large overhang at a short incut corner. Climb this to the grass ledge at 5 metres. Continue more easily up the wall above, trending left into the top of an overhung wall. Move right and up past the roof of the large overhang into a diminishing groove. Escape is possible via a hold on the left edge, then a line of vertical cracks.

8. Conception Corner 23m HVS 5b **
Takes the crack that splits the large overhang.
Climb the wall, then the overhang direct and
follow the crack to the top. Strenuous but well
protected.

9. Long John 23m S 4b *
A fine climb, of increasing interest and exposure.
Start at a rib below a large whitened stance (The
Platform). Climb the rib to The Platform, then
continue diagonally left up to the right end of the
large overhang. Climb the flake on the wall to the
right until it is possible to traverse back left into a
vertical crack, which is followed to the top.

10. Platform and Chimney 25m D *
An interesting climb. Start at the lowest point of
the buttress and climb up to the short chimney at
12 metres. Climb the chimney to a platform, then
traverse into Central Gully and so to the top.

11. Yellow Slab 25m VD
Start as for Platform and Chimney to the foot
of the short chimney. Make a delicate move up
right onto the steep red wall bounding Central
Gully and climb it to a ledge. Finish up the left
wall and arête of the gully.

12. Alligator Crawl 25m HS 4b
A poor climb, usually wet and slimy and with
a dirty finish. If you still want to do the climb,
start in the corner of Central Gully and climb to
a junction with Yellow Slab. Finish up the dirty
crack on the left wall.

13. The Chicken 25m S 4b
Starts in the right corner of Central Gully. Climb
the left trending ribs until it is possible to move
out of the gully by a weakness on the right.
Continue up the steep wall above which eases
near the top.

14. Forgotten Wall 25m VS 5a *
The undercut wall left of College Grooves. Start
about 2 metres right of The Chicken, climb a
short left facing corner to the overhang, move
right then directly up the wall above. Continue
via the shallow left facing groove to a ledge, then
follow steep but easier rock to the top. Quite
delicate.

Direct Start 5b
Once at the overhang, reach right and climb up
through the notch.

15. College Grooves 30m HS 4b ***
One of the classic routes on the crag, providing
some of the best Severe climbing in the county.
Start 6 metres to the right of Central Gully below
an overhanging groove in the face of the steep
slab. Pull up the groove onto the slab above,
which leads to a V groove. A second groove
above ends below an easier little chimney and
the steep but easy rocks lead to the top.

16. Zig Zag 30m D
A pleasant climb. Start beneath the right angled
corner to the right of College Grooves. Climb this
to an open chimney, exiting left where it narrows,
then traverse right across a steep wall to a
shallow groove. Go up the groove or the wall on
its right to finish up an easy gully.

17. Right Hand Rib 18m VD
Climb the rib that forms the right edge of the wall
to gain an open slab where a steep move leads
to a second slab. Finish up the right edge of the
buttress.

Karin Magog enjoying the classic
15. College Grooves (HS 4b)
Photo: Steve Crowe

Cannon Hole Rake

Cannon Hole Buttress

This is right of and at a lower level than Henhole Wall. The left half of the face is split halfway up by the Cannon Hole Rake, which slopes upwards from left to right, starting as a large grass platform and ending as a narrow rock ledge. At the foot of the face, below the termination of the rake, an overhanging corner has been walled in to form a shelter. To the right of the shelter is a steep face containing the Cannon Hole.

Cannon Hole Rake

The following climbs start from the Cannon Hole Rake.

18. Grooved Corner 15m D

Follows the grooved corner of the buttress to the right of a small cave to a yellow wall. Move left into the corner then easily to the top.

19. Continuation 16m D

Start 6 metres right of Grooved Corner. Ascend diagonally leftwards to join Grooved Corner and finish directly up the yellow wall.

20. Conclusion 18m VD

Starts as for Continuation. Climb straight up the slab to the overhang. Traverse left round the corner to a crack line which splits the back of the overhang. Climb the crack on good holds to the top.

21. Conclusion Super Direct 14m E3 5c *

Climb Conclusion to the overhang. Surmount this direct using a hanging flake just above the lip to gain crimps and better holds. A bold and powerful excursion.

22. The Brute 14m HVS 5a **

A bold route, both steep and exposed. Start two metres from the right end of the Rake on the face to the right of the red slab and left of the small rib. Climb the steep wall with difficulty to gain the open groove above, which is followed to the overhang. A strenuous pull up the corner leads to the foot of the final easier groove.

23. Fingery Jim 12m E1 5b *

A steep climb on small holds on the most exposed part of the buttress. Starts at the right end of the Rake up the small rib. Climb the right side of the rib to a bulge at 4 metres. Move onto the right wall and then make a difficult move left onto the small sloping top of the bulge. A crack in the wall above is used to gain a sloping ledge at its left end from where the face above is climbed straight to the top.

Various parties leading
22. The Brute (HVS 5a)
and **30. Cannon Hole Direct (MVS 4b)**
Photo: Andy Birtwistle

Cannon Hole Buttress, Shelter Wall

Shelter Wall

The next climbs start at the foot of the crag.

24. The Arête 12m M

The sharp rib at the left end of the buttress.

25. West Wall 12m D

Start between the rib and the shelter. Climb the wall initially up the left sloping fault, traverse diagonally left to the Rake to finish.

26. Shelter Wall 14m S 4b *

A good route. Start in the shelter in the left corner. Climb the corner by the left wall until the overhang forces a move out left onto the face. Ascend direct to a mantelshelf and continue up to the Rake.

27. Hooly's Horror 14m HVS 5b*

A direct and fairly strenuous line from the shelter to the Rake, starting 2 metres left of Hooly's Delight. Climb steeply up to the cracks, then make a hard move to gain the niche and move left to the base of the obvious corner crack. Follow this to a good spike and continue more easily up the pillar above, finishing just right of Shelter Wall

28. Hooly's Delight 16m S 4b

Starts at a short, narrow chimney 1 metre right of the shelter. Climb the chimney to a small platform. Continue straight up for 1 metre before traversing diagonally left across the wall above the shelter to reach the foot of a hanging corner. Climb the corner to the Rake.

29. Tombstone 18m S 4b *

An excellent climb, sustained for its grade. Start as for Hooly's Delight. From the platform continue up via a short right angled corner to a tall block. Climb this on its left side and continue up the open corner above to reach the Rake.

30. Cannon Hole Direct 38m MVS 4b ***

A classic, exposed line up the steep crack beneath the Cannon Hole. Climb the crack then continue directly to the Cannon Hole. The steep wall above the Cannon Hole is climbed to a niche below an overhang. An exposed traverse up a ramp to the right leads to the top.

31. Zeus the Mighty Bull 33m E1 5b ***

The Cannon Hole superdirect. Climb Cannon Hole Direct to the block and overhang. Gain the block and make a long reach to climb directly to the top on large holds. Excellent and exposed.

32. Black Adam's Corner 30m D *
Climb the crack of Cannon Hole Direct until it is possible to make a right traverse across the slab. Follow the edge of the slab to a sloping platform, then continue to the top via a short chimney.

33. Double Variation 30m VD
Climb Cannon Hole Direct to a higher traverse, leading diagonally right to the sloping platform. Follow Black Adam's to the top of the chimney, then traverse round the corner onto the right wall of the buttress and so to the top.

On the opposite side of the College Burn to Cannon Hole Buttress is Peake's Buttress. It faces north and consists of a stepped central buttress and a long green gully to its right.

Peake's Buttress

34. Titus Alone 42m VD
Climb the left side of the buttress via the left trending groove to the grass ledge at 12 metres. Traverse left and up a crack to reach the large grass ledge below a short steep wall. Climb the wall via a vertical crack line to the top.

35. Titus Groan 48m HS 4b
Climbs the central buttress, starting left of the central gully.
1. 15m Climb up the wall to a ledge below a contorted wall.
2. 15m Pass two ledges to reach a right angled corner and climb it with difficulty (crux).
3. 18m Climb the broken wall above, exiting right.

36. Steerpike 30m MVS 4c
To the right of the central gully is an overhang below a wall covered with light green moss. Climb up to the left of the overhang and continue to a ledge below an overhanging corner. Stand on the pinnacle and climb the corner. Continue up the crack to a large shelf, which is left by a weakness on the right.

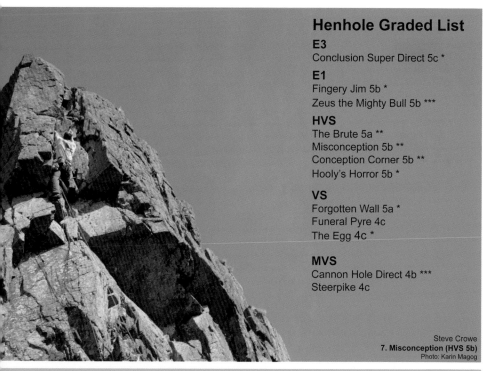

Henhole Graded List
E3
Conclusion Super Direct 5c *

E1
Fingery Jim 5b *
Zeus the Mighty Bull 5b ***

HVS
The Brute 5a **
Misconception 5b **
Conception Corner 5b **
Hooly's Horror 5b *

VS
Forgotten Wall 5a *
Funeral Pyre 4c
The Egg 4c *

MVS
Cannon Hole Direct 4b ***
Steerpike 4c

Steve Crowe
7. Misconception (HVS 5b)
Photo: Karin Magog

Howlerhirst Crag
Steve Crowe and Karin Magog

History
It is not known who first discovered, or climbed on, Howlerhirst Crag but Howlerhirst Crack, Overlapping Corner, Harris Tweed and Howlerhirst Chimney were mentioned in the 1970 guide. Most of these, if not all, were the work of Gordon Thompson in the late sixties. The next recorded developments came in 1979. Whilst brother Bob played April Fool, Tommy Smith climbed an impressive blank looking arête protected only by his Guardian Angel. Climbed in E.B.'s this superb route was well ahead of its time in boldness. Slightly later Paul Stewart and Bob Smith added Mad March Hare and Autumn respectively. Richard Davies led Devils Soulmate in September 1989. Dave Pegg added Where Angels Fear to Tread in October 1991. The latest additions, Crazy Diamond and Shine On were by Steve Crowe and Karin Magog whilst checking the text for this edition.

Situation and Character
An impressive sandstone outcrop in a fine remote position west of Bellingham. This west-facing suntrap is well worth a visit.

Approaches and Access
From the south take the B6320 towards Bellingham. Just after the passing the Kielder Resource Centre and before crossing the River North Tyne, take the left turn signposted to Hesleyside (opposite the cemetery). After 3 miles and after passing Low and High Carriteth farms a cottage on the right is passed. Almost opposite is a gate into a shallow valley (limited parking). Follow the shallow valley passing an isolated cottage. At some small rocks gain the valley rim on the true right bank. There is a right of access to the crag under CRoW.

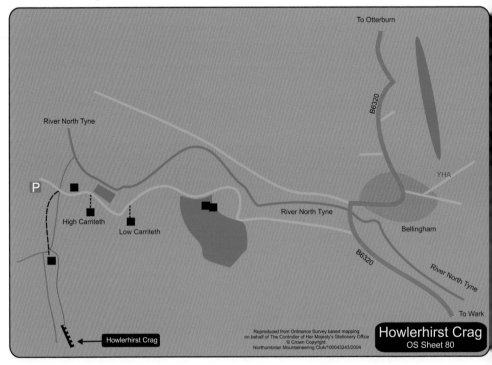

Steve Crowe relies on his
7. Guardian Angel (E5 6a)
An exercise in terror.
Photo: Karin Magog

Howlerhirst Crag

The Climbs

These are described on the highest central part of the crag and are described from left to right.

1. Buggy 5m VD
Start below the large nose of rock. Climb up to pass the roof on the left hand side.

2. Bogey 5m VD
Start below the large nose of rock. Climb up to squeeze past the roof on the right hand side.

3. Short Wall 5m VS
The short wall to the left of the V chimney.

4. Howlerhirst Chimney 5m S *
The V chimney towards the left end of the buttress provides a classic thrutch.

5. Harris Tweed 9m VS 5a
5 metres left a ramp can be reached by a dubious flake and quitted by an airy finish.

6. Devils Soul Mate 10m E6 6b **
A very bold route giving hard climbing. Start 2 metres to the left of Guardian Angel and climb up the wall to a very long reach above an appalling boulder for a good hold. A further long reach gains pockets in the overhanging wall above. Finish more easily.

7. Guardian Angel 11m E5 6a ***
Gain the undercut arête from the left hand side. Reach up to gain a positive intrusion and from here reach right to small pockets on the right hand side of the arête. From these move up to a thin finish via a broken flake and a further large pocket. A superb and committing climb, requiring a long reach, and an even longer neck.

8. Where Angels Fear to Tread 10m E6 6b **
Immaculate climbing up the hanging slab and flakes right of Guardian Angel. Infinitely harder for short people. Start just right of the arête and gain a ledge at 3 metres. Make hard moves over the bulge to gain the slab and a junction with Guardian Angel. Finish up this route via a long reach for the pocket.

9. Overlapping Corner 5m HVS 5a *
The overlapping walls with an obvious gap situated in the corner. A fine line.

10. Autumn 8m E1 5b
Solo the unprotected wall right of Overlapping Corner.

11. Crazy Diamond 8m E4 5c
The wall past the prominent but very dubious flake leads to a finish on pockets.

12. Shine On 8m E3 5c **
The smoothest section of the wall is climbed starting up the left edge of the large detached block.

13. Mad March Hare 9m E1 5b *
Start up the right edge of the detached block to gain the flake. Move right and up the wall.

14. July Fate 8m E3 5c
A bold start just left of the undercut section leads to an easier finish.

15. April Fool 9m E2 5b **
From the large ledge to the left of Howlerhirst Crack gain the arête. Climb the left side on suspect but big holds.

16. Howlerhirst Crack 8m HVS 5a *
The wide crack at the right of the highest part of
the crag is harder than it looks.

17. The Bleating of the Lambs 4m S
The centre of the short buttress to the right of the
main crag.

18. Endangered Species 4m HVS 5b
The end wall of the buttress to the right of the
main crag.

To either side of the main crag are smaller rocks,
which give many short routes and problems.
Below the crag the largest boulder provides an
excellent warm up traverse at 5b/c. Many short
up problems have also been worked out.

Karin Magog bounding up
13. Mad March Hare (E1 5b)
Photo: Steve Crowe

Howlerhirst Crag Graded List

E6
Where Angels Fear to Tread 6b ***
Devils Soul Mate 6b **

E5
Guardian Angel 6a ***

E4
Crazy Diamond 5c

E3
Shine On 5c **
July Fate 5c

E2
April Fool 5b **

E1
Autumn 5b
Mad March Hare 5b *

HVS
Endangered Species 5b
Overlapping Corner 5a *
Howlerhirst Crack 5a *

VS
Harris Tweed 5a

Jack Rock

Malcolm Lowerson

NU 233044
North Facing
30m
2 minutes

History

Malcolm Lowerson was the first person to discover the climbing potential of this crag in 1959, putting up most of the popular routes. Many of the first ascents were soloed including most of the Severes and Very Severes and the difficult Wet Fly. On the first attempt Malcolm was unable to summon up courage for the top wall. He also failed to make the moves back down to the ledge which resulted in a long jump into the river below.

The second phase of development was by Bob Hutchinson and John Earl. This started in 1973 with The Butcher and in the period up to 1976 they freed Ancient Briton and the Girdle Traverse and climbed, amongst others, The Angler and Greenwells Glory. Tommy and Bob Smith climbed the ferocious Barracuda Roof in 1979 and 9 years later Breakout was added by Kevin Howett and Andy Nelson.

Since the 1989 guide, further development has resulted in a dozen new routes of all grades. Of note is the 1999 ascent by Paul Smith of Little Mermaid which provides bold and powerful climbing up the left side of the overhanging Upstream Buttress and Steve Crowe's 2002 ascent of the technical and sensational Bigger Splash.

Situation and Character

The Jack Rock has an atmosphere that is unique in Northumberland climbing. It is a weathered sandstone crag of a vertical nature which rises up on the south bank of the Coquet and in part overhangs the river.

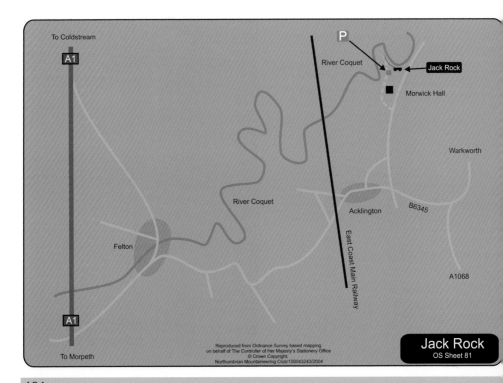

Reproduced from Ordnance Survey based mapping on behalf of The Controller of Her Majesty's Stationery Office © Crown Copyright. Northumbrian Mountaineering Club/100043243/2004

Jack Rock
OS Sheet 81

Karin Magog takes the
13. High Board (HS)
Photo: Steve Crowe

The left hand end of the crag is bounded by the overhanging Downstream Buttress. The next prominent buttress to the right is Tree Buttress which has a square incut corner, running vertically up its centre, topped by a pine. To the right and centre of the crag is Hanging Buttress which overhangs the river. A deep groove divides the upper part of Hanging Buttress from Wedge Buttress which juts out over the river and forms the left hand wall of the recess. The rock in the recess is the easiest angled on the whole crag but is topped by overhangs. To the right is Upstream Buttress which gently overhangs to its tree crested top and bounds the west end of the crag.

The rock contains some interesting fossils and has a number of ancient cup and ring marks inscribed upon it, particularly high on the arête to the right of Ancient Briton. One can only speculate at the climbing ability of those who carved them and care should be taken not to damage them.

Approaches and Access

The crag lies on the south bank of the River Coquet, facing north, 400 metres downstream from Morwick Mill. Morwick Village is about 3 miles south west of Warkworth. The crag is best reached from the Felton/Acklington Village B6345 road. From the centre of Acklington take the minor road north signed Warkworth. Follow this for 2 miles then take a left turn, signposted to Morwick Mill. Follow a rough track down towards the river where there is limited parking on the left. The crag is reached along the river bank. Access can be awkward during periods of high water or in summer when the vegetation is thick, when It may be better to approach along the top of the crag.

The Climbs

The climbs are described from right to left.

1. Bruin 10m HS
The route takes the upstream facing wall where the approach path meets the crag. Climb the steep wall left of the recess via the horizontal ledges to a sloping ledge and finish up the buttress to the left.

2. Straight Up 9m S
Climb the flake crack 1metre right of the arête to a ledge and continue up the buttress to the left to reach the top.

3. Pause and Ponder 15m VS 4c *
The right hand face of Upstream Buttress. The climb starts at the right edge of the wall. Climb the right side of the arête for 3 metres when a delicate traverse can be made across the face to the left edge. Move up on small holds until a good hold on the edge is reached. Continue straight up then trend right to the top on good holds. A good route in an excellent position.

4. The Poacher 11m E1 5b
An artificial but technically interesting route up the centre of the upstream wall of the crag. Start up the wall about 1 metre left of the arête of Pause and Ponder. Move up and left to a sloping foothold beneath a small overhang, climb straight up the centre of the traverse on Pause and Ponder and continue direct to the top.

Variation 15m E2 5b
Climb up for 3 metres and traverse left using the footholds of Pause and Ponder as handholds to reach the small roof at the left arête. Make a couple of interesting moves up the arête and finish as for The Poacher or The Butcher.

5. Greenwells Glory 17m E3 5c *
An exposed route that takes the steep face between The Butcher and the right arête of Upstream Buttress to finish by a traverse left above the cave in the upper tier. Start just left of Pause and Ponder and move round immediately onto the overhanging face. Climb steeply to gain two large horizontal ledges then move up left to the cave in the centre of the buttress. Traverse right (as for The Butcher) and climb up for 3 metres to the right end of a large sloping ledge, which runs diagonally upwards above the cave. Traverse across this to the left arête and finish as for The Angler.

6. The Angler 15m E3 5c *
Make awkward moves to gain direct the groove of The Butcher and follow it to the cave in the middle of the buttress. Finish sensationally up the bulging arête on the left of the buttress on good holds.

7. The Butcher 20m E3 5c ***
Takes the obvious groove on the front of Upstream Buttress. Start 4 metres left of the groove. Pull up to a ledge and hand traverse along this to the bottom of the groove. Move up the groove and exit right up to a cave in the middle of the buttress. Move horizontally right then climb the overhanging face left of the arête to finish. The classic of Upstream Buttress.

8. The Little Mermaid 15m E5 6b *
Takes the line of the blunt overhanging arête left of The Butcher groove via a small hanging groove. Start below the hand traverse of The Butcher and climb up steeply towards the groove to reach a crouch position beneath the roof. Move up the groove capped by a small roof on crimps and smears and slap for a jug (crux). Pull over the bulge and continue up the headwall to finish at the same point as the Angler.

9. Dry Fly Corner 12m VS 4c *
The square cut corner on the left hand edge of Upstream Buttress. Climb straight up the corner, using the horizontal cracks radiating from it to finish via tree roots.

Alternative HVS 5a
Climb up the corner for 3 metres and traverse out on the right wall along a crack for 2 metres to below the small recess. Climb up to the recess and finish spectacularly straight up..

10. Humpback 12m E1 5b
Climbs the blunt rib left of Dry Fly Corner. Start 2 metres left of the corner below a short groove. Climb the groove to a ledge, then boldly up the front of the rib to a sloping ledge at the top.

11. Brown Trout 10m S
The groove on the left side of the blunt rib, 3 metres left of Dry Fly Corner. Climb the groove to a sloping ledge followed by a short chimney.

12. Stickleback 10m S
Start from the centre of the upper ledge below the large overhang and go up diagonally to the right, to the rounded nose beneath the overhang. To the right of the nose is a large round block, which can be passed to reach the corner by a strenuous pull round on its top or a hand traverse beneath it. From the sloping ledge in the corner climb the small chimney.

Direct Start S
Climb the corner direct and thence to the sloping ledge.

13. High Board 18m HS ***
A climb of increasing interest and exposure with a fine finish. Start in the left of the recess below the left end of the ledge. Climb onto the left end of the ledge and continue up the corner until it is possible to move left onto the sloping ramp. Move along the ramp, which is forsaken for a hand traverse along the horizontal crack to a sentry box on the front of the buttress. Climb straight up out of the sentry box on good holds, to the top.

Alternative Finish HS
From the sentry box traverse down left onto the ledge on Devil's Wedge. Follow the groove to the top.

14. The Plummet 12m E2 5b
Climb directly up the corner, left of the start of High Board, to the sloping ramp. Pull up into the overhanging breach above, moving up right above the overhang to a small conifer and a vegetated finish. An intimidating pitch.

Graeme Read tackles
6. The Angler (E3 5c)
Photo: Richard Pow

15. A Bigger Splash 14m E5 6b *
Start 2 metres left of The Plummet below the hanging groove in the right side of Wedge Buttress. Pull up into the groove with difficulty (crux), and continue up, crossing High Board up into the overhanging breach of Plummet but exiting left in a sensational position.

16. Devil's Disciple 15m HVS 5b
Climb the overhanging crack to the right of Devil's Wedge and then go up to the ledge in the groove to the left. Ascend the right wall of the groove to finish as for High Board.

17. Devil's Wedge 15m VS 4c *
Start at the right side of Hanging Buttress, in the corner. Climb strenuously straight up the overhanging crack and pull up over the wedged blocks onto the ledge in the groove of the previous route. Ascend the slightly overhanging groove above to finish at a large tree.

18. Wet Fly 15m HVS 5a **
Start at the right side of Hanging Buttress below Devil's Wedge. Pull up on holds in the corner and move out left onto the ledge. The overhanging wall above is climbed directly up to and over the small overhang to a sloping ledge on the left and finish up a short wall to the top. Excellent climbing.

19. Criss Cross 18m MVS 4c
From the corner on the right side of Hanging Buttress follow the first 4 metres of Wet Fly to the ledge. From the ledge traverse back right and pull up over the wedged blocks onto the ledge in the groove. From the groove move out right diagonally upwards to the sentry box on High Board. Climb up out of the sentry box to the top as for High Board. A rather contrived line.

20. Ancient Briton 12m E2 5b ***
The corner topped by an overhang on the left of Hanging Buttress. The ancient inscriptions on the right wall of the corner further identify it. Climb the overhanging base with difficulty and follow the crack to the roof. Move right and surmount the roof by means of the crack. An excellent well-protected route, the start of which is unfortunately becoming harder as the river erodes the bank below.

21. Jack of all Trades 14m E2 5c
Climb Ancient Briton for 5 metres. Traverse horizontally right to the arête and move up to below the roof (junction with the girdle traverse). Pull over the overhang and finish sensationally up the arête.

22. Salmon Leap Variation 10m VS 5a
Start at the groove 5 metres left of Ancient Briton. Climb the groove, crossing the traverse of Salmon Leap and move up right to a sloping ramp to gain a groove above which is followed, moving right to finish.

23. Salmon Leap 15m VS 5a *

Start 2 metres right of a corner groove, below a small but prominent nose. Gain the nose with difficulty (due to bank erosion). From the top of the nose, traverse right to the corner. Go up to a sloping ramp, then traverse out to the right along a horizontal crack, until it is possible to climb straight up to the small chimney at the top.

Alternative Start E2 5c

Climb the arête on the right of Salmon Leap Variation until stopped by the overhang and then move left until the horizontal crack can be gained.

24. Kelt 11m HS 4c

Start at the foot of a corner groove. Climb up right across the steep slab onto the nose of Salmon Leap to gain the groove above, which is followed moving left at the top to a vegetated finish.

25. Sardine Sandwich 10m E1 5b

Start at the foot of the corner groove. Climb the right wall of the corner on small holds until forced right into the top of a groove. Climb up and left to a vegetated finish.

26. Deep Fry 10m HS 4c

Climb the corner groove. Awkward to start.

27. Fish Supper 10m HS 4c

Start at the foot of the corner groove. Climb up in the corner and move onto the left wall and up to a short vertical crack to finish at a tree.

28. Blazin' Aces 10m E1 5b

Start at the foot of the corner groove. Climb the edge of the left wall past a small ledge to the overhang. Move left onto the face and climb a thin vertical crack to finish at a tree.

29. Gibbet 10m E2 5b

Climb the undercut arête immediately right of the steep corner of Hanging Tree.

30. Hanging Tree 10m HVS 5b *

The tree that gave this climb its name has disappeared but a root remains embedded in the crack. Climb the corner direct to the top. The hard start is usually damp but the crack above gives good climbing. The left hand start via the missing tree is now significantly harder (6a)

31. Minnow 10m HS

The left arête of Hanging Tree gives an indistinguished climb.

32. Boreal Edge 6m HVS 5b

The sharp green arête left of the vegetated gully provides an unpleasant climb.

33. Smolt 8m HS

The dark groove topped by a large tree. Move left below the tree to finish. A poor route.

34. Flounder 8m VS 5a

Start 5 metres right of Mouldy Corner at a vertical crack. Climb up a short blunt rib and move left up a steep slab and wall, to finish up the short groove at the top.

35. Shark Attack 9m E2 5c

Start 2 metres right of Mouldy Corner at a vertical crack. Climb the crack and make an awkward move to stand on the ledge below the bulging wall. Overcome the bulge with difficulty moving up and slightly right to finish.

Malcolm Lowerson returns to the scene...
18. Wet Fly (HVS 5a)
Photo: Rick Barnes

36. Mouldy Corner 10m VS 4c
The slightly overhanging, incut corner on the right edge of Downstream Buttress. Climb the corner over a loose block to the small overhang and move up on the left wall on a small foothold, using the crack in the corner, until the top is gained. Alternatively from the overhang make a short, strenuous hand traverse on small holds out onto the left hand wall and pull up.

37. Barracuda Roof 12m E5 6a **
An exposed route in a fine position. Climb the right arête of Downstream Buttress, make a sustained traverse left under the overhang to a crouching position on the arête, pull over and climb the wall above on small widely spaced holds.

38. Breakout 10m E5 6b *
Starts at the central arête of Downstream Buttress. Climb the arête direct or traverse in from the left or right. Move up to good holds, then pull out left and make a long reach to the lip of the overhang above. Hand traverse left along the lip until it is possible to move up and finish up the arête on the left.

39. Spate Wall 7m HVS 5b
A short but technically interesting route up the arête at the extreme left end of the crag. Start in the corner, traverse right to the arête and ascend the wall via a long reach and strenuous pull.

Direct Start HVS 6b
Climb the arête to join the original route.

40. Girdle Traverse 56m HVS 5b
A good route particularly when combined with the extension. It starts at the same point as Pause and Ponder on Upstream Buttress.

1. 24m The first 10 metres of Pause and Ponder onto the edge of the buttress. (A runner can be arranged here to protect the second). Traverse the recessed face to the left edge of the buttress then round it to the corner on Dry Fly on a level with the small recess. The corner on the left is rounded on delicate holds to gain the sloping ledge beneath the small chimney on Stickleback

2. 12m Move round on the top of the large block on Stickleback or hand traverse beneath it. Continue the traverse using the horizontal crack beneath the overhangs in the recess, until the ramp on High Board is reached. Follow High Board to the sentry box.

3. 20m Climb down onto the ledge in the groove on Devil's Wedge. Step onto the left edge of the groove to gain the face of Hanging Buttress and move left on small holds to the corner of Wet Fly. Descend Wet Fly to the level of the large overhang on the left. Swing round the corner to beneath the final overhang of Ancient Briton. Surmount the roof by means of the crack which is climbed to the top.

Extension 26m E2 5c
To avoid rope drag, it is necessary to extend pitch 2 by 6 metres and take a stance and good thread belay on a ledge above the descent on Wet Fly.

3. 20m Follow the original route down Wet Fly and round the arête to the final crack of Ancient Briton. Continue into the overhung corner then move out left on improving holds round on to the slab of Salmon Leap (runner high up to protect second). Continue at the same level and belay in the corner groove of Deep Fry. (A backrope can be arranged to protect the second on this pitch).

4 6m Climb left onto the arête and move round to gain good jams which lead to Hanging Tree near its top, finish up this.

Dave Kirton leading
30. Hanging Tree (HVS 5b)
Photo: Steve Crowe

Steve Nagy powering up
37. Barracuda Roof (E5 6a)
Photo: Richard Pow

Jack Rock Graded List

E5
Breakout 6b *
The Little Mermaid 6b *
A Bigger Splash 6b *
Barracuda Roof 6a **

E3
The Butcher 5c ***
The Angler 5c *
Greenwells Glory 5c *

E2
Extension to Girdle Traverse 5c
Jack of all Trades 5c
Shark Attack 5c
Gibbet 5b
Salmon Leap Alternative Start 5c
Ancient Briton 5b ***
The Poacher Variation 5b
The Plummet 5b

E1
Blazin' Aces 5b
The Poacher 5b
Humpback 5b
Sardine Sandwich 5b

HVS
Devil's Disciple 5b
Hanging Tree 5b *
Spate Wall 5b
Dry Fly Corner Alternative 5a
Wet Fly 5a **
Girdle Traverse 5b
Boreal Edge 5b

VS
Flounder 5a
Devil's Wedge 4c *
Pause and Ponder 4c *
Dry Fly Corner 4c *
Mouldy Corner 4c
Salmon Leap 5a *
Salmon Leap Variation 5a

Kyloe Crag (Collar Heugh)

Martin Waugh

NU 040395
South West Facing
108m
10 minutes

History

The crag was probably climbed on in the early part of the century but there is no record of any lines ascended. Visitors also frequented the area in the late 1940's and early 1950's but the first recorded activity was not until the late fifties when the NMC produced a short guide showing sixteen routes, most of which followed the obvious lines. These were largely the products of Eric Clarke, Gil Lewis and Basil Butcher and included the fine Deception Crack and the awkward Trinity. 1957 was a prime year with Devil's Edge by Geoff Oliver accompanied by Derek Walton and Nev Hannaby, the latter also leading the superb flake crack of Tacitation to create one of the crags classic Very Severes. This brief surge in activity was followed by a long lull which lasted throughout the 1960's and although the crag was visited by the NMC and the Border Climbing Club nothing of worth was recorded. The next routes were done in September 1970 by Allan Austin who regularly visited the area with Dave Roberts. The companion routes of Penitent's Walk and the testing Coldstream Corner typified Austin's ability to tackle the harder lines. Around this time, in early 1971, Dave Ladkin also added the excellent Elevator. Hugh Banner had spied the line but was injured with a bad elbow (perhaps an early case of tendonitis) and urged Ladkin to attempt the route before the dynamic duo of Austin and Roberts had the chance to clean up. With the publication of the 1970 guide interest was spurred and Bob Hutchinson who had already made a big impression, jumped a quantum leap in grades by climbing the extremely testing Australia Crack. This remained unrepeated for two years and not surprisingly at its present E3 6b standing. The 1976 New Climbs Supplement stimulated further activity by John Earl, Paul Stewart, Steve Blake and Bob and Tommy Smith. In 1978 some excellent test pieces were found, notably Blake's technical and strenuous Prime Time and the necky Original Sin, which was done with Bob Smith, so named because of the first known use of chalk on a new route in the county by a local.

In 1980 Bob Smith discovered The Sabbath and Baptism and went on to celebrate the arrival of his son with the difficult First Born, demonstrating his bold approach and an eye for a good line. Also around this time, Earl and Bob Smith shared leads on Hot Spring and Paternoster. Elder Brother was also added, a very bold and determined statement by Tommy Smith and Tim Gallagher on one of Tom's many returns from retirement. Hugh Harris contributed a number of hard routes, culminating in Seventh Day in 1991.

Recent developments have largely been a mopping up process with few completely new lines, the only major advance being Albatross, circa 1995 courtesy of Andrew Earl and Steve Crowe (though the purists may still be looking for the RP to be placed on the lead).

Situation and Character

This superb sandstone crag is located in the north of the region on the flank of the Kyloe Hills. It lies on the northern boundary of Kyloe Wood, about 2 kilometres east of the village of Lowick. Its situation on the side of a small valley with a south westerly aspect and bounded by forest makes it very sheltered and the crags are often in perfect condition on dry winter days. This situation, combined with its beautiful setting, gives pleasant routes as well as some hard technical ones. It consists of a quarried section and a series of isolated buttresses which provide varied climbing in both character and difficulty, offering some of the best routes in the county. Protection is reasonable but as often the case with sandstone, not always trustworthy, even on the easier routes. Particular care should be taken after wet weather when the rock is much weaker.

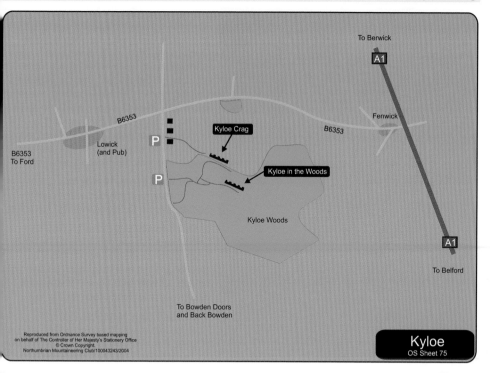

Approaches and Access

The crag is easily reached from the A1 trunk road 5 miles north of Belford. Turn west and follow the B6353 for 2 miles towards Lowick. At the crossroads turn due south, continue for half a mile and park beyond a large farm on the left. The approach to the crag is by a farm track, often very muddy in wet weather, which leaves the road at this point. Follow the track until it branches. Take the right fork through a gated field. A well worn path winds up through bracken to the crag. The distance is about 800 metres and takes ten minutes. Please take care not to harm relations with the local farmer which are very cordial at the time of writing. Electric fences should not be climbed and there is no need to deviate from the described approach. Take care when parking not to block the entrance to fields. The approach paths are showing considerable wear and tear and the crag itself is beginning to suffer from erosion, though less marked than Bowden Doors. At least it seems to be spared excessive attention from the dreaded abseiling groups and their mucky boots. Please consider the environment so that others may enjoy it and take your litter home.

The Climbs

The first buttress to be reached after walking uphill on the path is Saints Wall. The quarry routes are described from right to left and are found by turning left at Saint's Wall. The rest of the crag has names allocated to the buttresses and the climbs are described from left to right beginning at Saint's Wall and ending at Twin Cracks Buttress.

The Quarry

Reached by turning left at Saint's Wall on the approach and following a path over a slight rise next to a disintegrating boundary fence into the quarry. The climbs are described from right to left.

Steve Brewis going
3. Back to the Egg (E2 5c)
Photo: Andy Birtwistle

1. Fat Slags 15m E2 5c
Rarely in condition but worth catching!! The first section features as a good boulder problem sticking strictly to the crack, head north earlier to keep at the grade. Start 3m right of Prickly Corner at the leftward slanting crack. Climb the crack to the break and mantelshelf to a good hold and up to a sloping ledge. Climb the overhang on the right to another break, then traverse left around the corner and finish on rounded holds. A pleasant and varied outing.

2. Prickly Corner 10m S 5a
The large corner adorned with gorse bushes is hard to start and prickly to finish.

3. Back to the Egg 11m E2 5c
Climb the arête and move right to a small ledge beneath the overhang. Move up steeply and make a long reach up and right for a good hold. Pull up and bridge right, making another long reach for the top.

4. Devils Edge 10m HVS 5a **
An excellent route. The impending arête is climbed first on the right to half height then on the left wall to finish. Other variations have been climbed on this arete starting on the left or finishing on the right.

5. The Faggot 10m E2 6a
The wall left of Devil's Edge. From the diagonal crack on the left swing across right to the break and climb the centre of the wall to the top.

6. Peewit 10m S
Climbs a left facing crack on the right wall into the corner, then the crack in the right wall to the top.

7. Birds Nest Corner 10m VD
The crack in the corner goes direct.

8. Chicken Run 16m E1 5b
A traverse along the obvious horizontal break from Bird's Nest Corner to Prickly Corner. Traverse to the arête, move round and hand traverse on good holds to the corner. The dirty wall that follows is optional.

9. Dogleg 15m E1 5b
Climb the slab, via the flake just left of the corner, with one awkward move at mid height.

10. Canine Wall 15m D
A slab and series of mantelshelves to the left are taken direct.

11. New Recruit 6m E2 5c
A one move wonder of a climb up the centre of the wall above the slabs. Climb the wall right of the two gorse bushes to the horizontal break. A mantelshelf leads to a finish through a gap in the bushes. No gear and an ankle bender landing.

12. Incisor 8m S
Start right of the arête. Climb on sloping holds to easy rock.

13. Active Service 8m HVS 5b
Take the left arête which leads awkwardly to easy slabs.

14. Baptism 16m E2 5c *
The obvious traverse across the main quarry face from right to left. Start at the arête. Climb this to the break and finger traverse to a rest on Original Sin. Continue to finish at Fence Post Corner.

15. Tsar Bomba 15m E5 6c
Climb the arete of Active Service and follow the traverse of Baptism for 3 metres before making hard moves up to a curving crack, then finish direct.

16. Original Sin 11m E4 6a ***
A fine and difficult climb that takes the central weakness in the large quarry wall. Start slightly right of the flake and move up to its top. Move awkwardly left and mantelshelf into the scoop with difficulty. Continue up and right on good but well spaced holds.

17. The Sabbath 16m E4 6a **
A good and sustained route. Start 3 metres left of Original Sin. Climb the quarried wall to the break, traverse right and climb the crux of Original Sin to the obvious high traverse line which is followed rightwards to finish.

18. The Seventh Day 11m E5 6c *
Start as for The Sabbath to the first break. Make an awkward move straight up to gain an obvious hold. The crux is to manage to stand up on this hold and hence reach the next break without testing the, by this time, distant gear. Finish more easily on suspect rock.

19. Fencepost Corner 13m VD
The left corner. Ascend the crack direct finishing through gorse bushes.

In the back of the quarry to the left is a large area of generally scrappy rock. Various lines have been climbed but are not recommended.

Saint's Wall

This is the first buttress to be reached after walking uphill on the path. It consists of a fine slab with a deep cut chimney, Temptation, near the centre.

The first routes begin at the base of a crack 6 metres left of Temptation. Some short problems on the wall left of this have been climbed.

20. Parity 12m HS 4c *
Climb the first step of the crack as for Trinity, move left for 2 metres and ascend the short groove and mantelshelf to a large ledge. The slanting crack in the wall above is climbed, followed by an awkward move to the top.

21. Trinity 12m VS 4c **
A Kyloe classic. Climb the crack direct in three steps, each harder than the previous one. The final bulge is overcome by a layback which all too often spits out aspiring leaders.

22. Waverly Wafer 14m E2 5c
An eliminate which tackles the centre of the wall between Trinity and the chimney. Climb to the first break by the slab or the crack, then take the flake crack to the second break. Move right along this and finish with difficulty up the arête.

Variation Finish VS 4c
More logically but much easier, finish up the chimney. This reduces the grade to VS 4c.

23. Temptation 10m M
The deep chimney is a traditional beginner's route. Climb it to the top on the inside or by bridging.

24. Threadbare 11m HVS 5a
Climbs the wall immediately right of the chimney passing a drilled hole to a large break, finish straight up to a rounded mantelshelf.

25. Pink Socks on Top 11m E1 5b
Start 1metre Right of Temptation, below the cave. Gain the cave direct. Exit the cave by layaways on the left to gain a standing position below the heathery break. Mantelshelf the break making a long reach up the wall above to a good hold (crux). Finish directly up the wall above.

26. Saint's Progress 14m S 4b
Starts immediately right of the chimney. Climb to the obvious traverse line and follow it to the foot of the green groove. Ascend this to the ledge at two thirds height and follow this leftwards to finish up a flake crack.

27. Holy Mother of Inspiration (Don't Fail Me Now) 12m E2 6a

Start as for Saint's Progress. Using the pothole, gain the second break, 2 metres right of the cave. Climb very delicately up the steep slab above (crux), trending slightly left and onto the big ledge. Climb the upper wall direct, just right of the upper crack of Saint's Progress. Protecting the crux is only feasible with side runners, which are likely to be of psychological benefit only.

28. St. Ivel 12m VS 4c **

An excellent climb. Begin just to the left of the undercut section and follow the green stain and groove of Saint's Progress to the ledge, then the wall immediately above direct.

29. Litany 12m MVS 5a *

Quite a good climb with an interesting finish. Begin where the buttress is undercut. Make awkward moves up and rightwards to the large ledge, then climb the left crack in the overhang to finish on good holds.

30. Saint's Arête 14m HVS 5b

Interesting climbing with the start now more difficult as the concrete shelter from which it started has disintegrated. Gain the arête with difficulty and follow it to the break. Finish up the corner crack above.

31. Bede 7m E2 6a

The right side of the arête is climbed to a pothole, then the slab to finish. The grade assumes a crash mat on the grotty landing, otherwise give yourself E3.

A poor route has been climbed up the right wall to twin cracks, then moving over the roof on the right.

The crag now fades into the hillside and a track runs along past a small buttress to the impressive Overhanging Buttress 90 metres to the right.

Neil Baxter
21. Trinity (VS 4c)
Photo: Mark Savage

Overhanging Buttress

The large rounded buttress with a double overhang and split at mid height by a large sloping shelf. The upper tier, can itself be girdled at Very Severe. The first pitches of Coldstream Corner and Penitents Walk have been exchanged to produce more logical lines.

32. Just Passing 15m MVS 5a

The left arête of Overhanging Buttress. Tricky moves to reach the break. Good biceps and bendy legs assist in getting past it onto the undercut wall above, to the left of the arête. Climb directly up to finish.

33. Easy Traverse 10m D

The obvious traverse on pocket holds starting on the left of the crag and finishing at the ledge.

34. Cloister Wall 23m HS 4c **

A good route, the easiest way up the buttress. Start 2 metres right of the traverse. Climb the steep wall immediately left of the overhang and continue to the break. Move left to the end of the ledge and climb up past horizontal breaks to finish up a rightward slanting groove.

35. Lost Property 18m HVS 5a *

A direct line which climbs the buttress at a reasonable standard. Begin about 3 metres left of the obvious crack (Birdlime Crack) and climb the overhang on flakes and the wall above to the ledge. Move onto the upper wall and continue to the top using horizontal breaks, taking care when passing some doubtful blocks in the lower break.

36. Hot Spring 18m E3 6a 6a *

Starts just left of Birdlime Crack under the overhangs.
1. Surmount the roof to good holds at the base of flutes which are climbed with difficulty.
2. From the ledge, climb the blunt rib 2 metres left of the rock ladder on widely spaced holds to the break. Pull out right over the roof and straight up to finish.

37. Birdlime Crack 8m MS *

The obvious crack in the lower tier provides a good climb to the ledge.

38. The Elevator 10m HVS 5a **
A very good climb which takes the top tier. Start from the half way ledge, 2 metres left of Coldstream Corner. Intimidating and bold but easier than it looks. Climb the obvious rock ladder and traverse left to a resting place. Move up the groove above on improving holds to reach the top.

Direct Finish E3 6a
From the top of the rock ladder continue straight over the bulge. At the top of its grade.

39. Irresistible Compulsion 10m E3 5c
Starts right of Elevator below the obvious shelves left of Coldstream Corner. Climb the two shelves and the wall above, resisting the urge to use Coldstream Corner.

40. Coldstream Corner 18m HVS 5a 5a ***
A magnificent top pitch, strenuous but well protected, makes this route a classic of the crag. Start just right of Birdlime Crack.
1. Move up trending right to a short crack which leads to the ledge. Belay at the bottom of the corner.
2. Climb the superb impending wall and crack into the corner and finish up this.

41. Albatross 8m E6 6c
The wide roof right of the second pitch of Coldstream Corner. (Pre-placed RP on lip of roof). A massive wingspan and unfeasibly large testicles are likely to be of benefit here.

42. Penitent's Walk 20m HVS 4c 5a *
Good climbing with an unusual move on the second pitch.
1. Climb the crack 5 metres right of Birdlime Crack moving right to the ledge. Belay on the shelf right of the corner.
2. Climb the bulging wall, using a hand jam in the horizontal crack, to reach a good hold on the lip of the overhang. Pull onto the slab and finish leftwards up the rising shelf.

43. Paternoster 18m E3 6a 6b
1. The blunt nose right of Penitent's Walk is gained from the left or right and followed to the ledge.
2. Continue over the roof just left of Penitent's Walk to finish on the rising shelf.

44. Oxter Wall 13m E1 5b 5b
A route for connoisseurs of mantelshelves.
1. Climb the scoop in the overhang at the right end of the lower tier to a rounded awkward mantelshelf onto the ledge.
2. Move up then tackle the second overhang on large holds, move right and finish by another teetery mantelshelf.

The quality of the rock on the **Short Wall** set back between Overhanging Buttress and Neb Buttress is not as good but one climb is still worthwhile. Every part of this buttress has been climbed on in years gone by and there is no room for more routes!

45. Cheviot Charlie 8m E1 5b
Climb the wall and crack at the left hand end. An interesting series of moves. Worthwhile.

46. Giblets 6m E1 5b
A real leftover. The middle crack is climbed with difficulty.

47. Dirty Bum 6m VS 5a
The right hand crack should be cleaned.

48. Pellagra 6m E2 5c
The wall right of Dirty Bum is climbed past a horizontal break, thin and reachy to the top.

Neb Buttress
A buttress that is rapidly becoming dwarfed by an adjacent conifer. It consists of a broken nose with a wall to its left.

49. Burns Offering 10m M
Start 3 metres left of the left arête and climb a wall for 5 metres to a ledge. Walk left and finish up a narrow chimney or, alternatively, climb the wall about 3 metres along the ledge.

50. Upstarts Downfall 18m VD
Begin directly beneath the left arête. Climb the short groove awkwardly to a ledge then traverse left for 3 metres, move up to another ledge then climb the wall above.

51. Hoglet 10m VD
Climb up the preceding route to the ledge and finish up the wall just left of the arête.

52. Conifer Direct 11m S 4b
Start at the base of the tree. Climb the crack and bridge the overhung corner. Finish up the overhang between two gorse bushes. At the present rate of growth, it will not be long before the route realises its name.

53. Ramp and Wall 10m S
Climb the ramp and wall right of Conifer Direct.

54. Double Decker 10m E1 5b
The double overhang on the right side of the buttress is climbed with interest.
A vegetated recess separates the next buttress.

Fir Tree Buttress
This buttress is in two tiers and is again masked by a large fir tree. Two worthwhile routes have been recorded and other variations are possible.

55. Fawlty Towers 11m VS 4c
Good climbing with a hard start. The top section, like Sybil, appears much more intimidating than it is. Take the left wall of the arête and continue to a ledge, then follow the crest of the upper tier in a fine position to the top.

56. Diminuendo 13m S 4b
The crack in the lower buttress is climbed through pine branches to the gorse covered break. A head torch is optional. The upper tier is taken on the left.

Central Wall
This section contains some of the best climbing on the crag. It consists of a steep wall with some fine and obvious lines and a small overhang which provides some of the most difficult routes at Kyloe.

57. Headbanger 6m E1 5c
The slightly undercut wall provides an awkward problem. Climb it on small rounded holds moving slightly left after 2 metres. Climb straight up after the break.

58. The Pincer 8m HVS 5b *
A good route. Start 2 metres right of Headbanger and climb the wall on undercuts leading right, then straight up to a good hold. Climb to the top of the crag.

Direct Finish E1 5c
Climb direct from the first pinch.

59. Oral Spout 8m E2 6a
The wall right of The Pincer is climbed on very sharp fingerholds.

60. Flake Crack 11m S 4b **
A classic of the grade. Starts 3 metres right of The Pincer. Climb the steep crack to an obvious ledge and follow the crack above to the top. An excellent climb.

61. Wasted Time 11m E1 5b *
Something of a misnomer. It is, in fact, a good route; with thin climbing up the wall between Flake Crack and Tacitation. Start 1 metre left of Tacitation and climb up to the leftward trending flake. Follow this to the overhang, moving left and over on thin holds to a good flake and continue to the top.

Direct Finish E2 5c
From the top of the flake finish direct.

62. Tacitation 11m VS 5a ***
A brilliant route directly up the flake crack. Gain the crack by a gymnastic move and climb it to the top on layaways. Superb climbing. An alternative finish is available by moving right after 6 metres to climb a black groove.

63. Prime Time 11m E4 6b *
An extremely technical problem. The overhanging wall at the base of the buttress is negotiated using pinches and incuts and the wall above is gained precariously, then followed boldly to the top via the nubbin on the right edge.

64. Australia Crack 13m E3 6b ***
The county's first 6b and a breakthrough in Northumberland climbing. So named because you spend most time upside down. This fine and difficult route starts at a prominent undercut pod and crack. Enter the overhanging pod with difficulty and climb until it is possible to gain the crack. Make some final punishing moves and finish up the slab above.

65. Oversight 10m HS 4b *
The corner groove right of Australia Crack.

66. Cataclysm 13m E6 7a
Climb Oversight to the obvious pocket, then make some desperate moves left and up across the wall, to finish above Australia Crack.

67. Holly Tree Arête 10m S
Of greatest interest to those of arboreal inclination, possibly best avoided if you can't see the wood for the tree! Start at the foot of the groove just right of Oversight. Climb the groove to the tree, step off this onto the right arête and climb direct to the top.

68. The Glade 10m MVS 4c
A good route which takes the hanging slab split by a crack near the back of the recess. Climb to the overhang, pull onto the slab and finish up the crack above.

A large oak grows from the back of the recess and to the right of this is a wall which sports a number of short climbs. Take your pick.

69. Eeny 8m VD
Take the left corner to the overhang, step left and finish straight up.

70. Meeny 8m VD
The crack 2 metres right of the corner is climbed direct.

71. Miny 8m S
Climb the centre of the wall by the flakes and the crack.

72. Mo 8m S
Climb the right hand side of the wall by the flakes and the groove.

The crag now opens out again to a slab bounded by a rib on the left and a large overhang above, this is Space Buttress. The next climb begins at the base of the rib.

Richard Duffy
63. Prime Time (E4 6b)
Photo: Darren Stevenson

Space Buttress

73. Christmas Tree Arête 13m D **
Climb the crack or nose and rib to a stance beneath the overhangs. Move left to avoid the bulge and up to a large Christmas tree.
Direct Finish VS 4c
Continue straight up the overhanging crack. Easier than it looks.

74. Gargarin's Groove 13m HVS 5a *
An interesting climb which takes the hanging groove at the left end of the overhang. Start at the crack of the previous route and climb the left end of the slab, moving up through the first overhang to a small slab. Climb the groove using a flexing flake with care.

75. Elder Brother 13m E4 6b **
A bold and powerful route that climbs the overhang at its left end. Climb the previous route and from the horizontal crack under the overhang move up the blunt arête to a rest and friend placement in a hanging flake. From this, move up the wall above to a necky finish.
Direct start 6m E3 6b
The steep slab to the right of Gragarin's Groove is climbed direct above a bad landing without using the left hand crack.

76. An Anniversary Waltz 20m E5 6b *
Start as for Elder Brother. Traverse under the lip using the First Born friend placement as an undercut. Continue as for First Born over the roof but then continue rightwards to finish up Space Walk.

77. First Born 10m E4 6b ***
A tremendous route over the centre of the overhang. Start at the right hand end and move diagonally left via horizontal cracks to the bottomless corner beneath the roof (friend on the left). Using the undercut pull over the roof to a large pothole and move up and left on flutings to finish.
An eliminate has been climbed through the roof right of First Born.

78. Spacewalk 11m E2 5c *
An airy excursion. Start up the slab and groove directly beneath the overhanging arête. Climb to a large spike high on the gully wall. Step down and move delicately across to reach the arête. Move round and continue on good holds to the top. The arête was originally gained lower down and this way it is at least a grade harder, as is the direct finish up the wall right of the arête.

A descent gully separates the next buttress.

Tony Lickes leading
Coldstream Corner (HVS 5a)
Photo: Mark Savage

Deception Buttress

The first climbs start up the easy descent gully.

79. Spirit on Mars 7m MVS 4c

Pleasant going but poorly protected climbing up the arête 1.5 metres left of West Wall Groove.

80. West Wall Groove 8m VS 5a

The groove and wall two thirds of the way up the gully.

81. West Wall 9m HVS 5a

The thin crack 2 metres lower down and the wall above.

82. Deception Wall 10m HS 4c *

A steep and interesting climb. Start 3 metres left of the prominent 'V' groove beneath an undercut wall. Climb this on good holds.

83. Deceiver 10m HVS 5b

Climb the wall between Deception Wall and Deception Crack on friable flakes with larger holds to finish.

84. Deception Crack 10m HS 4b ***

An excellent climb, justifiably popular. The prominent 'V' groove is climbed on good holds and jams.

85. Wilfred Prickles 10m VS 5a **

A fine, steep route which takes the flaky wall right of Deception Crack. Start below the centre of the wall and climb it on flakes to the horizontal break. Finish direct on surprisingly large holds. Unfortunately the large gorse bush which gave the climb its name has been vandalised.

86. Fakir's Crack 10m VD

Climb the crack at the right end of the wall.

87. Fakir's Groove 10m VD

Climb the deep groove right of Fakir's Crack.

88. Fakir's Slab 10m VD

The slabby arête is taken direct.

Nev Hannaby
94. Chris's Arete (HS 4b)
Photo: Nev Hannaby Collection

89. Slab and Groove 13m VS 5a *
Balance up the left edge of the slab and finish up the corner groove left of the crack.

Alternative Finish E1 5c
Takes the top wall above the slab, after traversing right between the crack of Slab and Wall and the right arête.

90. Slab and Wall 13m VS 4c **
Interesting and varied climbing. Climb the right side of the slab by delicate moves to a ledge then take the steep crack in the wall above.

91. Slab and Arête 10m E1 5b
Start as for Slab and Wall. Climb the slab to gain the right hand end of the wall above. Climb the arête, passing a narrow vertical crack.

92. The Adder 30m HS 4c
A left to right traverse of the buttress. Start just right of West Wall climb. Gain the horizontal crack and traverse right to Deception Crack. Continue across Wilfred Prickles to a recess. Traverse right again, on a line beneath a large slab and wall, to a short chimney. Move up this, step right then easily to the top.

The crag now breaks down again before the fina buttress.

Twin Cracks Buttress
The final buttress with a prominent arete.

93. John's Wall 15m S 4b
Start in the small recess at the left end and from the highest block step onto the wall. Go directly up and exit just right of a small overhang or alternatively, move left at the break and climb past flakes to finish between two prows.

94. Chris's Arête 11m HS 4b *
Good climbing, the arête is taken finishing slightly left. It can be finished direct at HVS 5b.

95. Twin Cracks 11m S 4b
The cracked front of the buttress may be climbec as a single route or the cracks can be ascended separately.

The short wall at the right end can be climbed or small holds to a ledge on the right at 5b. A direct finish is possible.

Kyloe Crag Graded List

E6

Albatross 6c
Cataclysm 7a

E5

The Seventh Day 6c *
An Anniversary Waltz 6b *
Tsar Bomba 6c

E4

Elder Brother 6b **
First Born 6b ***
The Sabbath 6a **
Prime Time 6b *
Original Sin 6a ***

E3

Australia Crack 6b ***
The Elevator Direct Finish 6a
Hot Spring 6a *
Paternoster 6b
Friday the Thirteenth 6b
Irresistible Compulsion 5c

E2

Bede 6a
Oral Spout 6a
The Faggot 6a
Wasted Time Direct Finish 5c
Back to the Egg 5c
New Recruit 5c
Baptism 5c *
Giblets 5c
Waverly Wafer 5c
Holy Mother of Inspiration 6a
Fat Slags 5c
Spacewalk 5c *
Pellagra 5c

E1

Wasted Time 5b *
Double Decker 5b
Headbanger 5c
Slab and Arête 5b
Chicken Run 5b
Cheviot Charlie 5b
Oxter Wall 5b
Dogleg 5b
Pink Socks on Top 5b
Giblets 5b

HVS

Coldstream Corner 5a ***
Lost Property 5a *
Devil's Edge 5a **
The Elevator 5a **
The Pincer 5b *
Deceiver 5b
Active Service 5b
Threadbare 5a
Saint's Arête 5b
Gargarin's Groove 5a *
Penitent's Walk 5a *
West Wall 5a

VS

Slab and Groove 5a *
Wilfred Prickles 5a **
Tacitation 5a ***
Trinity 4c **
St Ivel 4c **
West Wall Groove 5a
Dirty Bum 5a
Slab and Wall 4c **
Fawlty Towers 4c
Christmas Tree Arête Direct Finish 4c

Kyloe in the Woods (Dues Heugh)

NU 045388
South West Facing
154m
15 minutes

Alec Burns

History

Hidden deep in a forest Kyloe-in-the-Wood was only discovered in the sixties, the earliest recorded route being Zed Climb by Frank Montgomery in 1966. Three years later, in January, the very good lines of Fluted Crack and Crack of Gloom were climbed by Allan Austin with Dave Miller and Dave Roberts respectively. When the 1971 guide was published, however, forty routes were recorded - the efforts of Hugh Banner, John Earl, John Hiron, Geoff Jackson, Dennis Lee, Malcolm Lowerson, Ken Mcdonald and Jim Patchett. Notable routes climbed during this period were The Elf, The Harp, Thin Hand Special (since mistakenly called Thin Finger Special) and The Crucifix, the latter two routes by Hugh Banner showing local climbers the niceties of jamming technique. Dennis Lee was responsible for writing up and renaming many of the climbs. The 1976 supplement recorded a number of less significant new climbs although Bob Hutchinson and John Earl had added Badfinger, the first of the overhanging fingery routes. Following the 1976 supplement routes fell thick and fast. The Pearler, Entertainer and Red Rum fell to Hutchinson and Earl (Earl leading the first one) while Paul Stewart fell in with Bad Company, later given an independent finish by Earl and Steve Blake bouldered out Elf Direct. Scottish invader, Dave 'Cubby' Cuthbertson raised bouldering standards with the free ascent of Monty Python's Flying Circus, although introducing chalk for the first time on a new route in the county. In 1978 Hutchinson and Earl invited all to High T, a very fine addition to the crag. In the build up to the 1979 guide, Paul Stewart climbed Trouble Shooter whilst Steve Blake claimed the first ascent of Hitchhiker's Guide to the Galaxy. The fine Bobby Dazzler wall was initially developed by Bob Hutchinson and John Earl and completed by Paul Stewart and Bob Smith. It was 1981 before any further routes of significance were added with John Earl digging out Bad News, Bob Smith on the hard stuff with Hard Liquor and Smith, Earl and Ian Kyle completing Jocks and Geordies, the initial crack having been climbed by Dave Cuthbertson and Murray Hamilton. The crag lay fallow until late 1986 when Tim Gallagher terrified himself with a fine lead of High Society - an often eyed line. Bob Smith swiftly responded with the Upper Crust, another fine addition to the High T Wall.

Since the last edition of the guide not a lot has been done. At the beginning of the 90's there was some filling in by the locals. The crag has been used mostly for bouldering since then. Few people ever finish at the top of the crag. Leviathan by Malcolm Smith is a route, but a boulder problem, never getting more that 1½ m above the ground until it's finish, even then you can jump off. However, it is included here as it requires an amount of effort matched by only the hardest bolt routes. Arch Rivals was climbed in 2001 by Andrew Earl. That too was basically a boulder problem, but unfortunately you have to finish at the top of the crag, as jumping off would be painful. In 2003 Andrew Earl climbed one of the last great problems of the County with his ascent of The Prow which is very hard and very bold. Darren Stevenson stepped up in a vain attempt to put this guide out of date by climbing the very thin Feanor up the centre of the High Tea headwall during a dry spell in the damp summer of 2004. There is still scope here for new routes, but they will also be very hard and bold.

Situation and Character

This fine crag is hidden away in the centre of the woods and the steep, solid sandstone provides many splendid and enticing lines. The very flora which gives the crag its unique atmosphere, however, does encroach on the finishes of many of the climbs and some cleaning prior to an ascent may be necessary, or even recommended. This is a situation that is getting worse as more people just come here to boulder nowadays. The wooded atmosphere certainly does not detract from the climbing which is usually very technical and can vary from delicate to strenuous. At the time of going to print there has been considerable felling in the vicinity of the crag. This should improve the air circulation around the crag and hopefully improve the condition of the finishes of many of the routes.

Approaches and Access

The crag is reached easily from the A1, 5 miles north of Belford. Turn west and follow the B6353 for 2 miles towards Lowick. At the crossroads turn due south and continue past the parking for Kyloe Crag for half a mile where a gated forest road leads into the woods. Cars must be left on the main road. Care should be taken not to obstruct the gate. Follow the forest road for about 500 metres to a junction with a red 'WS' sign pointing left. Pass to the right of the sign and follow the track straight on at this point for 300 metres turning right at a vague crossroads with a 'WS 1' sign pointing left. The rocks soon appear to the left of the track (about 15 minutes). The woods are privately owned and there is no right of way. See the approach map on page 173.

Trees in the Woods
Photo: Steve Crowe

The Climbs

The routes are described from left to right. The first section to be reached is an undercut slab with an overhang at the left side. Beneath the overhang is a short, green slab.

1. Crickhollow Corner D 9m
Climb the green slab beneath the overhang to a ledge. Move left round the corner to finish up either the slab on the left or the short crack.

2. The Balrog 9m MVS 4c
Climb the overhang at the right end of Crickhollow Corner and pull awkwardly round onto the slab. Continue up the left edge to the top.

3. The Dainty Stair 9m D
Gain the undercut slab at the right hand end and make a rising leftwards traverse, to finish as for The Balrog.

4. Treebeard 9m VD
Start as for the previous route but climb directly up the slab via the flutings.

5. Bombadil Slab 9m VD
Climb the right edge of the mossy slab containing Treebeard.

6. The Shire 9m E2 5c
Climb the left wall of Green Cleft using two horizontals to gain the obvious break, step left and climb the arête to finish.

7. The Green Cleft 9m VD
The deep-cut groove on the right of the slab is more difficult than first appearance would suggest.

The once gardened buttress to the right of The Green Cleft has four routes but recent growth has rendered access difficult and the climbs overgrown. Briefly, they are :-

8. Squelchy Wall 9m MVS 4b
The mossy wall and slab.

9. Impromptu 9m VS 5a
The overhanging front of the buttress via a thin crack and flake.

10. Carpet Crack 9m S
The crack to the right of Impromptu.

11. Lichen Groove 8m S
The V groove high up to the right of the previous route.

After a vegetated section is another once gardened slab, which contains the next two routes.

12. Crumbly Crack 8m S
The left groove is climbed starting at a small tree.

13. Mardale 8m VD
The right hand groove with a tree at the top.

3 metres left of the edge of the next buttress lies the next route.

14. Rivendell Crack 9m VS 5a *
The obvious crack in the upper half of the wall. Pull up the bottom wall to some ledges below and to the left of the crack. An awkward move over the slight bulge leads to the crack which is followed to the top. A good climb.

15. Mordor Front 9m HVS 5a
3 metres right of Rivendell Crack. Climb the front of the buttress direct; undercut at the start.

16. Shelob 9m HVS 5b
Climb the wall 4 metres left of Evendim Corner, via the obvious potholes which run left to right.

17. Tea Break 9m HVS 5b
The hanging crack/groove to the right of Shelob finishing up slabs. Bridging on the arête behind is basically cheating, reducing the grade to 5a.

18. Evendim Corner 9m D
The deep corner to the right of the last climb. A short crack leads into a chimney about 3 metres up. Climb the chimney near the back.

19. Aragorn 9m HS 4c
The steep broken wall 1 metre to the right of the corner is split by a crack. The climb follows this line.

20. Time for Tea 9m HS 4b
Climb the arête to the right of Aragorn to a large ledge. Continue straight up to the right of that route.

21. Frodo 9m HS 4c
2 metres to the right, a second crack follows the line of a shallow groove with a bulge at half height.

22. Legolas 9m MVS 4c
To the right again a third crack twists up the wall.

23. The Black Rider 10m MVS 4c
Right of Legolas the wall bulges forming an undercut black slab. The bulge is surmounted on the right followed by a leftwards traverse out onto the slab, finishing just right of Legolas.

24. The Hobbit 9m VD
The awkward slanting corner and wide crack gives an unusual problem.

25. Bilbo 8m S 4b
Climb the wall between The Hobbit and the easy way down to a ledge and thence by a crack high up.

Round to the right is a dirty cleft which provides the only way down in the centre of the crag.

Steve Crowe on the popular
28. Swan Wall Direct (E1 5c)
Photo: Karin Magog

26. Little Arête 6m D
The rib left of the way down gives a short climb.

27. Swan Wall Arête 6m E2 5c
The arête right of the way down.

28. Swan Wall 6m MVS 4c
To the right of the way down is a pair of cracks. Jam the left crack until it becomes extinct at half height. Traverse out left and up the rib to the top.

Direct Start 6m E1 5c *
Climb straight up the wall 1 metre left of the ordinary start to join the middle of the traverse.

Alternative Finish VS 5a
From the top of the crack, climb the bulges mainly on good holds.

29. Ostrich Crack 10m VD
The right hand crack is climbed direct. No good will come of burying one's head in the crack when the final bulge is reached.

30. Marmoset 10m MVS 4c
3 metres to the right, the wall is climbed with the aid of a flake. This leads to some flutings and a final scoop.

31. Pink Gin 12m E2 6a *
Climb 1 metre left of Red Rum to gain the prominent flake. Traverse horizontally right to Elf Direct. Finish up this.

32. Red Rum 12m E2 6a ***
Start at the groove 2 metres right of Marmoset and climb up slightly left to gain a prominent flake. Make a long reach up to a good hold then left into a mossy scoop to finish.

Alternative Finish 12m E2 6a
Instead of moving left from the good hold, traverse right to The Elf finishing up this. Slightly easier than the original.

33. The Elf Direct 10m E1 5c *
The wall 3 metres left of the ordinary start can be climbed, with long reaches, joining The Elf at the end of the overhang.

34. The Elf 12m VS 5a *
Ascends the left side of the recess. Climb the centre of the left wall until it is possible to move out left to the arête. Climb up to the overhang near the left end and move left round the end of the roof to splendid finishing holds.

35. Bad News 9m E3 6a
Climb the left hand crack of the recess until it is possible to hand traverse right beneath the roof, which is climbed at the obvious weakness with a long reach to gain a shallow scoop.

36. Right Hand Recess Crack 9m VD *
Climb straight up the crack in the right corner. A move right at the top enables fine holds to be reached for the move onto the finishing platform.

37. The Twitch 7m HS 4c
The right hand wall can be climbed at the edge. Getting started is the problem.

The wall right of the recess overhangs steeply.

38. Badfinger 9m E2 5c **
Climb directly up the bulging wall 1 metre right of the arête; the lower section is the most difficult.

39. Bad Company 9m E2 5c **
Gain and climb the bottomless flake 1 metre right of Badfinger. From the top of the flake move slightly left and then straight up the wall to finish.

Direct Finish 9m E3 5c
From the top of the flake move slightly right then up the wall and trend right to finish by means of a tree root (but which one?).

Sadie Renwick soloing
32. Red Rum (E2 6a)
Photo: Dave Cuthbertson/Cubby Images

Right Hand Finish 10m E4 6a
From the top of the flake traverse right for 2 metres along the fault to a good hold. Move over the bulge and up the wall with difficulty.

40. Sex and Brutality 11m E4 6a
From the Right Hand Finish of Bad Company, continue along the obvious line; strike diagonally right to a good hold (short flute) to finish on rounded holds.

41. Monty Python's Flying Circus 10m VS 6a ***
In the centre of the wall is a small niche, with a crack slanting up to it from the right. Gain the niche with difficulty and follow the crack above on good holds. If the niche is gained traditionally by means of a shoulder, the standard of the route is reduced to 4b.

42. Crack of Gloom 10m MVS 4c ***
The obvious overhanging corner crack.

43. The Pearler 13m E3 5c
3 metres right of Crack of Gloom is a crack which runs halfway up the wall. Climb this to its top and move up the overhanging wall above until it is possible to move left to the arête, which is followed to the top.

44. Woodlark 17m E2 5b **
Climb the crack of The Pearler to where it peters out, then traverse strenuously right along the obvious line to Thin Hand Special. Continue rightwards beneath the overhang onto The Rack. Finish directly up the slab above.

Alternative Start One Third E2 6a
From Crack of Gloom traverse the horizontal fault at one third height to the Pearler.

Alternative Start Two Thirds E2 6a
From Crack of Gloom traverse the horizontal fault at two thirds height to the Pearler.

45. Jocks and Geordies 10m E3 6b **
The short crack 2 metres left of Thin Hand Special is climbed to the break and then up the wall to a diagonal crack slanting up left. A hybric route.

The Yorkshireman, a short hard crack immediately to the right provides a dynamic boulder problem at 6c.

46. Thin Hand Special 10m E1 5c ***
8 metres right of Crack of Gloom a thin crack splits the bulging wall. A good test of jamming proficiency. Often mistakenly called Thin Finger Special.

47. Hitchhiker's Guide to the Galaxy 9m 6c **
The flake in the middle of the wall to the right of Thin Hand Special is gained and then climbed with some difficulty.

The next feature is a pair of short cracks slantin to the left, above which the crag lies back forming a slab and groove.

48. The Rack 13m HS 4c
Start in the overhung corner and using the uppe crack, gain the ledge above. Follow the broken groove to the top. Some stretching moves.

Alternative Start VS 5b
The lower of the two cracks may also be climbed to the platform.

49. Playing Rudies 5m 6c
The small bulging wall right of The Rack with some naughty moves.

50. The Slide 13m VD
A diagonal line up the slab to the left of the gully which lies 4 metres right of The Rack, starting up the gully.

Direct Start VS 5a
Start 1 metre left and use lay-aways to gain the ordinary route.

51. Leviathan Font 8b+ *
The classic traverse, from Badfinger to The Rack. This 'problem' is included as a route as it is longer than any in the County, and requires the stamina of the hardest bolt routes. There are rules: no jamming in the cracks and no foot edge below Monty Python's Flying Circus.

The next routes lie up the green mossy wall to the right of The Slide.

52. The Duffer 8m MVS 4c
The flake at the left end of the wall is climbed to the overhang which is taken direct.

Direct Start 8m 5c
The rounded rib to the left of the original start.

53. Solo Trumpet 9m E1 5b
The wall right of The Duffer on small holds to the overhang. Straight over this.

54. Trumpet Solo 9m HVS 5a
Climb the wall just left of Beorn, finishing at the large block on top of the crag.

55. Beorn 10m VS 5a
7 metres right of the gully is a slight depression in the steep wall. Climb this to a small overhanging crack.

56. Hard Liquor 10m E3 5c
The wall between Beorn and Beorn Too Late. Climb the shallow flakes to a good hold at the horizontal break, continue directly up the overhanging wall.

57. Beorn Too Late 10m E1 5b
Takes the steep wall immediately right of Hard Liquor. Start at the base of an indefinite ramp. Move right along the ramp to reach a good pocket. Move up and diagonally left to finish

58. The Flying Scotsman 9m E1 5b
Start beneath a small hanging flake. Using two small pockets to gain better holds above, continue up the wall to the hanging flake and move over this to the top.

59. The Mallard 9m E1 5b
The wall between Flying Scotsman and Root Scoop.

60. Root Scoop 8m HVS 4c
The scoop at the right hand end of the wall.

61. Forest Rib 8m VD
Climb the slab then the arête immediately right of the previous route.

Andrew Earl
47. Hitchhikers Guide to the Galaxy (6c)
Photo: Steve Crowe

62. Yseut 22m E1 5b
A traverse at two thirds height. Climb the flake of The Duffer then hand traverse rightwards beneath the overhang, move up and right to a short crack. Step down and cross the bulging wall, continue rightwards along the break to finish up the final groove of Root Scoop.

The next route lies past a tree-filled break in the wall.

63. Greensleaves 8m S 4b
Climb the short jamming crack to its finish and then delicately up the wall above.

64. The Missing Link 9m HVS 5b *
Just to the right of Greensleaves a crack slants up from the foot of the crag. It ends 1 metre below a second crack which extends from the top of the wall. The route follows these cracks, the crux being the move between the two cracks.

65. Stirring up Trouble 9m E3 5c *
The arête left of The Flutings Direct is followed until forced left onto the wall to the right of The Missing Link.

66. Trouble Shooter 11m E3 6a **
The wall left of The Flutings Direct is climbed via The Ear and The Chicken Head to reach a single fluting.

67. The Flutings Direct 11m VS 4c **
The climb ascends the shallow fluted groove on the left wall of the recess.
The wall to the right of The Flutings Direct has also been climbed.

68. Piccolo 12m S **
The steep chimney-crack in the left corner is a fine line.

69. Verticality 12m E1 5a *
The steep wall right of the corner is climbed direct with a mossy finish. A good route spoilt.

70. Zed Climb 12m VS 4c **
The right wall of the recess contains a slanting crack. Climb this, moving left at the top under the overhang. Exit direct through the roof on good holds.

71. The Harp 10m VS 5a ***
Climb the wall just right of Zed Climb until it is possible to move via a flake onto a rightward hand traverse, which is followed to the edge of the buttress. Pull up onto the slab to finish.

72. Orpheus 12m E3 5c
Start 2 metres right of The Harp. Climb the wall and flake to the traverse of The Harp. Move up to gain a horizontal break above the overhang then move left and make a long reach to good finishing holds.

Alternative Start 6a
From the blunt rib 3 metres right of The Harp climb straight up the wall to the hand traverse.

73. The Mite 6m VS 4c
The hanging corner of the buttress is taken direct starting high on the right and finishing as for The Harp.

74. The Mitre 6m VS 5a
The arête immediately right of The Mite is climbed direct.

The ground level now rises and the crag lies back about 9 metres. A ramp slants down from the left, ending 1 metre off the ground.

75. The Nadser 5m 6c
The wall to the left of the ramp is climbed on quarried holds.

76. Forgotten Wall 8m MVS 4c
Climb the wall between the ramp and the chimney in the corner by means of a faint groove. Aptly named.

In the corner is a narrow chimney which opens out deeper in the crag. It provides an amusing descent. A crack just left of the chimney also gives a short climb, or descent. To the right of the Chimney is a pocketed green wall.

77. The Hulk 9m E1 5c
Climb the centre of the wall left of Green Man with a long reach at the top.

78. Green Man 9m VS 4c *
Climb the strangely pocketed wall to the right, moving right near the top.

79. Not-so-Green 6m HVS 5b
The arête to the left of Evergreen Corner right of Green Man.

80. Evergreen Corner 9m S 4b
The green, stepped corner at the right hand end of the wall.

81. Evergreen Wall 9m VS 5b
The wall left of Primitive Crack with a difficult start.

Percy Bishton
75. Nadser (6c)
Photo: Steve Crowe

82. Primitive Crack 9m MS *
The excellent jamming crack provides very pleasant climbing.

83. Dingly Dell 10m HVS 5c *
Climb the wall 1 metre right of Primitive Crack. Trend right to the large horizontal break and finish directly above.

84. Bobby Dazzler HVS 5c **
The fluted wall 4 metres to the right of Primitive Crack is climbed via the left flute with difficult initial moves.

85. Autowind 11m HVS 6a *
Just right of Bobby Dazzler. Climb directly up the wall with occasional use of the right hand flute to handholds on the left edge of the ramp. Finish direct on easier ground.

86. Robber's Dog 11m HVS 5c
The wall to the left of the arête of Fluted Crack is climbed direct. Finish easily up the wall above. Using the arête is a steal.

A number of other variations have been climbed on this wall, the best being the pockets between Autowind and Robber's Dog at 6b.

The wall ends with a large obvious crack.

87. Fluted Crack 15m S 4b
The long boot-wide crack, the first few moves of which are awkward.

88. Piano 15m S 4c *
Starts up Fluted Crack. Climb 3 metres up the crack to where a traverse leads delicately left. Move across the flutings and up the wall to the top.

To the right of Fluted Crack is an impressive wall with some very fine routes. They do, however, become lichenous and may require cleaning.

89. Penny Whistle 12m E2 5c *
Starts 1 metre to the right of Fluted Crack. Climb the wall on small holds to a small flake. Continue up the wall and the flutings above. Runners in Fluted Crack blow the whistle.

90. The Entertainer 14m E3 5c *
Takes a line up the left side of the wall. Start 3 metres right of Fluted Crack at a large hold. Use the hold to gain a ledge then climb directly up the wall moving right, then back left at two thirds height. An excellent climb.

The following route is a harder variation on The Entertainer.

Darren Stevenson
on the first ascent of
91. Feanor (E6 6b)
Photo: Steve Crowe

91. Feanor 15m E6 6b **
Start as for The Entertainer and traverse 3m until below the blankest section of the wall. Ascend this on very small slopers and pockets to rejoin The Entertainer at the good hold below the top and welcome protection. Finish direct.

92. Upper Crust 15m E5 6b **
Start as for The Entertainer and traverse diagonally rightwards to join High T at the large pocket. Continue right to the bottom of the obvious ramp which is climbed to a horizontal break. Step right and finish awkwardly. Excellent.

93. High Society 15m E6 6b **
Start just left of the crack of High T, make a long reach to pockets and climb the bulge above to the 'T'. Traverse right to a large 'cauliflower' foothold. Move right and up to finish. Another superb climb.

94. High T 15m E3 5c ***
Start at the right hand side of the wall. Gain the obvious horizontal crack - the 'T' via a short crack and traverse. Stand on the 'T', move left and up to a good rest. Step left and make a long reach to good finishing holds. A great climb.

Moving right, an obvious overhanging crack is seen. It is split by a horizontal fissure at two thirds height.

95. The Crucifix 12m HVS 5a ***
The crack begins some 4 metres up the wall. Move up on fingerholds until the crack is reached. The overhanging crack is climbed to the top. Excellent.

96. Crucifixion 13m E3 5c *
From high up The Crucifix follow a horizontal line of pockets rightwards to finish at a fluted crown of rock.

97. The Prow 13m E9 7a ***
The blunt arête to the right of The Crucifix provides one of the hardest and best routes in the County. From the boulder climb the arête direct on a number of small shallow pockets.

98. Hourglass Chimney 11m S 4b
The narrow chimney in the next corner to the right. A wet crack is climbed up to the chimney. The chimney is very tight and gives a strenuous, but short, struggle.

99. Hostile Environment 13m E4 6a
Climb Hour Glass Chimney to 2/3 height.
Traverse left along the line of pockets to the
arête and up this to finish. A display of courage
will keep you on your way.

100. Pigs and Truffles 11m E3 6a
Start at the small groove/crack right of Hourglass
Chimney. Climb up, then right to an oval rock
feature. Finish up and leftwards, with long
reaches. Potential ascentionists will be grateful
to know it is seldom dry.

101. The Gauntlet 10m E1 5b ***
The blunt rib with an obvious crack 5 metres
right   of Hourglass Chimney is difficult to start.
Continue up the wall above. Very good.

102. Machinate 15m E3 5c
Follow The Gauntlet to just below the top then
traverse left into Hourglass Chimney. Finish up
this.

103. The Iron Fist 10m E1 5c
The wall 1 metre right of The Gauntlet is climbed
on small holds to a mantelshelf move onto a
rounded ledge. Move left and finish as for The
Gauntlet.

104. Plastic Novelties 10m E1 5b
Climb the wall just right of The Iron Fist, first right
and then left to gain the upper break. Move left
to finish up The Gauntlet.

105. Loam Crack 8m HS 4c
5 metres right of the previous route a rather dirty
crack slants up to the right.

106. Southerner 8m MS
Just right of Loam Crack. A boot jamming crack,
bulging slightly at the start, but easing off when
the left wall lies back.

Right of Southerner there is a large overhang.
Right again are the final climbs on the crag.

107. Ta-Ta Crack 6m D
A broken crack to the right of the overhang.

108. Dog Turd 7m E1 5c
The friable bulging wall right of Ta-Ta Crack, with
a well-named hold. Disgusting.

109. Arch Rivals 7m E3 6c
Start at the right lip of the cave, reach out to a
boss, then a seam with difficulty, then easier to
the top. Protection by crashmat.

Darren Stevenson on
101. The Gauntlet (E1 5b)
Photo: Steve Crowe

Kyloe in the Woods Graded List

E9
The Prow 7a ***

E6
High Society 6b **
Feanor 6b **

E5
Upper Crust 6b **

E4
Bad Company Right Hand Finish 6a
Sex and Brutality 6a
Hostile Environment 6a

E3
Arch Rivals 6c
The Entertainer 5c *
High T 5c ***
The Pearler 5c
Bad Company Direct Finish 5c
Trouble Shooter 6a **
Jocks and Geordies 6b **
Bad News 6a
Machinate 5c
Pigs and Truffles 6a
Crucifixion 5c *
Stirring Up Trouble 5c *
Hard Liquor 5c
Orpheus 5c

E2
Bad Company 5c **
Badfinger 5c **
Woodlark Alternative Start 1 6a
Woodlark Alternative Start 2 6a
Red Rum 6a ***
Red Rum Alternative Finish 6a
Swan Wall Arête 5c
Pink Gin 6a*
Penny Whistle 5c *
The Shire 5c
Woodlark 5b**

E1
Iron Fist 5c
Dog Turd 5c
Yseut 5b
Thin Hand Special 5c ***
The Gauntlet 5b ***
The Hulk 5c
Beorn Too Late 5b
The Elf Direct 5c *
Swan Wall Direct 5c *
The Mallard 5b
The Flying Scotsman 5b
Plastic Novelties 5b
Solo Trumpet 5b
Verticality 5a *

HVS
Autowind 6a *
Robber's Dog 5c
Bobby Dazzler 5c **
Dingly Dell 5c *
The Crucifix 5a ***
Shelob 5b
Mordor Front 5a
The Missing Link 5b *
Tea Break 5b
Trumpet Solo 5a
Root Scoop 4c
Not So Green 5b

VS
Beorn 5a
The Mitre 5a
Impromptu 5a
Evergreen Wall 5b
The Elf 5a *
Rivendell Crack 5a *
The Harp 5a ***
Zed Climb 4c **
Swan Wall Alternative Finish 5a
The Flutings Direct 4c **
The Rack Alternative Finish 5b
The Slide Direct Start 5a
Green Man 4c *
The Mite 4c
Monty Pythons Flying Circus 6a ***

Andrew Earl on the first ascent of
97. The Prow (E9 7a)
Photo: Steve Crowe

Linshiels One

Tim Catterall

NT 897054
South Facing
215 m
20 minutes

History
Bob Hutchinson, John Earl, Hugh Banner and Ian Cranston developed Linshiels One between September and November in 1973. The most notable routes being The Mirage led by Hutchinson and The Phantom by Earl. Bob and Tommy Smith added The Mercenary later in 1973, subsequently straightened by Bob in 1982. Steve Crowe and Karin Magog added a number of lines including A Chance Remark, Offensive and Stealth during the spring of 2000.

Situation and Character
This remote but pleasant crag lies in the upper Coquet Valley on the Ministry of Defence Artillery Range. The rock is sound and a number of very good routes on steep rock have been recorded. The crag consists of two buttresses, the left hand Two Tier Buttress and to the right, Pinnacle Buttress.

Approaches and Access
Follow the road west from Alwinton for about 2 miles and park near Linshiels Farm. The track leads south to the crag after about 1 kilometre. Visits should be restricted to periods when the red flags are not flying as the crag lies on a Ministry of Defence Artillery Range. It is advisable to contact the Otterburn Range Control on 01912394261 / 01830520569 who will provide information on firing times and when access is permitted. Do not pick up, kick or remove anything from the Otterburn Training Area IT COULD KILL. Avoid visiting if Ravens are nesting.
There is no CRoW right of access to the crag. It is on land regulated by military bylaws and as this is excepted land under the Act, it is excluded from the right of access

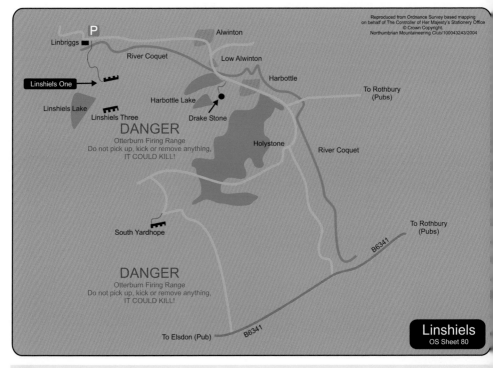

The Climbs
The routes are described from left to right.

Two Tier Buttress

1. Commando Crack 15m HVS 5b
This fine climb ascends the left hand of the two cracks. Climb the overhang by means of the crack at the right end of the cave and continue to a flake. The overhanging crack above is climbed on good jams.

2. The Phantom 15m E2 5b *
Climb the slab about 3 metres right of the previous climb and trend left to its flake. Make a sensational hand traverse right, by means of the horizontal flake crack, until an awkward move can be made onto the ledge at the arête. Climb the slab above.

3. Captive's Crack 12m VS 5a
Climb the slab immediately beneath the right hand crack to a ledge. Continue to beneath the overhang. Then traverse right until an awkward move can be made to gain the upper crack, which leads to the top.

4. Escapee 10m E3 5c
Start up Captive's Crack until it is possible to hand traverse boldly right to gain the toe of the hanging slab (crucial rock 1 difficult to place). Pull up to small friend behind the flake. Continue directly up the slab to finish.

Direct Start 10m E5 6a
Attack the most overhanging section of the buttress, directly below the slab and above a heinous landing. Follow the lip leftwards on good but snappy holds, to a junction with Escapee at the toe of the slab. Continue boldly up the slab to finish. This route was climbed with a pre-placed runner in the start.

5. A Chance Remark 12m E5 6b **
Start 2 metres right of the prow in a shallow scoop. Testing moves lead boldly to a break, which is followed left to a good slot. Reach left to a good pocket, reach up then trend left to gain the toe of the slab. Finish up this as for Escapee. A bold route.

Direct Finish 10m E5 6b
A safer but harder variation. From the good slot power up to reach small holds on the edge of the slab and trend right to finish with care up the flutings.

6. Sidewinder 4m VS 4c
The short but perfectly formed crack in the wall right of A Chance Remark is followed to a tricky mantle finish.

Pinnacle Buttress
The impressive buttress 20 metres further right.

7. Private's Passage 9m S
Climb the crack formed between the pinnacle and the buttress, to the top of the pinnacle. From here, climb the wall to reach the indefinite crack and so the top.

8. Ripcord 13m VS 4c
Climb Private's Passage to gain the obvious horizontal crack, which is followed across the smooth wall and round the arête until easy climbing leads to the top.

9. The Mercenary 9m E5 6a **
A very bold unprotected route. Start 3 metres left of The Mirage directly beneath the upper rib. Make an awkward move to gain the slabs and traverse left and then back right to gain the rib, which is climbed to the horizontal break. Climb the wall above direct.

10. Stealth 9m E3 5c *
Tackles the smooth wall, just right of the rib of The Mercenary. Start at two pockets immediately beneath a heather ledge. Reach the heather ledge as for The Mirage. Step left and continue directly up the wall on improving holds. Small sliding nuts essential.

11. The Mirage 11m E3 5b **
An excellent route, which climbs the impressive wall on the right side of the arête. Start at two pockets immediately beneath a heather ledge. Make an awkward move to reach the right end of the steeply sloping ledge and then up to the heather ledge. Make a thin move right and up to reach the thin crack, finish directly up the wall.

12. Flanking Arete 12m MVS 4c
The arête at the right end of the wall is climbed direct.

13. Gully Wall 10m S
The wall to the right of the arête is climbed in its centre, until a move left can be made to finish.

14. Capstone Gully 9m VD
The obvious gully to the right of the previous climb.

15. Private's Part 9m HS
The wide twisting crack, in the right wall of the gully, leads with surprising difficulty to the top.

16. Offensive 9m VS 5a
The thin crack just right of Private's Part. Pull straight up to finish just right of a large clump of heather.

Linshiels One Graded List

E5
A Chance Remark Direct Finish 6b
A Chance Remark 6b
Escapee Direct Start 6a
The Mercenary 6a

E3
Escapee 5c
Stealth 5c
The Mirage 5b

E2
The Phantom 5b

HVS
Commando Crack 5b

VS
Captive's Crack 5a
Offensive 5a
Ripcord 4c
Sidewinder 4c

Karin Magog on the first ascent of
10. Stealth (E3 5c)
Sliding micro wires provide essential protection.
Photo: Steve Crowe

Linshiels Three

Tim Catterall

History

All of the routes were climbed in the autumn of 1973 by Bob Hutchinson and John Earl accompanied by Hugh Banner and Ian Cranston, with the exception of Montgomery and Rommel, which were added nine years later by Tommy and Bob Smith.

Situation and Character

This remote crag is on the Ministry of Defence Artillery Range and has a very unspoilt secluded feel to it. The routes described are situated on the impressive overhanging buttresses above the shallow boggy lake. Although the routes are of good quality and on sound rock they have unfortunately become somewhat overgrown in recent years, but for those who want to get away from the crowds the remoteness and beauty of the crag cannot be beaten.

Approaches and Access

As for Linshiels One, drive west from Alwinton and park near Linshiels Farm. Follow the track south past Linshiels One to the copse of old pine trees and then to the large overhanging buttress at the extreme right end of the crag. Visits should be restricted to periods when the red flags are not flying as the crag is lies on a Ministry of Defence Artillery Range. It is advisable to contact the Otterburn Range Control on 01912394261 / 01830520569 who will provide information on firing times and when access is permitted. Do not pick up, kick or remove anything from Otterburn Training Area IT COULD KILL. See the approach map on page 206.

There is no CRoW right of access to the crag. It is on land regulated by military bylaws and as this is excepted land under the Act, it is excluded from the right of access.

The Climbs

The climbs are described from right to left.

Buttress One

1. Khaki Crack 9m VS 5a

In the bay towards the right end of the buttress is an impressive crack which leads over bulges to beneath an overhang, whence a traverse right under the roof is made to a heathery slab.

2. AWOL 9m MVS 4c

To the left of Khaki Crack is a left facing corner groove starting 3 metres off the ground. This is entered from the left and followed to the top.

3. Pinnacle Face 9m S

The next feature to the left of a Scots pine is a pinnacle. This route takes the front face of the pinnacle starting on the left.

4. Shell Shock 8m E1 5b

Behind the pinnacle is an overhung bay. The crack in the roof is gained by means of a flake on the left and is then climbed on jams to a heather slab. Awkward climbing with good protection.

Continuing left there is an overgrown, overhanging area with a shallow, square cut, overhanging groove.

5. The Deserter 11m MVS 4c

Climb the groove to a heather ledge and then finishes up the wall above.

Buttress Two

The enormous slanting overhang to the left of The Deserter. The next route takes the rightward facing wall at its right end.

6. Green Beret 9m MS

Climb the blocks until it is possible to step left onto a ledge and then climb the jagged crack.

7. A.R.P. 15m VS 5a

Start as for Green Beret until the obvious traverse line can be followed leftwards.

Buttress Three

8. Alwinton Annual Show 8m HVS 5a
Takes the thin crack at the left end of the loose looking buttress to the left of a dirty gully.

Buttress Four
This is separated from Buttress Three by a grassy break and has a hanging chimney containing a number of horizontal flakes at its right end and a large overhang to the left of this.

9. Howitzer Chimney 9m S
The obvious hanging chimney at the right end of the buttress.

10. Shrapnel Crack 9m MVS 4c
On the left of the chimney is a leftward facing corner with an overhang at its top. Climb up to the overhang, traverse right, then make an awkward move into the top groove.

Continuing left there are several buttresses up to 9 metres in height which contain a number of climbs of all grades up to Very Severe.

The recess at the far left end of the crag contains two good routes.

11. Montgomery 8m HVS 5a
The right hand crack.

12. Rommel 8m E1 5b
The left hand crack.

Linshiels Three Graded List

E1
Shell Shock 5b
Rommel 5b

HVS
Alwinton Annual Show 5a
Montgomery 5a

VS
A.R.P. 5a
Khaki Crack 5a

PaddaCrag

Chris Davis

History
The crag was discovered by John Earl, Bob Hutchinson and Tim Edmundson in 1973, Padda Wall, Churnsike Crack and the difficult Sike Wall all dating from this time. A further nine routes were added by Dave Bowen and Stewart Wilson in 1978 beginning the tradition of wild west names. A few more routes were literally unearthed by Colin Murley during the production of the 1989 guide. The most noteworthy was Almighty Voice although this is likely to be the same line as Four Horns which was claimed some years earlier. The crag was extensively cleaned during preparations for this guide and Bald Eagle and Little Squawk added.

Situation and Character
This is the most westerly crag in the guide and one of the most remote. The crag has a superb situation occupying a hilltop clearing within coniferous forest, with good views of the fells to the south of Haltwhistle and Brampton. Padda Crag is south facing and formed of excellent quality Fell Sandstone, the crag dries quickly after rain and is particularly recommended to those who seek to escape the madding crowd. The lack of traffic does result in many of the holds being somewhat lichenous. The semi-mature forest trees, set back at the top of the crag provide good belay points. The crag provides plentiful opportunities for bouldering, generally with reasonable landings, although care is required on the brittle Seventh Wall.

Approaches and Access
The crag is approached from Gilsland (1 mile from Greenhead on the A69). Follow the Spadeadam road north for 1 mile to Moscow Farm and turn right onto a good but narrow road. Follow this road through forests and across open moorland for 6 miles passing through a gate and a shallow ford at Butterburn. The tarmac ends at a wooden bridge about half a mile before Chumsike Lodge. It is possible to obtain permission from the Forestry Commission at Bellingham (tel. 01434 220242) to continue by car almost to the foot of the crag. Those without permission can park between the bridge and the forest gate. Walk through the gate and follow the road round to the left to reach Churnsike Lodge. Take the left fork here and continue past a ruined barn on the left to reach a second junction. Turn right and continue for a further half a mile ignoring a junction on the right after half a mile to reach a dip in the road over a stream (culvert). A small layby is situated just beyond the culvert, park here. The crag is just visible on the right through the trees and is reached by following the stream. Care should be taken on warm summer days as adders enjoy basking on the large grass tufts in the lower section of the moor, just above the forest. From Chumsike Lodge allow 5-6 minutes by car, a mountain bike provides a good alternative to the 40-45 minute walk in.

The Climbs
The climbs are described from left to right.

First Wall
The first outcrop of rock at the westem end of the crag, terminated on its right by a chimney full of jammed blocks.

1. Piute 6m S
Start 2 metres right of the left hand end of the wall, climb diagonally right via the shallow recess finishing just right of the tiny overhang.

2. Padda Wall 5m HS 4b
A pleasant wall climb on superb rock. Start at the twin cracks 1/2 metre left of the arête. Climb the wall by the line of least resistance.

3. Oregon Trail 5m MS
Climb the arête at the right boundary of First Wall.

210

Second Wall
This is set back from First Wall and extends to a large cave.

4. Whoops 6m MVS 4b
Start at the boulder that leans against the foot of the wall, climb straight up on good holds.

5. Bald Eagle 6m HS 4b
Start at the right hand side of a small roof/overlap 1 metre above ground level, trend rightways using undercuts to an ear shaped flake and scoop. Climb directly up the wall to finish. Can be climbed directly above the roof at 5b.

6. Sioux Hare 5m VD
Climb the short hand-width crack 5 metres left of the cave and continue up the wider cleft above.

7. Rooster Cogburn 6m D
Climb the arête that forms the left edge of the cave and continue up the juggy wall above.

Main Wall
Extends rightwards for 10 metres to the easy angled arête and is distinguished by the square shaped roof at two thirds height.

8. Creak 5m D
Climb the rightward slanting crack, 1 metre right of the cave.

9. Four Horns 9m E1 5b
Climb directly up the centre of the wall between the cave and the prominent stepped corner, on small, but positive holds.

10. The Funnel 9m VS 5a
The prominent stepped corner is ascended by strenuous laybacking and wide bridging.

11. Sike Wall 9m HVS 5b*
Climbs the prominent roof by means of the large crescent shaped flake crack. Start at the indistinct rib below the left hand end of the roof.

12. Red Cloud 9m HVS 5b
Start 2 metres right of Sike Wall. Climb the smooth wall direct to a break in the widest part of the overlap. Finish through this.

13. Lone Ranger 9m HVS 5b
Follow Red Cloud to finish up a short groove at the right end of the overlap.

14. Churnsike Crack 9m S
The obvious steep bulging crack 1 metre right of the square roof becomes easier as one gains height.

15. Witch Hunt 8m HVS 5b*
Climb the steep wall on small holds 1 metre right of Churnsike Crack.

16. Arête Direct 8m HS
The arête at the right hand end of main wall.

Boulder Slab
The slab to the right and at an angle to Main Wall. It lies between the arête and the easy cleft, which has flakes jammed in its upper part.

17. Chisholm Trail 9m D
Climb the centre of the slab, which steepens near the top.

Third Wall

Extends from the easy angled slab to the overhanging nose above a ledge, on which grows two rowan trees.

18. Leaning Crack 8m S

The right trending crackline 1 metre right of the corner.

19. The Niggler 8m MVS 4b

Start 2 metres left of the rotten tree and attempt to gain a small ledge. Continue with greater certainty to the top.

20. Vital Signs 9m VS 5b**

A good wall climb. Start 1 metre right of the thin birch growing on the face. Climb a very thin crack with difficulty to a good jug. The steep wall above is an excellent finish.

21. Pipe of Peace 10m MVS 4c**

Start as for Vital Signs. Instead of climbing the thin crack, follow the overlap rightwards until some fingery moves lead to better holds. Swing across the wall on the left to gain the jug of Vital Signs and finish as for that route.

22. Padda Stairs 8m D

Start at the left hand end of the ledge with the two rowan trees and follow the huge steps to the top.

Fourth Wall

This extends from the birches to the isolated pinnacle.

23. Forked Tongue 8m D

An interesting climb. Start 2 metres right of the two birches at the foot of the crack and groove. Climb the lower cracks and continue straight up, or step right into the groove to finish.

24. Tomahawk 5m HS

Climb the shallow groove 2 metres right of the crack and groove of Forked Tongue.

25. Hiding to Nothing 8m HVS 4c*

Climb the fine arête, which bounds the right hand end of the Fourth Wall. The finish is intimidating.

Padda Tower

The isolated pinnacle.

26. The Tower Crack 6m M

Start in the gully on the left hand side of the pinnacle, climb the crack.

27. Teton 6m VD

The wall and arête on the left hand side of the tower.

28. Ojibwa 6m MS

The arête and wall on the right hand side of the tower.

29. The Tower Ordinary 5m Easy

Start below a short crack on the west side of the Tower where it abuts against the fellside. Climb a short crack onto a pedestal, a pull up gains the summit.

The Fifth and Sixth Walls are respectively 50 and 60 metres east of Padda Tower. Fifth Wall has a band of overhangs at 1.5 metres; Sixth Wall has a band of overhangs at 2 metres.

The Playground

This is the name given to the 50 metre stretch of small outcrops and boulders between Padda Tower and the next continuous rock; Fifth Wall. One minor route is described in this area.

30. Nasty Knobbles 5m S
Starts between a prominent flake and a vegetated crack on the steep wall 10 metres right of the Tower. Climb directly up the steep wall on small holds to finish at a pointed block.

Fifth Wall
The steep wall to the right of The Playground has in its centre a huge detached block in a dark corner. The wall to the left of this corner has an overhang at chest height, whilst the wall to the right of this corner has a prominent jutting neb ow down.

31. One-Eyed Jack 8m VS 4c*
A very pleasant climb but with no protection. Start at the left-hand end of the wall below a steep shallow scoop. Climb over a small overlap and finish up the steep, shallow scoop.

32. Muleskinner 8m D
Start at the right-hand crack of the huge detached block in the corner. Climb the crack and exit on the right.

33. The Nebbish 7m HVS 5b
Starts below the neb. Pull up on good holds and make a hard move to stand on them. Climb up to and out of a sentry-box.

Sixth Wall is a further 12 metres to the right of Fifth Wall. It consists of a line of walls and buttresses ranging in height from 5-7 metres. Sixth Wall is divided into two halves by a gully. To the left of the gully is a smooth left-slanting groove and beyond this to the left a barrier of overhangs at head height guard the wall. To the right of the gully is a false wall leaning against the foot of the crag. The wall then ends in a jutting tooth-like arête on the right.

Sixth Wall

34. Little Groove 5m MVS 4c
Climb the left-slanting, smooth groove.

35. Tusk 7m MVS 4c
Climb the jutting tooth-like arête.

Seventh Wall
This is the very steep wall of bubbly rock immediately right of the tooth-like arête. Seventh Wall terminates in a very deep recessed corner, which has a fist-wide crack in the angle.

The steep overhanging wall can be climbed directly, in the middle at 5b and to the left of Hiawatha at 6a, care should be taken as the extrusions are very brittle.

36. Little Squawk 6m VS 5a
A leftwards trending ramp leads to the top of the crag. Start 2 metres to the left of the ramp and climb the wall directly to jugs on the overhang and an awkward finish.

37. Hiawatha 6m HVS 5a**
An excellent steep climb up the obvious flake crack. Attack the crack by strenuous laybacking, then retreat from the crack by bridging to a rounded finish. The protection is good.

38. Papoose 6m MS
Starts in the deep comer and climbs the wall on the right to a good flake and then the top.

Padda Crag Graded List

Peel Crag

Chris Davis and Rick Barnes

NY 755677
North Facing
250m
5 minutes

History

M.B. Heywood is attributed the discovery of Peel Crag along with Crag Lough. In the C.C. Journal for 1912 which contained a long article and a sketch of Crag Lough, Heywood described Peel Crag as too broken to offer many definite climbs and included a description of only one route at the west end of the crag; a clean line up a very stiff slab which necessitates exceptional contortions.

In the years that followed, Peel Crag appears to have been neglected. By the mid 1930's most of the county's crags had been climbed on but Crag Lough and to a greater extent Peel Crag did not seem to be popular. It was not until the late 1930's that Basil Butcher and Keith Gregory began their exploration of Crag Lough and to a lesser extent Peel Crag. In the 1940's development of Crag Lough was in full swing but Peel Crag was still regarded as too loose and broken for good routes, with the exception of Sunset Buttress which had a route called Zig-Zag, which we now know as Sunset.

It was the formation of the Crag Lough Club in 1952 with Albert Rosher as the key figure that was responsible for the major development of Peel Crag. Early members, Frank Carroll, Don Laws and Geoff Oliver, were joined in the late fifties by Nev Hannaby who was responsible for a number of new routes and by Eric Rayson, Terry Sullivan and John Cheesmond. It was during this period and the early sixties that most of the classic routes were climbed; Certificate X, Locomotion, Grooves, Ace of Spades, Overhanging Crack and Rock Island Line are all attributed to Rosher. During this time lines that could not be free climbed were pegged, with the aid progressively reduced until climbed free. Examples were Rock Island Line, Green Line and Chocolate Deirdre, which was not climbed free until 1978. Twenty-two routes on Peel Crag were included in the 1964 N.M.C. guide, but this was probably not a true record of the development at that time for shortly afterwards Rosher brought out a small guide at his own expense, with some seventy new routes added to Peel Crag and Crag Lough.

By the publication of the 1971 N.M.C. guide the number of routes on Peel had risen to seventy-one due mainly to the continued efforts of Rosher and the newly formed Border Climbing Club.

In the 1970's the pace of development slackened as interest moved away from Peel Crag and Crag Lough to the sandstone outcrops in the north of the county. By the time of the publication of the 1979 N.M.C. guide only half a dozen routes had been added. The most significant of these was the free ascent of Ritual by Bill Wayman.

In the 1980's Peel Crag continued to decline in popularity. The nature of the rock, unable to offer the potential for harder lines provided by the sandstone elsewhere in the county had little for the 'extreme' rock climber. Despite having a range of good quality Severes and Very Severes, Peel had to compete with Crag Lough for the Very Severe climber's attention. Consequently, a large number of routes have become overgrown, with only the popular climbs receiving enough traffic to keep them clean. Some of the half dozen new routes put up since the 1979 guide are of a rather artificial or eliminate nature and would suggest that Peel Crag has little scope for new routes. This is not necessarily the case however, as Malcolm Lowerson's Albert's Wall (named in tribute to Albert Rosher) and more recently, Steve Nagy's Whinstone Cowboy prove. Finally, during the preparation for this guide, Chris Davis and Rick Barnes discovered that the buttress at the west end of the crag had been inexplicably omitted from previous guides, even though the central crack appears to have been regularly climbed. The pair added two worthwhile routes, Phoebus Maximus and Clear As Crystal to this popular end of the crag. Overall, Peel Crag has enough good quality routes to deserve better attention in the future.

Situation and Character

Peel Crag is a long outcrop that runs west for 800 metres from the big gap in the escarpment which separates this crag from Crag Lough. The Roman wall follows the line of its crest. Buttresses of clean, compact rock are interspersed with broken, overgrown areas that predominate towards the eastern end of the crag.

As with Crag Lough the rock is the quartz dolerite of the Whin Sill. It is hard and smooth and weathers along vertical and horizontal planes to give it its typical block-like appearance. In the main the rock is sound, providing steep exposed climbs, the majority of which are in the Severe/Very Severe grades.

Approaches and Access

Turn right off the Military road (B6318) at the crossroads near the Once Brewed National Park Information Centre, 35 miles west of Newcastle. Follow the road for about half a mile to the Steel Rigg car park at the top of the hill from where the crag is clearly visible. The National Park charge for parking at Steel Rigg, it's worth it for the situation alone! An annual pass for this car park and all the other Trust car parks on the wall can be obtained from Housesteads or the National Park centre at Once Brewed. The public footpath leads south to the Roman Wall, which is followed to the foot of the crag in about five minutes. This land is National Trust property and camping is not permitted but rights of way from both directions are secure. For approach map see page 101.

Peel Crag has not been mapped as CRoW access land. It is, though, on National Trust land and so will be shown as open country on the new Explorer map. Access rights and arrangements remain as they are at present.

Approaching
Peel Crag
Photo: Steve Crowe

Sunset Buttress

The Climbs

For identification purposes the crag has been divided into several areas, described from right to left as you approach the crag from Steel Rigg car park. The most obvious feature at the west end of the crag is the high, prominent buttress with a large, unstable-looking block at the top. This is Sunset Buttress. The first buttress of any substance rises immediately adjacent to the approach path, 30m right of Sunset Buttress. It has been omitted from previous guides but provides three worthwhile lines.

1. Phoebus Maximus 10m HVS 5b
Climb the blunt arête to the right of the central crack using horizontal breaks to reach a large ledge. Cross some easy rock before following the V-groove and steep wall to finish direct.

2. Route One 10m VD
The obvious clean corner crack provides a pleasant climb.

3. Clear As Crystal 10m VS 5a
Starts at the same place as the previous route but soon moves left to a right facing corner. Climb the slab to a large hold on the right, move left, mantelshelf onto the ledge and follow the arête direct to the top.

The next routes are located on the small buttress situated above a grassy recess. The steep wall split by a slotted crack provides a route that bears no relation to its Llanberis namesake.

4. Ribstone Crack 9m VD
Climb the crack direct.

5. Crackstone Rib 9m D
The obvious line just left of the previous climb. Follow the right side of the corner to the top.

6. Layback Buttress 18m VD
Situated on the right wall of the grassy recess overlooked by Sunset Buttress. Just left of the toe of the buttress is an obvious layback crack, which proves awkward. The wide crack and ridge can be followed, past a Rowan tree, easily to the top.

7. Jackdaw 18m D
Immediately left of Layback Buttress. Climb the wide crack to the right, then follow the ridge.

8. Suicide 11m S
A bulging wall with cracks up the centre, high up at the back of the grassy recess. Climb the airy wall, which has an awkward move at the top.

Sunset Buttress

9. Meridian 27m S

An indefinite line crossing Sunset Buttress. Start at the right of the buttress to the right of Twin Cracks. Climb a short, vegetated chimney and traverse into Twin Cracks above the difficult moves of that route. Ascend, then work round left to the large ledge on Sunset. Mantelshelf onto a ledge and climb up diagonally left to the top.

10. Twin Cracks 20m VS 5a *

The bottom section contains all the technical difficulties. It follows the line of two thin cracks, which slant up the right side of Sunset Buttress. Climb delicately up the cracks until the bottom edge of a rectangular brown patch can be used in conjunction with a jammed right foot for an awkward move up. Move slightly right into a recess, then follow the cracks again to the top.

11. Whinstone Cowboy 20m E1 5b

Start left of Twin Cracks and climb the wall on small holds to a crescent shaped feature. Use this to gain a good hold at the base of the crack in the wall above. Follow the crack, using layaways to each side, to a ledge. Finish as for Scratch.

2. Scratch 21m HVS 5a

Just left of Whinstone Cowboy. A mantelshelf move leads onto a ledge. Climb up left of a rib for a few moves until it is possible to swing right onto the steep wall. Very precarious climbing leads right onto Twin Cracks. Climb up the wall, moving slightly left to a ledge below the summit. Pull over the overhang and climb the crack on the right of the block.

3. Exasperation 15m S

Climb the mantelshelf of Scratch and continue up to the platform on Sunset. Move down slightly until the face on the left can be traversed. Climb the vegetated groove until the face on the right can be regained. Cross over to a ledge on the right and follow the crack above to the top. A wandering sort of route.

4. Sunset 23m MS ***

A superb route, the classic of Peel Crag. Start at the lowest point of the buttress in a corner. Climb the corner, moving slightly right to a ledge. Go up a short wall to a platform at the foot of a big corner with a deeply cracked right wall. Climb the corner, first by bridging, to a ledge. Either mantelshelf to a ledge on the left or continue up the corner to a platform and then traverse left and up.

15. Sunset Direct 26m VS 5a *

A good route which finishes up the improbable looking ridge of stacked blocks. Although high in the grade, the line is spoiled by the availability of escape. Start left of Sunset at the bottom of the narrow ridge. Climb the wall moving right to a V-groove. From a ledge at the top of the groove step left onto the front of the buttress and ignoring the temptations of the easy corner to your left, make delicate moves to the big ledge. Swing right onto the front of the ridge and follow it to the top. No purpose will be served at this point by considering the possibility of the blocks ever becoming unstacked!

1 metre to the left is an open chimney.which has been subject to a recent rockfall and is currently unstable making the following poor route even less appealing than before.

16. Rainy Day 23m MVS 4c

In theory, climb the thin crack on the right side of the groove to a junction with Chockstone Chimney. In practice, you are likely to have at least one foot on each route for this part of the climb, in which case you are downgraded to HS! Climb the scoop above, soon moving left to finish up the chimney. All in all, a bit pointless and not recommended!

17. Chockstone Chimney 24m D *

Climb the wide chimney on big holds to a grass ledge (some loose rocks). Move left and up to the tree. Round to the left again is a chimney which, if you have a botanical interest, can be followed to the top. Far more pleasant is the alternative, direct finish past a chockstone. A good route at the grade.

18. Easy Street 23m MVS 4c

On the other side of the arête, to the left of Chockstone Chimney is a wide crack. Climb it, trend left to a tree, then climb the bulging nose above.

The next routes start 8 metres to the left and above a grassy slope.

Red Wall

Blasphemy Wall

19. Grog 18m S
At the top of the recess to the left of the previous climb is a wall split by a crack. Jam the crack to the top or, alternatively, move right and climb the crack through the overhangs to the top.

2 metres to the left is a completely overgrown crack which used to provide the line of.........

20. Hanging Crack 15m S
Follow the crack throughout, if you can find it!

21. Ulysses 15m VD*
To the left is a buttress at an easier angle. At its base is a rowan tree with a small jammed block behind. Climb up on the right of the tree to a corner. Make a rather awkward move left onto the long narrow slab, which is followed to the top.

22. Odysseus 15m S
Start as for Ulysses but move right and climb the overhanging corner above the tree to a ledge. Follow the corner crack and then direct over the final overhangs.

Further to the left is a deep, rather dirty gully with an earthy ramp leading up to it; this provides a quick means of descent. Beyond this broken area is a buttress with a sharp arête containing a sharply cut overhang. To the right is a well-defined crack, which is the start of the next two routes.

Blasphemy Wall

23. Easy Crack 15m VD
Follow the crack to the top of the small pillar. Gain a crack on the left wall to reach the top.

24. Swing Up 18m HS 4b
From the top of the pillar on Easy Crack make a long reach for a handhold on the arête. With a foot on a high hold round the corner, pull gingerl across. Finish straight up.

25. C'est La Vie 18m E3 6a
Climb the easy wall and shattered arête right of Overhanging Crack to a small ledge beneath the overhang. Climb the short wall on layaways and surmount the overhang to gain the arête, which is followed to join Swing Up.

26. Overhanging Crack 18m MVS 4c ***
A rewarding line. On the left side of the buttress, 3 metres left of Easy Crack, is a short wall with twin, broken cracks, topped by a wider overhanging crack. Climb the wall on small hold to a ledge below the crack. The crack provides good jams and eases towards the top.

27. Albert's Wall 18m E1 5a *
An enjoyable route with some delicate and strenuous moves. Start 1 metre left of Overhanging Crack. Climb the wall up its centre to the top.

28. Apollo 18m MS
On the buttress wall facing Overhanging Crack.
Scramble up to and climb the obvious fern filled
crack. Above, climb dubious rocks to easier
ground.

29. Blasphemy Wall 21m HVS 5a *
To the left of Apollo on the other side of the
buttress is a steep wall with a detached tower
leaning against it. Climb the arête at the right
side of the wall, traversing left to the top of the
tower. From the gap between it and the face,
traverse right and climb the centre of the wall
or 3 metres. Move right to the arête, which is
followed to the top. The tower has also been
climbed at a similar grade.

30. Shadow Wall 11m VD
Immediately left of the detached tower of
Blasphemy Wall is an overgrown buttress with a
large rowan tree at its foot. The route follows the
right side to a ledge high up from where escape
is made left.

Red Wall
Left of Shadow Wall lies the steep and compact
Red Wall.

31. Red Wall 20m VS 4c
On the right side of the wall, climb a short wall
to a crack, which is followed to a tree. Move up
or 4 metres then traverse left into the vegetated
V corner. Climb this for 3 metres moving back
right. Delicate climbing leads into the final
groove.

32. Red Chimney 18m VD
The obvious rather vegetated V chimney. Climb
the chimney until it becomes difficult. Step left
and climb the wall above to finish.

33. Jester 20m VS 5a *
A fine route. Start at the foot of an obvious
green corner on the front of the buttress with a
small overhang at its head. Climb the corner,
moving right onto footholds on the wall. Pull up
and layback the overhang. Climb past some
alarmingly stacked blocks, trending right across
a slab to the top.

To the left the rocks are broken by tree-filled
gullies for about 25 metres. A number of routes
have been climbed but the area is generally
loose. The more solid buttress in the middle has
a reasonable climb straight up the middle (Very
Difficult).

Mark Weatherhead seconding
26. Overhanging Crack (MVS 4c)
Photo: Steve Crowe

Tigers Wall | Central Wall

Central Wall

The broken area terminates in a high, solid wall with a large brown scoop at the right end and high, stepped overhangs at the left end. The brown overhung groove is a prominent feature.

34. Myxomatosis 15m S
The crack to the right of the brown scoop. A short wall leads to a crack with an ash tree at its head. Climb to the tree, move left onto a slab and climb this.

35. Sacrifice 20m E3 6a
The brown scoop was originally an artificial route (Chocolate Deirdre). Climb the scoop to the roof. The roof is overcome on the left on small rounded holds, which lead to a small boss above. A more delicate move enables the final, easier crack to be reached.

36. Ace of Spades 20m HVS 5a *
Ascend the right side of the broken pinnacle, which lies against the face to the left of Sacrifice. From the top of the pinnacle climb the centre of the wall using a crack. Move right after a short way then go straight up.

37. Ritual 21m E4 6a **
A sustained wall climb. To the left of Ace of Spaces lies a high, steep wall with an inverted staircase of overhangs low down. Go up the V groove and pull round the overhangs onto the wall. Follow the crack to a good hold (ancient peg for protection). Make a dynamic move to reach a small, sloping ramp above the right crack. Good holds lead to the top of the wall.

38. Green Line 15m E1 5b *
To the left of the stepped overhangs is a wall split by a thin crack. From the small pinnacle at the base, climb the wall and crack. A good climb that gets easier, and better protected, the higher you go.

39. Zig Zag 15m VD
Left of Green Line is a shrub-filled gully. Start just left of this and climb the wall to a tree. Traverse right across the gully and continue across the top of Green Line to another tree.

40. Green Chimney 20m S
2 metres left of Zig Zag is a green, dirty-looking chimney. Climb the chimney to the high overhang. Step left below the overhang and pull up. Continue moving left until the top is reached

1. Certificate X 21m E1 5a **

A few metres left of Green Chimney a rib protrudes from the face and on its left is a small cave. Climb out of the cave to a ledge on the rib. Go up the wall above, trending left into a corner. Move up the corner for a short way to a horizontal line. Traverse delicately right towards two hairline cracks a few centimetres apart. At the top of these cracks are two small holds which are used to pull up to a good jug. Good holds lead to the finish.

2. Trilogy 21m E2 5b *

At the foot of the buttress is a small cave. Climb the left wall of the cave to the hanging corner. Continue straight up the corner groove to the top.

3. Parental Guidance E2 5c *

Start below the centre of the wall to the right of Rock Island Line. Climb the centre of the wall until forced to move right into the groove by a small overhang. Move left onto the wall above the small overhang and make difficult moves up into the hanging corner below a small roof. Strenuous moves up over the roof brings easier climbing up the buttress above.

4. Rock Island Line 21m E1 5b ***

An excellent route, one of the best in the County at its grade, which climbs the wall below the conspicuous stepped overhang. Start 2 metres left of the cave. Climb the centre of the wall via the cracks to the overhangs. Pull strenuously left over the roof and finish up a deep crack.

5. The Intruder 21m E2 5c *

Climb the wall left of Rock Island Line to the square notch in the overhang. Surmount this with difficulty and keeping to the left edge, climb the thin V crack to the top.

To the left of The Intruder is a rotten chimney full of nettles and tree roots; this is Central Chimney (Difficult and unpleasant). To the left lies: -

Malcolm Lowerson on
44. Rock Island Line (E1 5b)
Photo: Rick Barnes

Tigers Wall

Tiger Wall

A clean, narrow buttress immediately above the dry stone wall.

46. Trinity 21m S
Follow a V corner on the right edge of the buttress to a ledge. From the ledge move up to the final crack of Grooves. Traverse left for 2 metres, mantelshelf and finish up a groove.

47. Grooves 21m S 4b **
A fine, airy route up the highest part of the buttress. Climb up cracks to the sentry box, pull out and up to a ledge. Climb the groove behind making an awkward move right into a wide crack. Finish up the crack to the tree.

48. Tiger's Chimney 18m VD
2 metres left of Grooves. Climb the corner until the chimney is reached. Then, either ascend the chimney direct, or traverse left above the overhang and climb up the centre of the wall.

49. Tiger's Overhang 18m VS 4c **
Start beneath the prominent roof. Climb up the centre of the wall to the roof. Bridge across and pull up on good holds. Climb straight up to the top.

50. Kamikaze Sex Pilot 17m E2 5c *
Climb the wall immediately left of Tigers Overhang to a crack system in the middle of the wall.

The wall has also been climbed via the jagged overlap at E4 6a.

51. The Left Edge 15m VD
Climb the left edge of the wall to the small nose. Pull over it, move right and climb the crack to the top.

52. Peel Crag Central Girdle 60m VS 4c
The route traverses Tiger Wall and Central Wall. Start as for the The Left Edge. Climb this until level with the roof of Tiger's Overhang. Swing across, originally accomplished by the use of a peg and move round under the roof. Traverse right across Tiger's Chimney, round onto Grooves, round the corner and across to Central Gully. Descend the gully for 3 metres, step round the rib and move across to Rock Island Line. Traverse right on big handholds and swing round onto Certificate X. Descend 2 metres. Move right and step across Green Chimney, then climb up to the tree on Zig Zag.

Left of Tiger Wall the rock becomes less continuous and more overgrown. A number of lines are possible but only a couple are worthy of mention. These lie on a small tree shrouded buttress with a wide crack containing a large jammed block, some 12 metres left of Tiger Wall.

53. Consternation 11m VS 4c
Climb the crack to the jammed block. Traverse right to a small ledge then follow the right edge to the top.

54. Caesar 11m S
Climb the crack up to and over the jammed block.

The next area is situated above the remains of a dry stone enclosure, which lies between the path at the bottom and the base of the crag. On the right hand of two towers is......

55. Tiger's Hangover 20m VS 4c
Climb up the front of the buttress to the overhang. Pull over the overhang and climb the crack on the left to the top.

Alternative Finish S 4b
From below the overhang move right and pull round the rib. Make a layback move then continue moving right and up to the top.

56. Verdant Groove 17m MVS 4b
3 metres left of Tiger's Hangover and 1metre left of a deep, green chimney, climb the crack. Step right and pull into the groove. Move up to the overhang; step left and go up the steep groove and a grassy finish.

57. Locomotion 15m E2 5c *
Start below the huge, scooped overhang above the enclosure. Climb the crack to the foot of a V groove. Move up the groove. A balance move on undercuts enables a good right handhold to be reached. Pull up to the tree, then move right into the nose and gain the gangway. Pull up to the top.

58. Flamingo 14m VD
Left of Locomotion is a heavily vegetated slab. Stroll up through the garden to the top (please shut the gate and keep your dog under control). The continuation corner, on the right, is a little leaner and therefore of less interest to those of a horticultural persuasion!

59. Denizen 11m VS 4c
2 metres left of Flamingo is a steep, narrow corner with a small triangular overhang at 3 metres. Pull up on the left, then step back right above the small overhang and continue straight up the crack.

60. Vindication 12m VS 4c
The large, open corner below a tree-filled gully just left of Denizen. Climb the corner to a large ledge on the right. Take the crack up the steep wall finishing up an open corner.

61. Tanya 18m VS 4c
Start a couple of metres round to the left of Vindication. Climb the right edge of the wall to a thin crack. Go up the crack, then step right and move up to a large jug. Move right and up to a ledge. Traverse left under a roof to finish up a groove.

8 metres to the left of the previous route and above two rocks embedded in the grass near the path, is an obvious narrow buttress.

62. Cynic 17m S
Takes direct the attractive buttress right of Bookworm.

Broken, vegetated rocks continue. The following route has been recorded somewhere here, take your pick from a number of vegetated grooves and chimneys. Better still, leave this area to Mother Nature and press on to the Eastern Wall.

63. Bookworm 17m VD
Climb the chimney on the left of a pillar for 6 metres. Step right onto the face and climb to the top.

64. Fissure-La-Boot 12m VS 4c
10 metres left of Bookworm is a right facing 6 metre crack, 17 centimetres in width and with a large ash tree at the top. The crack is easier if done in big boots.

65. Panorama 15m VD
Start at a small overhang on the buttress 20 metres left of Fissure-La-Boot and with two rowan trees at the top. Climb up to the overhang, step right and move up for 2 metres. Move back left above the overhang, then straight up.

Rick Barnes leading
49. Tigers Overhang (VS 4c)
Photo: Steve Crowe

Eastern Wall

15 metres further left the buttresses come together again to form a more continuous wall - Eastern Wall, which is home to some fine routes that deserve greater attention.

66. Caution Corner 18m MS
A green stained roof is at the right end of the wall. Start just to the right. Climb a short wall to gain the corner and finish up it.

67. Adolphus 17m VS 5a
Start below the roof. Good holds lead to the roof, move right and climb to a horizontal crack. Move back left above the overhang. Climb straight up.

68. College Girl 18m VD
Start 3 metres left of Adolphus. After a difficult move, ascend the steep wall on good holds moving left to a grass ledge. Climb the wall above moving left until a step back right can be made and the top so reached.

69. Hepple Wall 15m VD
Follow the right side of a steep arête 5 metres left of the last climb then go up the corner. A pull up and two mantelshelf moves lead to easier ground.

70. Perseverance 14m VS 4c
Start just right of the big open corner. Climb the crack in the left side of the arête.

71. The Corner 14m VS 4c
Climb a short wall to the prominent corner. Ascend the corner.

72. Kurt 14m VS 4c
The groove to the left of The Corner with a small triangular overhang. Follow the crack and groove straight up.

73. John Peel 14m S
Start just left of Kurt. Climb the open corner until a step left can be made and continue straight to the top.
At the top of a grassy bank starts.......

74. A.S.B. 12m VS 4c
Climb the centre of the wall to the right of a vegetated groove. Move right at the top onto easier rock.

Prow Buttress
6 metres left of A.S.B. is a green corner with a prominent fin and roof at head height. This marks the beginning of the Prow Buttress area.

75. Dice 14m HS 4b
Start below the green corner. Climb up to the 1 metre overhang. Using the jammed blocks pull out and over it and climb straight up to the tree. Just left of Dice is the interesting problem of obtaining lodgement in the bottomless V groove

76. Trog 15m MVS 4b
Start in a short groove round to the left of Dice. Move into the groove and mantelshelf out onto a ledge. Climb the groove above then step left onto the arête. Pull up and climb to the top.

The following routes start from a large grassy ledge with a horizontal 2 metres long rock at the eastern end.

77. Triton 14m VD
The wide, vegetated groove to the left of Trog.

78. Grim Wall 14m MVS 4b
2 metres left of Triton above the horizontal rock. Climb the wide crack to the top of the pinnacle, then the wall above using side holds until a ledge is seen on the right. Traverse along the ledge to the corner then up. The wall may be climbed direct (Hard Very Severe).

9. Nimbus 12m D
limb the wide groove to the left of Grim Wall,
loving left at the top.

0. Prow Buttress Route One 14m S
tart below a projecting block at the top of the
ag (the prow). Climb up the wall to the sentry
ox. Move up and left onto a detached block.
limb up moving right to finish up the right side
the prow.

1. Prow Buttress Route Two 15m VS 4c
tart below and to the left of the prow. Climb up
e wall for 2 metres moving left into the crack.
limb the crack to the detached block. Finish up
e open chimney to the left of the prow.

2. Mortician 18m E1 5c *
tart 4 metres left of Route Two at the foot of the
uttress. Climb the front of the buttress using a
ghtward trending deep crack to a ledge. Climb
e thin vertical crack in the leaning wall above.
ne initial moves from the ledge are difficult. A
ne climb worth the exploration.

3. Hammer 17m VD
ollow the corner-crack 2 metres left of
ortician, two rowan trees mark the top.

4. Capitan 17m E1 5b *
xposed and delicate. Climb up the centre of the
ulging, fissured wall just left of Hammer, moving
ght to the tree at the top.

5. Practitioner 15m MS
art below the very green V chimney left of
apitan. Climb up to the chimney, which is
scended. Move left and up, then back right.

5. Mac 18m S
art below the short steep wall with the
ndercut base. Climb the right edge of the wall,
lit by a thin crack to a ledge, stepping right
to a groove. This is climbed, moving right at
e top. Traverse diagonally rightwards crossing
apitan to the tree.

7. Sickle 15m D
o either left or right of the short, steep wall of
ac, up easy rock to the ledge above the wall
d then straight up.

8. Autobahn 15m VD
imb the prominent chimney moving left to the
ack and across the slab at the top.

89. Siesta 15m D
Start to the left of the chimney. Climb up to a
large leaning block. Mantelshelf onto it then
climb straight up to finish.

90. Shake 15m VD
5 metres left of Siesta by the multi stemmed
rowan. Climb up a wall of loose blocks then the
crack above.

Numerous short walls and pinnacles continue
to the east for those seeking further horticultural
adventures but are best passed quickly by for
the classics of Crag Lough.

Graeme Read enjoying the
37. Ritual (E4 6a)
Photo: Malcolm Lowerson

Peel Crag Graded List

E4
Ritual 6a **

E3
Sacrifice 6a
C'est La Vie 6a

E2
Parental Guidance 5c *
Kamikaze Sex Pilot 5c *
Locomotion 5c *
The Intruder 5c *
Trilogy 5b *

E1
Capitan 5b *
Mortician 5c *
Rock Island Line 5b ***
Green Line 5b *
Certificate X 5a **
Albert's Wall 5a *
Whinstone Cowboy 5b

HVS
Phoebus Maximus 5b
Scratch 5a
Ace of Spades 5a *
Blasphemy Wall 5a *

VS
Twin Cracks 5a *
Jester 5a *
Sunset Direct 5a *
Clear as Crystal 5a
Adolphus 5a
Tiger's Overhang 4c **
Central Girdle 4c
Tiger's Hangover 4c
Tanya 4c
Prow Buttress Route Two 4c
Red Wall 4c
Consternation 4c
Denizen 4c
Vindication 4c
Perseverance 4c
The Corner 4c
Kurt 4c
A.S.B. 4c
Fissure-La-Boot 4c

John and Chris Hammerton
14. Sunset (MS)
Photo: Steve Crowe

Chris Davis leading
5. Sunset Direct (VS 5a)
No purpose will be served by considering the
possibility of the blocks ever becoming unstacked.
Photo: Rick Barnes

Queens Crag
Martin Waugh

History

Information for this guide has been largely plundered from 'North of England Rock Climbs' by Stewart Wilson (Published by CORDEE) with the Author's kind permission. A goodly selection of the climbs were repeated to check grades and route descriptions. In particular, these Lakeland boys were obviously hard men not given to overgrading and though overall grades are fine one or two of the technical grades are harsh even by Northumberland standards and the routes, though on very sound rock, have been so little climbed as to make prior cleaning a necessity. One new route was added during preparation for this guide, Andrew Earl hugging his way up the difficult Magician's Nephew. A number of excellent boulder problems have also been discovered. The remainder of the routes recorded here are all the work of Pete Whillance, Pete Botterill and Dave Armstrong who in 1982 'blitzed the crag and recorded their efforts. However, this is not the full stor as Whillance states "Some of the very easy lines must have been climbed before, but there is no evidence of this at all. The state of most of the routes leads me to think that probably nothing of VS or above had been previously climbed...." and, "Geoff Oliver admits to having pegged Rabbit crack many years ago!"

Situation and Character

Queens Crag is situated in the wild and remote-feeling country north of the Roman Wall at Housesteads. It faces North towards the Wark Forest and a landscape of moss and cotton grass. A lonely place, but in good weather a fine place to climb. The escarpment is nowhere higher than 8 metres and because 6 metres is more or less constant, heights are omitted. Many of the climbs, though short, are of excellent quality but because few people have climbed there as a result of lack of information, star ratings have been used sparingly until such time as a consensus is reached.

Approaches and Access

Follow the Military Road (B6318) west to where a gated track runs north from the road to Sewingshields Farm 8 miles west of Chollerford. Permission to drive along this unmetalled road may be sought at the cottage by the gate or at the main farmhouse, found to the left side of the track as it rises and turns 90 degrees right 600metres beyond the gate. Continue past the farm house to a sharp left hander after which the track curves right and down crossing a cattle grid 1 mile from the main road. Park carefully up on the left verge as the track turns 90 degrees to the right, the east end of the crag can be seen 10 minutes easy walk to the west. Alternatively park by the verge on the side road south to Haydon Bridge, reached just before the track to Sewingshields. See approach map on page 101.

The Climbs

The routes are described from right to left. A drystone wall runs uphill to meet the right hand end of the main crag at a prominent cave (usual base of operations). From here and leftwards the Main Crag extends to a region of short easy slabs and cracks located by the presence of a large boulder on the slope below. This is Boulder 2; the largest boulder on the crag. The section left of this more broken region is known as The Prows on account of the three jutting prows towards its left hand end.

To the right of the cave and across the drystone wall faces continue for about 100 metres to a prominent pinnacle – The Rabbit Stone.

Main Crag

. Boudicca HVS 6a
tart in the cave just right of where an obvious
ain crack cuts the roof. Pull over the roof on
mall holds to reach a horizontal crack. Hand
averse right and climb the arête to the top.

. Cleopatra HVS 5c
tart below the thin crack through the left hand
ide of the cave. Climb the crack and the slim
orner crack above. Possibly 5c for an orang
tang or someone who has just sat on an asp.

. Salote VD
limb the easy crack just left of the cave,
identified by a large block and several
hockstones. Dirty.

. Hera HVS 5b
limb the arête direct, immediately left of the
rack, to a sloping shelf. Finish above via an
wkward mantelshelf.

. Layback HS
he wide crack with an overhang at half height,
climbed by any appropriate method.

he next prominent buttress is identified by three
ood cracks on it's front face.

. Bicycle Race VS 5a
limb the right hand crack which has an
ndercut base and awkward jamming higher up.

7. Fat Bottomed Girls HS
Climb the central crack direct.

8. Jazz VS 5a *
A good route. Start in a groove set back from
the other two cracks. Climb the thin crack in the
groove by laybacking.

9. Grumble and Grunt S
Deep in the corner on the left is a crack formed
by two huge flakes sat one upon the other. Climb
the dirty crack.

The next prominent buttress has two very fine
climbs and between them an unclimbed thin,
snaking crack.

10. Gloriana E2 5b **
Start just left of a pedestal below the prominent
arête. Climb the arête direct just left of the
pedestal, then follow hollow flakes on the right
side to gain an awkward sloping ledge just below
the top. Bold!

11. Marie Celeste HVS 5b ***
Climb the striking corner to the left of the
unclimbed wall. Superb!

The next feature is a hanging rib above a nasty
looking block. It is unclimbed!

The buttress to the left has a wide crack on
either side.

12. Juno VS 4c
Start below the right hand crack. Climb the crack, which curves steeply up to a ledge on the left. Easier than it looks.

13. Dream Of Wet Corgies S
An annoying thrutch. Climb the left hand chimney/crack.

The next buttress has a very thin crack in its front face.

14. Security Risk HVS 5c
Start from a glacis and climb the thin crack in a slim groove on finger slots.

15. O. H. M. S. VD
Start round the corner on the left below a dirty, open groove. Climb the groove which has jammed flakes protruding from it.

About 3 metres further left of the dirty groove with the protruding flakes is a bulge with a thin crack running through it.

16. Queen Of Hearts HVS 6a
Start below the cracked bulge. Climb the bulge using the crack and the wall on the right. Move right to finish.

The scooped wall direct is so far unclimbed.

17. Etoile Vert VS 5b
Start at a green flared chimney just left of the cracked bulge. Climb the chimney to a large, wedged block. The finish is dirty and the climb is harder than it looks.

To the left of the green, flared chimney is an inset, square grooved recess containing a number of sandwiched flakes and cracks.

18. Stell Green Groove VS 4c
Climb the groove/recess via a pull on a jammed block and back and foot to exit right at the top. (Harder variations and eliminates are possible depending on what you choose to ignore – aren' there always?)

The final feature of the main crag is an overhanging rib.

19. Retch For The Stars HVS 5b
Start on the left side of the rib. Pull on a faint, flake crack on the left side of the rib to reach a horizontal break. A flake on the wall above is then used to finish by a mantelshelf. Alternatively, hand traverse right onto the hanging rib and pull up to a good finishing jug.

Left is a section of short, easy slabs and cracks providing quick ways up and down. 10 metres left is a thin, curved crack in a scooped wall which will give a short desperate problem.

20. Starstruck VS 5a
Climb the arête direct, just right of the curving crack.

There is another, short, easier crack before the rocks gain more height.

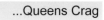

Ian Murray
14. Security Risk (HVS 5c)
Photo: Mike MacFarlane

The Prows

This is the name given to the section of the crag to the left of the area of easy slabs and cracks. The three prows of rock after which the section is named are in the latter half of the described climbs, i.e. at the left hand end.

The first climbs here are found on the first buttress to the left of the lower rocks described. This buttress is identified by a short crack on its front which ends in a sloping shelf. To the right of the crack is a curving rib.

21. The Furry Quean HVS 5b

Climb the curving rib to gain the sloping shelf. The arête above has an awkward move.

22. Queen Bee VS 5b

Climb the short crack on the front of the buttress to gain the sloping shelf. Climb the wall above to the top.

23. Bumble D

Climb the obvious blocky chimney just left of Queen Bee.

24. The Sting HVS 5b

Start immediately left of the chimney (and unfortunately within reach of it) below a short, sharp arête. Climb the arête direct to good finishing holds.

A bubbly wall (unclimbed!) on the left of the arête is followed by shorter rocks and a series of tightly packed, loose looking flakes and cracks which provide the next two climbs.

25. The Haggler HS 4c

Start at the short, thin rightmost crack which is solid. Climb the crack to an overhang and then follow the twin cracks to the top.

26. Left-Hand Crack VS 4c

Climb the left hand crack of the group via an overhanging start to gain a ledge on the left. Finish easily.

The left hand end of the crag has three distinct prows.

27. Prow Three VS 5a

Start on the right hand side of the prow. Pull up to a sentry box and climb the groove above.

Just left of Prow Two is short, green groove (VS 5a), then easy slabs and a tiny prow before Prow Two.

28. Prow Two HVS 5b

Start directly below the sharp arête. Climb the arête direct to start, then on its scooped right side to the top. (stepping off the large block on the left to start lowers the grade to VS 5a)

Short rocks and problems lead to Prow One.

29. Prow One VS 5b

Only a short problem. Use a pocket to reach up left to a ledge above the undercut base (or jump!). Use the rib to gain a standing position and reach the top.

The left side of Prow One is much easier and a few more problems exist.

There are several large boulders about 100 metres further left, but better boulders are to be found down the slope below the Main Crag. Many problems are possible. Particularly worthy of note are:-

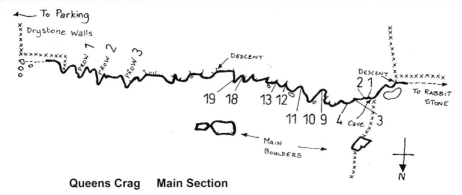

Queens Crag   Main Section

Boulder 1

The large boulder directly below the cave at the right end of the crag. It actually forms part of the drystone wall. The west face has two short routes of interest.

30. The Flutings VS 5a

Climb flutings in the centre of the wall to a break. Continue directly up the wall above on pockets.

31. Stewpot HVS 5b

Climb the wall to the right of the flutings to an obvious large pocket. Straight up to finish.

Boulder 2

The largest of the boulders, lying below the centre of the Main Crag. The north side presents a slabby face guarded by a bulging wall. The best three routes are recorded.

32. Sigg Arete HVS 5c *

Start at the curving arête on the right side of the bulging wall. Climb the overhanging right side of the arête and pull over onto the left side to finish.

33. Botterill's Shelf HVS 6a *

Start at the foot of the curving arête. Make a hard pull up left onto a very sloping shelf. Climb the slab diagonally leftwards to the top.

34. Brighton Rock HVS 5b

Start at the left hand side of the bulging wall. Climb a rightward slanting crack for a metre. Pull over the overlap and continue delicately to the top.

To the right of the Main Crag short faces continue for almost 100 metres to a prominent pinnacle – The Rabbit Stone

The Rabbit Stone

35. Rabbitstone Crack HVS 5b **

Start below the thin crack on the south side. Climb the thin crack in a slight corner by layback to big, spanking jugs at the top. Classic.

36. You Asked Ferret S

Start at the foot of the north west arête. Follow the edge all the way or climb the wide, left-slanting crack in the west face to meet the arête at half height.

37. Lapine It Up HVS 5b

Star at the lowest point at the foot of the north east arête. Move up the arête, then go right (crux) and up, to finish up the middle of the slabby north face.

38. The Snare VS 4c

Climb the east face, steeply at first, on a series of flakes. A slabby face is climbed above these to reach the top.

39. The Magician's Hat HVS 5b

Start from a pocket just left of Rabbitstone Crack. Pull around the arête to small holds on the west face. Climb straight up using the edge to a large flake and the top.

40. The Magician's Nephew E1 6b

Climbs the blunt arete at the south west corner of the Rabbit Stone by some precarious bearhugging to finally finish on good holds.

The crag facing the Rabbit Stone offers several hard possibilities. Short routes and problems have been done on the left of the prominent overhang.

Martin Waugh
8. Jazz (VS 5a)
Photo: Mike Macfarlane

Johnny Edwards
7. Fat Bottomed Girls (HS)
Photo: Mike MacFarlane

Queens Crag Graded List

E2
Gloriana 5b **

E1
The Magician's Nephew 6b

HVS
Botterill's Shelf 6a *
Queen of Hearts 6a
Left Hand Crack 4c
Sigg Arete 5c *
Security Risk 5c
Marie Celeste 5b ***
Hera 5b
Retch for the Stars 5b
The Furry Quean 5b
The Sting 5b
Prow Two 5b
Stewpot 5b
Brighton Rock 5b
Rabbitstone Crack 5b **
Lapine It Up 5b
The Magician's Hat 5b

VS
Queen Bee 5b
Etoile Vert 5b
Prow One 5b
Jazz 5a *
Bicycle Race 5a
Starstruck 5a
The Flutings 5a
Boudicca 6a
Prow Three 5a
The Snare 4c
Cleopatra 5c
Stell Green Groove 4c
Juno 4c

Ravensheugh Crag

Hugh Harris

NZ 013991
Norh West Facing
392 m
45 minutes

History

Climbing on Ravensheugh lagged somewhat behind its less hostile neighbour Simonside. In fact the real development of the crag did not take place until the late sixties and early seventies when a group of N.M.C. members were preparing the 1971 guide. The significant routes recorded at this time included Pendulum, Half Minute Crack and Baluster Crack by Allan Austin and Dave Roberts and Ravensheugh Crack, Wild West Show, Honeymoon Crack (with a shoulder) and The Trouser Legs by Hugh Banner.

In 1974 Bob Hutchinson and John Earl added the impressive Sandrider up the front of the first pinnacle. 1975 saw the addition of two superb bold routes up the west face of the second pinnacle - Gates of Eden by Earl and Candle in the Wind by Hutchinson; an electric storm caught Earl on the top of the pinnacle after completing Gates of Eden necessitating a swift descent and preventing Hutchinson from following. Hutchinson and Earl were again in action in 1976 freeing Honeymoon Crack to provide a very hard start to a superb route and exchanging leads for the bold, unprotected Plumbline. In 1978 Hutchinson added the deceptive Plumber whilst Earl lunged his way up Octopus. Steve Blake added Grease and Mimic which in the days prior to 'sticky boots' were bold and precarious pieces of climbing. Sadly in the same year Hutchinson led what was his last new route in Northumberland, Childhood's End, an excellent climb up the hanging crack right of Ravensheugh Crack.

Bob Smith made his first contribution in 1979 with Billy Biscuit and The Judas Hole raising the standard of the routes to E5. Bob Smith returned with Earl in 1984 to climb Rock and Roll Star, yet another good route up the west face of the second pinnacle. The following year he succeeded where many had failed and climbed the left arête of The Mole to give Bonneville. Finally, in 1987 he soloed the hard Trial Separation to complete the lines on the west face of the second pinnacle.

The new 1989 guide only succeeded in pointing out the obvious gaps and Hugh Harris was first to exploit these, soloing a Lapse of Reason up the obvious scoop right of Billy Biscuit. This was followed by First Among Equals up the immaculate fading crack left of Ravensheugh Crack - an oft-eyed line with many aspirants and the crag's first E6. Later that year Tim Gallagher climbed Castaway; a very bold direct version of Sandrider and another E6. Richard Davies got in on the action with the third E6; the well named Agape that goes straight up where Brown Trousers slides right. Harris added Paradise Lost in 1991, climbing direct out of Gates of Eden and adding another fine route to the second pinnacle.

As is usual at Ravensheugh there followed a lull of 5 years until 1996, when one of the most tried lines there, was finally completed by Noel Crane to give the totally unprotected and very reachy Reiver, up the blunt arête on the wall facing the back of the second pinnacle - a possible contender to be the crag's first E7. In the same year Nick Dixon completed his audacious hop step and jump to give a 7b Direct Start to Verbal Abuse.

After another 5 years in the summer of 2001, Andrew Earl climbed the bouldery Overpowered and in 2003 the impressive left arête of The Second Pinnacle to produce, the crags second E7, Crocodile Arête. On the same day Alec Burns was caught Chasing Sheep.

Situation and Character

This magnificent crag lies 1mile west of Simonside and faces north west with a commanding aspect over the Coquet Valley, in a setting which is unsurpassed anywhere in the county. The rock is compact sandstone, which is generally of good quality, though there are occasional sandy areas where the harder surface has eroded. Cracks and chimneys are plentiful offering obvious lines. The open walls and buttresses, which are often rounded and with small holds, provide many of the harder routes. In general the climbing is reminiscent of gritstone and proficiency in jamming is

Steve Crowe grappling with
27. The Trouser Legs (E1 5b)
Photo: Karin Magog

essential on many of the middle grade routes. Some of the best climbs in Northumberland are to be found on this crag, although early in the season they may be lichenous and the harder ones may require cleaning (as if the visitors need an excuse).

Approaches and Access

The rocks can be reached in about forty five minutes from the Forestry Commission car park on the road between Great Tosson and Lordenshaw (037997). The Forestry Commission road is followed through the forest to beneath the west end of Simonside where a minor track leads west across the plateau to a stile. Follow a faint track 100 metres further to reach the top of the crag. An alternative approach can be made in about the same time from Great Tosson by following the Simonside track to the 300 metre contour line, then branching off right along a forestry road which is followed until just after a hairpin bend to the left where the trees stop. Cut up the hillside to gain the minor track and continue to the stile just before the crag.

No right of way exists from the stile to the crag. At the time of writing there is no access problem but climbers must not stray across the moor. There is a right of access to the crag under CRoW.

The Climbs

At the eastern end of the crag the unique Block Pinnacles are easily identified and it is in this area that the best routes are concentrated. The western section is broken into a number of outcrops separated by heather slopes. The routes are described from left to right and on the pinnacles in an anticlockwise direction commencing from the left hand front corner (north east). Starting from the eastern end, the most obvious feature is the vertical wall containing the Parallel Cracks. Round the corner to the left is a shorter wall that provides some easy scrambles. The first climb is in the centre of this short wall.

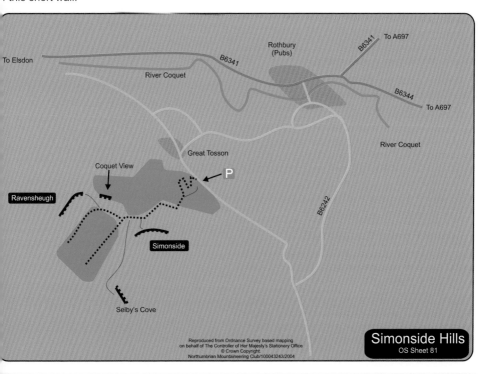

Simonside Hills
OS Sheet 81

Parallel Crack Area

Parallel Crack Area

1. Easy Cave 6m M
Climb the wall into the cave and continue up the short chimney.

2. Stomach Traverse 7m D
Just right of the previous climb. The right hand edge of the wall is followed to a ledge beneath the overhang from which a stomach traverse is made to exit on the right. An alternative start can be made just left of the direct start.

3. Amanda 8m HVS 5b
Start 3 metres right of Easy Cave. Climb the wall direct and pull over the overhang.

4. Rubberneck 6m HVS 5b
The wall 3 metres left of Left Parallel Crack.

5. Dark Passage 15m 6a
A popular finger traverse of the wall. Start at Rubberneck and follow the obvious traverse line to the Right Parallel Crack. The climb now gets interesting, follow the thin crack across Big Daddy and finish up one of the problems at the right hand end.

6. Left Parallel Crack 6m VD

7. Central Parallel Crack 6m VD
The wall between Central Parallel Crack and Limbo has been climbed at 5c.

8. Limbo 6m E1 5c
The overhanging wall between the Central and Right Parallel Cracks. A large hold above head height is gained; standing on this provides the crux. Continue directly up the wall above.

9. Arête-shun 6m E1 5b
The left arête of Right Parallel Crack, direct to the large break from where a large jug can be attained via crimps.

10. Right Parallel Crack 6m VD

11. Little Idi 6m E1 5b
Climb the wall 3 metres right of Right Parallel Crack and then move left to a dubious looking flake which is used to gain the break.

12. Big Daddy 6m 6a
Dynamically climb the wall right of Little Idi by the vague flake.

To the right of Big Daddy, leftward trending holds are followed by ledges at 5c.

Slightly downhill and 50 metres to the east of the Parallel Cracks is a 6 metre buttress with an overhang split by twin cracks 5c.

East Buttress
Immediately right of a grassy slope is a wall with the well defined crack of Pendulum in its upper half.

13. Pete's Ploy 7m E2 5b
The wall left of the arête provides a deceptively serious route.

14. Plumbline 9m E4 5c ***
The fine arête is climbed direct without protection and gives a superb but serious climb

Jenny Hogarth leading
7. Central Parallel Crack (VD)
Photo: Steve Crowe

East Buttress

First and Second Pinnacles

15. The Judas Hole 9m E5 6a **
Another good hard climb, up the wall between Plumbline and Pendulum. Follow the deceptive groove left of Pendulum Direct to a horizontal break. Using a small, deep pothole, (wobbly 21/2 Friend or better Tricam 4) and small holds climb the wall above.

16. Pendulum 9m VS 4c ***
A good route. Start in the corner to the right of the direct line to the crack, follow a leftward sloping crack and make a traverse left to gain the bottom of the deep crack (crux). The crack is then climbed more easily on good jams to the top.

Direct Start HVS 5a
The thin crack direct to the upper deep crack.

17. Hanging Chimney 6m S
The conspicuous chimney in the corner on the right. Climb by the slab and crack into the cave. Work out beneath the overhang and make a strenuous exit facing right.

18. Billy Biscuit 9m E5 6a ***
The fine unprotected arête right of Hanging Chimney leads dynamically to a good hold at 6 metres. Continue up the black wall above.

19. Lapse of Reason 10m E5 6a
Climb the wall 2m right of Billy Biscuit, passing the obvious large pocket, until moves rightward lead to the sloping ledge at 6m. Finish direct on rounded breaks.

20. Easter Grooves 12m E2 5b *
Follows the obvious series of grooves overlooking First Pinnacle Gully. Start up a crack at the toe of the buttress, then move right to gain a slabby groove which runs up rightwards. Climb this and the steeper groove above, then move left onto a good ledge on the arête. Finish more easily up the slabs above.

21. Ginger Snap 8m HVS 5b
The wall right of Easter Grooves is climbed via the obvious T shaped hold.

22. Easter Bunny 8m HVS 4c
A right to left traverse on the wall right of Easter Grooves.

The First Pinnacle

23. Verbal Abuse 9m E2 5c
The arête left of Baluster Crack which is reached by a traverse from the left.

Direct Start E2 7b
Take a boulder hopping, running jump then smear and slap to gain the arête direct.

24. Baluster Crack 12m HVS 5b **
The impressive fist jam crack on the front of the pinnacle. Climb the first overhang by strenuous jamming followed by a further bulge to a ledge. Continue up the easier angled crack to the top.

Variation Finish 5b
The overhanging crack to the right is harder.

Bob Hogarth avoiding the good jams on
16. Pendulum (VS 4c)
Photo: Steve Crowe

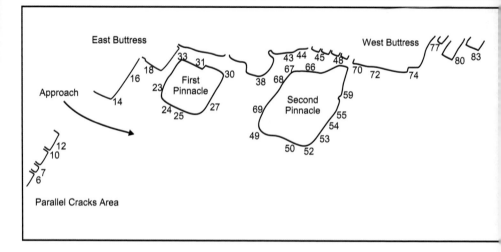

25. The Sandrider 15m E3 5c **
An excellent route. Climb the crack 3 metres right of Baluster Crack until a move left can be made onto the ledge. Climb the bulge above by a crack which fades out onto flat holds. Traverse right and finish up the fine crack in the centre of the top tier of the pinnacle.

26. Castaway 13m E6 6a**
Start as for Sandrider and climb the initial crack to the ledge. From here make a long reach from the undercut crack straight up for good holds. Unprotected moves then lead slightly right to the shelf. Move left and finish up the top crack as for the normal route.

27. The Trouser Legs 15m E1 5b ***
This classic route up the west face of the pinnacle follows the obvious scoop divided by a rib (the trouser legs). Start in the corner, left of the scoop and climb a difficult wall to reach a crack in which protection can be arranged. Traverse right, round the bulge to gain access to the bottom of the scoop. Climb the scoop with difficulty to a resting place below the overhang. Traverse right to a short crack, which leads to a final finishing crack.

Direct Start 5c
Gain the scoop direct, a long reach being useful.

28. Brown Trousers 15m E2 5c
Start as for The Trouser Legs then climb the arête to the break. Traverse right to finish at the crack right of The Trouser Legs.

29. Agape 13m E6 6a
Start as for The Trouser Legs and climb direct to a good rest and runners. Swing up left and then move up to a large hole. From good holds above this, traverse right to a hands-off rest below another hole and further runners, then up the overhanging wall above to a rounded finish.

30. Stay With Me 6m E2 5c
Twin cracks immediately right of the arête right of The Trouser Legs are climbed to a sloping ledge, when a move left to another crack around the arête leads to the top (no stepping off).

31. Easter Crack 6m VD
Right of the previous route on the back wall of the pinnacle. It is the easiest route down from the top.

32. E Star HVS 5a
The wall just right of Easter Crack.

33. Platform Route 6m VD
Start at the south east corner of the pinnacle. Pull up onto a platform then climb the wall above, either by a direct line or diagonally to the right.

34. Tea Break Wall 9m MVS
Start half way up the gully between the East Buttress and the First Pinnacle. Traverse right to below a flake. Pull up to this and continue straight up to a good ledge. Finish easily up the short, wide crack above.

35. Coffee Time 8m MVS 4b
A vague corner groove right of Tea Break Wall.

36. First Pinnacle Traverse 24m E2 5c
Start up Easter Crack, traverse to Platform
Route and climb easily to below the final crack of
Baluster Crack. Good holds under the overhang
lead to protection then to the final crack of The
Trouser Legs.

An easy route over large boulders separates the
First Pinnacle from Intermediate Buttress.

Intermediate Buttress

37. Lazy Afternoon 8m E2 5b
Start left of Pussyfoot and go straight up the
bulging wall.

38. Pussyfoot 8m VS 5a
Climb directly up the slabby front of Intermediate
Buttress. Pull awkwardly onto the slab on
the right, then move across up left to join
Catwalk below the final crack. Finish up this or
alternatively move right and finish up Felix.

39. Catwalk 10m D
An interesting route starting high up on the right
wall of the buttress. Traverse left along a ledge
and make an exposed move round the corner
onto the front of the buttress. Finish up the
crack.

40. Felix 10m VS 5a
Climb the obvious, thin, rightward sloping crack
in the wall above the Catwalk traverse.

To the right of the start of Catwalk is the curious
recess known as the Box Office. There is a short
crack climb on the right of the entrance which is
of Difficult standard. The next climbs are to the
right of the Box Office on the steep wall facing
the back of the Second Pinnacle.

41. Index Breaker 6m E3 6a
The wall left of Octopus. A snappy route.

42. Octopus E3 6b *
An extending problem up the curved, shallow
groove in the wall. Climb the groove until a long
reach or slap can be made to gain the ledge.
Move right and climb to the top. Only those with
long tentacles need apply.

43. Reiver 9m E7 6c **
The oft-tried blunt arête between Octopus and
Smarty Pants. From a standing position on
the sloping hold at head height, a long reach
may gain the ramp line up and left and further
committing moves to the break. The first
ascensionist was 6' 4" with long arms.

44. Smarty Pants 9m E2 5c **
The fine, open corner dominating the wall gives
an excellent climb. Well suited to pyschedaelic
tights.

45. Half Minute Crack 8m VS 5a **
The thin, leaning crack near the centre of the
wall provides a thirty second exercise in hand
jamming but can take much longer.

46. Chasing Sheep 8m E3 6b
The crack just to the right of Half Minute Crack,
which is hard to start, is climbed direct.

47. One Boot Crack 8m VS 5a *
The wide crack right of the previous climb. The
start is the crux and the route is deceptively
difficult and strenuous.

48. The Backdoor 5m M
The corner to the right provides an easy way
down.

Alec Burns on the first ascent of
46. Chasing Sheep (E3 6b)
Photo: Andrew Earl

Andrew Earl
on the first ascent of
49. Crocodile Arete (E7 6c)
Photo: Alec Burns

The Second Pinnacle

49. Crocodile Arête 14m E7 6c **

This fine line takes the imposing left hand arête of the Second Pinnacle. From the boulder reach a jug, campus to the break, move left to the arête and up to the ledge. A tricky sequence up the final section of the arête leads to a good jug to finish.

50. Honeymoon Crack 14m E3 6b ***

The front of the Second Pinnacle is protected by a huge overhang. This fine climb follows the crack, starting near the right edge of the overhang. Climb the roof to gain the crack with difficulty, follow it to the ledge above then traverse left and gain access to a second wide crack which leads awkwardly to the top. Traditionally a shoulder was used to gain the initial crack, this reduces the grade to 5b.

51. Old Man River 13m E4 6b *

Climb Honeymoon Crack until the obvious rising crack line can be gained by a traverse left. Follow it to the arête which is climbed on the left to a ledge. Finish left.

The following four routes ascend the impressive west face of the pinnacle.

52. Trial Separation 18m E4 6b **

Start 2 metres right of Honeymoon Crack at the obvious pothole in the roof. Use this to swing left to another pothole, then swing back right to a further large pothole above the roof. Swing back left to a jam in a horizontal break and continue to the ledge (The Balcony). Finish up Candle in the Wind.

53. Rock and Roll Star 18m E5 6a *

A good hard route starting up the wall left of Candle in the Wind and finishing up the arête right of Honeymoon Crack. Climb the wall on rounded holds to gain some small pot holes, use these to gain the rounded break and then move up to the cave of Gates of Eden. Traverse The Balcony to the arête at the left hand end and climb this direct to flutings.

54. Candle in the Wind 18m E3 5c ***

A magnificent route. Gain the left parallel line of flakes with difficulty and follow them to the overhung ledge (The Balcony). Traverse left along this, move up and then continue leftwards to an awkward finish up the groove immediately right of the arête (it is possible to continue the traverse left for a runner in Honeymoon Crack).

Second Pinnacle, Crescent Wall

55. Gates of Eden 18m E2 5c ***
A fitting companion to the previous route. Climb the right parallel line of flakes to the cave. Traverse left and make an awkward move onto the overhung ledge. From its right end make a difficult move to gain the slab, which is climbed to the top. The short may find it impossible to gain the slab direct and an alternative entry is possible on the left.

56. Paradise Lost 12m E5 6b **
Start as for Gates of Eden and climb the right parallel line of flakes to the cave. Pull through the roof of the cave and go straight up the wall above to a worrying move onto the slab and a sloping finish.

57. Borstal Boy 12m E1 5b
The wall right of Gates of Eden. Climb to the platform and then up the flutings to join Crescent Wall, continue via the arête on the left.

58. Crescent Wall 12m MVS 4b **
Climb to the platform as for The Crescent. Continue straight up to a second platform then climb the slightly overhanging wall above, taking care with the dubious flake.

59. The Crescent 13m S *
The conspicuous curving crack on the west wall of the pinnacle. Climb the crack or wall to a platform, move up then traverse out on the right wall and make a pull up into the crack. Work up and through the crack to join Layback which is followed to the top. More akin to potholing.

60. Wide Eyed &Legless 8m E4 5c *
The arêtes right of Backdoor and left of Layback are bridged. Exit left or right.

61. Layback 8m VD
An obvious wide crack on the back of the pinnacle. It can be climbed by thrutching or more elegantly by laybacking. The easiest climb down the pinnacle.

62. The Nark 8m MVS 4c
Just right of Layback. An awkward start and short slab lead to the wall which is climbed with the aid of some incipient cracks and a shallow corner on the left.

63. Dawes Route 8m E5 6c
Climb the arête right of The Nark. A hard start is followed to a delicate finish.

64. The Squealer 8m E2 5c
Start up the wall on the right until the arête can be gained more easily.

65. Scoop Crack 8m HS 4b
Starts at the centre of the back wall of the Second Pinnacle. Climb the scoop with the aid of the thin crack.

66. Cat's Whiskers 8m E1 5b *
The obvious scoop to the right of Scoop Crack is ascended direct by delicate climbing.

67. Hot Bricks 8m E1 5c
Climb the wall just right of the arête via the small pothole. More serious than it looks.

68. East Wall 10m S
From the jammed blocks near the left end of the east face move diagonally right to a large ledge. Climb straight up either from the left or right end of the ledge.

69. Sunny Sunday 10m E2 5c
Start right of East Wall. From the top point of a large boulder climb straight up the wall.

West Buttress Area

West Buttress

West Buttress lies on the right of the Second Pinnacle and is bounded on the left by the Backdoor.

70. Cave Crack 11m VS 4c

Start below the cave on the left hand edge of West Buttress. Easy climbing leads to the cave from which the undercut crack is reached. Follow this until near the top, where a bridge across onto the Second Pinnacle then a step back into the top of the crack makes an awkward finish.

71. First Among Equals 12m E6 6b ***

The superlative hard classic up the fading crackline left of Ravensheugh Crack. Climb the initial shallow corner of Ravensheugh Crack to the shelf. Pull into the crack directly above and gain a standing position on the large flat hold. A hard sequence leads to the next rounded break and then a long reach is made to finish just left of the chicken head.

72. Ravensheugh Crack 12m HVS 5a ***

An exhilarating classic up the crack which splits the upper section of West Buttress right of Cave Crack. Climb the lower wall by a strenuous shallow corner to reach the ledge below the crack. Move right and pull up into the crack, continue to the top on good jams.

73. Childhood's End 13m E4 6a ***

A superb route up the hanging crack right of Ravensheugh Crack. Pull up just left of Wild West Show and move left to a ledge beneath the crack. An awkward runner placement is possible in the base of the crack. Gain the crack precariously, climb it to just below its top, then traverse left into Ravensheugh Crack to finish.

Direct Start 6a

Climb the wall direct to the crack.

74. Wild West Show 15m HVS 5a **

Yet another classic. Start near the right hand edge of West Buttress. Climb the wall by a shallow corner to attain a flat ledge. Hand traverse left to reach the bottom of a fine crack. Climb the crack, which eases back near the top, to finish over slabs.

The following routes provide delicate and unprotected climbing up the smooth slab on the extreme right hand side of West Buttress.

75. Redskin 11m E2 5b *

Start a metre right of the start of Wild West Show and climb straight up to the base of the slab. Pull onto the slab and continue directly upwards to join the last section of Buckskin.

76. Sitting Bull 9m E2 5b

Start just right of the nose. Climb to the ledge left of Moccasin Slab and then over the overhang using the obvious pot holes.

77. Moccasin Slab 8m HVS 5a *

At the right side of the slab is a detached block. Bridge up between this and the wall then step across with difficulty onto the slab. Climb straight up on small holds.

78. Buckskin 11m VS 4c **

Start as for the previous route then take an independent line diagonally left across the slab.

Little Leaner Area

The next section of the crag is separated from West Buttress by a short gully and extends as far as Zig Zag Slab.

79. Bonneville 6m E3 6c *
The left arête provides a very hard micro route.

80. T.C. 6m E3 5c
Climb the Mole to a horizontal crack, hand traverse left along this to the arête and up this via the obvious pot hole.

81. Mole 6m MS
The corner crack.

82. Just Arrested 8m E2 5b
Climb the Mole to half height, step right onto the edge then right again to the groove which leads awkwardly to the top.

83. Just Ice 8m E3 6a
Start 2 metres right of the Mole. Make a long reach to gain a small layaway and climb the wall tending left to join and finish up the shallow groove of Just Arrested.

The boulder forming the left wall of Out On The Wall Gully gives two 4b arête problems.

84. Out On The Wall Gully 10m D
An obvious feature 7 metres right of the previous route. Climb the chimney below the main part of the gully and continue up the right wall. An easier but less worthwhile start can be made round the corner on the left.

85. Overpowered 8m E5 6c
The overhanging wall to the left of the arête left of Pink Lane. Climb the wall on positive holds to a break, then make powerful and delicate moves to gain the top.

86. Pink Lane 8m E1 5b *
Start a metre left of Little Leaner. Climb up then traverse left to a ledge on the right of the arête. Move back right and climb the wall to finish.

87. Facing Facts 6m E2 5c
The wall just left of Little Leaner. Climb the horizontals to the faint flakes, up these to the horizontal break and the top.

88. Little Leaner 6m VS 5a **
A good little route up the next corner to the right. Ascend the left wall and the overhanging corner then finish over the prow of the leaning right wall.

89. Bede Crack 6m MS
The obvious corner crack just right of Little Leaner gives a good climb in spite of its rather dirty finish.

90. Grease 8m E4 6a **
Serious and thin slab climbing. Traverse right from Bede Crack along the lip of the slab. From a pocket in the centre of the slab move up on small holds to the top.

Direct Start 6b
Gain the pocket direct by means of shallow pockets.

91. Mimic 6m E3 5c
The arête right of Grease. Pull over the bulge onto the slab, step up onto the arête and finish direct.

92. St. Cuthbert's Crack 6m VS 5a *
The layback crack to the right, in a shallow corner. Climb the crack to reach a ledge on the left. Continue easily to the top.

Graeme Read leading
73. Childhood's End (E4 6a)
Photo: Richard Pow

Capstan Rock

The next obvious feature to the right is Zig Zag Slab on which there are a number of variations. A ledge divides the slab at half height and the lower section has two faces divided by a rounded rib.

93. Slab Corner 9m VD
Climb the corner on the left of the left hand slab, to the ledge. Continue easily up the wide crack above.

94. Zig Zag Slab, Route One 9m S
Climb the left hand slab starting just right of Slab Corner and trend right to gain the right hand edge of the ledge. Traverse left (or continue straight up, harder) and ascend the corner crack for a short distance until it is possible to move back right and ascend the upper slab near its right hand edge.

95. Zig Zag Slab, Route Two 10m S
The steepest slab, on the right of the rib, is climbed to the half way ledge. Some thin, incut holds on the middle section lead to the right hand edge of the upper slab.

Right of Zig Zag Slab is a boulder strewn heather slope. Capstan Rock is set back at the top of the slope and on the short wall behind and left of it, is a crack of Very Difficult standard.

Capstan Rock
The next route takes the wall left of the groove/crack immediately behind the Capstan.

96. Capstan Full Strength 5m E2 5c
The wall is climbed direct.

97. Capstan Crack 5m VS
The groove/crack immediately behind the Capstan.

98. Funeral for a Friend 6m E4 6a
The arête left of The Convict (a runner can be placed in the crack to the left).

99. The Convict 6m E2 5b
Start on the shelf beneath the steep wall on the right. Climb the flake and move diagonally right for a metre then climb the wall direct.

Heather Slab
Some 25 metres west across the heather slope is the easy angled Heather Slab.

100. Heather Slab 11m M
Climb the slab by starting on the left. Finish up the short wall above.

101. The One That Got Away 8m VS 5a
The route takes a flake crack in the wall around to the right of Heather Slab. Climb the crack and then make difficult moves up and left to gain the right edge of the slab.

104 105   107   Plumber Buttress

further heather slope follows, the **Split Blocks** et back near the top of the slope provide some hort problems. Further across this heather lope is another outcrop which provides the ollowing routes:-

'lumber Buttress

02. Green Gully 6m D
limb a short wall to enter the gully then either nish steeply to the left or traverse out to the ght across a slab.

03. Steeple Crack 6m VS 5a
he shallow corner just right of Green Gully. limb the corner or the green wall to the break. inish up the crack above.

04. The Plumber 9m E5 6b *
good route giving deceptively thin climbing on ounded holds up the wall left of The Sewer.

05. The Sewer 8m S
he deep, straight chimney right of Green Gully ives a strenuous climb.

06. Soil Stack Crack 8m VS 5a *
he thin crack right of The Sewer.

The slab on the right which leads to the layback crack has been chiselled and is not recorded, even though it has since been climbed avoiding the chipped holds.

107. Badger 6m S
The corner crack near the right edge of the outcrop which runs out short of the top.

Trident Buttress
A short walk leads to the Trident which is set back up the slope and is split by two chimneys. The left hand chimney is short and of no interest.

108. Neptune 8m VS 5a
Start up the arête left of Trident Chimney. Move left along the break to surmount the upper wall direct.

109. Trident Chimney 6m VD
The right hand of the two chimneys. A typical Ravensheugh chimney. Thrutch up to the large capstone and climb round it on the outside.

Right of Trident Buttress and slightly down the hillside is a short wall split by four cracks. This forms the left end of the Garden Wall.

The Garden Wall

110. Titch 4m HVS 5b
The short arête left of Left Hand Crack, starting on the right and finishing on the left.

111. Left Hand Crack 5m S
The left-hand crack of the twin cracks.

112. Right Hand Crack 5m S
Climb the right hand of the twin cracks which is very narrow initially but widens at the top.

113. Northern Rock 6m E1 5c
Start 1 metre right of Right Hand Crack and climb the left side of the wall using the arête for assistance.

114. Northern Line 6m E3 6b
The thin crack left of Mouldy Corner is short and sharp.

115. Mouldy Corner 5m HS
The damp corner.

116. Acne Vulgaris 8m HVS 5a
The unpleasant wall right of Mouldy Corner.

117. Sleight of Hand 6m MVS 4c
Start 3 metres right of Mouldy Corner. Gain a grass ledge 3 metres off the ground. Move up and right to finish on the slab at the top.

At this point the crag is split into two tiers. On the left is the shattered Castle Pinnacle and right of this the large and vegetated face of the Garden Wall, where three routes and a start to Wombat have been cleaned and climbed. They have however long since become overgrown and are best forgotten. The next four climbs start above and behind the pinnacle.

118. Balmoral Groover 8m HVS 5a
The obvious groove left of Castle Chimney.

119. Castle Chimney 8m D
The square cut chimney is awkward and dirty.

120. Gone Fishing 9m E3 5c
Climb the wall to the left of Rampart Crack.

121. Rampart Crack 9m HVS 5b *
The rightward slanting crack up the overhanging wall to the right of Castle Chimney. A fine climb.

122. Wombat 9m S
Scramble slightly down and right from Castle Chimney. Ascend to a constricted cave below the overhang in the corner. Climb out of the overhang on its left (crux).

123. Battlements 12m VS 4c
This takes the front of the Castle Pinnacle starting at the left hand corner. An awkward move enables the flake to be gained direct; this is then followed to a ledge below the final overhang. Move right and surmount the overhang to gain the top of the pinnacle.

124. Pigeon's Nest Crack 9m MVS 4c
The prominent off width crack at the right end of the Garden Wall.

Far West Buttress
This buttress marks the western end of Ravensheugh Crag and is set back from the Garden Wall. Near its left hand edge is Waterpipe Chimney, an easy scramble.

125. Downcomer Crack 8m MVS 4c
Takes the crack and groove up the centre of the left flank of the buttress.

126. West Wall Variant 10m E1 5b
Climb the wall left of Far West Chimney to an awkward pull onto a ledge. Move right and finish up Far West Chimney.

127. Far West Chimney 10m MVS 4c
The obvious undercut chimney splitting Far West Buttress. The final overhanging chimney providing the crux.

Variation Finish 13m VD
Ascend to beneath the final overhanging chimney and avoid the crux by traversing left along an exposed ledge to reach the upper part of Waterpipe Chimney.

128. Futility 13m VS 4c *
Starts round the corner to the right of Far West Chimney, beneath an overhang. Climb the crack up to the overhang and traverse left on undercuts until access to the crack above can be gained. This is followed to a ledge from which the overhanging corner is climbed, until a move left can be made onto a ledge leading easily to the top.

129. Scoop Right Hand 8m VD
This climb is on the short right hand wall of Far West Buttress. A scoop is a prominent feature. Climb a short wall to reach the right hand edge of the scoop then continue diagonally right along a wide flake crack.

130. Little Crack 6m S
Climb the crack on the left of the small stepped buttress. The finish is quite awkward.

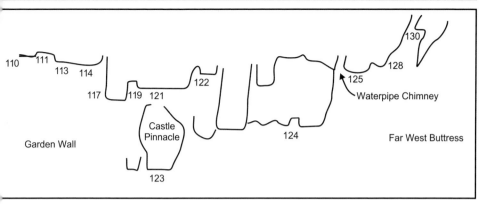

Ravensheugh Crag Graded List

E7
Reiver 6c **
Crocodile Arête 6c **

E6
Castaway 6a **
Agape 6a
First Among Equals 6b ***

E5
Judas Hole 6a **
Paradise Lost 6b **
Overpowered 6c
Silly Biscuit 6a ***
Lapse of Reason 6a
Rock and Roll Star 6a *
Pawe's Route 6c
The Plumber 6b *

E4
Plumbline 5c ***
Grease Direct Start 6b
Trial Separation 6b **
Funeral for a Friend 6a
Grease 6a **
Childhood's End 6a ***
Old Man River 6b *
Wide Eyed & Legless 5c *

E3
Bonneville 6c *
Octopus 6b *
Chasing Sheep 6b
Mimic 5c
Candle in the Wind 5c ***
Honeymoon Crack 6b ***

Index Breaker 6a
Just Ice 6a
Northern Line 6b
T.C. 5c
Gone Fishing 5c
The Sandrider 5c **

E2
Verbal Abuse Direct Start 7b
Gates of Eden 5c ***
The Convict 5b
Verbal Abuse 5c
Capstan Full Strength 5c
Easter Grooves 5b *
Smarty Pants 5c **
Brown Trousers 5c
Pete's Ploy 5b
The Squealer 5c
First Pinnacle Traverse 5c
Sunny Sunday 5c
Sitting Bull 5b
Stay With Me 5c
Lazy Afternoon 5b
Facing Facts 5c
Redskin 5b *
Just Arrested 5b

E1
Borstal Boy 5b
The Trouser Legs 5b ***
Hot Bricks 5c
Limbo 5c
Pink Lane 5b *
Little Idi 5b
West Wall Variant 5b
Northern Rock 5c

Arête-shun 5b
Cat's Whisker 5b *

HVS

Baluster Crack 5b **
Ginger Snap 5b
Easter Bunny 4c
Rampart Crack 5b *
Rubberneck 5b
Balmoral Groover 5a
Acne Vulgaris 5a
Amanda 5b
Moccasin Slab 5a *
Wild West Show 5a **
Ravensheugh Crack 5a ***
Pendulum D.S. 5a
E Star 5a
Titch 5b

VS
Felix 5a
Half Minute Crack 5a **
Little Leaner 5a **
Neptune 5a
Battlements 4c
Buckskin 4c **
Cave Crack 4c
One Boot Crack 5a *
Pendulum 4c ***
Futility 4c *
Pussyfoot 5a
Soil Stack Crack 5a *
St. Cuthbert's Crack 5a *
Steeple Crack 5a
The One That Got Away 5a

Rothley Crag

Tim Catterall

History

The crag was first mentioned briefly in an article by Jack Longland in 1928, although the first route was not recorded until 1940 when he climbed Rothley Crack. This excellent line which still demands respect may well have been the hardest climb in the county at that time. Little else was recorded until a concerted effort in the early 1980's by Martin Doyle, Karl Telfer and friends produced a number of routes culminating in the bold and difficult Master Blaster led by Don Barr. This was followed by Bob Smith and John Earl's ascent of Muscular Eruption and finally Hugh Harris's lead on The Taste of Someone Else. New routes at the crag then lay dormant until a spell of activity in 1999 when Andy Cowley added Water Torture. Then in 2000 Masterstroke was added by Steve Crowe which filled the gap right of Master Blaster and Andrew Earl added Masterclass and Master Blaster Arête. 2002 saw Karin Magog and Steve Crowe add Swing Time and Jane Lies Agape respectively to Tarzan Buttress and finally The Cattleburners on the main buttress.

Situation and Character

The crag lies about 2 miles north of Scots Gap just east of the unclassified road which leads to the B6342 Rothbury road. Most of the routes lie upon the large buttress split by a prominent crack which is clearly visible from the road. This is Rothley Crack. The crag is composed of rough and usually sound sandstone which can be lichenous because of the north westerly aspect. There is a pleasing view to the west towards the Wanneys and added interest is provided by the folly 100 metres or so to the east of the main crag. To the south of and below the main crag are numerous small buttresses which contain many enjoyable and quite testing boulder problems. Although a number of routes have been named on these buttresses they have not been described in this guide as they are short and the keen boulderer is left to explore at leisure. A number of routes reported prior to the last guide have again not been included because the first ascentionist resorted to the totally unaccepted practice of chipping holds. This is a stance which the current guide book team wishes to endorse. Person or persons unknown, have been involved in frequent wire brushing, particularly on Master Blaster Arête. This is a totally unaccepted practice which has already changed the route and will, if it continues, destroy it.

Approaches and Access

Cars must be parked in the lay-by at the crossroads just north of the crag and must not be parked on the road in front of the crag. At the east end of the lay-by a track leads through the woods and then across the moor to boulders at the north end of the crag. There is a right of access to the crag under CRoW.

Rothley from the air.
Photo: Mark Savage

Andrew Earl enjoys his own
7. Masterclass (E7 6c)
Photo: Steve Crowe

Rothley Crag

The Climbs

The climbs are described from left to right beginning at the obvious thin crack which gives the first route.

Main Crag

1. Shades of Green 5m VS 4b
Climb the thin crack and finish up the small fluted arête.

2. After the Blast 6m E1 5c
The pod round to the right is climbed to the overhang, move left then step back right onto the slab and to the top.

3. Water Torture 11m E5 6a
Climb After the Blast until it is possible to reach right to a large pothole. Move right and climb the wall above on edges and pockets to a ledge just below the top. Traverse right onto and up Master Blaster to finish.

Two routes to the left of the arête have been excluded because they were chipped.

4. Master Blaster Arête 15m E7 6c **
This serious route provides excellent climbing directly up the blunt arête of Master Blaster.

Gain the ledge immediately beneath the arête. The routes only protection can be placed from this ledge; it is good in the break at foot level but very poor just above it. The first few moves above the ledge are the hardest. The technical difficulty eases when Master Blaster is reached but the seriousness increases.

An eliminate has been climbed between Master Blaster Arête and Master Blaster (6a) and can be combined with Masterstroke.

5. Master Blaster 15m E5 6a **
A good route which fineshes up the blunt arête left of Rothley Crack. Start 3 metres right of the arête, climb to the diagonal break on small holds, move up to a pocket, traverse left to the arête and climb to the top using the flute.

6. Masterstroke 15m E4 6b
Start as for Master Blaster. Cross the diagonal break and continue to the good pocket. (cam). Step up and right (crucial small Slider to left), then continue direct via a long reach to pockets and edges to the upper break and good protection (small cams). Finish direct.

A route has been climbed to the left but has been excluded because it was chipped.

. Masterclass 15m E7 6c ***
Hard, technical and serious. Start midway
between Rothley Crack and Master Blaster
Arête. Climb up to good gear in the break.
Follow the vague rib direct past a small side pull
or your right hand and make two or three hard
moves going straight up on several poor slopers
to a sloping pocket in the upper break. Finish
direct.

. The Taste of Someone Else 14m E6 6b *
A serious route. Start 3 metres left of Rothley
Crack. Climb easily up to the horizontal break,
stand up and move slightly right, then climb the
wall above past a small pocket to the next break.
Move left to a good pocket and pull over the top.

. Rothley Crack 14m VS 5a ***
The crack up the centre of the wall. A superb
classic line which provides the best route on the
crag at its grade.

0. Muscular Eruption 25m E3 5c *
An excellent sustained climb traversing from
Rothley Crack to Master Blaster about 2.5
metres below the top of the crag. Well protected
with Friends and nuts.

1. The Cattleburners E4 6a
Reach the runnel direct. Continue straight up
avoiding the crack on the left and the runnel of
Dog Burner on the right.

2. Dogburner 12m E4 5c *
Another good route. Start 3 metres right of
Rothley Crack. Climb to the crack in the overlap
and up to a ledge. Reach left for finger holds,
then using holds on both sides of the main
runnel climb up to the top.

3. Deerkiller 11m E3 5b
Start 2 metres right of Dogburner. Climb up to a
halfway runnel. Continue up the wall to rightward
tending ledges and past these to an awkward
pull over at the top.

4. The Fort 11m E2 5b
The wall between the Deerkiller and the right
arête. Climb up to the grassy ledge, then straight
up past a line of four small pockets to a flat hold
and a rounded finish.

5. Walton's Wall 10m VS 5a *
Start right of the four pockets and just left of the
arête. Make a hard move past the large intrusion
to reach the break. Continue using the arête for
the right hand to a well protected finish.

16. Spirit 8m VS 4c
Climb the right arête. Harder if the boulder isn't
used.

17. For Your Eyes Only 8m VS 4c
The wall and blunt arête right of Spirit. Also
harder without the boulder.

18. Sally 8m S
Climb into the cave right of For Your Eyes Only
and exit using the thin left hand crack.

19. Viper Crack 8m E2 6a
Climb the thin crack in the roof opposite Sally. An
enormous reach is needed at the top.

20. Longland's Traverse 30m VS 4c
Start on the left of the main face. Follow the
main fault rightwards to Rothley Crack, follow
this for 2 metres then move below the flutes and
follow the ledges to finish up Spirit.

Jo George leading
9. Rothley Crack (VS 5a)
Photo: Dave Cuthbertson/Cubby Images

Tarzan Buttress

Tarzan Buttress

Tarzan Buttress lies some 300 metres to the south of the main crag and is easily identified by a large overhang on the left hand side. It is also the tallest of the scattered buttresses in this area.

21. Sideline 6m S
Traverse right from the sidewall to gain the top of the arête of Swing Time.

22. Swing Time 10m E3 5c
Gain the left arête of the overhang at the lip. Swing up and lay off the arête to gain good holds.

23. Tarzan Going Ape 10m E4 6a
Climb the prominent overhang to the lip at its widest point. Swing out and pull blindly to adequate holds and the top.

24. Jane Lies Agape 10m E3 5c
Climbs the roof at its right side. A micro cam or small wire protects the hard move over the lip, to gain a good finger flake. Pull up and continue slightly leftwards on better holds.

25. Battle With Thunder 10m S 4b
Climb to the right side of the roof. Pass this at the large runnel and continue to the top up the fading crack.

26. Flies 10m S 4b
Climb the wall right of Battle With Thunder starting up the short corner. Step right and climb the bulge on good holds to the top.

27. Mystique 10m VS 4c
Climb the wall right of Flies on rounded green holds.

28. On the Edge of Insanity 10m E1 5c
Start low down in the cave to the right of the arête. Climb easily up to a desperate finish above a dangerous landing.

Various other things have been recorded in this area, most of these are included in the Northumberland Bouldering Guide and online at www.**climb**online.co.uk.

Rothley Crag Graded List

E7
Masterclass 6c ***
Master Blaster Arête 6c **

E6
The Taste of Someone Else 6b *

E5
Master Blaster 6a **
Water Torture 6a

E4
Masterstroke 6b
Tarzan Going Ape 6a
The Cattleburners 6a
Dogburner 5c *

E3
Muscular Eruption 5c *
Swing Time 5c
Deerkiller 5b
Jane Lies Agape 5c

E2
The Fort 5b
Viper Crack 6a

E1
After the Blast 5c
On the Edge of Insanity 5c

S
Rothley Crack 5a ***
Walton's Wall 5a *
For Your Eyes Only 4c
Longlands Traverse 4c
Mystique 4c
Shades of Green 4b
Spirit 4c
Rothley Crack 5a ***
Walton's Wall 5a *

Erin Magog leading
. Muscular Eruption (E3 5c)
wild trip on crimps!
Photo: Steve Crowe

Sandy Crag (Key Heugh)

Hugh Harris and John Wallace

NY 96897:
West Facing
270m
45 minutes

History

The first routes on Sandy Crag were climbed in the 1950's by the College Club which may well have been Question Mark Crack and the Vertical Vice but the details were not accurately recorded. In 1974 however, a new approach was taken to the development of the crag. Over the next few years John Earl and Bob Hutchinson largely had it to themselves for the quality lines. They cleaned out the large rotting wooden wedges from cracks to free the excellent Angel Fingers and climbed the aesthetic and compelling Sandy Crack, another originally aided line, both of which are now definitive sandstone classics. In 1977 they climbed the very bold, committing and fabulous arête of Salvation and added Goldfinger in the same year. 1978 gave them another hard line in Vincent which was the crags first E5. Vincent was so named because an ear of rock broke off during cleaning and nearly made the route a non-starter. Steve Blake stopped the clean sweep with his bold and brittle Basil Brush, cleaned with the help of a yard broom. 1979 only had one recorded new route, Pall Arête by Bob Smith.

The next phase of development came from Tommy and Bob Smith in 1980 with The Anvil, Classroom Worm and the very technical and worrying Greenford Road, the crag's first 6b. Nothing else happened until 1985, when Bob Smith and John Earl climbed the very powerful and sustained Leonardo which has had few, if any, repeats and deserves E6. They then reversed leads for the problematical Corporal Punishment. Not recorded at the time but circa 1989, Karl Telfer climbed the Direct Start to Greenford Road stepping left to place gear in the bottom of Sandy Crack. (In 2003 Mark Savage repeated the route without this runner.)

Another 5 years passed until photos of the crag reminded Hugh Harris of the gaps he had seen a few years earlier and two visits, a week apart in 1990, resulted in the fine Victim of Circumstance climbed with Rhian Webb and then a solo of Living on Borrowed Time. Then in 1991 Joe Webb threw sanity out of the window and soloed the immaculate Time and Motion above six very worried but thankfully redundant, spotters to give the crags first E7 - his best previous lead was E4!

Since then the crag has waited expectantly for the next 'wave' of development. There are some obvious lines left, but they are extremely hard and devoid of any gear, so it may be a while coming.

Situation and Character

This large, quarry-like face is situated at the end of a spur overlooking the Darden Burn. The crag is not marked on the 1:50,000 OS map although clearly shown on the larger scale maps as Key Heugh. The Sandy Crags marked on both maps are a collection of boulders 1 kilometre east which are of no real climbing interest.

Whilst the number of routes is relatively few, some of them stand out as amongst the finest in the county. They are improved further by the secluded feel of the whole area and the fact that you will probably never have to queue. The downside of this is that some of the less travelled routes may suffer from being dirty. The rock is less compact than the other Simonside outcrops but this has no bearing on the quality routes. The most impressive climbing is to be found on the continuous central section of the crag, which attains a height of over 20 metres. On either side of this central section are lower, more discontinuous buttresses.

The hillside below the main face consists of chaotically arranged boulders and tilted blocks, which give boulder problems and routes up to 6 metres. They provide good sport, though some of the landings are appalling and it is a very long way to carry a mat.

Approaches and Access

The crag is easily seen to the south of the Elsdon-Hepple road in the centre of a large grouse moor. Take a mental note of where the crag lies because it isn't visible from the car park at the picnic site (NGR 970995). Go right along the road to the bridge then take the track signposted Midgy House. Follow this for about 1 kilometre to the house. Take the bridge over the stream past the house, then follow the track up the crest of the spur (true left bank of the stream) to the plantation of Humble Law. When the crag is sighted on the left, strike straight for it down across the Darden Burn and up the moor to the base of the crag. Access was previously very restricted but it is now possible to climb throughout the year subject to obtaining permission first from the gamekeeper, Stuart Whitfield on 01669 640272. Permission will normally be granted. However, exceptionally the landlord may not wish to have people on the moor. Please help to preserve long term access by complying with his wishes. There is a right of access to the crag under CRoW.

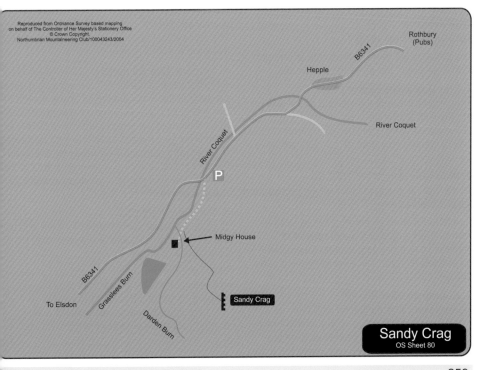

The Climbs

The crag runs across the hillside, below the edge of the moor plateau and the routes are described from left to right.

The extreme left hand buttress abuts an open stretch of slope and gives the first routes.

1. The Spelk 7m E2 5c*
The smooth arête at the left end of the wall gives a good little thorny problem. It may be started on either side and then finished direct or up the left wall. If you are less than 5' 10" you can have a 6a tick.

2. Weetabix Crack 7m HVS 5b
To the right is a jagged crack which proves more difficult than it looks.

A number of small buttresses follow, until 40 metres further right is a red buttress with an impressive overhanging leaning groove, with an arête to its right. The next route climbs the groove.

3. Leonardo 12m E6 6b**
Powerful and very sustained with hard-to-place-gear that fills up your handholds. Follow the clean-cut groove on layaways to its top when a sloping hold enables a move left to be made to a broken flake and an easy escape up the dirty corner to the top. A very good route slightly spoiled by being forced to finish left. The somewhat harder direct finish awaits the inventive touch of genius.

4. Vincent 12m E5 6a***
A masterpiece of sustained, technical and neck climbing at the lower limit of its grade, based on the arête just right of Leonardo. Start 2 metres right of the arête and move left with difficulty to a small ledge 2 metres up it. The ground seems to drop away alarmingly at this point. Climb up, heart in mouth, trending slightly leftwards to the famous broken flake then continue straight up the wall above.

5. The Bite 8m E1 5a
Start up the bank to the right of Vincent and tak the leftward-trending line across the wall. More serious than it appears.

The next buttress bounds the left end of the main crag and is clearly identified by the big arête of Salvation. The next route is left of this and takes the thin crack rising out of a cleft formed by a boulder in front of the buttress.

. The Bark 7m VS 5a
:limb the crack resisting the temptation to step
ack onto the boulder.

. Salvation 14m E4 5c***
he magnificent, bold route up the big arête is
 highly memorable experience. Not technically
esperate but not much in the way of gear either.
:limb the arête directly until a move left can be
1ade. Summon up your courage and carefully
1ove up the short wall above. Fantastic!

he next three routes are scrappy and not very
njoyable.

. Chimney and Crack 10m M
,round right from Salvation climb the broken
himney to a ledge. Continue up the corner
rack above.

. Denture Route 14m D
metres right of the last route is an obvious,
roken corner near the left edge of the big wall.
:limb it to a grassy ledge. The corner crack in
1e short wall above is climbed to an awkward
1ish.

John Earl
20. Angel Fingers (HVS 5b)
Photo: Andy Birtwistle

10. False Tooth 14m S
This route starts 3 metres right of Denture Route
and is often confused with it. It consists of a
steep, wide crack full of wedged blocks.

Things now start to improve a little.

11. Fang Crack 15m VS 5a*
To the right of False Tooth is an incipient
crack slanting from left to right. This is gained
awkwardly from the left and followed to the
terrace. The smooth groove above leads to the
top of the crag.

12. Basil Brush 10m E4 6a
The bold wall to the right of Fang Crack suffers
from the accumulation of fluff. You might want to
clean this one before you launch up it. Climb the
shallow scoop coming in from the right. Continue
very carefully up the wall on very friable holds to
the terrace. You have been warned.

13. McAlpine's Groove 15m S
Right of the last route the obvious groove in the
corner is climbed to the terrace where a traverse
left is made, before finishing up the chimney.

The crag starts to increase in height and the next
routes follow some great lines.

ob Smith
5. Sandy Crack (E2 5c)
hoto: Andy Birtwistle

14. Question Mark Crack 17m VS 4c**
This prominent crack is the most conspicuous feature on the left of the main face of the crag and gives a sustained route at its grade. Reach the edge of the flake and continue to reach a ledge on top of the flake. Finish up the vegetated corner to the left.

15. Raven's Nest Crack 17m VS 5a **
The thin crack immediately right of Question Mark Crack is another good route. Climb direct to attain the crack, which is followed to the top.

16. Raven's Nest Chimney 17m HS *
The narrow chimney just right of the crack gives a testing exercise in very traditional techniques. Easy climbing leads to a chockstone. Then a strenuous section follows before the unfortunately broken finish, which requires care.

17. Victim of Circumstance 18m E5 6a**
An atmospheric route that tackles the top part of the scooped arête right of Raven's Nest Chimney. Climb the chimney to the chockstone. Step right onto the front of the buttress using a deep pocket and rounded foot ledge. Traverse right to the blunt arête where hard exposed moves lead up into the open scoop, which is then ascended more easily, to finish.

The next part of the crag is broken by a large, vegetated ledge at half height and a dirty corner above. This is Sandy Corner. Right of Sandy Corner is the highest section of the crag. Two steep walls with the vertical cracks of Angel Fingers and Sandy Crack are separated by the chimney of the The Vertical Vice. Also, in front of this area of the crag sits Pall Arête.

18. Pall Arête 7m E3 6a
Takes the short blunt arête in front of the crag beneath Sandy Corner. Climb the arête moving left at the top. Funny that; it feels higher than it is.

19. Rake End Crack 20m S
Climb easily up the groove immediately to the right of Sandy Corner to a grass ledge. The steep crack above is climbed to the top.

20. Angel Fingers 20m HVS 5b***
A superb climb taking the thin crack just right of Rake End Crack and one of the 'must-do' routes on any Northumbrian HVS climber's hit-list. Climb the crack direct, which is awkward and committing to start, to a horizontal break at 10 metres. Then follow the two disjointed cracks to the top. For those less committed, start up Rake End Crack.

1. Goldfinger 20m HVS 5b**

Provides a fine finish up the groove on the arête between Angel Fingers and The Vertical Vice. Start the crack of Angel Fingers and continue for 10 metres to the first horizontal break. Move right along this to the arête and climb this direct to the foot of a groove. Finish up the groove in a fine position.

2. Living on Borrowed Time 20m E5 6a*

Boldly climbs the blunt arête between Angel Fingers and The Vertical Vice without any gear where it matters. Start from the platform 1 metre up The Vertical Vice and take a rising left traverse to the good ledge on the arête. Climb the steep slab above (crux) trending right to a single fluting, then up and left to a fluted ledge and a finish up Goldfinger.

3. The Vertical Vice 20m HVS 5a*

A strangely compelling cleft that gives a well named classic struggle. Easy climbing leads to the constricted and strenuous lower section of the vice. This is followed to a shallow cave beneath the final overhanging crack. A precarious back and foot technique can then be used to gain access to the final crack, which leads thankfully to the top.

4. The Anvil 44m E2 5b 6a*

1. 24m. Climb The Vertical Vice to the tree on the right, then traverse left to the arête of Goldfinger. Go up this to the top horizontal break, move left and hand traverse to a large ledge.

2. 20m. The 1cm wide crack running across the wall is hand traversed left with difficulty. Move round the arête, cross Raven's Nest Chimney and Raven's Nest Crack, then follow a final hand traverse to the top of Question Mark Crack.

5. Sandy Crack 25m E2 5c***

This brilliant and impressive crack-line splits the wall to the right of The Vertical Vice and is a contender for the finest E2 in Northumberland. Climb the strenuous overhang via the crack to a resting place at the base of the slab. The narrowing crack up the centre of the slab succumbs to increasingly difficult jamming to gain the horizontal crack. Step right and move up into the shallow scoop near the arête. Move back left to finish on good holds beside the thin crack.

26. Greenford Road 25m E5 6b***

A tremendous route up the enticing groove right of Sandy Crack with a technical move just where you don't want it. Climb Sandy Crack to the base of the slab. Traverse right and climb the wall above until a foothold and a hidden hold on the right lead to the bottom of the groove, which is followed to the ledge. Finish up the short arête above.

Direct Start E8 6b

Climb the overhanging arête direct and continue straight up Greenford Road. This is graded for not using a runner in Sandy Crack.

Mark Savage
26. Greenford Road Direct (E8 6b)
Photo: Mark Savage Collection

27. The Jaws 25m VS 5a**

This impressive traverse crosses the two big walls on either side of The Vertical Vice along the obvious lower horizontal fault. From Rake End Crack hand-traverse out to rest on a foot ledge in the middle of the wall, then continue around the arête to The Vertical Vice and a possible belay. Traverse out right along a horizontal crack onto the face of the buttress. Move up and right to a ledge round the corner. Climb vegetated slabs to the top.

28. Arkley's Wall 16m HVS 5a

The slabby wall round to the right of Greenford Road is climbed starting a little way up the slope. Beware the hollow flake.

There is a break in the buttresses at this point, followed by a lower section of rocks which provide the next routes. The crack of The Slit is the obvious landmark.

29. Corporal Punishment 10m E4 6b

The short but awkward, prominent arête 1 metre left of The Slit. Climb the arête, with the aid of the foothold on the slab, to the big jug. Use a precarious pinch on the arête to make a long reach to a small hold and then the ledge above. Mantel the ledge and then continue easily to the top.

30. The Slit 7m MVS 4c

Climb the aforementioned gradually widening crack.

31. Classroom Worm 10m E4 6a*

The hanging thread-like crack just right of The Slit. From the base of The Slit traverse right to the crack and climb this with difficulty to its top. Move right to the arête, then around the corner and up the wall to a diagonal fault and an awkward finish.

The next corner crack to the right starts at a lower level.

32. The Slot 10m MS

Climb the dirty crack and right wall to a grass ledge with a mountain ash on the right. Continue up the grassy corner to a poor finish on the heather slopes above.

33. Time and Motion 10m E7 6b***

An epic route up the immaculate arête right of The Slot and the most serious route on the crag. It offers delicate, insecure, hard climbing devoid of any gear and with a fall potential far longer than the route. Starting from the left, climb the arête to a crux far too near the top.

4. Christmas Crack 10m MVS 4c

The obvious wide crack 7 metres right of The Slot is easier once the start is overcome.

A couple of hundred metres right of the main crag is an overhanging block set low down and facing east. It has a cracked face that gives five climbs, which may be dry when the rest of the crag is wet.

5. Pudsey Zaps Clingons 10m E2 5c

Climb the orange wall left of the cracks. Pull over the overhang and climb the widening crack above.

6. Gingersnap 8m VS 5a

The left hand of the two cracks with a chockstone at the top.

7. Ginger Biscuit 8m VS 5b

The obvious rightward leaning off-width crack.

8. The Clingons Strike Back 10m E1 5b

Climb the wall and thin crack right of Ginger Biscuit finishing rightwards.

9. Dreaming of Hownsgill 6m HVS 4c

Climb the right arête. Throw the loose bits into the heather.

Joe Webb on the first ascent of
33. Time and Motion (E7 6b)
Photo: Rhian Cross

Sandy Crag Graded List

E8
Greenford Road Direct Start (no side runner) 6b

E7
Time and Motion 6b ***

E6
Leonardo 6b **

E5
Greenford Road 6b ***
Living on Borrowed Time 6a *
Victim of Circumstance 6a **
Vincent 6a ***

E4
Corporal Punishment 6b
Basil Brush 6a
Classroom Worm 6a *
Salvation 5c ***

E3
Pall Arête 6a

E2
The Anvil 5b 6a *
Sandy Crack 5c ***
The Spelk 5c *
Pudsey Zaps Clingons 5c

E1
The Clingons Strike Back 5b
The Bite 5a

HVS
Goldfinger 5b **
Angel Fingers 5b ***
The Vertical Vice 5a *
Weetabix Crack 5b
Arkley's Wall 5a
Dreaming of Hownsgill 4c

VS
The Bark 5a
Fang Crack 5a *
Ginger Biscuit 5b
Ginger Snap 5a
The Jaws 5a **
Question Mark Crack 4c **
Raven's Nest Crack 5a **

Selby's Cove

Ian Murray

NZ 023976
West Facing
320m
45 minutes

History

Selby's Cove is a well-known feature in the Simonside Hills. It is not surprising that many good lines were climbed early in Northumberland climbing history but by who is not recorded. The Corner, Holly Tree Wall, The Arête, Overhanging Chimney and The Traverse were all included in the 1950 guide. The fine Overhanging Groove (with the traverse start) succumbed to Eric Rayson, David Moy and Frank Montgomery during Easter 1964. The crag then saw little development until 1976 when John Earl on the day before his 30th birthday and reliving his youth, finished with the Roaring 20's. The fine Bowline and technical Fosbury's Crack fell to Bob Hutchinson and John Earl also in the mid seventies. In 1978 Tommy Smith accompanied by brother Bob just beat Paul Stewart to the first free ascent of Holly Tree Corner and in 1984 Peter Kirton, accompanied by Andy Moss (recorded as A. Non. A Moss) took his bouldering to new heights with the ascent of Fosbury's Crack Direct Finish. There was no further development for 11 years until Tim Catterall added a direct finish to Holly Tree corner in 1995. Steve Crowe added the direct start to Roaring 20's during the preparation of this guide

Situation and Character

Although remote, this outcrop of superb sandstone is well worth a visit. The westerly aspect of the rocks, combined with the shelter of the cove makes it a pleasant suntrap. Though limited in number the available routes are of high quality. The crag was named after a border reiver who used the cove. Which routes are his, however, are lost to antiquity.

Approaches and Access

From the Forestry Commission car park (NZ037997) follow marked tracks to a point west of the Simonside summit plateau (NZ 022988). Just before the forest starts there is a path heading south follow this for 1 kilometre until a fence is reached. Turn immediately right, cross a small, deep stream via a wooden rail then follow the fence to a slight rise until the valley containing Selby's Cove is entered. Shortcuts over the Simonside plateau are not recommended. See approach map on page 237. There is a right of access to the crag under CRoW.

The Climbs

The climbs are described from left to right. The Corner is an obvious feature of the left end of the crag and the first route follows a line up the arête on the small prow shaped buttress further left.

1. The Arête 15m D
Climb the arête on the left of the corner either by starting direct or by a pleasant traverse starting near the corner on the right.

2. Lichen Wall 9m VD
Start just right of The Arête. Climb the face, moving 1 metre right to the obvious crack at half height and thence to the top.

Direct Start HVS 5b
The thin crack directly below the upper crack.

3. The Corner 11m S ***
An excellent route up the obvious corner. The standard is maintained throughout.

4. Diagonal 13m VS 4c *
Starts awkwardly just right of The Corner. Climb the diagonal line of flakes across the lower wall to reach the large break. Follow this to the right until a move can be made onto the upper wall and the top gained.

5. Fosbury's Crack 13m E2 6a
A metre right of Diagonal is a thin, bottomless crack. Gain this with difficulty, the name may give a clue, and climb it direct until it is possible to finish up Diagonal.

Direct Finish 12m E5 6b
Finish up the wall above the break, just right of The Corner.

6. Bowline 13m E4 6a **
Climb the arête right of Fosbury's Crack to gain the wall above. Move up and right to a scoop. Follow this to a break and finish straight up.

I Horsfield leading
. **Fosbury's Crack (E2 6a)**
hoto: Steve Crowe

7. Holly Tree Corner 13m E2 5c **
The overhanging corner to the right of Bowline. Climb the corner to the overhang, gain the upper groove with difficulty and follow it to its top. Traverse right to the tree on Holly Tree Wall.
Direct Finish 13m E2 5b
Finish through the overhang.

8. Gymnast 11m VS 5b
Climb a crack in the wall to the right of Holly Tree Corner to its top. Continue direct or rightwards to finish up Holly Tree Wall. The arête to the right provides an alternative, harder start.

9. Holly Tree Wall 11m S *
Funnily enough, a conspicuous holly tree near the top identifies the climb. An enclosing wall runs up on the right and a crack runs up on the left. Climb the corner on the right and traverse left to the crack or climb the crack direct. Continue up the crack for a short distance, then traverse right and pass the holly tree to the top.

10. Flexing Flake Finish 10m E2 5b
Take the obvious flake cracks high on the right wall with much trepidation, if not terror, to finish up an easy groove above.

11. Overhanging Groove 13m HVS 5a ***
The V groove in the nose of the buttress is gained direct by means of the overhanging arête. Follow the groove to the top. Very good.

12. The Roaring 20's 10m E1 5b **
Follow Overhanging Chimney until it is possible to move left into a leaning crack. Climb this direct to the top. An interesting exercise in jamming, if you can jam. Well protected.
Direct Start 13m E2 5c *
Pull over the roof and climb the wall, moving right to gain the leaning crack. Bold.

13. Overhanging Chimney 9m VS 4c *
The chimney on the right hand edge of the rocks. An interesting route with a strenuous pullout at the top.

14. Giants Fall 9m HVS 5b
The juggy arête right of Overhanging Chimney. Start by traversing left from the niche then climb the arête without bridging. Provides a pleasant route.

5. The Traverse 30m S *

Starting on the extreme right of the crag at a high level, traverse left along an easy overgrown edge, over a nose, to the holly tree, where a stance is taken. Climb down 1 metre and continue the traverse round an arête on to a stance in The Corner. Then across The Arête to lower crags. A good second pitch.

Alternative Finish E1 5b

From Bowline move down the groove and traverse left to the corner, thence to the arête.

6. Low Level Girdle 30m HVS 4c, 5b *

. 12m Start in a recess just up to the right of Overhanging Chimney and traverse left onto . Climb up for 2 metres then traverse into Overhanging Groove. Move awkwardly left onto Holly Tree Wall and take a stance low down.
. 13m Move up left onto the large spike block overlooking Holly Tree Corner, reach across the corner and hand traverse sensationally round the arête into the scoop of Bowline. Continue to the Corner and either climb this or finish as for The Traverse.

Alex Smith powering up
12. The Roaring 20's (E1 5b)
Photo: Steve Crowe

Steve Crowe on the first ascent
12. The Roaring 20's Direct Start (E2 5c)
Photo: Karin Magog

Selby's Cove Graded List

E5
Fosbury's Crack Direct Finish 6b

E4
Bowline 6a **

E2
Holly Tree Corner 5c **
Holly Tree Corner Direct Finish 5b
The Roaring 20's Direct Start 5c *
Fosbury's Crack 6a
Flexing Flake Finish 5b

E1
The Traverse Alternative Finish 5b
The Roaring 20's 5b **

HVS
Giants Fall 5b
Overhanging Groove 5a ***
Low Level Girdle 5b *
Lichen Wall Direct Start 5b

VS
Gymnast 5b
Diagonal 4c
Overhanging Chimney 4c *

Simonside North Face

Karl and Graham Telfer

History

Simonside although always popular has probably never been a forcing ground in Northumberland and its history can be seen as a reflection of developments elsewhere. Exact details of the early routes on Simonside are unknown but the crag was certainly visited by climbers in the early 1900's. It is likely that some of the first climbs were made by members of the Trevelyan family along with G.W. Young, M.B. Heywood and R. Bicknell who were joined in the 1920's by F.R.G. Chew, Jack Longland, P. Bicknell and C. Bicknell. Later the King's College MC made frequent visits, eventually producing a short guidebook. Development continued during the 1940's and 1950's and routes such as Vibram Wall were probably climbed about this time, possibly by Eric Rayson. In 1959 Malcolm Lowerson claimed Delicatessen.

From the 1970s onwards the recording of new routes became more commonplace and in September 1972 George Micheson, John Earl and Ian Cranston claimed Les Perchass followed by Earl and Cranstons ascent of Nee Perchass. Hugh Banner climbing with Earl and Bob Hutchinson stormed up Thunder Crack in October of the same year. During the late seventies several teams were active on the crag, Geoff Lamb grabbing one of the best lines with his ascent of Over the Edge in 1978. The same year Martin Doyle discovered Dirty Thor't with Karl Telfer and Les Hibbert. Telfer returned in March 1979 to climb Gillette while Hutchinson added The Stoic.

Following publication of the 1979 Guide new route activity continued. Bob Smith added several routes including Cut Throat, On the Brink, Regular Nightmare and the hard Command Performance. Paul Stewart, partnered by Earl, climbed On The Border. Karl Telfer found several new climbs amongst them Gimme Wings, Bee Bumble and Golden Days, Graham Telfer was active too with the bold Master Plaster.

During work for the guide in August 1988 Andrew Moss and Mark Goodings developed South Buttress although Hutchinson had climbed Wise Crack during the 1970's. Routes included Wicked Child and the bold Top Gun both by Goodings while Moss led Smart Alec and Clever Dick.

Following the 1988 guide development continued to be sporadic but nonetheless routes of quality and difficulty continued to be climbed alongside several less significant problems. 1991 and 1992 saw Joe Webb produce The Outsider, The Secret Life and the serious Blood on the Rooftops. Mark Savage arrived at the crag in 1999 and left with Nine Inch Nails and a variation finish to Command Performance which became known as AKA Mr Vegas, this brought crag development to a close in the 20th century. Mark returned in 2004 to add an independent start to AKA Mr Vegas and give the independent route described here. There are few obvious quality lines left to be climbed in the new millennium, however this will not detract from the outstanding climbing that already exists.

Situation and Character

Located just below the summit of Simonside, this is an exposed sandstone escarpment. The lower tiers of the crag form rounded buttresses projecting from the hillside, while the upper tier is split by numerous vertical cracks and chimneys that form the basis of many of the routes. There are routes covering the whole range of grades on the crag with many that will match for quality any elsewhere.

To climb at Simonside on a summer evening with views over Coquetdale to the Cheviots and beyond is to experience Northumberland at its best.

Approaches and Access

The most popular approach is from the Forestry Commission picnic area and car park (NGR NZ 037997) on the minor road between Great Tosson and Lordenshaw. A footpath leads from the south east corner of the car park and soon bends round rightwards up the forested hillside. At the second forestry road turn left and follow the track until it reaches open moorland. Ignore the outcrops on the hillside above and continue along the track until the North Face comes into view. Numerous paths lead up through the heather most heading for a large boulder just below the central section of the crag - about thirty minutes. The forestry tracks are good and a cycle makes the approach and the descent much quicker. It is also possible to approach the crag by following the footpath from Great Tosson. See approach map on page 237. There is a right of access to the crag under CRoW.

The Climbs

The crag is divided into several buttresses. Immediately above the boulder is Boulder Face, to the left lies Window Buttress Face characterised by a jutting prow of rock with a hole right through it. Further left are the smaller East End and Far East Buttresses. Right of Boulder Face, A, B, C and D Buttresses project from the hillside with the Buttress Face being the tier of rock above them. The climbs are described from left (east) to right (west).

Far East Buttress

A small buttress and detached pinnacle 100 metres left of Window Buttress. It is most easily reached by walking east along the top of the crags to a line of fence posts, the buttress lies just below. Three routes of Difficult standard have been made; the west wall of the pinnacle, a high level rightwards traverse of the buttress and the slabs on its right side. Several short problems exist whose descriptions can be found in the Northumberland Bouldering Guide.

Simonside from the air.
Photo: Mark Savage

East End Buttress

15 metres east of Window Buttress Face. It contains an area of vegetated slabs with a clean rib on the right hand edge.

1. East End Buttress 14m D

The route takes the clean rib to a small turret. Continue easily to the top.

The slab just left can also be climbed.

Window Buttress Face

This face is in the form of a recess bounded by Window Buttress to the right and The Prow on the left. Many short climbs have been worked out hereabouts, those most worthwhile have been recorded.

2. The Prow 6m S

The small buttress which marks the left hand edge of Window Buttress Face. Start just left of the thin crack and climb diagonally right onto the front. Continue straight up to a mantelshelf finish.

3. Window Buttress Face One 6m VD

Start at the toe of the square cut buttress in the recess between The Prow and Window Buttress. Climb to a ledge and continue up the front of the buttress. The ledge can also be reached by traversing in on the right wall.

The two crack lines to the left have also been climbed.

4. Window Buttress Face Two 5m VD

The scruffy corner immediately right of the last climb. Finish on the left of the capstone.

5. Capstone Buttress 5m HS

The microscopic face just right of the previous climb. A thin crack is used to reach a recess beneath the precarious looking capstone, to avoid this finish rightwards.

6. The Flake 5m D

Just right of the corner. Climb the flake to a good finishing hold.

7. Slab and Chimney 7m M

Left of Window Buttress climb a cracked slab to the platform then the chimney above.

8. The Outsider 10m E4 6b *

Start left of Fenestration Front and climb the arête and slab to the roof. Move right along the obvious bracket hold and make a long reach/jump for the top.

9. Fenestration Front 12m HS

Start at the right hand side of the undercut base of Window Buttress. Climb the overhang on good holds, trending left up the slab beneath the large overhang. Move out onto the left wall and finish to the right on good holds.

10. The Secret Life 10m E4 6b

Start as for Fenestration Front and climb to the traverse line that moves out left under the finish of Peeping Tom. Move out left along this and finish up the wall right of The Outsider.

11. Window Buttress 9m M

An amusing route. Start on the right of the buttress. Climb up and through the window, with a smile, to join Slab and Chimney.

12. Peeping Tom 8m VS 4c

Start in the same place as Window Buttress. Climb the crack above the window until a horizontal crack can be followed leftwards.

Boulder Face
The most popular section of the crag, immediately behind the 'picnic' boulder.

13. Zig Zag Route 14m D
A seemingly rather pointless route which, nevertheless, offers some good climbing. Climb the crack on the left of the buttress to the half-way ledge. Traverse right past the first chimney and grovel up the second chimney to the top.

14. Swastika Chimney 8m D *
The chimney running up the centre of the buttress.

15. Swastika Face 8m HVD
The undercut wall, immediately right of Swastika Chimney is climbed direct to a ledge. Move right into the chimney and finish up its left wall.

16. Swastika Crack 5m S *
The undercut crack right of Swastika Face. Finish up the arête on the right.

17. Kyley's Route 5m HVS 5a *
The wall right of Swastika Crack is climbed rending leftwards.

18. Gaucherie Groove 5m VS 4c
The groove between Kyley's route and Boulder Face Chimney.

19. Boulder Face Chimney 7m M
The chimney set back on the right of Swastika Face.

20. Flying Nun 7m E1 5a *
Climb the crack in the prominent overhang immediately right of the previous route on a wing and a prayer.

21. Roth 7m VS 5a
Start up the right side of the overhang and climb diagonally up to a flat ledge. Gymnastic.

Lower rocks, leading to a deep corner, follow. The next three short routes are on this section.

22. Overhanging Chimney 4m VD

23. Flare Chimney 4m D

24. Boulder Face Corner 5m M

25. Nameless Wall 6m MVS 4c
A problem on the vertical wall right of the deep corner making use of the thin cracks. The wall just right can be climbed at a similar standard.

26. Boulder Face Crack 7m D
The wide crack on the front of the buttress

forming the right hand edge of Nameless Wall. The rock staircase just right provides a good descent route.

27. Innominate Crack 8m VD **
The crack on the left side of the next face.

The left side of the wall has also been climbed and is reached by a short hand traverse from Innominate Crack: Finger Clicker E1 5b.

28. Flake Corner 9m MVS 4c *
Starts just right. Climb the diagonal flake crack. Make a difficult move to stand on top of the flake then traverse right to join Flake Chimney. Climb the upper part of the chimney finishing by the left wall. Quite interesting.

Direct Finish VS 5a
From the top of the flake climb directly up the wall.

29. Flake Chimney 11m VD
The shallow corner chimney with a flake running up the right hand side.

30. Vibram Wall 11m HVS 5a **
The thin crack up the wall to the right. A good problem.

Jim Aiken Jnr. trucking up
66. Quartz Buttress (HVS 5a)
Photo: Andy Kirkup

31. On Edge 9m E2 5b
The right arête of Vibram Wall.

32. On the Brink 11m E3 5c
The narrow wall to the left of Long Layback.

33. Long Layback Crack 11m VS 4c **
The long, straight crack in the corner. A classic.

34. AKA Mr Vegas 11m E7 6c ***
A committing route which is not escapable until after the crux, which provides technical and sustained climbing up the wall left of Command Performance. Start at a sloping hold 1 metre right of Long Layback Crack. Climb up to a good hold beneath the overlap when a sequence of powerful moves leads to the crux lunge, a big move off a small crimp then leads to easier climbing up a vague groove to finish direct.

35. Command Performance 11m E4 6b ***
Start just left of the centre of the wall between Long Layback Crack and Over the Edge. Climb the wall on small 'chicken heads' to the overlap; move over this until a move right can be made to the overhang on Over the Edge. Using an undercut pull left past the overhang and boldly climb the wall.

36. Nine Inch Nails 12m E4 5c
Start as for Over the Edge. Undercut directly through the overhang then climb the wall and arête above to a poor thread. Finish up the arête direct.

37. Over the Edge 11m E3 5c ***
The arête to the right of Long Layback Crack. Climb the wall and undercut flake to the overhang, swing right to a thin crack and make some hard moves to the sloping ledge. An excellent route.

38. Dirty Corner 8m VD
The corner to the right. Better than it looks.

39. On the Border 9m E3 5c
Ascends the slim groove and crack in the wall right of Dirty Corner. Unfortunately slow to dry.

40. Dry Run E2 5b
Start as for On the Border. Climb diagonally right to the edge of the wall just below an obvious horizontal break, then straight up the arête to the top. The lower arête can also be climbed direct.

41. Staircase Chimney 8m D
The narrowest of the two chimneys on the left of 'A' Buttress.

42. Two-Way Chimney 7m VD
A scrappy route. The wide chimney right of the last climb. Start on the left, finish on the right.

43. Coquet Corner 7m VS 4c
The chossy corner. Climb to a block, overcome this and the vegetation above.

44. Chinese Crack 8m MVS 4b
The thin crack up the arête left of Little 'A' Climb Started on the left.

Mark Savage on the classic
35. Command Performance (E4 6b)
Photo: Paul Cosgrove

A Buttress B Buttress C Buttress D Buttress

45. Little 'A' Climb 8m MS
The dirty crack 3 metres right of Two-Way Chimney on the left hand edge of 'A' Buttress.

Below Little 'A' Climb is 'A' Buttress.

'A' Buttress
A' Buttress forms the right hand edge of the Boulder Face. It is a long, two-tier buttress with an obvious deep chimney splitting the lower tier.

The first two routes start left of the chimney.

46. The Privy 15m HVS 5b
Climb the scoop left of Giant's Stair to the overhang, move left to the arête and up to the heather plot using two large pot holes. Climb the rounded arête on the left and the slab above to finish.

47. Giant's Stair 15m VS 4c *
Climb the arête formed by the left wall of Great Chimney using a flake crack, then climb the overhang via the obvious crack to a ledge. The slab above is started on the right until a move to the centre can be made to gain another ledge. Finish up the final slab between the two overhangs.

48. Great Chimney 16m D ***
The chimney splitting 'A' Buttress. Climb the lower gully to an exit behind a massive boulder. Climb the crack above and finish up the final chimney.

49. 'A' Buttress Left Hand 5m VD
The short, wide crack on the left of 'A' Buttress Direct.

50. 'A' Buttress Direct 18m VD
Starts at the lowest part of the buttress. Climb direct to a prominent bulge which is turned on the right. Continue to the platform above

the gully of Great Chimney. The wall ahead is climbed on its right hand side. Finish up the final section of Great Chimney.

51. 'A' Buttress Right Hand 6m S *
The steep wall on the right of 'A' Buttress. Climb the wall and short crack above.

52. Eden Groove 6m M
The groove right of the last climb. Finishes on the platform of Great Chimney.

The next four routes start from the platform above Eden Groove.

53. The God Machine 11m E3 5c **
Climb the wall to the right of the crack of Great Chimney. Finish up the overhanging prow.

54. The Wind Tunnel 11m HVS 5a
The slab and groove left of Aeolian Wall and Delicatessen.

55. Aeolian Wall 11m VS 5a *
An exciting route giving a direct line up the wall to the left of Delicatessen. Start as for Delicatessen and move straight up the slab which leads to the left end of a large flake. Mantelshelf on the flake and climb over a bulge to a line of holds trending rightwards to the top o the upper wall.

56. Delicatessen 12m VS 4c **
A varied and interesting climb. From the right edge of the platform traverse delicately right across the slab, then up over a small overlap to reach the foot of the corner crack. Finish up this.

Direct Start 10m HS 4b
More direct. Begin 2 metres left of Chockstone Crack. Climb up then traverse left to good holds on a ledge. Continue to join the original route below the final crack.

Dave Rudge on
69. Gillette (E3 5c)
Photo: Mark Savage

Descent

63 64 65 66 67 68 69 70 71 72 73 74 75 76 77

Buttress Face

57. Golden Days 11m E1 5b *
Start directly below the final crack of
Delicatessen. Climb a faint groove/crack and
then up to the flake on Delicatessen. Step right
and up the wall.

58. Gimme Wings 11m E4 6a *
Start as for Delicatessen Direct. Move up to a
small niche on the right and arrange protection.
Step left and up the wall.

Buttress Face
In effect the continuation of 'A' Buttress.

59. Chockstone Crack 8m D
The wide crack dividing 'A' Buttress from the
Buttress Face.

60. The Whalers Thoughts 8m HVS 5a
The arête between Chockstone Crack and
Stepped Buttress finishing up either route.

61. Stepped Buttress 9m M
Start 2 metres right of Chockstone Crack and
follow a direct line up the ledges.

62. Archer's Chimney 8m D
The obvious, deep chimney just right of the
previous climb.

63. Sagittarius 9m VS 4c *
A good quality and quite strenuous route up
the crack on the wall right of Archer's Chimney.
Climb the crack to a resting place in a scoop
then continue up the steep corner above.

64. The Quiver 9m VS 5a *
Starts at the toe of the buttress immediately righ
of Sagittarius. Climb the crack up the front of
the buttress. There is an awkward move at half
height.

65. Wide Eyed and Witless 9m VS 4c
The thin crack immediately right of The Quiver
and the cracked scoop above.

66. Quartz Buttress 12m HVS 5a **
The smooth buttress capped by an overhang to
the right of The Quiver. Start up cracks on the
left side of the wall until a traverse right can be
made to the right arête. Move up to a ledge and
the top.

67. Regular Nightmare 10m E4 6a *
Climb the diagonal ramp right of Quartz Buttress
to the break, move left and climb the overhang
on good holds.

68. Blood on the Rooftops 10m E5 6b *
A boulder problem start leads to a bold finish.
Starting on the ground, boldly climb the arête
right of Regular Nightmare to the roof. Move
right and climb the wall right of the finish to
Quartz Buttress.

To the right an inclined block provides a
convenient means of descent. Beyond this an
obvious square cut pillar has been climbed by
three good routes:-

69. Gillette 10m E3 5c **
The left arête is climbed direct.

70. Cut Throat 10m E5 6a **
The wall between Gillette and The Stoic. Climb the centre of the wall to the overlap and using the vague crack gain and climb the wall above.

71. The Stoic 10m E2 5c **
The right arête is also climbed direct.

72. Loophole Crack 10m MS *
The corner crack provides a worthwhile route.

73. Les Perchass 9m HVS 5b *
The left hand crack which has a hard move to start.

74. Nee Perchass 9m VS 5a *
The right hand crack.

75. Broken Toe 8m HVS 5a
Just right of Nee Purchass, climb the overhang and wall above.

76. Cairn Crack 8m VD
Climb the crack, often dirty at the top.

77. Cairn Slab 8m S *
The wall on the right of Cairn Crack is climbed on its right side. The left side can also be climbed.

78. Cairn Scoop 8m VD
The shallow scoop with an undercut base right of the last climb. This is the usual finish to Cairn Wall.

79. Cairn Crack West 8m VD
The crack on the right of the scoop and near the right hand edge of the terrace provides an interesting alternative finish to Cairn Wall.

80. Sunset Wall 8m S
Starts on the extreme right of Buttress Face above the gully between 'B' and 'C' Buttresses. It can be reached by either a stomach traverse rightwards or by scrambling up the gully. Climb the undercut wall by a shallow scoop to an overhang. Move left and finish up a crack.

The walls either side of Sunset Wall can be climbed at a similar standard.

Joanne Edwards eying up the sequence on
28. Flake Corner Direct (VS 5a)
Photo: Mark Savage

Descent

A Buttress   B Buttress   C Buttress   D Buttress

'B' Buttress

'B' Buttress lies below the terrace of Buttress Face, it is split by a deep chimney which cuts right through the buttress. On the left of the Chimney the buttress forms a slab which gradually merges into the hillside.

81. 'B' Buttress Direct 15m HS *

Start at the left corner of the slab or alternatively climb the left bounding arête of 'B' Buttress Chimney. Traverse right towards the centre of the slab, then climb straight up the scoop moving right onto an earthy ledge below the steep upper section. Climb the steep right edge of the upper slab, then continue more easily to the terrace.

82. 'B' Buttress Chimney 15m S *

The deep chimney-crack splitting the front of 'B' Buttress. Thrutch up the constricted lower chimney to emerge at a resting place and good chockstone runner below the final section. This is climbed facing right and is less difficult than it appears. Climb the short wall ahead as for Cairn Wall and scramble up to the terrace.

83. Bee Bumble 11m E3 5c *

Climbs direct the bulging buttress right of the Chimney. Side runner in the Chimney (has been done without at E5 – the choice is yours).

84. Cairn Wall 21m MS *

Climb the prominent flake crack on the right wall of 'B' Buttress. The awkward short wall above leads to a good stance. Traverse across the wall on the right and up a groove to the terrace. Finish up Cairn Scoop or any of the Buttress Face routes.

85. Lightning Wall 12m HVS 5a *

The hanging crack to the right of Cairn Wall is gained by an ascending traverse from the right and quitted by an awkward move to a ledge on the left. The scoop to the right is then followed to the terrace.

86. Stormbringer 11m HVS 5a *

Climb direct to the flake 4 metres right of Lightning Wall. Continue straight to the top.

87. Fair Wind 11m E1 5b

The vague scoop 3 metres right of Stormbringer is gained by an awkward move over the bulge. Finish direct.

'C' and 'D' Buttresses are separated from 'B' Buttress by a gully. There is little worthwhile climbing on 'C' Buttress. The following routes are on the right wall of 'D' Buttress. Many of them are bold undertakings but are worthwhile.

C' And 'D' Buttresses

8. Go Skoda 7m MVS 4b
Start at the toe of 'D' Buttress just left of a large boulder. Climb directly to the heather ledge. Escape by a traverse rightwards below Thunder Crack.

9. Treebeard the Happy Rabbit 8m E1 5b
Start on the ledge where Go Skoda finishes and climb the sandy arête left of Thunder Crack.

0. The Naked Ledge 8m HVS 5a
About 4 metres right is a short crack 1 metre above the ground between two boulders. From the crack streak up and rightwards to the ledge. Traverse off to the right.

1. Thunder Crack 9m E1 5b **
The hanging crack on the left of the wall. Easy climbing leads to the cave. Reach and climb the crack above.

2. Master Plaster 14m E2 5b *
From the right side of the cave, climb directly to the break and use small holds above to reach the right side of the lower flutes. Gain good holds in the next break, then step left and up the wall moving left again to an awkward finish.

3. Dirty Thor't 12m E3 5c *
An unprotected route up the wall between Master Plaster and A-wristed that utilises the upper group of flutes.

4. A-wristed 10m HVS 5a
From the small hole just right of the cave climb direct on small holds to the second break, step right to 'D' Buttress Crack and climb the wall just to its left on good holds.

5. 'D' Buttress Crack 7m VS 4c *
High up on the extreme right hand edge of 'D' Buttress. Climb the wall on small holds to reach a crack, which is followed to the top.

West End Buttress
A small buttress with only one route which links together the available rock.

6. West End Buttress 14m D
Although not recommended the buttress can be climbed in four short pitches.

The next group of rocks are a few hundred metres south of the summit cairn of Simonside. The rock is of excellent quality and there are numerous possibilities for boulder problems on the many short walls.

South Buttress
The routes are described from right to left beginning with the buttress which has a pool at its foot.

97. Wellington Crack 11m S 4b
Climb the crack behind the pool to the break, continue up the wide crack just right.

98. Smart Alec 10m E3 6a
Start left of the pool. Follow the rounded arête to the second of two breaks. Pull straight over the overhang to gain the slab above which is climbed direct to the top.

99. Wise Crack 12m E1 5b *
Climb a wide crack and easy rocks just right of the cave to an overhang. Hand traverse right and make a strenuous move into the crack above. Continue up this to a rounded finish.

100. Clever Dick 11m E3 5c
As for Wise Crack until a move can be made onto the left wall. Follow the obvious weakness to a crack and the top.

About 30 metres left is another buttress with an obvious crack near its right edge.

101. Adidas 6m D
Lace up your trainers and sprint up the crack.

15 metres left is a smooth wall with a rounded arête to its left.

102. Top Gun 10m E1 5a
Start at the lowest point of the buttress and climb the arête on its right side until a delicate move enables improving holds trending right to be reached.

103. The Wicked Child 5m VS 5a
A good route up the cracks in the right wall of the stony gully just left of Top Gun. Climb the first crack to its end, step right to a second shorter crack and throw a tantrum over the top.

Left of the stony gully is a short wall giving two routes:

104. Shock 6m MVS 4c
The right side of the wall is climbed at its highest point.

105. Horror 5m MVS 4c
Climb the obvious feature just left.

Simonside Graded List

E7
AKA Mr. Vegas 6c ***

E5
Blood on the Rooftops 6b *
Bee Bumble (without side-runner)
Cut Throat 6a **

E4
Gimme Wings 6a *
Command Performance 6b ***
Regular Nightmare 6a *
The Outsider 6b *
The Secret Life 6b
Nine Inch Nails 5c

E3
Dirty Thor't 5c *
Smart Alec 6a
Over The Edge 5c *
The God Machine 5c **
On The Border 5c
Clever Dick 5c
On The Brink 5c
Bee Bumble 5c *
Gillette 5c **

E2
The Stoic 5c **
Master Plaster 5b *
On Edge 5b
Dry Run 5b

E1
Wise Crack 5b *
Fair Wind 5b
Thunder Crack 5b **
Golden Days 5b *
Finger Clicker 5b
Top Gun 5a
Flying Nun 5a *
Treebeard the Happy Rabbit 5b

HVS
Stormbringer 5a *
The Wind Tunnel 5a
The Privy 5b
A-wristed 5a
The Naked Ledge 5a
Kyley's Route 5a *
Lightning Wall 5a *
Vibram Wall 5a **
Les Perchass 5b *
The Whalers Thoughts 5a
Broken Toe 5a
Quartz Buttress 5a **

VS
Aeolian Wall 5a *
The Quiver 5a *
The Wicked Child 5a
'D' Buttress Crack 4c *
Nee Perchass 5a *
Roth 5a
Long Layback Crack 4c **
Gaucherie Groove 4c
Flake Corner Direct Finish 5a
Giant's Stair 4c *
Coquet Corner 4c
Delicatessen 4c **
Sagittarius 4c *
Wide Eyed and Witless 4c
Peeping Tom 4c

Liam Carr on
10. The Secret Life (E4 6b)
at 4.30 am!
Such an early start is not essential for success!
Photo: Mark Savage

South Yardhope

Karl and Graham Telfer

NT 924005
North West Facing
300m
15 minutes

History

Although climbs had been recorded in earlier times, the crag was not extensively developed until the seventies with ascents of The Arête by Bob Hutchinson, Original Route by Ken Macdonald and Hugh Banner's The Last Straw. With a clear indication of the quality of rock and routes available, John Earl and Bob Hutchinson provided the ability to climb The Reaper, Popcorn Surprise, Godzilla and The Camel's Back. The pace of development remained fierce even after the publication of the 1979 guide and a further fourteen routes were added. These routes included the superb Quiet County by Paul Stewart and John Earl along with other high standard, high quality routes such as: Funeral Drum by Bob Smith and Paul Stewart, The On Sight Gobbler and Footloose and Flying Free by Bob and Tommy Smith, Priapismic Failure by Bob Smith and Andy Moss and Stella by John Syrett.

Incredibly, development since the last guidebook has ceased completely. This may be due to a variety of factors: access problems, greater popularity of other crags, changes in climbing outlook. What it is not due to however, is the quality of remaining lines to be climbed, of which there are many and similarly, the excellent bouldering hereabouts.

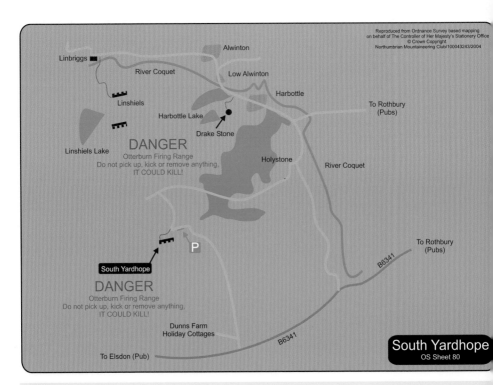

Situation and Character

South Yardhope has a splendid situation and outlook being only 400 metres from the road and is climbable for most of the year due to the lack of drainage on the pinnacles. The crag is situated high above a semi-wooded valley on the Otterburn Ranges, which gives it an air of remoteness and solitude out of all proportion to the distance of approach. This fine crag faces northwest and dries reasonably quickly in most places. The rock is of good quality but does not run to holds or protection; this, coupled with its steepness, means that many of the routes are of a high standard of difficulty. Between the crag and the road are some interesting caves where a small stream flows through the crag.

Approaches and Access

The crag lies 3 miles southwest of Holystone on the Ministry of Defence firing range. Although it is possible to climb on the crag at many times during the week throughout the year - do not climb when the red flags are flying. Permission should be sought in advance from Otterburn Range Control on 0191 2394261 or 01830 520 569. Follow the Ministry of Defence road out of Holystone to the edge of the 'danger area' then turn left and drive for 1 mile until the crag is seen a few hundred metres away on the right. Alternatively, turn left from the Elsdon-Rothbury road at the Billsmor View Point (signed towards Dunns Farm Holiday Cottages) and follow the winding, narrow lane until the crag is seen on the left. Do not touch any military ordnance that may be found lying around this area. It can be dangerous! There is no CRoW right of access to the crag. It is on land regulated by military bylaws and as this is excepted land under the Act it is excluded from the right of access.

Karl Telfer taking great care on
7. The Reaper (E4 5c)
Photo: Steve Crowe

The Climbs

These are described from left to right.

Though the authors are not responsible for the carved names at the bottom of some of the traditional routes, it has unfortunately been impossible to avoid their inclusion as blatantly obvious landmarks.

Far Left Buttress

The first climbs are on the buttress to the left of the caves.

1. Hush 6m VS 4c

The short left hand crack.

2. Quiet County 11m E6 6b ***

The impressive diagonal crack cleaving the front face of the buttress is the way of this fine climb. Follow the crack until it runs out into undercuts just below the top. Trend leftwards to a rounded exit.

200 metres further right is the left hand buttress of the crag.

Left Buttress

3. Slim 7m VD

The name is carved beside the base of the crack. A pleasant but undistinguished route.

4. The On Sight Gobbler 9m E4 6a **

Climb Slim for 1½ metres and then follow a rightward sloping ramp to good handholds (No. 1 Friend). A hard mantelshelf and a traverse of the ledge across Comfortably Numb leads to the Camel's Back.

5. Comfortably Numb 9m E4 6a **

The undercut scoop on the left of the obvious arête of the Camels Back is climbed until forced rightwards to the rib.

6. The Camel's Back 9m E3 5c ***

A bold route giving excellent climbing in a superb situation. Round to the right is a scoop. Start on the right and climb this up to the arête which is followed to a bald finish. An inferior alternative start on the left can be climbed to the rib.

7. The Reaper 7m E4 5c ***

The right arête provides an even more serious challenge. Climb the arête direct finishing by a difficult mantelshelf.

On the opposite face of the cleft running almost horizontally across the steep back wall is an obvious wide crack. This gives:-

8. Millstone Crack 7m HVS 5b

Start from the boulder at the back of the cleft and climb awkwardly along the crack passing a constriction to the top of the crack.

9. Grip Crack 7m HS 4b

A good climb up the wide crack to the right of Millstone Crack with the hardest moves near the top.

10. Yard of Hope 7m E3 6a **

The arête to the right of Grip Crack is climbed boldly past the pothole.

Further right are two small cracks which provide interesting short climbs. About 40 metres further right is a gardened wall with an overhang at half height. This gives three routes.

11. Hay Fever 7m S 4b

The gardened left hand groove is climbed throughout.

12. Straw Dogs 7m VS 5a

Climb the groove in the centre of the buttress and move over the overhang. Finish directly up the slab above.

13. The Vegetarian 6m HVS 5b

The corner right of Straw Dogs, better than it looks.

South Yardhope Pinnacle

Lower down the slope is a large pinnacle. The left arête gives a pleasant climb.

14. Alfalfa 12m D

Start at the lowest point of the pinnacle and climb the obvious chimney on its left side.

15. Heaven Can Wait 12m HVS 5b

Start just right of the Alfalfa chimney. Climb the left edge of the slab and pull left to a halfway ledge. Move back right then to the top via a diagonal crack and flutes.

16. No time for Prayers 11m E3 6a *

Starts 4 metres right of Heaven Can Wait. Climb directly up the centre of the slab until the small hole/undercut is used to escape left.

Steve Crowe attacks
35. Godzilla (E3 5c)
Photo: Karin Magog

Main Buttress

Up to the right of the pinnacle is the main buttress. The first climb is a crack of deceptively easy appearance which runs up the left hand side.

17. Haystack Crack 11m HS 4b

Climb the easy, wide crack to a ledge. Continue up the jam crack, which is more awkward than it looks, to a rounded finish.

A few metres right where the buttress begins to overhang is a wide crack, this is:-

18. The Long Straw 9m HVS 5b

Wedge round the overhang and move up the crack until an awkward move can be made to gain the top of a wedged flake. Continue up the crack to make an awkward mantelshelf finish.

19. The Straw 9m E2 6a

Climb the parallel cracks between The Long Straw and The Short Straw.

20. The Short Straw 9m HVS 5c

The thin crack 2 metres right is climbed by awkward jamming and laybacking. Move slightly left and finish up the vegetation above.

21. The Last Straw 9m E2 6a

A hard route but with bombproof protection. Start 1 metre right of the last climb and go up to a niche beneath the thin bulging crack. Make awkward and strenuous moves directly up the crack to a tree. Finish easily up the vegetation.

22. Footloose and Flying Free 12m E3 5c **

The hanging crack between The Last Straw and Bonds Folly which is gained from Bonds Folly. A lovely exercise in laybacking.

In the centre of the buttress is a large chimney with a slab running up its middle.

23. Bonds Folly 12m MS

Climb the chimney by jamming and bridging into its upper reaches. Finish with a few caving moves.

24. Bran Flakes 14m E1 5b *

Start to the right of Bonds Folly directly beneath a crack that splits the flakes. Climb the rough edged crack to the pinnacle, bridge across the chimney to the top.

5. Funeral Drum 14m E3 5c
limb the overhang 3 metre right of Bran Flakes
nd the wall above moving diagonally right to the
utes at the top of The Arête.

he next climbs are to be found round to the
ght on the impressive west-facing wall of the
rag and are among the best in the county.

6. The Arête 15m HVS 5b ***
akes the prominent arête which is the main
eature of the buttress. Start to the right of the
rête and follow the obvious traverse line to gain
e arête itself. Climb the flutes and reach over
the unusually good finishing holds.

irect Start HVS 5b
limb the overhang to the arête, more strenuous
an the original.

7. Stella 9m E4 5c *
his route climbs the dubious flakes between
he Arête and Original Route. Serious.

8. Original Route 12m VS 5a ***
n excellent climb. The original route on the
ain wall. Start in the centre of the wall beneath
large hanging flake. Climb up to the flake.
ove right then climb the steep crack above to a
ounded finish.

9. The Splits 16m HVS 5a **
long route which requires an unusual
anoeuvre in an excellent position. Follow
riginal Route to the top of the hanging flake.
ove right above the overhangs until a long
ride can be made through space onto a small
dge. (the 'splits' move). Pull round the rib and
imb delicately diagonally rightwards up the wall
an awkward finish.

0. Priapismic Failure 9m E4 6b *
he overhung crack and grooves left of Popcorn
urprise. A much stiffer proposition than the
ame would suggest. Climb up and traverse
ght along the overhung crack to join the groove
Popcorn Surprise, up this to its top. Pull out
ft and climb the obvious groove, then the right
and of the two cracks above.

1. Popcorn Surprise 9m E3 6a **
he unusual overhanging crack to the right
Original Route. Enter from the right, then
mb the difficult crack to a resting place on the
ose. Continue up the fading crack, then climb
elicately up the pillar to finish directly at its top.

Karin Magog on
26. The Arete (HVS 5b)
Photo: Steve Crowe

32. The Threshing Machine 6m HS
The funnel shaped chimney which bounds the wall on the right.

Far Right Buttress
50 metre further right from the main buttress is a large overhang split by two impressive cracks. The larger of the two cracks, which dominates the centre of the buttress supports two superb climbs.

33. Godzooki 7m E1 5c
The scoop on the left wall of the buttress 6 metres left of Godzilla.

34. Kong 11m E3 6a **
Climb Godzilla to the top of the bulging crack, then make a king size reach to the overhanging crack on the left (No. 1 Friend). Continue on good jams.

35. Godzilla 11m E3 5c ***
The overhang is climbed either statically or dynamically to gain the monster crack which is followed to beneath the roof. Make a long reach left where a difficult move is made to reach the top crack. Follow this to an awkward rounded finish.

36. Strawberry Crack 7m HVS 5b
Climb the overhang to the crack on the right side of the buttress and follow it on jams to a rounded finish and the sweet taste of success.

37. The Grinder 6m HVS 5c *
The obvious scoop round to the right of Strawberry Crack.

Down the slope beneath the main buttress is a large block split by a chimney.

38. Headbanger 7m VD
Climb the chimney and exit either over the block or through the narrow cave.

South Yardhope Graded List

E6
Quiet County 6b ***

E4
The On Sight Gobbler 6a ***
Priapismic Failure 6b *
Stella 5c
Comfortably Numb 6a *
The Reaper 5c ***

E3
The Camel's Back 5c ***
Yard of Hope 6a **
Popcorn Surprise 6a **
Footloose and Flying Free 5c **
Funeral Drum 5c
Kong 6a **
No Time for Prayers 6a *
Godzilla 5c ***

E2
The Straw 6a
The Last Straw 6a

E1
Bran Flakes 5b *
Godzooki 5c

HVS
The Short Straw 5c
The Grinder 5c *
The Long Straw 5b
The Arête 5b ***
Strawberry Crack 5b
Heaven Can Wait 5b
Millstone Crack 5b
The Vegetarian 5b
The Splits 5a **

VS
Hush 4c
Original Route 5a ***
Straw Dogs 5a

arl Telfer taking even more care on
7. Stella (E4 5c)
oto: Steve Crowe

Thrunton Wood

Ian Murray

History

The crag has been climbed on for some time, Thrunton Front was put up by Malcolm Rowe in 1968, but the main development was by Gordon Thompson together with John Grey, Kevin Watt, Bob Crossling, John Cummings and Tommy Carey in 1973. Most of the routes described here are the result of their work although George Micheson found the solution to Birthday Crack, Hugh Banner was responsible for Banner's Variation and Bob Hutchinson and John Earl discovered Lord of the Flies. Gordon Thompson originally supplied the information upon which this guide is based.

Situation and Character

The crag is situated in Thrunton Wood approximately 2½ km north of Coe Crag and commands an expansive view of Whittingham Vale to the Cheviots beyond. There are several independent buttresses spread across a steep and vegetated hillside and because of the difficulty in traversing that hillside, it is usually easier to use the forest track which runs above the crags to progress from buttress to buttress. It is not a popular crag and most of the routes may be dirty although West Buttress does see some traffic, is relatively clean and has a number of excellent routes.

Approaches and Access

Turn left off the A697 half a mile north of the cross-roads with the B6341 at a bend signposted Thrunton Wood and follow the road over the bridge at Rough Castles to park at the Forestry Commission car park. Continue along the road for a further 800 metres until a track is seen on the left. Follow the track west for about 2 kilometres until the crag is sighted stretching across the hillside to the right. See approach map on page 72.

The Climbs

First time visitors to the crag are advised to locate West Buttress from which the other buttresses can most easily be located.

East Buttress

This buttress is the first to be reached and though hidden beneath the scarp edge its position can be located by a track on the left and a seat on the right 100 metres before the main buttresses. An isolated scots pine marks the top of the buttress and from it a path descends leftwards. The climbs are described from right to left.

1. Tree Chimney 9m VD

The vertical crack leads to an undignified but practicable stomach traverse left. (As an alternative swing up left below the traverse)

2. West Wall Route 12m MS

Climb the bulging wall using an obvious flake then move delicately right to finish.

3. Long Chimney 15m D

The chimney on the front of the buttress.

4. Long Climb 17m VD

Climb the slab to the left of the previous route and follow the blunt arête to the top.

5. Short and Sweet 8m VD

The corner and crack on the eastern side of the buttress is climbed direct and is easier than it appears.

Flake Buttress
This buttress is 80 metres west of East Buttress and should be approached from the road with caution due to the steep and awkward descent. The climbs are described from left to right.

5. Ignoramus 6m VD
Follow the awkward flake crack on the left side of the buttress.

7. Watty's Route 8m VS 4c
The left hand crack gives good jamming to a holdless ledge which is gained by a precarious move.

8. John's Route 8m VS 4c
The right hand crack which is awkward and strenuous.

The two flakes on the right side of the buttress have been climbed, the left one being hardest.

No.7 Buttress Area
This area lies approximately 25 metres from Flake Buttress and the approach is awkward to say the least. There are two buttresses with a slab, The Great Slab, beneath the eastern one. The upper eastern buttress has potential for a couple of easier lines for the adventurous, but the upper western buttress is overgrown.

The Great Slab
This slab was originally dug out from the hillside, but has now been reclaimed by the vegetation and is so over grown that it is impossible to climb on. It has three lines, all being around Very Severe in standard. If you feel the need to do some extensive gardening good luck.

The Tower of Flints
Best approached by descending between No 7 Buttress and The Tower of Flints Buttress. This buttress is recognisable by means of the weird rock formations capping it. The rock is friable and the angle steep. The climbs are described from left to right.

9. Crown of Horns 11m HS 4b
Climb the chimney and traverse right under the overhang. Climb this, moving directly up to the crown.

10. The Tower of Flints 11m HS 4b
Start in the centre of the buttress. Climb the overhang direct to finish up the steep upper wall.

11. Corner Crack 11m VD
Climb the corner direct.

The Buttress of Peculiar Perversions
This second buttress lies immediately to the west of the Tower of Flints.

12. The Creeping Queer 11m E1 5b
Start at the left of the buttress beneath some overhanging blocks. Follow the traverse right and climb the overhang direct to an awkward finish.

13. Anal Intercourse 12m E1 5a
Climb direct to the hole. From there bridge out and go straight up on large friable holds.

Central Buttress lies about 50 metres west and down the hill side. The approach is awkward and overgrown.

Central Buttress
The climbs are described from left to right beginning in the overhung bay.

Warning: birds of prey sometimes nest in Savage Crack. Barbed wire has been placed around the bottom of the buttress to prevent access. Care should be taken not to disturb them.

14. Big Bad Ad 14m VS 5a
Climb the chimney in the right corner awkwardly and make a delicate rising traverse left and upwards. Move back right making for the obvious holds and follow a short layback to the top.

15. Banner's Variation E1 5b
Climb the roof crack direct.

16. Birthday Crack 9m E1 5b
The thin crack on the right wall is hard to start but becomes progressively easier.

17. Savage Crack 11m VS 4c
Climb the bulging crack in the front of the buttress and follow the easier corner to the top.

To the right is a square-cut bay in which there are several overgrown routes of Very Difficult/Severe standard.

18. The Unusual Wailing Wall 14m VS 4c
Follows the slabs to the right of the bay, moving right at the top.

19. Quicksand 9m HS 4b
The chimney on the west wall.

West Buttress Area

This is the prominent square-cut buttress, 150 metres west of Central Buttress, which is seen when approaching from the east. It is less obvious when directly above and can be found by walking along the track until three road side pines are reached on the left 60 metres past a seat. Head north and descend trending left of the buttress. The first five routes are described from left to right, the rest which are much cleaner are described from right to left.

20. Guillotine 9m VD

Climb the west-facing wall by a crack and over blocks.

21. Jugs Incredible 14m VD

Climb the corner on good holds then a small groove leads to the top.

22. Unfinished Arête 14m D

Go straight up the arête on good holds.

23. Wanderer's Return 14m VD

Climb the obvious gardened groove being wary of loose blocks.

24. Blind Pugh 15m VS 5a

Climb to the overhang and then up the awkward impending crack.

The right buttress is separated by a vegetated chimney though a few lines exist at Very Difficult/Severe standard in this area. The main buttress then rears up and the next route takes the shallow groove on its west side.

25. Thompson's Wonderful Route 17m HS 4b

Climb the deceptive scoop to a ledge and make an exposed traverse left until it is possible to move up. Follow a crack and wall to the top.

26. Thrunton Front 14m HVS 5a***

A classic route. Climb a diagonal jamming crack, then move straight up into a scoop. Trend rightwards then awkwardly back left to a ledge. The crack above leads to the top.

27. Lord of the Flies 18m E1 5b*

Climb the thin crack a metre left of Thrunton Front and continue to a leftward trending scoop which is followed to a foothold on the left edge of the buttress. Climb the arête passing a large ledge where the difficulty eases.

Lamb's Finish E1 5b

From the top of the initial crack continue up the crack above direct.

28. The Lurker 18m HS 4b

Climb the chimney at the east end of the buttress to the ledge above the chockstone. Climb the steep wall to a jammed block and over the capstone on good holds.

Further west are several scattered buttresses with a variety of routes which are suitable for those with exploratory or botanical interests.

Thrunton Crag Graded List

E1
The Creeping Queer 5b
Banner's Variation 5b
Birthday Crack 5b
Lord of the Flies 5b *
Lamb's Finish 5b
Anal Intercourse 5a

HVS
Thrunton Front 5a ***

VS
Blind Pugh 5a
Big Bad Ad 5a
John's Route 4c
Watty's Route 4c
The Unusual Wailing Wall 4c
Savage Crack 4c

Karin Magog making the second ascent of
14. Bones don't Bounce (E5 6b)
Andrew Earl took a nasty ground fall
prior to his succesful first ascent!
Photo: Steve Crowe

Whiteheugh Crag
Steve Crowe and Karin Magog

NY762940
South West Facing
310m
5 minutes

History

Whiteheugh has a very short history. The crag was climbed on by Barry Imeson and Gordon Thompson in the sixties and Steve Blake in the seventies. Bob Smith, John and Andrew Earl, Karin Magog and Steve Crowe revisited the crag during 1994-97, climbing all the lines described.

Situation and Character

The crag is beautifully situated in a sheltered position on the edge of a clearing in Kielder Forest. Most of the developed climbing is to the left of the spring but there is a lot of scope for bouldering at the right hand end of the crag, along with one route. The rock is of good quality and the routes are varied and interesting making it worth the trip.

Approaches and Access

Follow the B6320 west through Bellingham. Do not cross the River North Tyne but follow the minor road along the north bank of the river to Lanehead. Turn right at the crossroads and continue to the next crossroads, turn left here through Gatehouse and on to Comb. Continue past the Reivers of Tarset and follow the forestry road to park below the crag. The path up to Whiteheugh is invariably boggy due to the fact that a spring emanates from the crag. Climbers are requested to seek permission from Emblehope Farm or telephone 01434 240 267 before making a visit. Permission will not be granted during the bird-nesting season. There is a right of access to the crag under CRoW.

The Climbs

The climbs are described from right to left. There is a good low level warm up traverse from Canny Crack to Pride and Prejudice at 5b.

1. Lost Property 5m E1 5c *
At the far right end of the crag is a high south-facing wall. Gain and climb the crack just right of the arête with difficulty.

The next recorded line is to the left of the spring.

2. Thirty Something 4m S 4c
The first line to the left of the spring climbs a short staircase, which leads to the arête.

3. Whispering Grass 5m MVS
The short heather filled crack.

4. The Bulge 4m HVS 6a
Climb the bulging nose to the left to gain a ledge at half height, continue more easily.

5. Canny Crack 6m HVS 5b**
The wide corner crack.

6. True Grit 7m E4 6b ***
The obvious thin crack to the left.

7. Whiter than White 7m E5 6c**
Left again, climb the wall using a series of shallow pockets to gain a horizontal break. Move left then up to finish.

8. John's Route 7m E2 5b**
Just left of the arête is a line of large pockets. Study them well before you start! Follow these up to some rounded ledges then to the top.

9. Pride and Prejudice 7m E1 5c**
The obvious sickle shaped crack is gained with difficulty from the left then followed. Trend right to finish.

10. Whiteheugh Corner 7m VD
Climb the corner.

The next route is just left of a densely vegetated slab in a recess.

11. Clutching at Straws 7m E2 6a
Start to the left of the vegetation at a good pocket. From this gain a pocket on the left, good thread runner, then continue up and right to finish up the obvious crack.

2. Tears in Heaven 7m E3 6a
To the left is an obvious 'eye' shaped pocket. Gain this from the break below then finish direct by a series of thin cracks.

Left of the broken gully is an overhanging crack.

3. True Blue 7m HVS 5b
The powerful overhanging crack.

4. Bones don't Bounce 7m E5 6b ***
The wall to the left again is climbed to reach a flake. At the top of the flake a long, blind reach hopefully gains the finish.

5. Whiteheugh Slab 6m S
The slab round to the left is climbed via the pockets.

The next buttress is much further left and slightly forward of the main crag line. It has an impressive overhanging face, which is currently unclimbed.

16. White Noise 3m E1 5c
Under the right arête is a nasty jumble of unstable boulders. Climb the right side of the right arête using a one-finger pocket to gain a large sloping ledge, then the break.

17. White Heat 5m E4 6b **
Start to the left of the left arête. Move up then rightwards to gain a dubious wire placement behind a small hollow flake. Continue up this to the top.

18. The Whitest 4m HVS 5a**
Climb the crack just to the left of the start of the previous route, with an awkward move rightwards onto the ledge near the top.

Whiteheugh Crag Graded List

E5
Bones don't Bounce 6b ***
Whiter than White 6c ***

E4
True Grit 6b ***
White Heat 6b **

E3
Tears in Heaven 6a

E2
Clutching at Straws 6a
John's Route 5b **

E1
Pride and Prejudice 5c **
Lost Property 5c *
White Noise 5c

HVS
The Bulge 6a
True Blue 5b
Canny Crack 5b **
The Whitest 5a **

Wolf Crag

Malcolm Lowerson

History

Wolf Crag has only warranted a mention in the 'Other Crags' section of the last four N.M.C. guides as 'a pleasant spot for an hours soloing', without providing any route descriptions. When Malcolm Lowerson revisited the crag in 1997 he decided it was worth spending the time and effort of cleaning, climbing, recording and grading all the obvious lines and throw in some crag diagrams for good measure, to try and encourage others to visit this neglected crag. During the preparation for this guide it came to light that in 1964, Gordon Thompson had written a guide to the crag recording some 31 routes with a couple of friends. He intended to publish it along with guides to other lesser-known Northumbrian crags but these plans never came to fruition.

Situation and Character

A series of north facing buttresses up to 8 metres in height on an east-west ridge, composed of sound compact sandstone similar to that of Great Wanney. The routes described are on the main buttresses towards the west end of the crag. There are some bouldering lines at the east end where the crag is lower and more broken. The majority of the climbs are in the easier grades making it ideal for the VS climber or the competent soloer.

Approaches and Access

2 miles north of Knowesgate on the A696, plainly visible some 300 metres to the east side of the road. Cars can be parked on the roadside verge or on the access to a track 100 metres to the north of the crag. There is a right of access to the crag under CRoW.

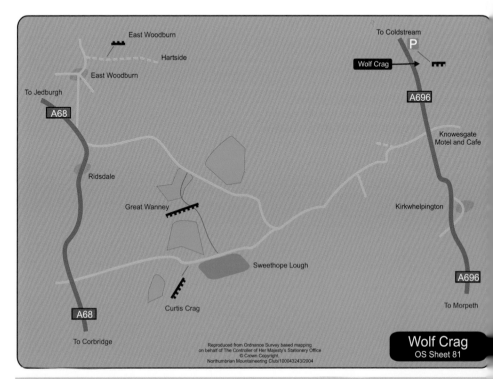

he Climbs

he climbs are described from right to left (west) east).

'row Buttress
he small prow shaped buttress 5 metres high.

. Snap Shot 5m VS 5a *
:limb the right wall via the pockets at half height, nishing right using the slot above the horizontal reak.

. Freeze Frame 5m VS 5a
:limb the arête.

. Still Motion 5m VS 4c *
:limb the left wall via the pockets at half height.

eabag Buttress
he next buttress with 5 metre high walls leading ito a deep gully, which provides an easy way own.

. Teabag 5m MVS 4c
tart 2 metres right of the vertical crack. Climb ɔ moving right onto the ledge below the verlap. Move round and up the right side of the ʻête.

. Drop Scone 5m VS 5a *
tart as for the previous route but climb straight ɔ over the overlap and continue to the top of e wall.

. String Bean 5m S
:limb the crack.

7. Angel Cake 5m HVS 5b
Climb the wall 1 metre left of the vertical crack.

8. Cucumber Sandwich 5m HVS 5b
Squeezed in between Angel Cake and Peapod with a large chockstone in its lower half. Climb the wall 1 metre right of the vertical crack directly to the top.

9. Peapod 5m VD
Climb the crack with the large block in its lower half.

Family Outing Buttress
The buttress on the left of the deep gully.

10. Dandelion 5m VS 4c
Climb the wall with a ledge at half height near its right edge.

11. Burdock 6m VS 4c
Climb the wall with a ledge at half height near its left edge from its undercut base.

12. Vimto 7m VS 5a
Start on the left side of the undercut corner and make a difficult move to reach the ledge. Continue up the arête on its left side to the top.

13. Family Outing 8m VD *
Start in the small overhung corner 3 metres left of the undercut arête (name on rock). Follow the stepped crack above, leading to the diagonal cleft and the top.

14. Picnic 8m VS 4c
Start 1 metre left of the small overhung corner. Climb the wall and follow the faint vertical crack line above, leading to the short vertical slot at the top.

15. Summer Holiday 7m VS 4c
Start 2 metres left of the small overhung corner. Climb up to the ledge and up the wall above on the left of the faint vertical crack line, finishing left of the short vertical slot at the top.

16. Day Away 7m VS 4c
Climb the narrow wall left of the gully. Continue up past the large block and finish up the right side of the arête.

17. Midsummer Madness 7m HVS 5b
Climb the edge of the small crescent shaped corner to the left end of the large block and finish up the left side of the arête.

18. Spring Fever 7m VS 5a
Climb up the centre of the wall left of the small crescent shaped corner to the horizontal break and up the headwall via a small flake.

19. Green Bean 7m D
Climb the green corner crack.

20. Fruit Salad 7m VD
Climb the crack 1 metre left of the green corner

21. Jelly and Cream 7m S
From the vertical cleft at its base, climb the wall passing on the left of a small roof to the top of a huge wobbly block.

The next routes are on the wall to the left of the easy block chimney.

22. Crusty Loaf 7m HVS 5b
Climb the wall right of the thin vertical crack up to the horizontal break below the bulging headwall and surmount the right end with difficulty.

23. Bread knife 7m S
Climb the central crack line up to and through the headwall at the top.

24. Bread Bun 7m MVS 4c
Climb the wall left of the central crack, past the horizontal break to the top.

ittle Layback Buttress

he small buttress with a central crack with immed blocks in its top half.

5. Small Matter 6m S
limb the stepped cracks right of the central rack, up to the ledge and finish up the top wall sing the narrow corner on the right.

6. Little Layback 6m D
tart where the name is etched on the rock and imb the central crack with jammed blocks.

7. Trivial Pursuit 6m E1 5c
limb the wall left of the central crack, moving the left edge to finish with difficulty over the oping top.

East Buttress

This buttress has a large overhang at half height on the right of a crack and chimney, with a wall on the left split by a horizontal crack at half height.

28. Adagio 7m VS 4c
Climb the wall on the right of the overhang up its centre, past the horizontal break at half height to the top.

29. High Note 8m VS 4c *
Climb the wall below the right end of the overhang on the right of the Y crack. Go up to and around the right end of the roof. Move back to the left of the arête to reach the top.

30. Sharp Practice 7m E4 6a
Climb the wall on the left of the Y crack to the roof. Pull up onto the wall above using poor chicken heads and finish direct to the top.

31. Lost Chord 7m D
Climb the central crack and chimney.

32. Perfect Pitch 7m S
Climb up the centre of the wall left of the central crack and chimney, past the horizontal crack, keeping left on the top wall to finish.

Far East Buttress

The buttress is split by a central crack with the right wall split by a ledge at half height and with a wall and overhang on the left of the crack.

33. Red Sky 8m VS 4c

Climb the right wall 1 metre left of its right edge, up to the ledge and finish up the right arête.

34. Shepherd's Warning 8m VS 4c

Climb up the centre of the right wall via the initial vertical crack, past the ledge and up the slab and wall to the top.

35. Fading Light 8m D

Climb the central crack.

36. Summer's End 8m HVS 5a *

Climb the left wall 2 metre left of the central crack, up over the overlap and past the right end of the overhang to finish up the shallow scooped wall above.

Wolf Crag Graded List

E4
Sharp Practice 6a

E1
Trivial Pursuit 5c

HVS
Midsummer Madness 5b
Angel Cake 5b
Cucumber Sandwich 5b
Crusty Loaf 5b
Summer's End 5a *

VS
Spring Fever 5a
Drop Scone 5a *
Snap Shot 5a *
Freeze Frame 5a
Vimto 5a
Still Motion 4c *
Picnic 4c
Shepherd's Warning 4c
High Note 4c *
Adagio 4c
Summer Holiday 4c
Red Sky 4c
Dandelion 4c
Burdock 4c
Day Away 4c

Karin Magog soloing
9. High Note (VS 4c)
Photo: Steve Crowe

Minor Crags
John Dalrymple

There are many crags in Northumberland which are either not high enough nor extensive enough to merit full descriptions in this guide. These can be delightful small sandstone outcrops on open moorland, large whinstone or sandstone quarries, lonely volcanic outcrops in the Cheviots, and wooded crags hidden away in denes and forests. Some of the best of these are described here with a selection of the better routes, the others are left for the more adventurous to discover.

Where they exist, full guides for these crags are all published in the online guide on the Northumbrian Mountaineering Club website at www.thenmc.org.uk. Crags with fuller information online are identified by "Web Guide" in the crag header.

Aid Crag   NY92083

Aid Crag lies north west of Great Wanney. The crag consists of a long string of isolated buttresses with a quarried area in the middle. About four dozen routes have been recorded but the majority are short and vegetated. A few of the better routes are listed below, working from east to west. When approaching the Wanneys on the Forestry track, keep to this as it swings round above Aid Crag. The crag is not visible but break off to the right when opposite the small lough and the top is soon reached. The walk in from Ridsdale is a good alternative, following the track by the mobile phone masts. There is a right of access to the crag under CRoW.

The climbs are described from left to right.

The first big buttress has a huge poised boulder on top and contains three cracks.

1. Cabbala 9m VS 4c
The left crack which has a kink right.

2. Cosmic Egg 8m MS
The central main crack.

3. Ankh 8m VS 5a
The thin right hand crack.

The quarry contains the following:-

4. Quaker 11m D
A route up the wall on the east side of the quarry.

5. Shaker 11m S 4b
The overhanging crack just to the right with poor protection and loose rock.

6. Faker 12m MVS 4c
Start beneath a small overhang in the central wall (arrow in rock). From a niche move right and up to a ledge. Continue up and right to a bulging wall and finish up left.

7. Just a Little Green 10m E2 5c
The green wall on the right hand side of the quarry. Better than it looks.

8. Sick, Sick, Sick (The Beast) 10m E1 5a
The unstable looking flake right of Green Wall is as unstable as it looks.

9. Hypotenuse 14m VD
The long buttress bounding the quarry on the right. A good climb. Go up the short arête, work across a wall to the right and finish up the crack.

The next buttress contains a recess. This can be climbed by the left crack or up the narrow wall, both Mild Very Severe. Further along is a buttress with two easy chimneys. The wall at the right end is Very Difficult. The next buttress has an overhang atop it. The bulging left wall is Severe and the right end past the overhang is Very Difficult.

Further right is a small buttress consisting of a slab topped by a rib which has a clean crack just left.

10. Thompsons Rib 7m E1 5b *
Climb the slab, pull up to the foot of the short rib which is followed to the top.

Further right is a higher quarried area with a thin crack on its right hand side.

11. Guilty 8m HVS 5a
Climb the crack, on doubtful rock and suspicious protection.

eanley Crag

mile south of Eglingham on the Eglingham
Beanley road a permissive track leads across
e moor. Follow this track for around 800
etres to where it swings rightwards, and then
alk along the foot of the small scarp on the left
the crag. There is a right of access to the crag
der CRoW. The climbs are described from left
right.

eorge's Buttress

e highest buttress, with two obvious
acklines.

The Ramp 7m HVD
imb the left to right rising ramp with a mantel
finish.

Janet and George 7m HS
imb the obvious flake to the right of The Ramp
ishing as for The Ramp.

3. Shunt 7m VS 4c
Climb the flake of Janet and George and finish
up to the right, up the scoop.

4. Gillian's Flute 7m HVS 4c
Climb the thin leaning groove to the right of
Shunt to the flutings on a slab. Ascend this and
mantel to finish.

Homestead Buttress
This is the last buttress and has an obvious
slanting crack rising out of an alcove.

5. 40 Years On 7m MVS 4c **
The slanting crack is interesting and well
protected.

6. Blondie 8m E1 5b **
Start at the foot of the twin runnels and move left
with difficulty to a foothold at the edge of the wall
and climb this to a testing finish.

izzle Crag

arge crag situated high on the northern slopes
The Cheviot above Dunsdale Farm. It can be
proached from the Harthope Valley via the
rthern flanks of Cheviot, or from the College
lley. A permit is required to drive up the valley,
d these can be obtained from John Sale and
rtners of Wooler. There is a right of access to
e crag under CRoW.

e classic "V Diff" Bizzle Chimney is the
vious line on the left of the crag, other routes
ve been recorded to the right.

e location of the crag means that it is often in
od winter condition and two routes are worthy
note. (See Winter Climbing Section on page
8)

Alan Hinkes in his element on
Bizzle Burn Waterfall (III)
Page 328
Photo: Steve Crowe

Boyes Quarry

NU11707

A sandstone quarry which, despite its rather dirty appearance, provides a couple of good routes. Park near a forest entrance on B6341 Alnwick/Rothbury road about 1/2 mile north of the A697 crossroads (the first plantation going north from the crossroads, just after Caller Crag). About 30 metres north of the plantation is a small gate, through this and up the hill for 250 metres to the quarry. There is a right of access to the crag under CRoW.

The routes described all lie on the high wall on the right hand side of the quarry.

1. One Small Step 16m VS 4b *
The obvious thin corner (hard for the short) and continuation crack above.

2. Mental Block 18m E1 5a
Up a short flake to a recess (sapling). Move righ then back left and up to the top.

3. The Jupiter Collision 20m HVS 5a **
From the left side of the small cave make some hard moves up and right onto the wall (5c for th short). Trend left and finish up the obvious crac

4. Arrested Development 18m HVS 4c
From right of the cave move up then left toward Jupiter Collision finishing trending right.

5. Blagdon Panther 16m HVS 5a **
Starts between the cave and a pointed block. L the wall via ledges to reach a short crack and a long reach to finish.

6. Nanny Felton 12m S
Cracks and ledges on the right side of the wall

Broomlee Lough Crag

NY79469

Situated about 1 kilometre north west of the B6318 Military Road, access is via a public right of way from Moss Kennels to Hadrian's Wall, about half a mile west of Housesteads fort. A boggy moor must be crossed before the crag is reached. There is a right of access to the crag under CRoW.

Facing north over the southern shore of Broomlee Lough, this crag consists of a number of buttresses composed of rough and sometimes friable sandstone. There are a number of obvious lines, but only the best are described here.

1. Consolation 15m HVS 5a
Takes the overhanging wall to the right of the b roof.

2. Brutus 15m HVS 5b
The crack to the left of the roof will appeal to masochistic off-width enthusiasts.

3. The Throwback 16m E4 5c
Start just left of the previous route. Climb the wall to the horizontal break. Follow this rightwards, crossing the wide crack and contin to the nose. Move round the nose and up the wall to a slabby finish or a knock back.

Caller Crag

NU1140

Caller Crag is clearly visible from the B6341 Alnwick-Rothbury road, on the north west facing hillside. There is a right of access to the crag under CRoW. The crag is split into two sections, a group of three pillars on the right and a buttress on the left split by a cave.

1. Summer Lightning 7m E1 5b
Start on theleft- buttress, to the left of the roof on the wall left of the cave. Follow flakes rightwards up to the roof, move left and up the rib to finish.

2. The Far Country 7m E2 6a **
A well protected route just left of the cave. Clim the runnel up to the roof and surmount it with difficulty using the flake crack.

3. Touch and Go E2 6a *
The obvious curving scoop/slab on the centre pinnacle of the right side.

Cartington Crag
NU047051

Cartington Crag is on the western slopes of Cartington Hill with fine views up the Coquet Valley and across to the Simonsides. From the Thropton - Whittingham road, half a mile north of Cartington Farm, a track leads off rightwards, through a gate, past a large wooden hut and towards Cartington Hill. The crags are on the hillside 5 minutes away.

The crag consists of two groups of outcrops, the northernmost offering a couple of short routes, while the southernmost has two pinnacles with a few routes of 7 metres. A very pleasant spot indeed.

A group of buttresses spread along the escarpment in Edlingham Wood.

Causey Quarry
NZ204560

Reference to this old sandstone quarry appears in the historical section as it featured in the NMC 1979 edition 'Northumberland a Rock Climbing Guide'. It has not been included in subsequent editions as it is situated outside of Northumberland. Full details of this crag are to be found in 'Climbing in North East England' published by Smartboys Publishing. ISBN 0-9525765-1-1

Cawfields Crag
NY718668

Turn north off the B6318 Military Road opposite the Milecastle Inn, 4 miles east of Greenhead. Follow the road for 1 mile to the car park and picnic area next to the flooded quarry. Walk along the road towards Cawfields Farm and the crag soon comes into view on the right.

Cawfields Crag is half a kilometre long and, in places, a good 20 metres high. Unfortunately it is broken and vegetated and has received little attention. Two lines are described here, but there are more available. The crag is very similar in character to the other Whin Sill crags and also has the Roman Wall running along the top. The impressive quarried section above the pool has, as far as is known, been sensibly ignored. It is rumoured that Mick Johnston has done some new routes of up to HVS here, but details are not available.

1. Earth Invasion 23m HVS 5b
Start at the foot of a buttress 18 metres left of an obvious triangular block below the scree. Climb the corner to reach a sloping ledge beneath sinuous cracks. Gain the sloping niche above, move right to a crack in a pinnacle and climb this to its top. Step right to a huge flake and work back left to good holds on the face. Finish up cracks in the arête in a fine position.

2. Engineers Buttress 15m MVS 4c
On the prominent buttress at the right (west) end of the crag. Start at the lowest point. A few easy moves lead to the foot of a crack which is climbed to a ledge. Traverse right to the foot of a second crack which is climbed to another ledge. A wide crack above is then climbed to a small ledge on the right. Step left and finish straight up.

Church Rock
NZ026996
Web Guide

Two small sandstone buttresses in the wooded area around the Simonside Forestry picnic site. They can easily be combined with a visit to Simonside North Face, but by comparison the buttresses are poor fare and are mentioned solely because of their convenient location. From the Simonside forestry picnic site follow the red and yellow waymarked track west and the crag is rather conveniently signed.

Corbies Fortress

The crag which faces west is situated in a sheltered narrow secluded valley on Bewick Moor and can be reached in 40 minutes. The rock is sandstone and unfortunately varies in quality from poor to very poor; chicken heads in particular should be used with caution. Leave Eglingham heading north west towards Chatton on the B6346, after half mile turn right at a sign for Harehope farm. Park at the entrance to the quarry, being careful not to block the gate. DO NOT PARK NEAR THE FARM, Walk up the hill and past the farm to where the road ends.

Follow the bridleway across the field and throug a gate on the left, turn right and follow the path until a field opens out on your left. Cross the fie and over the wooden footbridge to the burn on the far side, cross the burn at its junction with th fence on the left of the wall and head diagonally up and left across the moor towards the large isolated boulder. A path from the left hand side of this contours round to the top of the crag afte a further two minutes. Alternatively follow the description for Harehope Canyon and carry on down the burn for a further 10 minutes to this crag. There is a right of access to the crag und CRoW.

Tim Catterall leadin
2. Skin Graft (E5 6l
Photo: Steve Nac

Brook Brow 8m VS 4c
Climb the overhanging niche and rounded
breaks above at the left hand end to the large
ledge.

Skin Graft 14m E5 6b
Climbs the wall and large roof above. Start 2
metres right of the overhanging niche at a small
side pull. Use this to gain some sloping holds,
a dynamic move gains the right hand end of a
small ledge above. Stand up awkwardly and
climb the wall right of the rounded arête to the
roof. Use a slot on the left side of the triangular
roof to gain the nose, gear placed blind. Slap for
the outer lip of the roof at its widest part and pull
up if your technique allows.

Snakes Skin Flake 13m HVS 5a
Start at the obvious S shaped large flake. Move
up the flake until it is possible to step left onto
a narrow ledge. Move up onto a larger ledge
and the right side of the roof. Move right into the
recess and climb the slab on the left where it
forms a vague corner.

The Wriggler 14m E1 5b
Start at the two rounded caves. Climb up to gain
the wide crack above which gradually narrows,
gain the ledge and move up and right to an off-
width body sized crack. Enter this and do as the
name suggests to the top.

Frowzy Fortress 14m HVS 5a
Climbs the off-width, narrowing crack to the top.

Intergalactic Storm Trooper 13m E6 6b
Start at the obvious pothole to the left of the
arête. Use this to gain the small bottomless
crack, move left and climb the centre of the wall
to a sloping ledge. Climb the blank wall above to
the roof, where welcome gear can be arranged.
Make very strenuous moves out of the roof and
to the wall above, passing another pothole to
better holds and the top.

The Executioners Tale 13m E4 5c
Climbs the arête in the centre of the crag. Start
at the pointed block, gain the overhanging nose
and follow the arête to the obvious break. Move
slightly right and climb the blank wall to the top.

8. Garrotted Chicken 13m E5 6a
Start just left of the large flat boulder in the
boulder filled pool. Climb the wall 4 metres right
of the arête, just left of the vague weakness
to a small rounded ledge. Use this to gain the
rounded break. Climb the wall above to the blunt
arête, just left of the cave. A sloping ramp leads
via some rounded breaks to the top.

9. The Whaling Wall 10m E1 5a
Climb the wall 2 metres left of the obvious
bottomless crack.

10. Cateran Crack 10m VS 4c
Climb the bottomless crack at the right hand end
of the crag.

11. The Wicker Man 10m E1 5a
Climb the right hand arête to a rounded ledge.

Bracken Buttress
This buttress lies at the southern end of the
crag and is set slightly up the slope on the east
side of the burn. A small clean buttress with a
blackened arête in its middle.

12. Bruised and Bracken 8m VS 4c
Start below the left arête. Climb the arête to
the break where an awkward move leads to a
hidden hold. Continue just right of the arête.

13. Paws In My Lunch 8m HS 4a
Start in the centre of the left wall, directly below
the small cave. Climb the wall to the break, pull
up and right. Move back left over the roof via
small hidden holds which lead to the top.

14. Border Raider 10m VS 4b
Start right of the arête in the centre of the
buttress. Climb the blank looking wall to the
ledge, and then climb the fluted wall above on
the right of the projection to the top.

Crag Point   NZ34376

A reference to this crag appears in the historical section and details that were correct at the time are included in the 1979 edition 'Northumberland a Rock Climbing Guide' It has not however been included in subsequent guides due to the loose and dangerous nature of the cliff.

Cullernose Point   NU26118
Web Guide

The crag lies on the coast 1 mile south of Craster near the hamlet of Howick. Cars should be parked in the lay-by, from where a path leads down to the foreshore and thence to the base of the crag in 5 minutes. The routes on the eastern end of the crag are inaccessible at high tide, and the whole crag is out of bounds during April to August because of the nesting Kittiwakes, and their guano means that it is best to wait until the winter storms do their cleaning job. The crag does face south, and can be very pleasant on a sunny winters day.

Dovehole Boulders   NT96636

A collection of boulders and pinnacles of quite soft, but reliable, sandstone on a south facing hillside near Kimmerston. most notable for their fine bouldering.

Turn off the A697 Wooler-Coldstream road just as you enter Millfield and continue along the unclassified road to Kimmerston. Take the second left and the crag soon comes into view. Turn right onto a No Through Road (to Fordwood House). Go to the farm to ask permission.

The routes are on the west wall of the largest block and are described from left to right.

1. Chicken Drumstick Legs 7m HVS 5a
The left arête is followed on the right side, moving round left to finish.

2. Grandad Slap 8m E3 6a
The classic of the main buttress. Move right from the arête to gain a flake crack. Follow this direct past pockets to gain flutes above. Finish up these.

3. The 'D.B.' 8m E1 5a
Start on the left hand side of the ledge. Pass overhangs on the left to gain runnels. Follow these to the top.

4. Legal Loophole 8m E1 5b
Gain the hole direct from the ledge to gain the obvious runnel. Step right and up to a break the up the wall above.

5. Too Hard for a Couch 8m E2 5b
From the middle of the ledge gain good holds above the overhang. Use these to gain the flake crack. Finish up this moving right to a ledge and the top.

Dunsdale Crag   NT897234

This quite large, easy angled crag sits low on the south facing hillside at Dunsdale Farm in the Cheviots. It offers many lines up to VS, but has always had a reputation for looseness. The crag is by the side of the road in the College Valley, and a permit can be obtained from John Sale and Partners of Wooler to drive up the valley. There is a right of access to the crag under RoW.

Edlingham Crag   NU112074

From the A697 7km north of Longframlington, take the B6341 (Alnwick Rothbury road) towards Alnwick. After 1.5km there is a layby at a gate and fingerpost. The scattered rocks of Edlingham Crag can currently be seen in the remains of the wood left of the moor. There are a few poor routes.

Ellis Crag   NT746010

Sits on top of the hill south of Catcleugh Reservoir. The easiest access is via forestry tracks from Cottonshopeburnfoot where the Kielder Forest Drive starts (2 miles), the shortest is a desperate thrash uphill through the forest after crossing the Catcleugh dam (one and a half miles). There is a right of access to the crag under CRoW.

There are a dozen or so short routes and a conspicuous 9 metre high overhang which awaits an unaided ascent.

Goats Buttress   NT985362

A compact buttress in a sheltered position in trees and rhododendron bushes. There is no agreement with the landowner and CLIMBING IS CURRENTLY STRICTLY FORBIDDEN.

Were climbing allowed, you would get there by following the unclassified road between Milford and Lowick to Roughting Linn and park opposite the farm track. Follow the road south towards Fenton for about 400 metres and the crag lies across a couple of fields on the left.

Cockchafer Crack 9m VS 5a
The left hand crack. Quite pokey.

The Dungeon E6 6a **
Start beneath the left hand side of the main overhang. Gain an obvious boss and move onto the overhanging wall, making awkward and airy moves to finish on good holds directly above.

3. The Hesitant Roofer E3 5c **
Start as for The Leaf moving up to the obvious roof. Make long reaches over the roof and an awkward move left to finish.

4. The Leaf 11m E1 5c
The overhang between the cracks is climbed at the obvious break.

5. Cricket Crack 9m MVS
The right hand crack.

6. Gamekeeper Crack 8m HVS 5a
The crack on the right hand side of the crag.

Great Dour Crag

NY79203

This large rambling crag is very dirty and has been subject to quarrying and is loose in part. Despite this, routes have been reported and there is scope for more. The crag is situated on the northern edge of Great Dour Hill above Byrness in Redesdale, 8 miles north of Otterburn on the A696.

The crag is best approached from the Cottonshopeburn forestry picnic site. Drive up the track and park at the first ford. Walk along the riverside track, plodging through several fords en route until the edge of the forest is seen. Head for the fence on the right and follow it up to about level with the crag, then traverse the hillside to the crag. There is a right of access to the crag under CRoW.

The climbs are described from left to right and lie on the right hand side of the quarried bay in the centre of the crag.

1. Rob Roy 12m VS 5a
Climb the wall left of the chimney to the flake and layback this to the thin crack which is climbed to an awkward finish.

Direct Start HVS 5b
Climb the fine arête and wall directly beneath the thin crack to join it at its foot.

2. Great Dour Chimney 12m VD
Climb the chimney on the left and exit through the cave at the back taking care with loose blocks.

Direct Finish HVS 5b
The overhang is climbed direct and though safe is awkward, strenuous and dirty.

3. Chimney Variant 10m MVS 4c
Climb Great Dour Chimney for 7 metres then ex along an obvious ledge on its right wall. Move round the arete into a groove and climb this moving right to finish.

4. Culloden 15m E1 5c *
Climb the rather messy initial overhang of the central corner and continue up the groove to a good resting place beneath the roof. Surmount the roof and continue up the magnificent wide crack above.

5. The Bagpipes 15m S *
Surmount the overhang and continue up the corner direct.

Hard Heugh

NU05105

A small crag high on the Rothbury Moors, with fine views to the south west. The rock is a little friable, but otherwise quite good. Most of the obvious lines on the crag were climbed in the 60's - including the fine crack on the lower wall, which gives a good Severe.

Access is easiest from the approach used for Cartington Crag. From the Thropton - Whittingham road, half a mile north of Cartington Farm, a barely metalled road leads off rightwards, through a gate, past a large wooden hut and towards Cartington Hill. Park somewhere sensible, around where the track goes left and through another gate onto an open field. From here a grassy path goes through the reeds and over the shoulder of the hillside to a stone wall. Follow the wall up the hill to the crag. There is a right of access to the crag under CRoW.

Harehope Quarry

NU0922

Web Guide

A south facing sandstone quarry with some reasonable routes, but the ambience is marred somewhat by the fact that the quarry is used for disposal of rubbish, which has also led to the reduction in length of some of the routes.

From the village of Eglingham on the B6346 road north of Alnwick, continue north for approximate 1 mile to a road junction on the right, signposted to Harehope. Follow this narrow road for about 100 metres to a gate on the left which gives access to the quarry.

Hareshaw Linn
Web Guide
NY842854

A well known local beauty spot, there are sandstone crags on both sides of the burn near the waterfall, the best known being the Main Overhang, a large roof atop a 10 metre wall. This has been climbed free.

On the opposite side of the burn there is a large crag of doubtful, vegetated rock which has had over 20 routes recorded.

The approach is from the Hareshaw Linn National Trust car park next to the small Industrial Estate in Bellingham.

Heckley
NU188164

This overhanging east facing crag is an old quarry situated in a sheltered position in a wood just north of Alnwick. There are some good routes, but the finishes are vegetated and slings round the trees for lower offs are recommended.

From the Alnwick bypass on the A1, turn off at the B1340 and at the T-junction turn left then immediately take the road on the right. Follow this for 1 kilometre to a roundabout, turn right and follow the B6341 up the hill to a large lay-by on the left. The crag is in a small wood behind a rocky knoll which can be seen across the fields on the other side of the road. Go north for a few metres to a gate, go through the gate in the field on the right then follow the fence on the left downhill to a gate. Go through the gate and continue to follow the other side of the fence until a gate on the right leads to the crag in the wood. There is no right of way, and there have been access problems in the past, so follow this route exactly and SHUT THE GATES.

The routes are described from left to right.

1. Black Hole 8m VS 5a
The roof flake above the pool.

2. Poisoning Pigeons in the Park 10m E4 6b
Climbs the impending wall to the right of the Black Hole. Climb as for the Black Hole to the roof. Swing out right to obvious holds and then directly up to a jug (Friends). Traverse right and up following the obvious line to the slight prow (Friend). Pull over with difficulty to finish.

3. Hunting the Badger by Owl Light 9m E4 6a
Climbs the roof between Black Hole and The Birch. Start at a short rib in the middle of the wall. Go up diagonally rightwards to a lurch over the overhang to jugs.

4. The Birch 10m E1 5c
The hanging corner in the centre of the crag.

5. Meteorite 2002 NY40 10m E5 6c
Climb the rib to the right of The Birch to the roof. THE MOVE is then made right and up to gain the shelf. Make easier moves to gain the top of the rock. Grapple with the vegetation to gain the top of the crag.

6. Jack by the Hedge 14m E3 6a
Climb the left wall of the large niche to the right of The Birch. From the horizontal flake make a long reach to the first break, continue up to a long traverse line and follow this to a tree.

7. Liquorice Torpedo 10m E3 6a
The overhangs to the right of previous route.

Hepburn

The crag at Hepburn is the big slab in the trees to the south of the main bouldering area and below the edge of the escarpment. The bouldering is described in detail in the Northumberland Bouldering Guide.

Take the B6346 Alnwick to Chatton road. About half a mile south of Chillingham Village turn east for Hepburn. The road follows the south wall of Chillingham Castle grounds. Go through the farm turning sharp left then right and park at the forest enterprise car park.

Take the path to the plateau. On the right a depression/small valley leads off and down, follow it for 20 metres, cross it and follow a faint path near the edge of another small drop. After about 125 metres you come to an old oak tree, pass it and drop down to the right for 30 metres to an old fence. This is just back from the top of the crag. Gain the foot of the crag on the right facing out.

The following two routes take the main buttress.

1. Long Lost E5 5c
The left hand line. Climb the wall to arrive at a pocket just left of the obvious overlap. Move right and surmount the overlap with difficulty. Finish more easily. Not many runners, but they may hold.

2. Mis-spent E4 6a
The central line Climb directly up the slab to a thin long overlap. Follow the undercuts right to a groove. Climb the groove until forced left along a fault. Finish easily from the end of the fault. You can place runners but do not fall on them.

The next route climbs the boulder on the left.

3. A Northern Soul E5 6b
The left hand arête of the boulder with a precarious finish.
The right hand edge of the boulder provides a testing boulder problem.

Paul Linfoot making the first ascent of
2. Mis-spent (E4 6a)
In September 1991 before it was rediscovered by
Alec Burns whose route names and
descriptions have been used here.
Photo: Anne Coxon

ousey and Langlee Crags   NY956218 & NY965221

Housey Crags and their neighbour, Langlee Crags, are small volcanic plugs on the ridge on the south side of the Harthope Burn in the Cheviot Hills, easily reached from the car park in the Harthope Valley. There is a right of access to the crag under CRoW. There are several short obvious routes on good volcanic rock.

Little Wanney Crags   NY925835

These crags lie about 360 metres north west of Great Wanney. There is a right of access to the crag under CRoW.

The eastern end consists of a few small buttresses containing a dozen or so routes of up to 6 metres. An impressive deep chimney towards the east end provides a good line. The hanging groove to the right of the chimney is E3 5a.

Further west are two higher sections: the first is known as Rickety Castle and the second as Buff Crag. About 12 routes are possible, some on doubtful rock. The best are described below. Much of the crag is dirty.

Eastern End

. Cave Chimney Ungradeable
Climb the right wall far back, then traverse forward over the mouth of the cave, and so up to the exit by the hole in the roof.

Rickety Castle

. Tau 6m D
From the left side make a rising traverse right (long step) to the ledge and exit horizontally left.

. Sigma 8m D
From a gully on the right side traverse left under the capstone and climb airily up on the right.

Buff Crag

4. Hairy Diplodocus 12m E2 5c
The obvious fin of rock left of Chiasmus Chimney is climbed starting on the right with interesting moves to start.

5. Chiasmus Chimney 11m D
The deep chimney on the left can be climbed in either corner.

6. Ghost of a Dog 12m E2 5c
Start left of Psyche, climb easy rock to the roof at the left side of the buttress. Pull over on good pockets and move up the wall to gain the base of the slab and climb this rightward to finish more easily. A pleasant route on good rock.

7. Psyche 12m HS 4b
The hanging chimney in the centre is reached direct. Wide bridging makes the upper chimney straightforward. A good line. A harder alternate is to gain the chimney by the broken crack on the left.

Maiden Chambers

A clean little crag set in a wood one kilometre south east of Lorbottle Hall on the Whittington-Thropton Road. It occupies a sheltered position but faces north and is slow to dry. During a dry spell however it offers worthwhile climbing in the lower grades.

Over 20 climbs have been recorded here by Ken Smith and members of the Wanneys Climbing Club.

Just to the south of Callaly Village a gate leads through a wall to a track running south alongside a small wood. This track traverses the hillside in a south south easterly direction to where a fence and wall join at a sparse wood. The crag sits on the northern edge of this wood. There is a right of access to the crag under CRoW.

The large buttress at the south end provides the best and most sustained routes and the four cracks provide identification features. The routes are described from right to left.

1. Greengage Summer 7m VS 5a
Starts up the undercut crack to reach good holds on the left edge. Easier climbing leads to the top

2. The Bullworker 7m MVS 4c
Climb the deep cleft to the left of the previous route and follow the crack to large finishing holds.

3. Barnstormer 7m VS 5a *
Strenuously climbs the steep crack on the front of the buttress making an awkward move to finish. An excellent, sustained route.

4. Beetle Crusher 7m VS 5a
The thin crack 3 metres left of Bullworker. Join the crack to a ledge, move right and climb the short slab to the top.

5. The Hustler 9m S
Climbs the scarred wall some 10 metres left of the previous route. Reach a sharp flake in the centre of the wall and climb easily to a broken ledge. Finish up the twin cracks.

6. Narrow Buttress 9m VD
At the north end of the crag this pleasant route takes the left edge to a small sloping platform. The top is reached via large holds.

Ratcheugh Crag   NU224145

The crag is completely obscured by trees during the summer, and is at its best in the spring when the afternoon sun can get to the rock.

From the north end of the A1 Alnwick bypass take the Denwick exit and turn right where the road swings left just after the village. The folly on top of the crag is clearly visible. Turn right after one and a half miles and park at the entrance to the wood. A path leads directly up to the crag from the gate. Permission to climb should be sought from the tenant of the folly.

The climbs are described from right to left.

1. Delicado 10m S 4b
The large slab 5 metres right of a massive rotten tree stump is climbed via the left edge on small holds. At the steepening, step right to a horizontal break and finish via a mantelshelf. A good route.

The direct line up the wall gives a serious but artificial problem (5b) while the right hand edge can be climbed at Mild Severe.

2. Flying Mac 8m MS
Climb broken cracks on the left side of the slab to a V groove. Either follow the crack to finish or step right and climb the steeper wall.

3. Flash Harry 10m S 4b
Up the short, awkward wall immediately left of the rotten stump. Climb the slab near its left edge until it steepens. Move right and finish directly up the wall.

4. Ash Tree Slabs 6m VD
Three lines are possible on the slab set back and a little higher than the previous buttress. The best starts below a spindly tree growing out of the slab and climbs to the obvious thin crackline which is followed to the top.

The next main buttress has an overhung arête on the left side.

5. Girlfriend in a Coma   10m E5 6a
Start to the right of the lowest point of the face and climb the wall direct on sloping holds.

6. Adam's Folly 10m S *
Start to the right of the orange slab at the lowest point of the face. Move to a ledge at 3 metres and step left to the arête which is followed to the top.

7. Rabbits' Way 10m VD
10 metres left of the last route is a small slab with an obvious V groove at the base. Pull up on small holds to the right of the groove to a ledge, step left and finish directly up the wall above.

8. Narrow Buttress Direct 10m HVS 5a **
Probably the best climb on the crag, it takes the front of the pinnacle on small holds. Protection can be arranged to the sides.

The next worthwhile area is some distance to the left past an overgrown section of the crag. A large boulder with an undercut base sits next to a wall that appears to be made of stacked blocks.

9. Veterans Way 10m VD *
Climb to the crack in the middle of the wall and finish direct. A good route.

10. Kidology 8m HS 4b
The narrow wall to the left is climbed by a series of increasingly delicate mantelshelf moves.

11. Austerity 8m VS 4c
12 metres left is a narrow buttress with three small overhangs towards the top gives:
Climb the front of the buttress direct using small fingerholds. Interesting

12. Flibbertigibbet 6m HS 4b *
The thin crackline in the wall between Muscleman and Austerity gives an
interesting problem. The crack is difficult to start but holds improve at the overhang.

13. Muscleman 6m VS 4c
The obvious bow-shaped crack gives a very strenuous route. Pull out of
the crack to the left or right, both are hard, and finish up the wall above.
A long way left through dense undergrowth and past many pleasant, short routes is a buttress with a distinctive smooth orange corner and a small niche towards the top.

14. Senapod Corner 6m S 4b *
The obvious corner provides an entertaining climb.

15. Itchypaw 6m S 4b
The wall to the left provides a pleasant route if climbed direct, stepping off to avoid the bulge reduces the grade to Difficult.

The obvious broken buttress with a large overhang gives three lines, two of which are straightforward while the central one gives a strenuous problem.

16. Sorbandyguts 6m VS 4c **
Climb the slanting crack and take the overhang direct to a ledge. Finish directly up the rib via a delicate mantelshelf move. An excellent route.

Raven Crag (Kyloe)
Web Guide

NU04936

A small quarried outcrop on Rabbit Hill at the south of Kyloe in the Woods. Much of the rock is very poor, but there are several good routes.

Park at Holborn on the Chatton-Kyloe road, the farm road becomes a bridleway which winds past the crag at 1.5 kilometres.

1. Close Encounters 8m E2 5c **
From the sandy corner reach the thin crack and climb it, escaping left at its top. A classic.

2. Raven Mad 13m E4 5c
Climb Close Encounters and reach a large pocket directly above its thin crack, stride right on large sandy holds and pull up to the break. Climb the wall past a thin crack. Lunacy.

3. The Ayes Have It 11m E8 7a
Climb the centre of the wall to the right of Close Encounters via the two prominent eyes. Powerful and dynamic climbing is needed to gain the eye from where easier climbing leads to the top.

The corner and its right wall are loose and unpleasant. Further right the rock improves again and provides 3 routes of around VS on a short wall.

Bob Smith
1. Close Encounters (E2 5c
Photo: Alec Burn

Raven's Crag (Bowden)

NU07032

This interesting crag lies in front of the south end of Bowden Doors and deserves more attention as there are some fine routes. It is reached by walking over the moor from Bowden Doors.

The most prominent feature of the crag is a blunt, undercut prow with a bottomless crack in its left side. The first route described starts furrther round to the right at the end of the undercut section.

1. Raven's Crack 6m D
The wide flake crack.

2. Sand Lizard 8m E3 6a
Pull powerfully over the roof into the wide crack, step right and finish more delicately up the slabby bulge.

3. Orang Utang 8m VS 5a **
Starts 4 metres further left. Climb to a break in the overhang and surmount this, moving left to a good hold. Move directly to the top.

4. Bottomless Crack 8m HVS 5b ***
A brilliant route. Start directly beneath the overhanging prow and climb the strenuous wall, trending left to gain the undercut crack which is followed to the top.

5. Flake Crack 6m VS 5a
2 metres left of the previous route. The flake crack is gained by strenuous moves up the wall and is followed to the top.

6. The Pink Cone 6m VS 5a
3 metres left of the previous route. The pink, conical slab gives a delicate climb.

7. Poxywall 10m VS 4c
The longest, but not the best route on the crag. Start 3 metres left of The Pink Cone. Stand on a boulder and pull strenuously up the wall. Continue easily to the top.

8. Strain a Vein 8m E3 6b *
The obvious flutes at the end of the crag. Step left and climb the flutes via three small flakes, then up to better flakes to finish.

Redheugh Crag
Web Guide

NU119069

A pleasant, compact crag on the hillside above Caller Crag.

The approach is as for Caller Crag, then carry on over the top of the crag and up the hill. Redheugh Crag soon comes into view. There is right of access to the crag under CRoW.

The highest section has one good Very Severe and there are several shorter lines on the wall to the left. There is good bouldering at the crag.

1. The Crack 8m VS 4c *
The corner crack, escaping right at the bulge.

Rothbury Quarry

NU044018

This sandstone quarry lies in woodland on the hillside immediately above the western end of Rothbury. For a quarry, there is quite a pleasant ambience about the place and its ease of access makes it a good spot for an evening's exploration, with some quite hard climbing available on fairly poor rock. Many routes have been done here over the years, but only one is recorded. There are 3 sections. The first consists of a compact wall with few natural lines and impenetrable vegetation in summer; the central section is an impressive 12 metre high wall with natural lines; the last is a 7 metre high wall of good rock with a few short routes and an interesting traverse.

Follow the high level road up the hillside from opposite the County Hotel at the west end of the main street in Rothbury. Continue due west and parallel to the main road until a drive on the right leads through a gate and apparently up to a house. Follow the drive round to the left, through a gate and into the quarry.

1. Pilgrimage 12m E6 6b/c
The central section of the quarry is bounded on the left by a wall set at right angles to the main face. Climb the once pegged crack boldly up the leaning wall with sustained interest. In situ pegs may offer psychological protection.

Salters Nick, Shaftoe Crags
Photo: Steve Crowe

Shaftoe Crags

Local climbers have visited the crags for many years and in the early eighties a strong group of climbers based at Newcastle University climbed extensively on the crag but did not record their activities. It was not until the early nineties, when Shaftoe's true potential as a bouldering venue was realised, that a few good routes on the higher buttresses were climbed.

At present the only routes that have been recorded are on the partial wooded escarpment that faces south, the large neb with a westerly aspect and an isolated buttress on the south facing section of the northern escarpment. The crags have a pleasant sunny outlook and are situated on Shaftoe Moor.

The routes included are all of good quality, making it worthwhile to include a rope and harness along with your bouldering gear.The crag is situated about 18 miles from Newcastle on the A696 road to Jedburgh. The best and quickest approach is probably from the west. From Newcastle follow the A696 through Belsay towards Jedburgh, after about 3 miles the crag can be seen on the right about 1/2 a mile from the road. Park in the lay-by on the main road just past the turning for Ferney Chesters farm. Follow the footpath past the farm to the crag. There is a right of access to the crag under CRoW.

A point of reference for finding the buttresses is Cave Buttress, the large buttress on the left-hand side of the escarpment as you approach from the farm.

Cave Buttress

1. Cave Route Right Hand VS 4c
Start at the mouth of the cave. Climb the wall to gain the crack.

2. Cave Route Left Hand E3 6b
Climb the crack in the corner until undercuts lead awkwardly to the lip and an easier finish.

3. Flake Crack HVS 5a
5m left of the mouth of the cave is a layback flake. Climb this awkwardly.

Café Noir Buttress

From Cave Buttress head right into the wood until you reach the tall buttress with a large oak tree and, at the time of writing, a green barrel at its base. This is Café Noir Buttress.

4. Café Noir 10m E4 5c   **
Climb the arete on the left-hand side of the buttress. Quite delicate.

5. Cream Topping 10m E5 6c
Climb the crack just right of the left arete until its end, then make some very hard moves off a small crystal and finish up a faint groove.

Just beyond Café Noir Buttress is the Triple Boulder, which has a higher buttress above it. The next climb starts from the shelf on the top of the Triple Boulder.

Two Tier Buttress

6. Shafted 9m E3 5c
Powerfully gain a flake, then continue more delicately up the slab above.

Turtle Rock

From Cave Buttress contour round the hillside until travelling in a northerly direction. Follow the line of outcrops for a couple of hundred metres until you reach the massive neb.This is Turtle Rock, which has a westerly aspect.

7. Galapagos Turtle 8m E5 6a
Start at the centre of the south face of Turtle Rock. Gain the horizontal break and then traverse left along it until it is possible to gain the ledge above. Good protection can be arranged if you are strong enough to hang around.

Salters Nick

This is the escarpment which is about 200 metres north of Turtle Rock and terminates at the track next to the dry stone wall. Although it has a number of routlets and boulder problems, the only one described here takes the bottomless arête about 100m right of the track.

8. Syco Sheep E4 6b
Start directly below the the bottomless arête. Climb up under the roof, pull out left to a sloper and then up the arête and fluting to finish.

John Dalrymple
4. Cafe Noir (E4 5c)
Photo: Steve Nagy

Shitlington Crag

A long, low south facing outcrop of Fell Sandstone in the North Tyne Valley, straddling the Pennine Way on Wark Common.

Turn left off the B6320 2 miles north of Wark and one mile south of Bellingham. Follow this lane for ¼ mile and then take the Pennine Way past the radio mast and over the crag. There is a right of access to the crag, except Wood Buttress, under CRoW, but until the act is implemented climbing is banned.

Early climbing on the crag was by Keith Turnbull (who lived at the house half way along the crag), David Baihle and friends.

Wood Buttress

These routes lie on a buttress on the right hand side of the dirt track south of the farm.

1. Charity 8m E1 5b

The crack at the left end of the wall containing Jade. Climb the crack to a ledge and straight over the bulge to the top.

2. Plop 14m E1 5b

Climb the crack of Charity and hand traverse the obvious break rightward, with a move up then down at the corner. Cross the wall taken by Faith avoiding the temptation of the tree and finish up a wide flake crack and another tree at the extreme right of the wall.

3. Jade 10m E1 5b

Takes the wall left of the obvious corner in the centre of the buttress. Climb the overhanging wall to the roof, move right through the roof finishing on potholes.

4. Little Dave Horner 9m E2 5c

Climb the corner to the roof, over this to well spaced potholes and reach the top with difficulty.

5. Faith 11m E1 5b

Takes the wall right of the corner. Start at the dubious flake by the large tree, mantelshelf onto a sloping ledge and move up to the bulge, move right through this and straight up the wall to a rounded finish.

6. Under the Boardwalk 15m E3 6a

100 metres or so right of the Wood Buttress is an impressive roof. This is climbed from right to left along the obvious break to an awkward exit onto the ledge.

7. Grunt 6m E1 5b

The off width crack on the right gives a good thrutch.

Farm Buttress

The next 4 routes lie on the buttresses behind the farm and are described from right to left.

8. Lunacy 7m HVS 5a

The obvious weakness on the big buttress above the farm.

9. Deranged 7m E4 6b

The wall left of Lunacy is climbed on small holds.

10. Harvest 7m HVS 5b

The good groove up the buttress of pocketed rock right of the rusty wall.

11. Extraction 7m E4 6a

The obvious clean groove up the rusty wall above a rock pavement on the broken crag on the left. Climb the groove to a good hold below the roof, pull out left to finish.

Various small buttresses outcrop on the hillside but are not large enough to warrant separate description.

At the extreme left hand end the crag gains reasonable height and is split into five buttresses which have been numbered from left to right.

No. 1 Buttress

12. Sickle 6m E1 5b

Start from the ground just right of the gully. Move up to the pothole, reach for the flake, move right to another pothole, up and right to a layaway in the groove then straight up. There is a good hold on the break on the left. The large boulder should not be used.

13. Kremlin 6m E4 6c

The wall on the right is climbed by a series of very difficult moves.

No. 2 Buttress
The left hand arête provides a good V Diff and
the centre of the slab on the right is 5b.

No. 4 Buttress

4. Pitch 6m HVS 5a
Start at the boulder underneath the overhang
on the left hand side of the buttress. Climb up
to the right hand end of the roof, move up to the
obvious hole and finish up the right hand arête.

5. Fork 8m E1 5b
Up the crack on the right of the arête. Move
left onto the arête and then up and left to the
obvious hole, left again and finish up the slab.

No. 5 Buttress

6. Combine 8m E2 5c
On the right wall is a good layaway hold 2½
metres up. Use this to move left to two good
holds and then up to a jug on the arête. An
awkward move leads to the top. The two good
holds can be gained direct, which is harder.

7. Old MacDonald 6m E2 6a
From the good layaway hold reach up to another
layaway, then move slightly right and up to finish.

Spindlestone Heugh   NU152338
Web Guide

A south facing Whin Sill crag which, though broken, had over a dozen lines of up to 15 metres in
the 1979 guide. Aficionados of Whin Sill climbing may like it here, but sandstone lovers will hate
it. Several loose blocks were removed during preparations for the 1979 guide, but more will lurk,
waiting for the unwary. Access is by traversing the hillside to the south from Warren Mill Caravan
Site.

Swinburne Quarry   NY926757
Web Guide

A long Whin Sill quarry with over 30 routes up to HVS climbed and recorded, but the rock is loose
and protection is scarce. Currently cattle are overwintered in the quarry, making the place pretty
unpleasant underfoot.
A good track leads in from Gunnerton to the west.

The Tipalt

A compact, pleasant north facing sandstone crag with over a dozen routes up to HVS.

Turn north off the B6318 Military Road half a mile east of Greenhead along a no-through road, signposted to the Carvoran Roman Army Museum. Follow the road for about 1 mile past the museum until High Old Shields farm is reached on the left and the crag on the right. It is important to ask for permission, the landowner is sympathetic to climbers but asks that climbers see him at the farm before climbing. There is a right of access to the crag under CRoW.

The crag was discovered by Alan Stark and developed by members of Eden Valley M. C. in early 1976. The information was originally published in "North Of England Rock Climbs" in 1992, and is reproduced here with the permission of Stewart Wilson.

Seen from below the crag consists of 3 sections: Left Hand Buttress, Main Face and Right Hand Buttress. Steep grassy gullies separate each section. The best descent is to the right of Right Hand Buttress at the west end of the crag. The climbs are described from left to right as you face the crag.

Left Hand Buttress

A barrel shaped buttress with three faces. The front face is undercut.

1. Hopesike Wall 7m VD

Not an outstanding climb. Start 4 metres up the slope from the foot of the buttress at the foot of a broken groove. Climb the groove past a small jutting nose and after 3 metres step right and finish up rightwards on ledges.

2. Green Fingers 7m HVS 5b

Start just left of the front face at an obvious V-groove. Climb the V-groove to good holds in a break above the overhang. Pull over strenuously using a thin crack. Finish direct.

3. This 8m VS 4b *

A good little climb, steep and interesting. Start at the foot of the front face at a square hole-like recess. Climb to the prominent overhang and ascend the thin crack splitting its right hand side. Climb the wall direct on good holds.

4. That 6m S

A worthwhile, steep wall climb. Start below the centre of the steep right hand wall. Climb the wall on good holds.

Main Face

This is about 20 metres long and has a ledge system at half height. The upper left hand side is dominated by huge unclimbed roofs. The right hand part has an obvious green drainage line which ends as a deep chimney/crack and is the line of Walk Like A Dog. The main face ends at an arête identified by an arrow shaped overhang at 5 metres.

5. Snipe 8m HVD

Start at the foot of a dirty groove at the left side of the main face, at a point to the right of which the roofs start to develop. Climb the dirty groove until pleasant moves on good holds lead rightwards above the overhangs. A wide cleft is then followed to the top.

6. Here 9m MVS 4b

Start on the first patch of level ground on the left side of Main Face, just left of the prominent undercut rib of The Snout. Climb the shallow corner to a large flat ledge. From the left hand end of the ledge, pull over the overhang on good holds and traverse diagonally right to finish.

7. The Snout 5m MVS 4b

Good value. Start below the jutting prow. Climb the undercut arête. 'Thank God' holds appear when most needed. Finish on the ledge above.

8. There 11m VS 5a **

The most impressive natural line on the crag and at its grade a hard won though absorbing effort. Start 5 metres right of The Snout below the impressive V groove which cleaves the top overhangs. Climb the initial undercut wall via a thin crack to gain a ledge. Pull under the roof and gain the upper groove. Follow this to the top, moving out left to finish.

The base of the crag now forms a small bay or amphitheatre with a jutting roof at 2 metres.

9. Everywhere 11m MVS 4b

Start at the foot of the arête at the right hand end of the amphitheatre. Climb the arête by the shallow groove on its left to a good ledge. Move just over a metre to the right and climb the wall above using a thin crack which soon peters out.

Variation Finish VS 4c

From the ledge, surmount the bulge directly above the arête and move left to finish at some prominent knobs of rock.

10. Walk Like A Dog 11m S

Better than it looks with a steep finish. Start 2 metres right of the amphitheatre at the foot of the obvious green runnel. Race up the runnel to a ledge then struggle up the strenuous chimney above.

1. Crab Fair 16m D **
 fine combination of wall, traverse and slab; a
eginners dream. Start just right of the obvious
reen runnel. Climb the steep wall rightwards on
emorable holds to a good ledge. Traverse right
asily and swarm onto a higher ledge. Just around
ne corner on the right is a groove. Climb this until
 can be quitted for excellent jugs and a slab finish
n the left.

2. Goose Fair 11m HS
 good steep climb, but rather awkward. Start at the
oot of the arête with the arrow-shaped overhang at
ne right end of Main Face. Climb the arête, passing
ne overhang to gain the good ledge. Finish as for
rab Fair by climbing the groove on the right until
igs on the left lead to a slab finish.

Variation Finish VS 4c
rom the point of arrival on the ledge, climb directly
o and over bulges to gain the top slab of Crab Fair.

Right Hand Buttress
his is a smaller, scruffy and broken buttress at the
ght hand end of the crag. Short scrambles, but
othing of interest.

Steve Nagy
8. There (VS 5a)
Photo: John Dalrymple

Thrum Mill

NU068015

 quarried sandstone face on a bend of the
oquet, with copious amounts of vegetation
ncroaching on the finishes of the routes. It is
irectly opposite Thrum Mill, a popular tourist
oot 1 mile east of Rothbury just to the south of
ne B6344.

ark at the large lay-by and take the path
oward Thrum Mill. The crag may be reached
y fording the river after approximately 100
etres, depending on the height of the river. An
lternative is to approach from the end of the
dustrial estate on the south side of Rothbury.

. Hooker 10m   E4 6b
limb the left arête of the crag and climb round a
mall roof at the top.

. Joint Effort 10m E1 5c
tart right of Hooker, up a groove, then up
ne wall passing the left end of a larger roof to
dges.

3. The Final Cut 10m E4 5c
Start right of Joint Effort and pull onto the wall.
Move up right and climb the wall just left of a
faint rib to pull round the right side of the larger
roof and gain ledges.

4. Lethal Addiction 10m E3 5c
Start right of The Final Cut and make a horrible
mantel to gain the left side of a groove. Up this
pulling over roofs to finish.

5. Withdrawal Symptoms 10m E2 5b
The wall right of Lethal Addiction passing a flake
near the top.

6. Crack Attack 10m S 4a
The corner to the right of Withdrawal Symptoms.
The wall just left of this can also be climbed at a
similar standard.

Tosson Hill NZ00498

The buttress to the west and below the survey pillar unfortunately provides only limited climbing of an easy nature. Approximately 1 kilometre to the north west, on the hillside overlooking Hepple Whitefield, are a number of scattered buttresses which offer a couple of harder lines. There is a right of access to the crag under CRoW.

Titlington Mount NU09115

A very good little south facing crag low down on Titlington Pike, only 7 metres in height but offering some quite bold leads/solos and well worth a visit.

Turn east off the A697 just south of Powburn and signed for Eglingham. Follow this road for half a mile until a right turn signed for Titlington can be taken. A further half a mile along turn left for Titlington Mount. Continue for 200 metres to a lay-by on the left. The crag is on the hillside directly above this.

1. Bobby Brown 7m HVS 5a
At the left end is a vague scoop. Pull into this. Once stood in the shallow break step left onto the arête and follow this to the top.

2. Chicken Heed 7m E2 5c
Follow Bobby Brown to the break then the green streaked wall above to an interesting finish.

3. Reet Stunner 7m E1 5b
The obvious system of cracks to the right of Chicken Heed.

4. Pain or Pleasure 7m E3 6a
Climb the wall between Reet Stunner and the single runnel to the right, passing a horizontal break and a cluster of single finger pockets to thin holds and a rounded finish above.

5. Angry Welshman 7m E3 6a
Pull into the aforementioned single runnel and climb the wall above past a one-finger layaway to a tricky finish.

6. Cock Ya Leg 7m VS 5a
Right again is the obvious scoop. Follow this trending slightly rightward.

7. Unlucky Break 20m HVS 5b
Beginning at Cock Ya Leg, pull up diagonally left on thin holds to the obvious break. Follow this leftward across the wall to finish up the left arête of Bobby Brown.

Vindolanda Quarry NY77566
Web Guide

A small sandstone Roman quarry on the western slopes of Thorngrafton Common, just above Vindolanda. The setting is splendid and 26 routes are recorded mostly with good grassy landings. This is important as the rock is not the best; there is little protection and no belays available at the top. There is a right of access to the crag under CRoW.

Walltown Quarry NU15233
Web Guide

A Whin Sill quarry about 1km east of Greenhead on the Military Road. There is a right of access to the crag under CRoW. Over 20 routes have been done here.

Cliff Robson
The Golden Hind (VS 5a)
Page 121
Photo: Malcolm Lowerson

Winter Climbing

Rick Barnes

Winter climbing in Northumberland is not a new pursuit, the ice falls that form on Cheviot during extended periods of cold weather have long been an attraction to local climbers. However, following trends in other parts of the country, there has been some recent exploration of the higher crags of the area resulting in some routes of a more marginal nature. Typically, these are mixed routes requiring an extended spell of very cold temperatures to make them viable.

While this style of climbing may be acceptable on the hard rock of the Cheviot massif it will never be so on a sandstone crag, no matter how thick the build up of ice. Climbers are asked to act with responsibility to others and to future generations If you want to use axes and crampons do it on the Cheviot crags when there is sufficient snow and ice, otherwise go to Scotland!

History

No record has been found of the first winter ascent of the Bizzle Burn and undoubtedly there have been other exploratory, and unrecorded, climbs in the Cheviot Hills. However, most of the mixed routes described below were first climbed during a stable period of cold weather at the beginning of 2003.

Richard Pow and Rick Barnes started the ball rolling early in January by climbing the obvious, and well iced, line of Cool Alligator and several variations on the small icefalls to the left of the buttress At the same time on the opposite side of the valley, Scottish climber Graeme Little was soloing two obvious lines on Peake's Buttress; the right-hand ridge and the central gully via an entry from the left. This was sufficient to stir Tim Catterall into activity when he soloed seven lines on and around Peake's Buttress in one day, including variations and a direct start to the lines climbed by Little the previous month. Three days later Tim returned with Richard Pow to make the first ascent of the hard Dogs of War.

Access to these routes is as described in the Henhole section of the guide except for the Bizzle Burn. For this it is better to take the left fork in the road at the community hall and ascend the valley from Dunsdale. Note that the Estate will not issue permits to drive up the valley if there is snow on the road.

Away from Cheviot itself the only other decent ice might be found at Linhope Spout (NT958171). This requires a prolonged spell of cold temperatures to freeze properly and even then it is likely that the plunge pool will remain a danger to a falling leader.

Bizzle Crags

NT 885215
550m
East

1. Dogs of War VI,7 26m **
The route follows an impressive corner just left of the obvious undercut section in the middle of the front face. The route is both technical and strenuous. Climb the corner with increasing difficulty until below the overhang. Hard moves left lead to a ledge and a rest. The overhanging upper crack will test your belief in your own immortality, with the crux where it should be at the top in a very exposed position. The belay totally relies on the turf above the route being hard frozen. This is the only possible belay, Warthogs essential.

2. Bizzle Burn Waterfall II/III 22m
The waterfall lies below and to the left of the crag in a small amphitheatre, and comes in condition fairly quickly. Once past the main pitch it is worth continuing up the line of the stream to numerous small but interesting ice pitches.

. **Bizzle Burn Waterfall (III)**
hoto: Steve Crowe

The Henhole

Rowan Buttress

Jacob's Bladder   III,3   12m
Climb the large icicle that forms to the left of Jacob's Ladder in hard winters.

Henhole Wall

Cool Alligator   IV,5   23m
Start as for the summer line of Alligator Crawl and follow this until it moves left at the junction with Yellow Slab. Instead, continue straight up on vertical ice to reach a series of grooves leading to the top.

To the left of this buttress several worthwhile icefalls often form and provide a variety problems and an afternoon's sport.

Peake's Buttress

The north facing buttress on the opposite side of the burn from Henhole Wall
Note: These climbs should only be attempted if the turf is hard frozen; the Turfulator also needs a build up of ice on the first wall.

Titus Torquous   IV,5   54m   **
1. 26m. Start 10 metres left of the central gully. Climb a rightwards slanting, steep ramp to a ledge system, traverse right into the central gully and follow this to a steep step and belay.
2. 28m. Climb the step above then up to a constricted chimney, which slants up left. Technical moves lead to a grassy ledge. Follow the groove above to the top. The chimney represents the crux and is hard to protect unless well iced.

Turfulator   IV,5   52m   **
1. 24m. Start directly below the central gully. Technical climbing on ice smears and turf leads to a ledge at the bottom of the central gully. Follow the gully to a steep step and belay.
2. 28m. Climb the step and follow the gully until blocked by an overhang, make an exposed traverse right onto the crest of the buttress and follow the obvious turf line to the top.

Timmy Tiptoes   IV,3   30m
Start in a recess to the right and lower down than the central gully. There is a flat grassy ledg at 3 metres. Climb up onto this using good turf. Follow steep turf to a small triangular recess. A hard move out of this leads to a turf line, which is followed rightwards and then back leftwards to a large ledge left of the pinnacle. The route can be finished here by traversing off right along the ledge or continued up the buttress behind at III,3.

College Burn

College Burn Upper Falls   III,2   25m
The upper fall, 100 metres higher up the bur past Henhole Crag can be climbed on either th left or right side. This is dangerous unless the plunge pool at the bottom is well frozen. In ver hard winters the whole fall will form reducing th grade to II.

College Burn Upper falls ice slabs
There is some slabby ground on the same side c the stream as Peake's Buttress and a little belov the upper falls. Several routes at Grade II can b climbed here; they vary from between 15 metre to 20 metres.

There are also some excellent icefalls that form directly left of Peake's Buttress in a hard winter. Although short they are quite steep and give interesting ice bouldering.

Richard Pow
Henhole Wall Icefalls (II/III)
Photo: Rick Barnes

BMC - Working for Climbers, Hill Walkers & Mountaineers

• Negotiating access to cliffs and mountains all over England and Wales and funding work on footpaths, stiles, notice boards & good practice publications.

• Securing access through direct ownership and management of crags.

• Working with landowners to keep the crag environment clean and climbable.

• Organising regional climbers meetings to discuss key issues such as fixed equipment policies, guidebooks, access and how to keep the crags clean and climbable.

• Providing high quality services and products for over 65000 members - travel insurance, information and a wide range of publications.

British Mountaineering Council
177-179 Burton Road
Manchester
M20 2BB
0870 010 4878
www.thebmc.co.uk

Steve Crowe
**34. The Overhanging Crack,
Bowden Doors (E2 5c)**
Page 57
Photo: Karin Magog

Photo Index...

The Crag Table...

Page	Crags	Status	mins	Alt m	Aspect	Up to VS	VS to HVS	E1 to E2	E3 to E4	E5 above	Total Routes	Bouldering	Comment
29	Back Bowden Doors	*****	10	170m	W	16	8	17	16	25	82	***	A great collection of quality routes of every grade.
46	Berryhill	***	5	75m	S	13	11	2	5	1	32	*	Popular for groups but always ask at the farm first.
52	Bowden Doors	*****	2	170m	W	25	33	47	31	14	150	***	Very accessible, very good but very busy.
72	Callaly Crag	*	20	230m	N	0	2	3	3	1	9	none	Home to one of the hardest routes in the county.
74	Callerhues Crag	****	30	323m	SW	8	24	16	16	1	65	some	Tough grades but great routes.
86	Coe Crag	**	30	304m	N	8	12	3	2	0	25	none	Splendid summer evening venue.
90	Coquet View Crag	*	45	350m	N	0	7	4	2	0	13	none	Esoteric venue.
92	Corby's Crag	***	1	184m	NW	19	24	8	7	0	58	*	Accessible but overused by groups.
99	Crag Lough	*****	15	250m	N	60	31	8	5	0	104	none	Great for easier routes.
116	Curtis Crag	*	5	250m	N	15	19	6	1	0	41	none	Handy for an evening.
120	Drake Stone	**	10	275m	N	4	5	3	3	0	15	none	The largest single boulder in Northumberland.
122	East Woodburn	***	5	250m	S	6	5	11	1	0	23	none	A must for E1 leaders.
126	Goats Crag	****	10	115m	S	17	15	6	5	2	45	*	Very sunny aspect.
133	Great Wanney	*****	30	310m	NW	24	17	20	17	11	89	some	Well protected routes at all grades.
148	Harehope Canyon	*	40	200m	NW&E	6	5	9	6	1	27	some	Unusual venue, don't forget to take a plank!
152	Henhole	****	60	610m	S	26	7	2	1	0	36	none	Superb mountain setting.
160	Howlerhirst Crag	***	20	210m	W	5	4	3	3	3	18	some	Remote feel but good clean rock.
164	Jack Rock	***	2	30m	N	7	14	12	3	4	40	none	Unique riverside setting.
172	Kyloe Crag	*****	10	108m	SW	34	22	23	11	5	95	**	Very popular
188	Kyloe in the Woods	****	15	154m	SW	36	27	25	17	4	109	***	Many good routes and excellent bouldering in an idyllic setting.
204	Linshiels 1	***	20	215m	S	3	5	1	3	4	16	some	A small clean crag in a stunning situation.
208	Linshiels 3	*	30	215m	N	6	4	2	0	0	12	none	Not as popular as its neighbour.
210	Padda Crag	*	30	370m	S	26	11	1	0	0	38	none	Situated in Kielder forest to the west of Crag Lough.
214	Peel Crag	****	5	250m	N	52	23	12	3	0	90	none	Great summer evening venue.
228	Queens Crag	*	10	277m	N	9	29	2	0	0	40	*	Short routes with strong lines.
235	Ravensheugh Crag	*****	45	392m	NW	40	29	28	20	13	130	*	Gritstonesque, well worth the long walk in.
252	Rothley Crag	***	10	230m	NW	2	9	4	8	5	28	***	High concentration of hard routes.
258	Sandy Crag	****	45	270m	W	8	13	6	5	7	39	some	Sandy Crack is one of the best E2s in the county.
266	Selby's Cove	****	45	320m	W	1	7	6	1	1	16	some	Small but perfectly formed.
270	Simonside	*****	30	420m	N	47	27	12	15	4	105	some	Great summer venue.
284	South Yardhope	**	15	300m	NW	8	12	4	13	1	38	some	Good routes that deserve more attention.
292	Thrunton Wood	*	30	230m	N	15	7	6	0	0	28	none	Home to a great HVS if you can find it. Worth huntin' out!
295	Whiteheugh Crag	**	5	310m	SW	4	4	5	3	2	18	none	Secluded location, short protectable routes.
298	Wolf Crag	*	5	278m	N	14	20	1	1	0	36	solos	Small but useful for an evenings soloing.
304	Minor Crag Section										149		A selection of gems are hidden in here!
328	Winter Climbing												But NOT on the sandstone please.